MW00931904

EDITORIAL

HAPPY is the moment that has no history! At the beginning of our second year we have little to record but quiet steady growth, a gradual spreading of the Tree of Knowledge, a gradual awakening of interest in all parts of the earth, a gradual access of fellow-workers, some young and enthusiastic, others already weary of the search for Truth in a world where so many offer the Stone of dogma, so few the Bread of experience.

There! we had nothing to say, and we have said it very nicely.

Floreas!

$$* \quad * \quad * \quad * \quad *$$

We must apologise for the necessity of holding over our edition of Sir Edward Kelly's account of the Forty-Eight Angelical Keys, and other important articles. Considerations of space were imperative.

$$* \quad * \quad * \quad * \quad *$$

Two days after the bound advance copies of this Number were delivered by the printer, an order was made restraining publication, continued by Mr. JUSTICE BUCKNILL, and dissolved by the Court of Appeal.

NOTES OF THE SEMESTER

MR. SHERIDAN-BICKERS held a large meeting at Cambridge in November, as successful as one would expect from the intellectual preeminence of our great university.

We beg to extend our warmest sympathies to Brother Aloysius Crowley. It seems possible that some gang of swindlers, fearing exposure, and having failed to frighten Mr. Aleister Crowley, decided to assassinate him. Their hired ruffians seem to have been knaves as clumsy as themselves, and Brother Aloysius suffered in his stead, escaping death by a miracle.

If we do not extend our sympathy to Mr. Aleister Crowley also, it is from a conviction that he has probably deserved anything that he may get.

In order to cope with the constantly increasing budget of letters of inquiry and sympathy from every part of the world, we have moved into new premises at 124 Victoria Street, Westminster, to which address all communications should be directed. Callers will always be welcome, but it is advisable to make appointments by letter or telephone.

LIBER XIII

VEL

GRADUUM MONTIS ABIEGNI

A SYLLABUS OF THE STEPS UPON THE PATH

A∴ A∴ Publication in Class D.
Issued by Order:

D.D.S. $7° = 4°$ Præmonstrator
O.S.V. $6° = 5°$ Imperator
N.S.F. $5° = 6°$ Cancellarius

51. Let not the failure and the pain turn aside the worshippers. The foundations of the pyramid were hewn in the living rock ere sunset; did the king weep at dawn that the crown of the pyramid was as yet unquarried in the distant land?

52. There was also an humming-bird that spake unto the horned cerastes, and prayed him for poison. And the great snake of Khem the Holy One, the royal Uræus serpent, answered him and said:

53. I sailed over the sky of Nu in the car called Millions-of-Years, and I saw not any creature upon Seb that was equal to me. The venom of my fang is the inheritance of my father, and of my father's father; and how shall I give it unto thee? Live thou and thy children as I and my fathers have lived, even unto an hundred millions of generations, and it may be that the mercy of the Mighty Ones may bestow upon thy children a drop of the poison of eld.

54. Then the humming-bird was afflicted in his spirit, and he flew unto the flowers, and it was as if naught had been spoken between them. Yet in a little while a serpent struck him that he died.

55. But an Ibis that meditated upon the bank of Nile the beautiful god listened and heard. And he laid aside his Ibis ways, and became as a serpent, saying Peradventure in an hundred millions of millions of generations of my children, they shall attain to a drop of the poison of the fang of the Exalted One.

56. And behold! ere the moon waxed thrice he became an Uræus serpent, and the poison of the fang was established in him and his seed even for ever and for ever.

LIBER LXV. CAP.V.

4

LIBER XIII

VEL

GRADUUM MONTIS ABIEGNI

A SYLLABUS OF THE STEPS UPON THE PATH

Quote LXV. Cap. V. vv. 52-56

1. *The Probationer.* His duties are laid down in Paper A, Class D. Being *without*, they are vague and general. He rceives Liber LXI. and LXV.

[Certain Probationers are admitted after six months or more to Ritual XXVIII.]

At the end of the Probation he passes Ritual DCLXXI., which constitutes him a Neophyte.

2. *The Neophyte.* His duties are laid down in Paper B, Class D. He receives Liber VII.

Examination in Liber O, Caps I.-IV., Theoretical and Practical.

Examination in the Four Powers of the Sphinx. Practical.

Four Tests are set.

Further, he builds up the magic Pantacle.

Finally he passes Ritual CXX., which constitutes him a Zelator.

3. *The Zelator.* His duties are laid down in Paper E, Class D. He receives Liber CCXX., XXVII., and DCCCXIII.

Examinations in Posture and Control of Breath (see EQUINOX No. I). Practical.

Further, he is given two meditation-practices corresponding to the two rituals DCLXXI. and CXX.

(Examination is only in the knowledge of, and some little practical acquaintance with, these meditations. The complete results, if attained, would confer a much higher grade.)

Further, he forges the magic Sword.

No ritual admits to the grade of Practicus, which is conferred by authority when the task of the Zelator is accomplished.

4. *The Practicus.* His duties are laid down in Paper E, Class D.

Instruction and Examination in the Qabalah and Liber DCCLXXVII.

Instruction in Philosophical Meditation (Gnana-Yoga).*

Examination in some one mode of divination: *e.g.*, Geomancy, Astrology, the Tarot. Theoretical. He is given a meditation-practice on Expansion of Consciousness.

He is given a meditation-practice in the destruction of thoughts.

Instruction and Examination in Control of Speech. Practical.

Further, he casts the magic Cup.

No ritual admits to the grade of Philosophus, which is

---

* All these instructions will be issued openly in THE EQUINOX in due course, where this has not already been done.

conferred by authority when the Task of the Practicus is accomplished.

5. *The Philosophus.* His duties are laid down in Paper E, Class D.

He practises Devotion to the Order.

Instruction and Examination in Methods of Meditation by Devotion (Bhakti-Yoga).

Instruction and Examination in Construction and Consecration of Talismans, and in Evocation.

Theoretical and Practical.

Examination in Rising on the Planes (Liber O, Caps. V., VI.). Practical.

He is given a meditation-practice on the Senses, and the Sheaths of the Self, and the Practice called Mahasatipatthana.

(See The Sword of Song, "Science and Buddhism.")

Instruction and Examination in Control of Action.

Further, he cuts the Magic Wand.

Finally, the Title of Dominus Liminis is conferred upon him.

He is given meditation-practices on the Control of Thought, and is instructed in Raja-Yoga.

He receives Liber Mysteriorum and obtains a perfect understanding of the Formulae of Initiation.

He meditates upon the diverse knowledge and power that he has acquired, and harmonises it perfectly.

Further, he lights the Magic Lamp.

At last, Ritual VIII. admits him to the grade of Adeptus Minor.

The Adeptus Minor. His duty is laid down in Paper F, Class D.

It is to follow out the instruction given in the Vision of the Eighth Æthyr for the attainment of the Knowledge and Conversation of the Holy Guardian Angel.

[NOTE. This is in truth the sole task; the others are useful only as adjuvants to and preparations for the One Work. Moreover, once this task has been accomplished, there is no more need of human help or instruction; for by this alone may the highest attainment be reached.

All these grades are indeed but convenient landmarks, not necessarily significant. A person who had attained them all might be immeasurably the inferior of one who had attained none of them; it is Spiritual Experience alone that counts in the Result; the rest is but Method.

Yet it is important to possess knowledge and power, provided that it be devoted wholly to that One Work.]

AHA!

AHA! THE SEVENFOLD MYSTERY OF THE INEFFABLE
LOVE;
THE COMING OF THE LORD IN THE AIR AS KING AND JUDGE
OF THIS CORRUPTED WORLD;

WHEREIN
UNDER THE FORM OF A DISCOURSE BETWEEN MARSYAS AN ADEPT
AND OLYMPAS HIS PUPIL THE WHOLE SECRET OF THE WAY OF
INITIATION IS LAID OPEN FROM THE BEGINNING TO THE END;
FOR THE INSTRUCTION OF THE LITTLE CHILDREN OF THE LIGHT.

WRITTEN IN TREMBLING AND HUMILITY FOR THE BRETHREN
OF THE A∴ A∴ BY THEIR VERY DUTIFUL SERVANT, AN
ASPIRANT TO THEIR SUBLIME ORDER,

ALEISTER CROWLEY

THE ARGUMENTATION

A LITTLE before Dawn, the pupil comes to greet his Master, and begs instruction.

Inspired by his Angel, he demands the Doctrine of being rapt away into the Knowledge and Conversation of Him.

The Master discloses the doctrine of Passive Attention or Waiting.

This seeming hard to the Pupil, it is explained further, and the Method of Resignation, Constancy, and Patience inculcated. The Paradox of Equilibrium. The necessity of giving oneself wholly up the the new element. Egoism rebuked.

The Master, to illustrate this Destruction of the Ego, describes the Visions of Dhyana.

He further describes the defence of the Soul against assailing Thoughts, and shows that the duality of Consciousness is a blasphemy against the Unity of God; so that even the thought called God is a denial of God-as-He-is-in-Himself.

The pupil sees nothing but a blank midnight in this Emptying of the Soul. He is shown that this is the necessary condition of Illumination. Distinction is further made between these three Dhyanas, and those early visions in which things appear as objective. With these three Dhyanas, moreover, are Four other of the Four Elements: and many more.

Above these is the Veil of Paroketh. Its guardians.

The Rosy Cross lies beyond this veil, and therewith the vision called Vishvarupa-darshana. Moreover, there is the Knowledge and Conversation of the Holy Guardian Angel.

The infinite number and variety of these Visions.

The impossibility of revealing all these truths to the outer and uninitiated world.

The Vision of the Universal Peacock—Atmadarshana. The confusion of the Mind, and the Perception of its self-contradiction.

The Second Veil—the Veil of the Abyss.

The fatuity of Speech. {11}

THE EQUINOX

A discussion as to the means by which the vision arises in the pure Soul is useless; suffice it that in the impure Soul no Vision will arise. The practical course is therefore to cleanse the Soul.

The four powers of the Sphinx; even adepts hardly attain to one of them!

The final Destruction of the Ego.

The Master confesses that he has lured the disciple by the promise of Joy, as the only thing comprehensible by him, although pain and joy are transcended even in early visions.

Ananda (bliss)—and its opposite—mark the first steps of the path. Ultimately all things are transcended; and even so, this attainment of Peace is but as a scaffolding to the Palace of the King.

The sheaths of the soul. The abandonment of all is necessary; the adept recalls his own tortures, as all that he loved was torn away.

The Ordeal of the Veil of the Abyss; the Unbinding of the Fabric of Mind, and its ruin.

The distinction between philosophical credence and interior certitude.

Sammasati—the trance wherein the adept perceives his causal connection with the Universe; past, present, and future.

Mastering the Reason, he becomes as a little child, and invokes his Holy Guardian Angel, the Augoeides.

Atmadarshana arising is destroyed by the Opening of the Eye of Shiva; the annihilation of the Universe,. The adept is destroyed, and there arises the Master of the Temple.

The pupil, struck with awe, proclaims his devotion to the Master; whereat the latter bids him rather unite himself with the Augoeides.

Yet, following the great annihilation, the adept reappears as an Angel to instruct men in this doctrine.

The Majesty of the Master described.

The pupil, wonder-struck, swears to attain, and asks for further instruction.

The Master describes the Eight Limbs of Yoga.

The pupil lamenting the difficulty of attainment, the Master shows forth the sweetness of the hermit's life.

One doubt remains: will not the world be able instantly to recognise the Saint? The Master replies that only imperfect Saints reveal themselves as such. Of these are

THE ARGUMENTATION

the cranks and charlatans, and those that fear and deny Life. But let us fix our thoughts on Love, and not on the failings of others!

The Master invokes the Augoeides; the pupil through sympathy is almost rapt away.

The Augoeides hath given the Master a message; namely, to manifest the New Way of the Equinox of Horus, as revealed in Liber Legis.

He does so, and reconciles it with the Old Way by inviting the Test of Experiment. They would go therefore to the Desert or the Mountains ___ nay! here and now shall it be accomplished.

Peace to all beings!

AHA !

OLYMPAS: MASTER, ERE THE RUBY DAWN
Gild the dew of leaf and law,
Bidding the petals to unclose
Of heaven's imperishable Rose,
Brave heralds, banners flung afar
Of the lone and secret star,
I come to greet thee. Here I bow
To earth this consecrated brow!
As a lover woos the Moon
Aching in a silver swoon,
I reach my lips towards thy shoon
Mendicant of the mystic boon !

MARYSAS. What wilt thou?

OLYMPAS.   Let mine Angel say!
"Utterly to be rapt away!"

MARYSAS. How, whence, and whither?

OLYMPAS.   "By my kiss
From that abode to this—to this!"
My wings?

MARYSAS.   Thou hast no wings. But see
An eagle swooping from the Byss
Where God stands. Let him ravish thee
And bear thee to a boundless bliss!

OLYMPAS. How should I call him? How beseech?
MARYSAS. Silence is lovelier than Speech.
Only on a windless tree
Falls the dew, Felicity!
One ripple on the water mars
The magic mirror of the Stars.
OLYMPAS. My soul bends to the athletic stress
Of God's immortal loveliness.
Tell me, what wit avails the clod
To know the nearness of its God?
MARYSAS. First, let the soul be poised, and fledge
Truth's feather on mind's razor-edge.
Next, let no memory, feeling, hope
Stain all its starless horoscope.
Last, let it be content, twice void;
Not to be suffered or enjoyed;
Motionless, blind and deaf and dumb—
So may it to its kingdom come!
OLYMPAS. Dear master, can this be? The wine
Embittered with dark discipline?
For the soul loves her mate, the sense.
MARYSAS. This bed is sterile. Thou must fence
Thy soul from all her foes, the creatures
That by their soft and siren natures
Lure thee to shipwreck!
OLYMPAS.   Thou hast said:
"God is in all."
MARYSAS.   In sooth.
OLYMPAS.   Why dread
The Godhood?

AHA!

MARYSAS.   Only as the thought
Is God, adore it. But the soul creates
Misshapen fiends, incestuous mates.
Slay these: they are false shadows of
The never-waning moon of love.

OLYMPAS.   What thought is worthy?

MARYSAS.   Truly none
Save one, in that it is but one.
Keep the mind constant; thou shalt see
Ineffable felicity.
Increase the will, and thou shalt find
It hath the strength to be resigned.
Resign the will; and from the string
Will's arrow shall have taken wing,
And from the desolate abode
Found the immaculate heart of God!

OLYMPAS.   The word is hard!

MARYSAS.   All things excite
Their equal and their opposite.
Be great, and thou shalt be—how small!
Be naught, and thou shalt be the All!
Eat not; all meat shall fill thy mouth:
Drink, and thy soul shall die of drouth!
Fill thyself; and that thou seekest
Is diluted to its weakest.
Empty thyself; the ghosts of night
Flee before the living Light.
Who clutches straws is drowned; but he
That hath the secret of the sea,
Lives with the whole lust of his limbs,

Takes hold of water's self, and swims.
See, the ungainly albatross
Stumbles awkwardly across
Earth—one wing-beat, and he flies
Most graceful gallant in the skies!
So do thou leave thy thoughts, intent
On thy new noble element!
Throw the earth shackles off, and cling
To what imperishable thing
Arises from the Married death
Of thine own self in that whereon
Thou art fixed.

OLYMPAS.   Then all life's loyal breath
Is a waste wind. All joy forgone,
I must strive ever?

MARYSAS.   Cease to strive!
Destroy this partial I, this moan
Of an hurt beast! Sores keep alive
By scratching. Health is peace. Unknown
And unexpressed because at ease
Are the Most High Congruities.

OLYMPAS. Then death is thine "attainment"? I
Can do no better than to die!

MARYSAS. Indeed, that "I" that is not God
Is but a lion in the road!
Knowest thou not (even now!) how first
The fetters of Restriction burst?
In the rapture of the heart
Self hath neither lot nor part.

AHA!

OLYPMAS. Tell me, dear master, how the bud
          First breaks to brilliance of bloom:
          What ecstasy of brain and blood
          Shatters the seal upon the tomb
          Of him whose gain was the world's loss
          Our father Christian Rosycross!
MARYSAS. First, one is like a gnarled old oak
          On a waste heath. Shrill shrieks the wind.
          Night smothers earth. Storm swirls to choke
          The throat of silence! Hard behind
          Gathers a blacker cloud than all.
          But look! but look! it thrones a ball
          Of blistering fire. It breaks. The lash
          Of lightning snakes him forth. One crash
          Splits the old tree. One rending roar!—And
          night is darker than before.
OLYMPAS. Nay, master, master! Terror hath
          So fierce an hold upon the path?
          Life must lie crushed, a charred black swath,
          In that red harvest's aftermath!
MARYSAS. Life lives. Storm passes. Clouds dislimn.
          The night is clear. And now to him
          Who hath endured is given the boon
          Of an immeasurable moon.
          The air about the adept congeals
          To crystal; in his heart he feels
          One needle pang; then breaks that splendour
          Infinitely pure and tender . . .
          —And the ice drags him down!

OLYMPAS.   But may
Our trembling frame, our clumsy clay,
Endure such anguish?

MARYSAS.   In the worm
Lurks an unconquerable germ
Identical. A sparrow's fall
Were the Destruction of the All!
More; know that this surpasses skill
To express its ecstasy. The thrill
Burns in the memory like the glory
Of some far beaconed promontory
Where no light shines but on the comb
Of breakers, flickerings of the foam!

OLYMPAS. The path ends here?

MARYSAS.   Ingenuous one!
The path—the true path—scarce begun.
When does the night end?

OLYMPAS.   When the sun,
Crouching below the horizon,
Flings up his head, tosses his mane,
Ready to leap.

MARYSAS.   Even so. Again
The adept secures his subtle fence
Against the hostile shafts of sense,
Pins for a second his mind; as you
May have seen some huge wrestler do.
With all his gathered weight heaped, hurled,
Resistless as the whirling world,
He holds his foeman to the floor
For one great moment and no more.

AHA!

So—then the sun-blaze! All the night
Bursts to a vivid orb of light.
There is no shadow; nothing is,
But the intensity of bliss.
Being is blasted. That exists.

OLYMPAS.　Ah!

MARYSAS.　　　　　But the mind, that mothers mists,
Abides not there. The adept must fall
Exhausted.

OLYMPAS.　　　　　　There's an end of all?

MARYSAS.　But not an end of this! Above
All life as is the pulse of love,
So this transcends all love.

OLYMPAS.　　　　　　　　Ah me!
Who may attain?

MARYSAS.　　　　　Rare souls.

OLYMPAS.　　　　　　　　I see
Imaged a shadow of this light.

MARYSAS.　Such is its sacramental might
That to recall it radiates
Its symbol. The priest elevates
The Host, and instant blessing stirs
The hushed awaiting worshippers.

OLYMPAS.　Then how secure the soul's defence?
How baffle the besieger, Sense?

MARYSAS.　See the beleagured city, hurt
By hideous engines, sore begirt
And gripped by lines of death, well scored
With shell, nigh open to the sword!
Now comes the leader; courage, run

Contagious through the garrison!
Repair the trenches! Man the wall!
Restore the ruined arsenal!
Serve the great guns! The assailants blench;
They are driven from the foremost trench.
The deadliest batteries belch their hell
No more. So day by day fought well,
We silence gun by gun. At last
The fiercest of the fray is past;
The circling hills are ours. The attack
Is over, save for the rare crack,
Long dropping shots from hidden forts;—
— So is it with our thoughts!

OLYMPAS.　The hostile thoughts, the evil things!
They hover on majestic wings,
Like vultures waiting for a man
To drop from the slave-caravan!

MARYSAS.　All thoughts are evil. Thought is two:
The seer and the seen. Eschew
That supreme blasphemy, my son,
Remembering that God is One.

OLYMPAS.　God is a thought!

MARYSAS.　　　　　　The "thought" of God
Is but a shattered emerod:
A plague, an idol, a delusion,
Blasphemy, schism, and confusion!

OLYMPAS.　Banish my one high thought? The night
Indeed were starless.

MARSYAS.　　　　　　Very right!
But that impalpable inane

AHA!

Is the condition of success;
Even as earth lies black to gain
Spring's green and autumn's fruitfulness.

OLYMPAS. I dread this midnight of the soul.

MARYSAS. Welcome the herald!

OLYMPAS.   How control
The horror of the mind? The insane
Dead melancholy?

MARYSAS.   Trick is vain.
Sheer manhood must support the strife,
And the trained Will, the Root of Life,
Bear the adept triumphant.

OLYMPAS.   Else?

MARYSAS. The reason, like a chime of bells
Ripped by the lightning, cracks.

OLYMPAS.   And these
Are the first sights the magus sees?

MARYSAS. The first true sights. Bright images
Throng the clear mind at first, a crowd
Of Gods, lights, armies, landscapes; loud
Reverberations of the Light.
But these are dreams, things in the mind,
Reveries, idols. Thou shalt find
No rest therein. The former three
(Lightning, moon, sun) are royally
Liminal to the Hall of Truth.
Also there be with them, in sooth,
Their brethren. There's the vision called
The Lion of the Light, a brand
Of ruby flame and emerald

Waved by the Hermeneutic Hand.
There is the Chalice, whence the flood
Of God's beatitude of blood
Flames. O to sing those starry tunes!
O colder than a million moons!
O vestal waters! Wine of love
Wan as the lyric soul thereof!
There is the Wind, a whirling sword,
The savage rapture of the air
Tossed beyond space and time. My Lord,
My Lord, even now I see Thee there
In infinite motion! And beyond
There is the Disk, the wheel of things;
Like a black boundless diamond
Whirring with millions of wings!

OLYMPAS. Master!

MARSYAS.   Know also that above
These portents hangs no veil of love;
But, guarded by unsleeping eyes
Of twice seven score severities,
The Veil that only rips apart
When the spear strikes to Jesus' heart!
A mighty Guard of Fire are they
With sabres turning every way!
Their eyes are millstones greater than
The earth; their mouths run seas of blood.
Woe be to that accursèd man
Of whom they are the iniquities!
Swept in their wrath's avenging flood
To black immitigable seas!

AHA!

Woe to the seeker who shall fail
To rend that vexful virgin Veil!
Fashion thyself by austere craft
Into a single azure shaft
Loosed from the string of Will; behold
The Rainbow! Thou art shot, pure flame,
Past the reverberated Name
Into the Hall of Death. Therein
The Rosy Cross is subtly seen.

OLYMPAS. Is that a vision, then?

MARSYAS.   It is.

OLYMPAS. Tell me thereof!

MARSYAS.   O not of this!
Of all the flowers in God's field
We name not this. Our lips are sealed
In that the Universal Key
Lieth within its mystery.
But know thou this. These visions give
A hint both faint and fugitive
Yet haunting, that behind them lurks
Some Worker, greater than his works.

Yea, it is given to him who girds
His loins up, is not fooled by words,
Who takes life lightly in his hand
To throw away at Will's command,
To know that View beyond the Veil.

O petty purities and pale,
These visions I have spoken of!

THE EQUINOX

The infinite Lord of Light and Love
Breaks on the soul like dawn. See! See!
Great God of Might and Majesty!
Beyond sense, beyond sight, a brilliance
Burning from His glowing glance!
Formless, all the worlds of flame
Atoms of that fiery frame!
The adept caught up and broken;
Slain, before His Name be spoken!
In that fire the soul burns up.
One drop from that celestial cup
Is an abyss, an infinite sea
That sucks up immortality!
O but the Self is manifest
Through all that blaze! Memory stumbles
Like a blind man for all the rest.
Speech, like a crag of limestone, crumbles,
While this one soul of thought is sure
Through all confusion to endure,
Infinite Truth in one small span:
This that is God is Man.

OLYMPAS. Master! I tremble and rejoice.
MARSYAS. Before His own authentic voice
Doubt flees. The chattering choughs of talk
Scatter like sparrows from a hawk.
OLYMPAS. Thenceforth the adept is certain of
The mystic mountain? Light and Love
Are Life therein, and they are his?
MARSYAS. Even so. And One supreme there is
Whom I have known, being He. Withdrawn

AHA!

Within the curtains of the dawn
Dwells that concealed. Behold! he is
A blush, a breeze, a song, a kiss,
A rosy flame like Love, his eyes
Blue, the quintessence of all skies,
His hair a foam of gossamer
Pale gold as jasmine, lovelier
Than all the wheat of Paradise.
O the dim water-wells his eyes!
There is such depth of Love in them
That the adept is rapt away,
Dies on that mouth, a gleaming gem
Of dew caught in the boughs of Day!

OLYMPAS.   The hearing of it is so sweet
I swoon to silence at thy feet.

MARSYAS.   Rise! Let me tell thee, knowing Him,
The Path grows never wholly dim.
Lose Him, and thou indeed wert lost!
But He will not lose thee!

OLYMPAS.   Exhaust
The Word!

MARSYAS.   Had I a million songs,
And every song a million words,
And every word a million meanings,
I could not count the choral throngs
Of Beauty's beatific birds,
Or gather up the paltry gleanings
Of this great harvest of delight!
Hast thou not heard the word aright?
That world is truly infinite.

Even as a cube is to a square
Is that to this.

OLYMPAS.   Royal and rare!
Infinite light of burning wheels!

MARSYAS.   Ay! The imagination reels.
Thou must attain before thou know,
And when thou knowest—Mighty woe
That silence grips the willing lips!

OLYMPAS.   Ever was speech the thought's eclipse.

MARSYAS.   Ay, not to veil the truth to him
Who sought it, groping in the dim
Halls of illusion, said the sages
In all the realms, in all the ages,
"Keep silence." By a word should come
Your sight, and we who see are dumb!
We have sought a thousand times to teach
Our knowledge; we are mocked by speech.
So lewdly mocked, that all this word
Seems dead, a cloudy crystal blurred,
Though it cling closer to life's heart
Than the best rhapsodies of art!

OLYMPAS.   Yet speak!

MARSYAS.   Ah, could I tell thee of
These infinite things of Light and Love!
There is the Peacock; in his fan
Innumerable plumes of Pan!
Oh! every plume hath countless eyes;
—Crown of created mysteries!—
Each holds a Peacock like the First.

OLYMPAS.   How can this be?

28

AHA!

MARSYAS.   The mind's accurst.
It cannot be. It is. Behold,
Battalion on battalion rolled!
There is war in Heaven! The soul sings still,
Struck by the plectron of the Will;
But the mind's dumb; its only cry
The shriek of its last agony!

OLYMPAS. Surely it struggles.

MARSYAS.   Bitterly!
And, mark! it must be strong to die!
The weak and partial reason dips
One edge, another springs, as when
A melting iceberg reels and tips
Under the sun. Be mighty then,
A lord of Thought, beyond wit and wonder
Balanced—then push the whole mind under,
Sunk beyond chance of floating, blent
Rightly with its own element,
Not lifting jagged peaks and bare
To the unsympathetic air!

This is the second veil; and hence
As first we slew the things of sense
Upon the altar of their God,
So must the Second Period
Slay the ideas, to attain
To that which is, beyond the brain.

OLYMPAS. To that which is?—not thought? not sense?

MARSYAS. Knowledge is but experience
Made conscious of itself. The bee,

Past master of geometry,
Hath not one word of all of it;
For wisdom is not mother-wit!
So the adept is called insane
For his frank failure to explain.
Language creates false thoughts; the true
Breed language slowly. Following
Experience of a thing we knew
Arose the need to name the thing.
So, ancients likened a man's mind
To the untamed evasive wind.
Some fool thinks names are things; and boasts
Aloud of spirits and of ghosts.
Religion follows on a pun!
And we, who know that Holy One
Of whom I told thee, seek in vain
Figure or word to make it plain.

OLYMPAS. Despair of man!

MARSYAS.   Man is the seed
Of the unimaginable flower.
By singleness of thought and deed
It may bloom now—this actual hour!

OLYMPAS. The soul made safe, is vision sure
To rise therein?

MARSYAS.   Though calm and pure
It seem, maybe some thought hath crept
Into his mind to baulk the adept.
The expectation of success
Suffices to destroy the stress
Of the one thought. But then, what odds?

AHA!

"Man's vision goes, dissolves in God's;"
Or, "by God's grace the Light is given
To the elected heir of heaven."
These are but idle theses, dry
Dugs of the cow Theology.
Business is business. The one fact
That we know is: the gods exact
A stainless mirror. Cleanse thy soul!
Perfect the will's austere control!
For the rest, wait! The sky once clear,
Dawn needs no prompting to appear!

OLYMPAS. Enough! it shall be done.
MARSYAS.   Beware!
Easily trips the big word "dare."
Each man's an Œdipus, that thinks
He hath the four powers of the Sphinx,
Will, Courage, Knowledge, Silence. Son,
Even the adepts scarce win to one!
Thy Thoughts—they fall like rotten fruits.
But to destroy the power that makes
These thoughts—thy Self? A man it takes
To tear his soul up by the roots!
This is the mandrake fable, boy!

OLYMPAS. You told me that the Path was joy.
MARSYAS. A lie to lure thee!
OLYMPAS.   Master!
MARSYAS.   Pain
And joy are twin toys of the brain.
Even early visions pass beyond!

OLYMPAS. Not all the crabbed runes I have conned

Told me so plain a truth. I see,
Inscrutable Simplicity!
Crushed like a blind-worm by the heel
Of all I am, perceive, and feel,
My truth was but the partial pang
That chanced to strike me as I sang.

MARSYAS.   In the beginning, violence
Marks the extinction of the sense.
Anguish and rapture rack the soul.
These are disruptions of control.
Self-poised, a brooding hawk, there hangs
In the still air the adept. The bull
On the firm earth goes not so smooth!
So the first fine ecstatic pangs
Pass; balance comes.

OLYMPAS.   How wonderful
Are these tall avenues of truth!

MARSYAS.   So the first flash of light and terror
Is seen as shadow, known as error.
Next, light comes as light; as it grows
The sense of peace still steadier glows;
And the fierce lust, that linked the soul
To its God, attains a chaste control.
Intimate, an atomic bliss,
Is the last phrasing of that kiss.
Not ecstasy, but peace, pure peace!

Invisible the dew sublimes
From the great mother, subtly climbs
And loves the leaves! Yea, in the end,

AHA!

Vision all vision must transcend.
These glories are mere scaffolding
To the Closed Palace of the King.

OLYMPAS. Yet, saidst thou, ere the new flower shoots
The soul is torn up by the roots.

MARSYAS. Now come we to the intimate things
Known to how few! Man's being clings
First to the outer. Free from these
The inner sheathings, and he sees
Those sheathings as external. Strip
One after one each lovely lip
From the full rose-bud! Ever new
Leaps the next petal to the view.
What binds them by Desire? Disease
Most dire of direful Destiny's!

OLYMPAS. I have abandoned all to tread
The brilliant pathway overhead!

MARSYAS. Easy to say. To abandon all,
All must be first loved and possessed.
Nor thou nor I have burst the thrall.
All—as I offered half in jest,
Sceptic—was torn away from me.
Not without pain! THEY slew my child
Dragged my wife down to infamy
Loathlier than death, drove to the wild
My tortured body, stripped me of
Wealth, health, youth, beauty, ardour, love.
Thou has abandoned all? Then try
A speck of dust within the eye!

OLYMPAS. But that is different!

MARSYAS.   Life is one.
Magic is life. The physical
(Men name it) is a house of call
For the adept, heir of the sun!
Bombard the house! it groans and gapes.
The adept runs forth, and so escapes
That ruin!

OLYMPAS.   Smoothly parallel
The ruin of the mind as well?

MARSYAS.   Ay! Hear the Ordeal of the Veil,
The Second Veil! ... O spare me this
Magical memory! I pale
To show the Veil of the Abyss.
Nay, let confession be complete!

OLYMPAS.   Master, I bend me at thy feet—
Why do they sweat with blood and dew?

MARSYAS.   Blind horror catches at my breath.
The path of the abyss runs through
Things darker, dismaller than death!
Courage and will! What boots their force?
The mind rears like a frightened horse.
There is no memory possible
Of that unfathomable hell.
Even the shadows that arise
Are things too dreadful to recount!
There's no such doom in Destiny's
Harvest of horror. The white fount
Of speech is stifled at its source.
Know, the sane spirit keeps its course
By this, that everything it thinks
Hath causal or contingent links.

AHA!

Destroy them, and destroy the mind!
O bestial, bottomless, and blind
Black pit of all insanity!
The adept must make his way to thee!
This is the end of all our pain,
The dissolution of the brain!
For lo! in this no mortar sticks;
Down come the house—a hail of bricks!
The sense of all I hear is drowned;
Tap, tap, isolated sound,
Patters, clatters, batters, chatters,
Tap, tap, tap, and nothing matters!
Senseless hallucinations roll
Across the curtain of the soul.
Each ripple on the river seems
The madness of a maniac's dreams!
So in the self no memory-chain
Or causal wisp to bind the straws!
The Self disrupted! Blank, insane,
Both of existence and of laws,
The Ego and the Universe
Fall to one black chaotic curse.

OLYMPAS. So ends philosophy's inquiry:
"Summa scientia nihil scire."

MARSYAS. Ay, but that reasoned thesis lacks
The impact of reality.
This vision is a battle axe
Splitting the skull. O pardon me!
But my soul faints, my stomach sinks.
Let me pass on!

OLYMPAS.   My being drinks

THE EQUINOX

The nectar-poison of the Sphinx.
This is a bitter medicine!

MARSYAS.   Black snare that I was taken in!
How one may pass I hardly know.
Maybe time never blots the track.
Black, black, intolerably black!
Go, spectre of the ages, go!
Suffice it that I passed beyond.
I found the secret of the bond
Of thought to thought through countless years
Through many lives, in many spheres,
Brought to a point the dark design
Of this existence that is mine.
I knew my secret. *All I was*
I brought into the burning-glass,
And all its focussed light and heat
Charred *all I am*. The rune's complete
When *all I shall be* flashes by
Like a shadow on the sky.

Then I dropped my reasoning.
Vacant and accursed thing!
By my Will I swept away
The web of metaphysic, smiled
At the blind labyrinth, where the grey
Old snake of madness wove his wild
Curse! As I trod the trackless way
Through sunless gorges of Cathay,
I became a little child.
By nameless rivers, swirling through

AHA!

Chasms, a fantastic blue,
Month by month, on barren hills,
In burning heat, in bitter chills,
Tropic forest, Tartar snow,
Smaragdine archipelago,
See me—led by some wise hand
That I did not understand.
Morn and noon and eve and night
I, the forlorn eremite,
Called on Him with mild devotion,
As the dew-drop woos the ocean.

In my wanderings I came
To an ancient park aflame
With fairies' feet. Still wrapped in love
I was caught up, beyond, above
The tides of being. The great sight
Of the intolerable light
Of the whole universe that wove
The labyrinth of life and love
Blazed in me. Then some giant will,
Mine or another's thrust a thrill
Through the great vision. All the light
Went out in an immortal night,
The world annihilated by
The opening of the Master's Eye.
How can I tell it?

OLYMPAS.   Master, master!
A sense of some divine disaster
Abases me.

MARSYAS.   Indeed, the shrine
          Is desolate of the divine!
          But all the illusion gone, behold
          The one that is!
OLYMPAS.   Royally rolled,
          I hear strange music in the air!
MARSYAS. It is the angelic choir, aware
          Of the great Ordeal dared and done
          By one more Brother of the Sun!
OLYMPAS. Master, the shriek of a great bird
          Blends with the torrent of the thunder.
MARSYAS. It is the echo of the word
          That tore the universe asunder.
OLYMPAS. Master, thy stature spans the sky.
MARSYAS. Verily; but it is not I.
          The adept dissolves—pale phantom form
          Blown from the black mouth of the storm.
          It is another that arises!
OLYMPAS. Yet in thee, through thee!
MARSYAS.   I am not.
OLYMPAS. For me thou art.
MARSYAS.   So that suffices
          To seal thy will? To cast thy lot
          Into the lap of God? Then, well!
OLYMPAS. Ay, there is no more potent spell.
          Through life, through death, by land and sea
          Most surely will I follow thee.
MARSYAS. Follow thyself, not me. Thou hast
          An Holy Guardian Angel, bound
          To lead thee from thy bitter waste

AHA!

To the inscrutable profound
That is His covenanted ground.

OLYMPAS. Thou who hast known these master-keys
Of all creation's mysteries,
Tell me, what followed the great gust
Of God that blew his world to dust?

MARSYAS. I, even I the man, became
As a great sword of flashing flame.
My life, informed with holiness,
Conscious of its own loveliness,
Like a well that overflows
At the limit of the snows,
Sent its crystal stream to gladden
The hearts of men, their lives to madden
With the intoxicating bliss
(Wine mixed with myrrh and ambergris!)
Of this bitter-sweet perfume,
This gorse's blaze of prickly bloom
That is the Wisdom of the Way.
Then springs the statue from the clay,
And all God's doubted fatherhood
Is seen to be supremely good.

Live within the sane sweet sun!
Leave the shadow-world alone!

OLYMPAS. There is a crown for every one;
For every one there is a throne!

MARSYAS. That crown is Silence. Sealed and sure!
That throne is Knowledge perfect pure.
Below that throne adoring stand

THE EQUINOX

Virtues in a blissful band;
Mercy, majesty and power,
Beauty and harmony and strength,
Triumph and splendour, starry shower
Of flames that flake their lily length,
A necklet of pure light, far-flung
Down to the Base, from which is hung
A pearl, the Universe, whose sight
Is one globed jewel of delight.
Fallen no more! A bowered bride
Blushing to be satisfied!

OLYMPAS. All this, of once the Eye unclose?

MARSYAS. The golden cross, the ruby rose
Are gone, when flaming from afar
The Hawk's eye blinds the Silver Star.

O brothers of the Star, caressed
By its cool flames from brow to breast,
Is there some rapture yet to excite
This prone and pallid neophyte?

OLYMPAS. O but there is no need of this!
I burn toward the abyss of Bliss.
I call the Four Powers of the Name;
Earth, wind and cloud, sea, smoke and flame
To witness: by this triune Star
I swear to break the twi-forked bar.
But how to attain? Flexes and leans
The strongest will that lacks the means.

MARSYAS. There are seven keys to the great gate,
Being eight in one and one in eight.

AHA!

First, let the body of thee be still,
Bound by the cerements of will,
Corpse-rigid; thus thou mayst abort
The fidget-babes that tense the thought.
Next, let the breath-rhythm be low,
Easy, regular, and slow;
So that thy being be in tune
With the great sea's Pacific swoon.
Third, let thy life be pure and calm
Swayed softly as a windless palm.
Fourth, let the will-to-live be bound
To the one love of the Profound.
Fifth, let the thought, divinely free
From sense, observe its entity.
Watch every thought that springs; enhance
Hour after hour thy vigilance!
Intense and keen, turned inward, miss
No atom of analysis!
Sixth, on one thought securely pinned
Still every whisper of the wind!
So like a flame straight and unstirred
Burn up thy being in one word!
Next, still that ecstasy, prolong
Thy meditation steep and strong,
Slaying even God, should He distract
Thy attention from the chosen act!
Last, all these things in one o'erpowered,
Time that the midnight blossom flowered!
The oneness is. Yet even in this,
My son, thou shalt not do amiss

If thou restrain the expression, shoot
Thy glance to rapture's darkling root,
Discarding name, form, sight, and stress
Even of this high consciousness;
Pierce to the heart! I leave thee here:
Thou art the Master. I revere
Thy radiance that rolls afar,
O Brother of the Silver Star!

OLYMPAS.　Ah, but no ease may lap my limbs.
Giants and sorcerers oppose;
Ogres and dragons are my foes!
Leviathan against me swims,
And lions roar, and Boreas blows!
No Zephyrs woo, no happy hymns
Pæan the Pilgrim of the Rose!

MARSYAS.　I teach the royal road of light.
Be thou, devoutly eremite,
Free of thy fate. Choose tenderly
A place for thine Academy.
Let there be an holy wood
Of embowered solitude
By the still, the rainless river,
Underneath the tangled roots
Of majestic trees that quiver
In the quiet airs; where shoots
Of the kindly grass are green
Moss and ferns asleep between,
Lilies in the water lapped,
Sunbeams in the branches trapped
—Windless and eternal even!
Silenced all the birds of heaven

AHA!

By the low insistent call
Of the constant waterfall.
There, to such a setting be
Its carven gem of deity,
A central flawless fire, enthralled
Like Truth within an emerald!
Thou shalt have a birchen bark
On the river in the dark;
And at the midnight thou shalt go
To the mid-stream's smoothest flow,
And strike upon a golden bell
The spirit's call; then say the spell:
"Angel, mine angel, draw thee nigh!"
Making the Sign of Magistry
With wand of lapis lazuli.
Then, it may be, through the blind dumb
Night thou shalt see thine angel come,
Hear the faint whisper of his wings,
Behold the starry breast begemmed
With the twelve stones of the twelve kings!
His forehead shall be diademed
With the faint light of stars, wherein
The Eye gleams dominant and keen.
Thereat thou swoonest; and thy love
Shall catch the subtle voice thereof.
He shall inform his happy lover:
My foolish prating shall be over!

OLYMPAS.   O now I burn with holy haste.
This doctrine hath so sweet a taste
That all the other wine is sour.

MARSYAS.   Son, there's a bee for every flower.

Lie open, a chameleon cup,
And let Him suck thine honey up!

OLYMPAS. There is one doubt. When souls attain
Such an unimagined gain
Shall not others mark them, wise
Beyond mere mortal destinies?

MARSYAS. Such are not the perfect saints.
While the imagination faints
Before their truth, they veil it close
As amid the utmost snows
The tallest peaks most straitly hide
With clouds their holy heads. Divide
The planes! Be ever as you can
A simple honest gentleman!
Body and manners be at ease,
Not bloat with blazoned sanctities!
Who fights as fights the soldier-saint?
And see the artist-adept paint!
Weak are those souls that fear the stress
Of earth upon their holiness!
They fast, they eat fantastic food,
They prate of beans and brotherhood,
Wear sandals, and long hair, and spats,
And think that makes them Arahats!
How shall man still his spirit-storm?
Rational Dress and Food Reform!

OLYMPAS. I know such saints.

MARSYAS.   An easy vice:
So wondrous well they advertise!
O their mean souls are satisfied

AHA!

With wind of spiritual pride.
They're all negation. "Do not eat;
What poison to the soul is meat!
Drink not; smoke not; deny the will!
Wine and tobacco make us ill."
Magic is life; the Will to Live
Is one supreme Affirmative.
These things that flinch from Life are worth
No more to Heaven than to Earth.
Affirm the everlasting Yes!

OLYMPAS. Those saints at least score one success:
Perfection of their priggishness!

MARSYAS. Enough. The soul is subtlier fed
With meditation's wine and bread.
Forget their failings and our own;
Fix all our thoughts on Love alone!

Ah, boy, all crowns and thrones above
Is the sanctity of love.
In His warm and secret shrine
Is a cup of perfect wine,
Whereof one drop is medicine
Against all ills that hurt the soul.
A flaming daughter of the Jinn
Brought to me once a wingéd scroll,
Wherein I read the spell that brings
The knowledge of that King of Kings.
Angel, I invoke thee now!
Bend on me the starry brow!
Spread the eagle wings above

THE EQUINOX

The pavilion of our love! . . . .
Rise from your starry sapphire seats!
See, where through the quickening skies
The oriflamme of beauty beats
Heralding loyal legionaries,
Whose flame of golden javelins
Fences those peerless paladins.
There are the burning lamps of them,
Splendid star-clusters to begem
The trailing torrents of those blue
Bright wings that bear mine angel through!
O Thou art like an Hawk of Gold,
Miraculously manifold,
For all the sky's aflame to be
A mirror magical of Thee!
The stars seem comets, rushing down
To gem thy robes, bedew thy crown.
Like the moon-plumes of a strange bird
By a great wind sublimely stirred,
Thou drawest the light of all the skies
Into thy wake. The heaven dies
In bubbling froth of light, that foams
About thine ardour. All the domes
Of all the heavens close above thee
As thou art known of me who love thee.
Excellent kiss, thou fastenest on
This soul of mine, that it is gone,
Gone from all life, and rapt away
Into the infinite starry spray
Of thine own Æon . . . Alas for me!

I faint. Thy mystic majesty
Absorbs this spark.

OLYMPAS.   All hail! all hail!
White splendour through the viewless veil!
I am drawn with thee to rapture.

MARSYAS.   Stay!
I bear a message. Heaven hath sent
The knowledge of a new sweet way
Into the Secret Element.

OLYMPAS.   Master, while yet the glory clings
Declare this mystery magical!

MARSYAS.   I am yet borne on those blue wings
Into the Essence of the All.
Now, now I stand on earth again,
Though, blazing through each nerve and vein,
The light yet holds its choral course,
Filling my frame with fiery force
Like God's. Now hear the Apocalypse
New-fledged on these reluctant lips!

OLYMPAS.   I tremble like an aspen, quiver
Like light upon a rainy river!

MARSYAS.   Do what thou wilt! is the sole word
Of law that my attainment heard.
Arise, and lay thine hand on God!
Arise, and set a period
Unto Restriction! That is sin:
To hold thine holy spirit in!
O thou that chafest at thy bars,
Invoke Nuit beneath her stars
With a pure heart (Her incense burned

THE EQUINOX

Of gums and woods, in gold inurned),
And let the serpent flame therein
A little, and thy soul shall win
To lie within her bosom. Lo!
Thou wouldst give all—and she cries: No!
Take all, and take me! Gather spice
And virgins and great pearls of price!
Worship me in a single robe,
Crowned richly! Girdle of the globe,
I love thee! Pale and purple, veiled,
Voluptuous, swan silver-sailed,
I love thee. I am drunkness
Of the inmost sense; my soul's caress
Is toward thee! Let my priestess stand
Bare and rejoicing, softly fanned
By smooth-lipped acolytes, upon
Mine iridescent altar-stone,
And in her love-chaunt swooningly
Say evermore: To me! To me!
I am the azure-lidded daughter
Of sunset; the all-girdling water;
The naked brilliance of the sky
In the voluptuous night am I!
With song, with jewel, with perfume,
Wake all my rose's blush and bloom!
Drink to me! Love me! I love thee,
My love, my lord—to me! to me!

OLYMPAS.   There is no harshness in the breath
Of this—is life surpassed, and death?

MARSYAS.   There is the Snake that gives delight

48

AHA!

And Knowledge, stirs the heart aright
With drunkenness. Strange drugs are thine,
Hadit, and draughts of wizard wine!
These do no hurt. Thine hermits dwell
Not in the cold secretive cell,
But under purple canopies
With mighty-breasted mistresses
Magnificent as lionesses—
Tender and terrible caresses!
Fire lives, and light, in eager eyes;
And massed huge hair about them lies.
They lead their hosts to victory:
In every joy they are kings; then see
That secret serpent coiled to spring
And win the world! O priest and king,
Let there be feasting, foining, fighting,
A revel of lusting, singing, smiting!
Work; be the bed of work! Hold! Hold!
The stars' kiss is as molten gold.
Harden! Hold thyself up! now die—
Ah! Ah! Exceed! Exceed!

OLYMPAS.   And I?
MARSYAS.   My stature shall surpass the stars:
He hath said it! Men shall worship me
In hidden woods, on barren scaurs,
Henceforth to all eternity.
OLYMPAS.   Hail! I adore thee! Let us feast.
MARSYAS.   I am the consecrated Beast.
I build the Abominable House.
The Scarlet Woman is my Spouse—

OLYMPAS.   What is this word?

MARSYAS.   Thou canst not know
Till thou hast passed the Fourth Ordeal.

OLYMPAS.   I worship thee. The moon-rays flow
Masterfully rich and real
From thy red mouth, and burst, young suns
Chanting before the Holy Ones
Thine Eight Mysterious Orisons!

MARSYAS.   The last spell! The availing word!
The two completed by the third!
The Lord of War, of Vengeance
That slayeth with a single glance!
This light is in me of my Lord.
His Name is this far-whirling sword.
I push His order. Keen and swift
My Hawk's eye flames; these arms uplift
The Banner of Silence and of Strength—
Hail! Hail! thou art here, my Lord, at length!
Lo, the Hawk-Headed Lord am I:
My nemyss shrouds the night-blue sky.
Hail! ye twin warriors that guard
The pillars of the world! Your time
Is nigh at hand. The snake that marred
Heaven with his inexhaustible slime
Is slain; I bear the Wand of Power,
The Wand that waxes and that wanes;
I crush the Universe this hour
In my left hand; and naught remains!
Ho! for the splendour in my name
Hidden and glorious, a flame

AHA!

	Secretly shooting from the sun.
	Aum! Ha!—my destiny is done.
	The Word is spoken and concealed.
OLYMPAS.	I am stunned. What wonder was revealed?
MARSYAS.	The rite is secret.
OLYMPAS.	Profits it?
MARSYAS.	Only to wisdom and to wit.
OLYMPAS.	The other did no less.
MARSYAS.	Then prove
	Both by the master-key of Love.
	The lock turns stiffly? Shalt thou shirk
	To use the sacred oil of work?
	Not from the valley shalt thou test
	The eggs that line the eagle's nest!
	Climb, with thy life at stake, the ice,
	The sheer wall of the precipice!
	Master the cornice, gain the breach,
	And learn what next the ridge can teach!
	Yet—not the ridge itself may speak
	The secret of the final peak.
OLYMPAS.	All ridges join at last.
MARSYAS.	Admitted,
	O thou astute and subtle-witted!
	Yet one—loose, jaggéd, clad in mist!
	Another—firm, smooth, loved and kissed
	By the soft sun! Our order hath
	This secret of the solar path,
	Even as our Lord the Beast hath won
	The mystic Number of the Sun.
OLYMPAS.	These secrets are too high for me.

MARSYAS.	Nay, little brother! Come and see!
	Neither by faith nor fear nor awe
	Approach the doctrine of the Law!
	Truth, Courage, Love, shall win the bout,
	And those three others be cast out.
OLYMPAS.	Lead me, Master, by the hand
	Gently to this gracious land!
	Let me drink the doctrine in,
	An all-healing medicine!
	Let me rise, correct and firm,
	Steady striding to the term,
	Master of my fate, to rise
	To imperial destinies;
	With the sun's ensanguine dart
	Spear-bright in my blazing heart,
	And my being's basil-plant
	Bright and hard as adamant!
MARSYAS.	Yonder, faintly luminous,
	The yellow desert waits for us.
	Lithe and eager, hand in hand,
	We travel to the lonely land.
	There, beneath the stars, the smoke
	Of our incense shall invoke
	The Queen of Space; and subtly
	She Shall bend from Her infinity
	Like a lambent flame of blue,
	Touching us, and piercing through
	All the sense-webs that we are
	As the aethyr penetrates a star!
	Her hands caressing the black earth,

AHA!

Her sweet lithe body arched for love,
Her feet a Zephyr to the flowers,
She calls my name—she gives the sign
That she is mine, supremely mine,
And clinging to the infinite girth
My soul gets perfect joy thereof
Beyond the abysses and the hours;
So that—I kiss her lovely brows;
She bathes my body in perfume
Of sweat .... O thou my secret spouse,
Continuous One of Heaven! illume
My soul with this arcane delight,
Voluptuous Daughter of the Night!
Eat me up wholly with the glance
Of thy luxurious brilliance!

OLYMPAS. The desert calls.

MARSYAS.   Then let us go!
Or seek the sacramental snow,
Where like a high-priest I may stand
With acolytes on every hand,
The lesser peaks—my will withdrawn
To invoke the dayspring from the dawn,
Changing that rosy smoke of light
To a pure crystalline white;
Though the mist of mind, as draws
A dancer round her limbs the gauze,
Clothe Light, and show the virgin Sun
A lemon-pale medallion!
Thence leap we leashless to the goal,
Stainless star-rapture of the soul.

THE EQUINOX

So the altar-fires fade
As the Godhead is displayed.
Nay, we stir not. Everywhere
Is our temple right appointed.
All the earth is faery fair
For us. Am I not anointed?
The Sigil burns upon the brow
At the adjuration—here and now.

OLYMPAS.   The air is laden with perfumes.
MARSYAS.   Behold! It beams—it burns—it blooms.
  *   *   *   *   *

OLYMPAS.   Master, how subtly hast thou drawn
The daylight from the Golden Dawn,
Bidden the Cavernous Mount unfold
Its Ruby Rose, its Cross of Gold;
Until I saw, flashed from afar,
The Hawk's eye in the Silver Star!
MARSYAS.   Peace to all beings. Peace to thee,
Co-heir of mine eternity!
Peace to the greatest and the least,
To nebula and nenuphar!
Light in abundance be increased
On them that dream that shadows are!
OLYMPAS.   Blessing and worship to The Beast,
The prophet of the lovely Star!

THE HERB DANGEROUS

PART III

THE POEM OF HASHISH

THE POEM OF HASHISH

CHAPTER I

THE LONGING FOR INFINITY

THOSE who know how to observe themselves, and who preserve the memory of their impressions, those who, life Hoffmann, have known how to construct their spiritual barometer, have sometimes had to note in the observatory of their mind fine seasons, happy days, delicious minutes. There are days when man awakes with a young and vigorous genius. Though his eyelids be scarcely released from the slumber which sealed them, the exterior world shows itself to him with a powerful relief, a clearness of contour, and a richness of colour which are admirable. The moral world opens out its vast perspective, full of new clarities.

A man gratified by this happiness, unfortunately rare and transient, feels himself at once more an artist and more a just man; to say all in a word, a nobler being. But the most singular thing in this exceptional condition of the spirit and of the senses—which I may without exaggeration call heavenly, if I compare it with the heavy shadows of common and daily existence—is that it has not been created by any visible or easily definiable cause. Is it the result of a good hygeine and of a wise regimen? Such is the first explanation which suggests itself ; but we are obliged to recognise that often this marvel, this prodigy, so to say, produces itself as if it were the effect of a superior and invisible power, of a power exterior to man, after a period of the abuse of his physical faculties. Shall we say that it is the reward of assiduous prayer and spiritual ardour? It is certain that a constant elevation of the desire, a tension of the spiritual forces in a heavenly direction, would be the most proper regimen for creating this moral health, so brilliant and so glorious. But what absurd law causes it to manifest itself (as it sometimes does) after shameful orgies of the imagination; after a sophistical abuse of reason, which is, to its straight forward and rational use, that which the tricks of dislocation which some acrobats have taught themselves to perform are to sane gymnastics? For this reason I prefer to consider this abnormal condition of the spirit as a true "grace;" as a magic mirror wherein man is invited to see himself at his best; that is to say, as that which he should be, and might be; a kind of angelic excitement; a rehabilitation of the most flattering type. A certain Spiritualist School, largely represented in England and America, even considers supernatural phenomena, such as the apparition of phantoms, ghosts, &c., as manifestations of the Divine Will, ever anxious to awaken in the spirit of man the memory of invisible truths.

Besides this charming and singular state, where all the forces are balanced; where the imagination, though enormously powerful, does not drag after it into perilous adventures the moral sense; when an exquisite sensibility is no longer tortured by sick nerves, those councillors-in- ordinary of crime or despair: this marvellous

State, I say, has no prodromal symptoms. It is as unexpected as a ghost. It is a species of obsession, but of intermittent obsession; from which we should be able to draw, if we were but wise, the certainty of a nobler existence, and the hope of attaining to it by the daily exercise of our will. This sharpness of thought, this enthusiasm of the senses and of the spirit, must in every age have appeared to man as the chiefest of blessings; and for this reason, considering nothing but the immediate pleasure he has, without worrying himself as to whether he were violating the laws of his constitution, he has sought, in physical science, in pharmacy, in the grossest liquors, in the subtlest perfumes, in every climate and in every age, the means of fleeing, were it but for some hours only, his habitaculum of mire, and, as the author of "Lazare" says, "to carry Paradise at the first assault." Alas! the vices of man, full of horror as one must suppose them, contain the proof, even though it were nothing but their infinite expansion, of his hunger for the Infinite; only, it is a taste which often loses its way. One might take a proverbial metaphor, "All roads lead to Rome," and apply it to the moral world: all roads lead to reward or punishment; two forms of eternity. The mind of man is glutted with passion: he has, if I may use another familiar phrase, passion to burn. But this unhappy soul, whose natural depravity is equal to its sudden aptitude, paradoxical enough, for charity and the most arduous virtues, is full of paradoxes which allow him to turn to other purposes the overflow of this overmastering passion. He never imagines that he is selling himself wholesale: he forgets, in his infatuation, that he is matched against a player more cunning and more strong than he; and that the Spirit of Evil, though one give him but a hair, will not delay to carry off the whole head. This visible lord of visible nature—I speak of man—has, then, wished to create Paradise by chemistry, by fermented drinks; like a maniac who should replace solid furniture and real gardens by decorations painted on canvas and mounted on frames. It is in this degradation of the sense of the Infinite that lies, according to me, the reason of all guilty excesses; from the solitary and concentrated drunkenness of the man of letters, who, obliged to seek in opium and anodyne for a physical suffering, and having thus discovered a well of morbid pleasure, has made of it, little by little, his sole diet, and as it were the sum of his spiritual life; down to the most disgusting sot of the suburbs, who, his head full of flame and of glory, rolls ridiculously in the muck of the roads.

Among the drugs most efficient in creating what I call the artificial ideal, leaving on one side liquors, which rapidly exite gross frenzy and lay flat all spiritual force, and the perfumes, whose excessive use, while rendering more subtle man's imagination, wear out gradually his physical forces; the two most energetic substances, the most convenient and the most handy, are hashish and opium. The analysis of the mysterious effect and the diseased pleasures which these drugs beget, of the inevitable chastisement which results from their prolonged use, and finally the immorality necessarily employed in this pursuit of a false ideal, consititutes the subject of this study.

The subject of opium has been treated already, and in a manner at once so startling, so scientific, and so poetic that I shall not dare to add a word to it. I will therefore content myself in another study, with giving an analysis of this incomparable book, which has never been fully translated into French. The author, and illustrious man of a powerful and exquisite imagination, to-day retired and silent, has dared with tragic candour to write down the delights and the tortures which he once found in opium, and the most dramatic portion of his book is that where he speaks of the superhuman efforts of will which he found it necessary to bring into action in order to escape from the damnation which he had imprudently incurred. To-day I shall only speak of hashish, and I shall speak of it after numerous investigations and minute information; extracts from notes or confidences of intelligent men who had long been addicted to it; only, I shall combine these varied documents into a sort of monograph, choosing a particular soul, and one easy to explain and to define, as a type suitable to experiences of this nature.

CHAPTER II

WHAT IS HASHISH?

THE stories of Marco Polo, which have been so unjustly laughed at, as in the case of some other old travellers, have been verified by men of science, and deserve our belief. I shall not repeat his story of how, after having intoxicated them with hashish (whence the word "Assassin") the old Man of the Mountains shut up in a garden filled with delights those of his youngest disciples to whom he wished to give an idea of Paradise as an earnest of the reward, so to speak, of a passive and unreflecting obedience. The reader may consult, concerning the secret Society of Hashishins, the work of Von Hammer- Purgstall, and the note of M. Sylvestre de Sacy contained in vol. 16 of "Mémories de l'Académie des Inscriptions et Belles-Lettres"; and, with regard to the etymology of the word "assassin," his letter to the editor of the "Moniteur" in No. 359 of the year 1809. Herodotus tells us that the Syrians used to gather grains of hemp and throw red-hot stones upon them; so that it was like a vapour-bath, more perfumed than that of any Grecian stove; and the pleasure of it was so acute that it drew cries of joy from them.

Hashish, in effect, comes to us from the East. The exciting properties of hemp were well known in ancient Egypt, and the use of it is very widely spread under different names in

THE POEM OF HASHISH

India, Algeria, and Arabia Felix; but we have around us, under our eyes, curious examples of the intoxication caused by vegetable emanations. Without speaking of the children who, having played and rolled themselves in heaps of cut lucern, often experience singular attacks of vertigo, it is well known that during the hemp harvest both male and female workers undergo similar effects. One would say that from the harvest rises a miasma which troubles their brains despitefully. The head of the reaper is full of whirlwinds, sometimes laden with reveries; at certain moments the limbs grow weak and refuse their office. We have heard tell of crises of somnambulism as being frequent among the Russian peasants, whose cause, they say, must be attributed to the use of hempseed oil in the preparation of food. Who does not know the extravagant behaviour of hens which have eaten grains of hemp-seed, and the wild enthusiasm of the horses which the peasants, at weddings and on the feasts of their patron saints, prepare for a steeplechase by a ration of hemp-seed, sometimes sprinkled with wine? Nevertheless, French hemp is unsuitable for preparing hashish, or at least, as repeated experiments have shown, unfitted to give a drug which is equal in power to hashish. Hashish, or Indian hemp (*Cannabis indica*), is a plant of the family of *Urticacea*, resembling in every respect the hemp of our latitudes, except that it does not attain the same height. It possesses very extraordinary intoxicating properties, which for some years past have attracted in France the attention of men of science and of the world. It is more or less highly esteemed according to its different sources: that of Bengal is the most prized by Europeans; that, however, of Egypt, of Constantinople, of Persia, and of Algeria enjoys the same properties, but in an inferior degree.

Hashish (or grass; that is to say, *the* grass *par excellence*, as if the Arabs had wished to define in a single word the *grass* source of all material pleasures) has different names, according to its composition and the method of preparation which it has undergone in the country where it has been gathered: In India, *bhang*; in Africa, *teriaki*; in Algeria and in Arabia Felix, *madjound*, &c. It makes considerable difference at what season of the year it is gathered. It possesses its greatest energy when it is in flower. The flowering tops are in consequence the only parts employed in the different preparations of which we are about to speak. The *extrait gras* of hashish, as the Arabs prepare it, is obtained by boiling the tops of the fresh plant in butter, with a little water. It is strained, after complete evaporation of all humidity, and one thus obtains a preparation which has the appearance of a pomade, in colour greenish yellow, and which possesses a disagreeable odour of hashish and of rancid butter. Under this form it is employed in small pills of two to four grammes in weight, but on account of its objectionable smell, which increases with age, the Arabs conceal the *extrait gras* in sweetmeats.

The most commonly employed of these sweetmeats, *dawamesk*, is a mixture of *extrait gras*, sugar, and various other aromatic substances, such as vanilla, cinnamon, pistachio, almond, musk. Sometimes one even adds a little cantharides, with an object which has nothing in common with the ordinary results of hashish. Under this new form hashish has no disagreeable qualities, and one can take it in a dose of fifteen, twenty, and thirty grammes, either enveloped in a leaf of *pain à chanter* or in a cup of coffee.

The experiments made by Messrs. Smith, Gastinel, and Decourtive were directed towards the discovery of the active principles of hashish. Despite their efforts, its chemical combination is still little known, but one usually attributes its properties to a resinous matter which is found there in the proportion of about 10 per cent. To obtain this resin the dried plant is reduced to a course powder, which is then washed several times with alcohol; this is afterwards partially distilled and evaporated until it reaches the consistency of an extract; this extract is treated with water, which dissolves the gummy foreign matter, and the resin then remains in a pure condition.

This product is soft, of a dark green colour, and possesses to a high degree the characteristic smell of hashish. Five, ten, fifteen centigrammes are sufficient to produce surprising results. But the haschischine, which may be administered under the form of chocolate pastilles or small pills mixed with ginger, has, like the *dawamesk* and the *extrait gras*, effects more or less vigorous, and of an extremely varied nature, according to the individual temperament and nervous susceptibility of the hashish-eater; and, more than that, the result varies in the same individual. Sometimes he will experience an immoderate and irresistible gaiety, sometimes a sense of well-being and of abundance of life, sometimes a slumber doubtful and thronged with dreams. There are, however, some phenomena which occur regularly enough; above all, in the case of persons of a regular temperament and education; there is a kind of unity in its variety which will allow me to edit, without too much trouble, this monograph on hashish-drunkenness of which I spoke before.

At Constantinople, in Algeria, and even in France, some people smoke hashish mixed with tobacco, but then the phenomena in question only occur under a form much moderated, and, so to say, lazy. I have heard it said that recently, by means of distillation, an essential oil has been drawn from hashish which appears to possess a power much more active than all the preparations hitherto known, but it has not been sufficiently studied for me to speak with certainty of its results. Is it not superfluous to add that tea, coffee, and alcoholic drinks are powerful adjuvants which accelerate more or less the outbreak of this mysterious intoxication?

CHAPTER III

THE PLAYGROUND OF THE SERAPHIM

WHAT does one experience? What does one see? Marvellous things, is it not so? Wonderful sights? Is it very beautiful? and very terrible? and very dangerous? Such are the usual questions which, with a curiosity mingled with fear, those ignorant of hashish address to its adepts. It is, as it were, the childish impatience to know, resembling that of those people who have never quitted their firesides when they meet a man who returns from distant and unknown countries. They imagine hashish-drunkenness to themselves as a prodigious country, a vast theatre of sleight-of-hand and of juggling, where all is miraculous, all unforeseen.—That is a prejudice, a complete mistake. And since for the ordinary run of readers and of questioners the word "hashish" connotes the idea of a strange and topsy-turvy world, the expectation of prodigious dreams (it would be better to say hallucinations, which are, by the way, less frequent than people suppose), I will at once remark upon the important difference which separates the effects of hashish from the phenomena of dream. In dream, that adventurous voyage which we undertake every night, there is something positively miraculous. It is a miracle whose punctual occurrence has blunted its mystery. The dreams of man are of two classes. Some, full of his ordinary life, of his preoccupations, of his desires, of his vices, combine themselves in a manner more or less bizarre with the objects which he has met in his day's work, which have carelessly fixed themselves upon the vast canvas of his memory. That is the natural dream; it is the man himself. But the other kind of dream, the dream absurd and unforeseen, without meaning or connection with the character, the life, and the passions of the sleeper: this dream, which I shall call hieroglyphic, evidently represents the supernatural side of life, and it is exactly because it is absurd that the ancients believed it to be divine. As it is inexplicable by natural causes, they attributed to it a cause external to man, and even to-day, leaving out of account oneiromancers and the fooleries of a philosophical school which sees in dreams of this type sometimes a reproach, sometimes a warning; in short, a symbolic and moral picture begotten in the spirit itself of the sleeper. It is a dictionary which one must study; a language of which sages may obtain the key.

In the intoxication of hashish there is nothing like this. We shall not go outside the class of natural dream. The drunkenness, throughout its duration, it is true, will be nothing but an immense dream, thanks to the intensity of its colours and the rapidity of its conceptions. But it will always keep the idiosyncrasy of the individual. The man has desired to dream; the dream will govern the man. But this dream will be truly the son of its father. The idle man has taxed his ingenuity to introduce artificially the supernatural into his life and into his thought; but, after all, and despite the accidental energy of his experiences, he is nothing but the same man magnified, the same number raised to a very high power. He is brought into subjection, but, unhappily for him, it is not by himself; that is to say, by the part of himself which is already dominant. "He would be angel; he becomes a beast." Momentarily very powerful, if, indeed, one can give the name of power to what is merely excessive sensibility without the control which might moderate or make use of it.

Let it be well understood then, by worldly and ignorant folk, curious of acquaintance with exceptional joys, that they will find in hashish nothing miraculous, absolutely nothing but the natural in a superabundant degree. The brain and the organism upon which hashish operates will only give their ordinary and individual phenomena, magnified, it is true, both in quantity and quality, but always faithful to their origin. Man cannot escape the fatality of his mortal and physical temperament. Hashish will be, indeed, for the impressions and familiar thoughts of the man, a mirror which magnifies, yet no more than a mirror.

Here is the drug before your eyes: a little green sweet-meat, about as big as a nut, with a strange smell; so strange that it arouses a certain revulsion, and inclinations to nausea —as, indeed, any fine and even agreeable scent, exalted to its maximum strength and (so to say) density, would do.

Allow me to remark in passing that this proposition can be inverted, and that the most disgusting and revolting perfume would become perhaps a pleasure to inhale if it were reduced to its minimum quantity and intensity.

There! there is happiness; heaven in a teaspoon; happiness, with all its intoxication, all its folly, all its childishness. You can swallow it without fear; it is not fatal; it will in nowise injure your physical organs. Perhaps (later on) too frequent an employment of the sorcery will diminish the strength of your will; perhaps you will be less a man than you are today; but retribution is so far off, and the nature of the eventual disaster so difficult to define! What is it that you risk? A little nervous fatigue to-morrow—no more. Do you not every day risk greater punishments for less reward? Very good then; you have even, to make it act more quickly and vigorously, imbibed your dose of *extrait gras* in a cup of black coffee. You have taken care to have the stomach empty, postponing dinner till nine or ten o'clock, to give full liberty of action to the poison. At the very most you will take a little soup in an hour's time. You are now sufficiently provisioned for a long and strange journey; the steamer has whistled, the sails are trimmed; and you have this curious advantage over ordinary travellers, that you have no idea where you are going. You have made your choice; here's to luck!

I presume that you have taken the precaution to choose carefully your moment for setting out on this adventure. For every perfect debauch demands perfect leisure. You know, moreover, that hashish exaggerates, not only the individual, but also circumstances and environment. You have no duties to fulfil which require punctuality or exactitude; no domestic worries; no lover's sorrows. One must be careful on such points. Such a disappointment, an anxiety, an interior monition of a duty which demands your will and your attention, at some determinate moment, would ring like a funeral bell across your intoxication and poison your pleasure. Anxiety would become anguish, and disappointment torture. But if, having observed all these preliminary conditions, the weather is fine; if you are situated in favourable surroundings, such as a picturesque landscape or a room beautifully decorated; and if in particular you have at command a little music, then all is for the best.

Generally speaking, there are three phases in hashish intoxication, easy enough to distinguish, and it is not uncommon for beginners to obtain only the first symptoms of the first phase. You have heard vague chatter about the marvellous effects of hashish; your imagination has preconceived a special idea, an ideal intoxication, so to say. You long to know if the reality will indeed reach the height of your hope; that alone is sufficient to throw you from the very beginning into an anxious state, favourable enough to the conquering and enveloping tendency of the poison. Most novices, on their first initiation, complain of the slowness of the effects: they wait for them with a puerile impatience, and, the drug not acting quickly enough for their liking, they bluster long rigmaroles of incredulity, which are amusing enough for the old hands who know how hashish acts. The first attacks, like the symptoms of a storm which has held off for a long while, appear and multiply themselves in the bosom of this very incredulity. At first it is a certain hilarity, absurdly irresistible, which possesses you. These accesses of gaiety, without due cause, of which you are almost ashamed, frequently occur and divide the intervals of stupor, during which you seek in vain to pull yourself together. The simplest words, the most trivial ideas, take on a new and strange physiognomy. You are surprised at yourself for having up to now found them so simple. Incongruous likenesses and correspondences, impossible to foresee, interminable puns, comic sketches, spout eternally from your brain. The demon has encompassed you; it is useless to kick against the pricks of this hilarity, as painful as tickling is! From time to time you laugh to yourself at your stupidity and your madness, and your comrades, if you are with others, laugh also, both at your state and their own; but as they laugh without malice, so you are without resentment.

This gaiety, turn by turn idle or acute, this uneasiness in joy, this insecurity, this indecision, last, as a rule, but a very short time. Soon the meanings of ideas become so vague, the conducting thread which binds your conceptions together becomes so tenuous, that none but your accomplices can understand you. And, again, on this subject and from this point of view, no means of verifying it! Perhaps they only think that they understand you, and the illusion is reciprocal. This frivolity, these bursts of laughter, like explosions, seem like a true mania, or at least like the delusion of a maniac, to every man who is not in the same state as yourself. What is more, prudence and good sense, the regularity of the thoughts of him who witnesses, but has been careful not to intoxicate himself, rejoice you and amuse you as if they were a particular form of dementia. The parts are interchanged; his self-possession drives you to the last limits of irony. How monstrous comic is this situation, for a man who is enjoying a gaiety incomprehensible for him who is not placed in the same environment as he! The madman takes pity on the sage, and from that moment the idea of his superiority begins to dawn on the horizon of his intellect. Soon it will grow great and broad, and burst like a meteor.

I was once witness of a scene of this kind which was carried very far, and whose grotesqueness was only intelligible to those who were acquainted, at least by means of observation of others, with the effects of the substance and the enormous difference of diapason which it creates between two intelligences apparently equal. A famous musician, who was ignorant of the properties of hashish, who perhaps had never heard speak of it, finds himself in the midst of a company, several persons of which had taken a portion. They try to make him understand the marvellous effects of it; at these prodigious yarns he smiles courteously, by complaisance, like a man who is willing to play the fool for a minute or two. His contempt is quickly divined by these spirits, sharpened by the poison, and their laughter wounds him; these bursts of joy, this playing with words, these altered countenances—all this unwholesome atmosphere irritates him, and forces him to exclaim sooner, perhaps, than he would have wished that this is a poor *rôle*, and that, moreover, it must be very tiring for those who have undertaken it.

The comicality of it lightened them all like a flash; their joy boiled over. "This *rôle* may be good for you," said he, "but for me, no." "It is good for us; that is all we care about," replies egoistically one of the revellers.

Not knowing whether he is dealing with genuine madmen or only with people who are pretending to be mad, our friend thinks that the part of discretion is to go away; but somebody shuts the door and hides the key. Another, kneeling before him, asks his pardon, in the name of the company, and declares insolently, but with tears, that despite his mental inferiority, which perhaps excites a little pity, they are all filled with a profound friendship for him. He makes up his mind to remain, and even condescends, after pressure, to play a little music.

But the sounds of the violin, spreading themselves through

the room like a new contagion, stab—the word is not too strong—first one of the revellers, then another. There burst forth deep and raucous sighs, sudden sobs, streams of silent tears. The frightened musician stops, and, approaching him whose ecstasy is noisiest, asks him if he suffers much, and what must be done to relieve him. One of the persons present, a man of common sense, suggests lemonade and acids; but the "sick man," his eyes shining with ecstasy, looks on them both with ineffable contempt. To wish to cure a man "sick" of too much life, "sick" of joy!

As this anecdote shows, goodwill towards men has a sufficiently large place in the feelings excited by hashish: a soft, idle, dumb benevolence which springs from the relaxation of the nerves.

In support of this observation somebody once told me an adventure which had happened to him in this state of intoxication, and as he preserved a very exact memory of his feelings I understood perfectly into what grotesque and inextricable embarrassment this difference of diapason and of pity of which I was just speaking had thrown him. I do not remember if the man in question was at his first or his second experiment; had he taken a dose which was a little too strong, or was it that the hashish had produced, without any apparent cause, effects much more vigorous than the ordinary—a not infrequent occurrence?

He told me that across the scutcheon of his joy, this supreme delight of feeling oneself full of life and believing oneself full of genius, there had suddenly smitten the bar sinister of terror. At first dazzled by the beauty of his sensations, he had suddenly fallen into fear of them. He had asked himself the question: "What would become of my intelligence and of my bodily organs if this state" (which he took for a supernatural state) "went on always increasing; if my nerves became continually more and more delicate?" By the power of enlargement which the spiritual eye of the patient possesses, this fear must be an unspeakable torment. "I was," he said, "like a runaway horse galloping towards an abyss, wishing to stop and being unable to do so. Indeed, it was a frightful ride, and my thought, slave of circumstance, of *milieu*, of accident, and of all that may be implied by the word chance, had taken a turn of pure, absolute rhapsody. 'It is too late, it is too late!' I repeated to myself ceaselessly in despair. When this mood, which seemed to me to last for an infinite time, and which I daresay only occupied a few minutes, changed, when I thought that at last I might dive into the ocean of happiness so dear to Easterns which succeeds this furious phase, I was overwhelmed by a new misfortune; a new anxiety, trivial enough, puerile enough, tumbled upon me. I suddenly remembered that I was invited to dinner, to an evening party of respectable people. I foresaw myself in the midst of a well-behaved and discreet crowd, every one master of himself, where I should be obliged to conceal carefully the state of my mind while under the glare of many lamps. I was fairly certain of success, but at the same time my heart almost gave up at the thought of the efforts of will which it would be necessary to bring into line in order to win. By some accident, I know not what, the words of the Gospel, "Woe unto him by whom offences come!" leapt to the surface of my memory, and in the effort to forget them, in concentrating myself upon forgetting them, I repeated them to myself ceaselessly. My catastrophe, for it was indeed a catastrophe, then took a gigantic shape: despite my weakness, I resolved on vigorous action, and went to consult a chemist, for I did not know the antidotes, and I wished to go with a free and careless spirit to the circle where my duty called me; but on the threshold of the shop a sudden thought seized me, haunted me, forced me to reflect. As I passed I had just seen myself in the looking-glass of a shop-front, and my face had startled me. This paleness, these lips compressed, these starting eyes!—I shall frighten this good fellow, I said to myself, and for what a trifle! Add to that the ridicule which I wished to avoid, the fear of finding people in the shop. But my sudden goodwill towards this unknown apothecary mastered all my other feelings. I imagined to myself this man as being as sensitive as I myself was at this dreadful moment, and as I imagined also that his ear and his soul must, like my own, tremble at the slightest noise, I resolved to go in on tiptoe. 'It would be impossible,' I said to myself, 'to show too much discretion in dealing with a man on whose kindness I am about to intrude.' Then I resolved to deaden the sound of my voice, like the noise of my steps. You know it, this hashish voice: grave, deep, guttural; not unlike that of habitual opium-eaters. The result was the exact contrary of my intention; anxious to reassure the chemist, I frightened him. He was in no way acquainted with this illness; had never even heard of it; yet he looked at me with a curiosity strongly mingled with mistrust. Did he take me for a madman, a criminal, or a beggar? Nor the one nor the other, doubtless, but all these absurd ideas ploughed through my brain. I was obliged to explain to him at length (what weariness!) what the hemp sweetmeat was and what purpose it served, ceaselessly repeating to him that there was no danger, that there was, so far as he was concerned, no reason to be alarmed, and that all that I asked was a method of mitigating or neutralising it, frequently insisting upon the sincere disappointment I felt in troubling him. When I had quite finished (I beg you well to understand all the humiliation which these words contained for me) he asked me simply to go away. Such was the reward of my exaggerated thoughtfulness and goodwill. I went to my evening party; I scandalised nobody. No one guessed the superhuman struggles which I had to make to be like other people; but I shall never forget the tortures of an ultra-poetic intoxication constrained by decorum and antagonised by duty."

Although naturally prone to sympathise with every suffering which is born of the imagination, I could not prevent myself from laughing at this story. The man who told it to me is not cured. He continued to crave at the hands of the cursed confection the excitement which wisdom finds in itself; but as he is a prudent and settled man, a man of the world, he has diminished the doses, which has permitted him to increase their frequency. He will taste later the rotten fruit of his "prudence"!

I return to the regular development of the intoxication. After this first phase of childish gaiety there is, as it were, a momentary relaxation; but new events soon announce themselves by a sensation of coolth at the extremities—which may even become, in the case of certain persons, a bitter cold—and a great weakness in all the limbs. You have then "butter fingers"; and in your head, in all your being, you feel an embarrassing stupor and stupefaction. Your eyes

77

start from your head; it is as if they were drawn in every direction by implacable ecstasy. Your face is deluged with paleness; the lips draw themselves in, sucked into the mouth with that movement of breathlessness which characterises the ambition of a man who is the prey of his own great schemes, oppressed by enormous thoughts, or taking a long breath preparatory to a spring. The throat closes itself, so to say; the palate is dried up by a thirst which it would be infinitely sweet to satisfy, if the delights of laziness were not still more agreeable, and in opposition to the least disturbance of the body. Deep but hoarse sighs escape from your breast, as if the old bottle, your body, could not bear the passionate activity of the new wine, your new soul. From one time to another a spasm transfixes you and makes you quiver, like those muscular discharges which at the end of a day's work or on a stormy night precede definitive slumber.

Before going further I should like, *à propos* of this sensation of coolth of which I spoke above, to tell another story which will serve to show to what point the effects, even the purely physical effects, may vary according to the individual. This time it is a man of letters who speaks, and in some parts of his story one will (I think) be able to find the indications of the literary temperament. "I had taken," he told me, "a moderated dose of *extrait gras*, and all was going as well as possible. The crisis of gaiety had not lasted long, and I found myself in a state of languor and wonderment which was almost happiness. I looked forward, then, to a quiet and unworried evening: unfortunately chance urged me to go with a friend to the theatre. I took the heroic course, resolved to overcome my immense desire to to be idle and motionless. All the carriages in my district were engaged; I was obliged to walk a long distance amid the discordant noises of the traffic, the stupid conversation of the passers-by, a whole ocean of triviality. My finger-tips were already slightly cool; soon this turned into a most acute cold, as if I had plunged both hands into a bucket of ice-water. But this was not suffering; this needle-sharp sensation stabbed me rather like a pleasure. Yet it seemed to me that this cold enveloped me more and more as the interminable journey went on. I asked two or three times of the person with whom I was if it was actually very cold. He replied to me that, on the contrary, the temperature was more than warm. Installed at last in the room, shut up in the box which had been given me, with three or four hours of repose in front of me, I thought myself arrived at the Promised Land. The feelings on which I had trampled during the journey with all the little energy at my disposal now burst in, and I give myself up freely to my silent frenzy. The cold ever increased, and yet I saw people lightly clad, and even wiping their foreheads with an air of weariness. This delightful idea took hold of me, that I was a privileged man, to whom alone had been accorded the right to feel cold in summer in the auditorium of a theatre. This cold went on increasing until it became alarming; yet I was before all dominated by my curiosity to know to what degree it could possibly sink. At last it came to such a point, it was so complete, so general, that all my ideas froze, so to speak; I was a piece of thinking ice. I imagined myself as a statue carved in a block of ice, and this mad hallucination made me so proud, excited in me such a feeling of moral well-being, that I despair of defining it to you. What added to my abominable enjoyment was the certainty that all the other people present were ignorant of my nature and of the superiority that I had over them, and then with the pleasure of thinking that my companion never suspected for a moment with what strange feelings I was filled, I clasped the reward of my dissimulation, and my extraordinary pleasure was a veritable secret.

"Besides, I had scarcely entered the box when my eyes had been struck with an impression of darkness which seemed to me to have some relationship with the idea of cold; it is, however, possible that these two ideas had lent each other strength. You know that hashish always invokes magnificences of light, splendours of colour, cascades of liquid gold; all light is sympathetic to it, both that which streams in sheets and that which hangs like spangles to points and roughnesses; the candelabra of *salons*, the wax candles that people burn in May, the rosy avalanches of sunset. It seems that the miserable chandelier spread a light far too insignificant to quench this insatiable thirst of brilliance. I thought, as I told you, that I was entering a world of shadows, which, moreover, grew gradually thicker, while I dreamt of the Polar night and the eternal winter. As to the stage, it was a stage consecrated to the comic Muse; that alone was luminous; infinitely small and far off, very far, like a landscape seen through the wrong end of a telescope. I will not tell you that I listened to the actors; you know that that is impossible. From time to time my thoughts snapped up on the wing a fragment of a phrase, and like a clever dancing-girl used it as a spring-board to leap into far-distant reveries. You might suppose that a play heard in this manner would lack logic and coherence. Undeceive yourself! I discovered an exceeding subtle sense in the drama created by my distraction. Nothing jarred on me, and I resembled a little that poet who, seeing *Esther* played for the first time, found it quite natural that Haman should make a declaration of love to the queen. It was, as you guess, the moment where he throws himself at the feet of Esther to beg pardon of his crime. If all plays were listened to on these lines they all, even those of Racine, would gain enormously. The actors seemed to me exceedingly small, and bounded by a precise and clear-cut line, like the figures in Meissonier's pictures. I saw distinctly not only the most minute details of their costumes, their patterns, seams, buttons, and so on, but also the line of separation between the false forehead and the real; the white, the blue, and the red, and all the tricks of make-up; and these Lilliputians were clothed about with a cold and magical clearness, like that which a very clean glass adds to an oil-painting. When at last I was able to emerge from this cavern of frozen shadows, and when, the interior phantasmagoria being dissipated, I came to myself, I experienced a greater degree of weariness than prolonged and difficult work has ever caused me."

It is, in fact, at this period of the intoxication that is manifested a new delicacy, a superior sharpness in each of the senses: smell, sight, hearing, touch join equally in this onward march; the eyes behold the Infinite; the ear perceives almost inaudible sounds in the midst of the most tremendous tumult. It is then that the hallucinations begin; external objects take on wholly and successively most strange appearances; they are deformed and transformed. Then—the ambiguities, the misunderstandings, and the transpositions of ideas! Sounds cloak themselves with colour; colours blossom into music. That, you will say, is nothing but natural. Every poetic brain in its healthy, normal state, readily conceives these analogies. But I have already warned the reader that there is nothing of the positively supernatural in hashish intoxication; only those analogies possess an unaccustomed liveliness; they penetrate and they envelop; they overwhelm the mind with their masterfulness. Musical notes become numbers; and if your mind is gifted with some mathematical aptitude, the harmony to which you listen, while keeping its voluptuous and sensual character, transforms itself into a vast rhythmical operation, where numbers beget numbers, and whose phases and generation follow with an inexplicable ease and an agility which equals that of the person playing.

It happens sometimes that the sense of personality disappears, and that the objectivity which is the birthright of Pantheist poets develops itself in you so abnormally that the contemplation of exterior objects makes you forget your own existence and confound yourself with them. Your eye fixes itself upon a tree, bent by the wind into an harmonious curve; in some seconds that which in the brain of a poet would only be a very natural comparison becomes in yours a reality. At first you lend to the tree your passions, your desire, or your melancholy; its creakings and oscillations become yours, and soon you are the tree. In the same way with the bird which hovers in the abyss of azure: at first it represents symbolically your own immortal longing to float above things human; but soon you are the bird itself. Suppose, again, you are seated smoking; your attention will rest a little too long upon the bluish clouds which breathe forth from your pipe; the idea of a slow, continuous, eternal evaporation will possess itself of your spirit, and you will soon apply this idea to your own thoughts, to your own apparatus of thought. By a singular ambiguity, by a species of transposition or intellectual barter, you feel yourself evaporating, and you will attribute to your pipe, in which you feel yourself crouched and pressed down like the tobacco, the strange faculty of smoking you!

Luckily, this interminable imagination has only lasted a minute. For a lucid interval, seized with a great effort, has allowed you to look at the clock. But another current of ideas bears you away; it will roll you away for yet another minute in its living whirlwind, and this other minute will be an eternity. For the proportion of time and being are completely disordered by the multitude and intensity of your feelings and ideas. One may say that one lives many times the space of a man's life during a single hour. Are you not, then, like a fantastic novel, but alive instead of being written? There is no longer any equation between the physical organs and their enjoyments; and it is above all on this account that arises the blame which one must give to this dangerous exercise in which liberty is forfeited.

When I speak of hallucinations the word must not be taken in its strictest sense: a very important shade of difference distinguishes pure hallucination, such as doctors have often have occasion to study, from the hallucination, or rather of the misinterpretation of the senses, which arises in the mental state caused by the hashish. In the first case the hallucination is sudden, complete, and fatal; beside which, it finds neither pretext nor excuse in the exterior world. The sick man sees a shape or hears sounds where there are not any. In the second case, where hallucination is progressive, almost willed, and it does not become perfect, it only ripens under the action of imagination. Finally, it has a pretext. A sound will speak, utter distinct articulations; but there was a sound there. The enthusiast eye of the hashish drunkard will see strange forms, but before they were strange and monstrous these forms were simple and natural. The energy, the almost speaking liveliness of hallucination in this form of intoxication in no way invalidates this original difference: the one has root in the situation, and, at the present time, the other has not. Better to explain this boiling over of the imagination, this maturing of the dream, and this poetic childishness to which a hashish-intoxicated brain is condemned, I will tell yet another anecdote. This time it is not an idle young man who speaks, nor a man of letters. It is a woman; a woman no longer in her first youth; curious, with an excitable mind, and who, having yielded to the wish to make acquaintance with the poison, describes thus for another woman the most important of her phases. I transcribe literally.

"However strange and new may be the sensations which I have drawn from my twelve hours' madness—was it twelve or twenty? in sooth, I cannot tell—I shall never return to it. The spiritual excitement is too lively, the fatigue which results from it too great; and, to say all in a word, I find in this return to childhood something criminal. Ultimately (after many hesitations) I yielded to curiosity, since it was a folly shared with old friends, where I saw no great harm in lacking a little dignity. But first of all I must tell you that this cursèd hashish is a most treacherous substance. Sometimes one thinks oneself recovered from the intoxication; but it is only a deceitful peace. There are moments of rest, and then recrudescences. Thus, before ten o'clock in the evening I found myself in one of these momentary states; I thought myself escaped from this superabundance of life which had caused me so much enjoyment, it is true, but which was not without anxiety and fear. I sat down to supper with pleasure, like one in that state of irritable fatigue which a long journey produces; for till then, for prudence sake, I had abstained from eating; but even before I rose from the table my delirium had caught me up again as a cat catches a mouse, and the poison began anew to play with my poor brain. Although my house is quite close to that of our friends, and although there was a carriage at my disposal, I felt myself so overwhelmed with the necessity of dreaming, of abandoning myself to this irresistible madness, that I accepted joyfully their offer to keep me till the morning. You know the castle; you know that they have arranged, decorated, and fitted with conveniences in the modern style all that part in which they ordinarily live, but that the part which is usually unoccupied has been left as it was, with its old style and its old adornments. They determined to improvise for me a bedroom in this part of the castle, and for this purpose they chose the smallest room, a kind of boudoir, which, although somewhat faded and decrepit, is none the less charming. I must describe it for you as well as I can, so that you may understand the strange vision which I underwent, a vision which fulfilled me for a whole night, without ever leaving me the leisure to note the flight of the hours.

"This boudoir is very small, very narrow. From the height of the cornice the ceiling arches itself to a vault; the walls are covered with narrow, long mirrors, separated by panels, where landscapes, in the easy style of the decorations, are painted. On the frieze on the four walls various allegorical figures are represented, some in attitudes of repose, others running or flying; above them are brilliant birds and flowers. Behind the figures a trellis rises, painted so as to deceive the eye, and following naturally the curve of the ceiling; this ceiling is gilded. All the interstices between the woodwork and the trellis and the figures are then covered with gold, and at the centre the gold is only interrupted by the geometrical network of the false trellis; you see that that resembles somewhat a very distinguished cage, a very fine cage for a very big bird. I must add that the night was very fine, very clear, and the moon brightly shining; so much so that even after I had put out my candle all this decoration remained visible, not illuminated by my mind's eye, as you might think, but by this lovely night, whose lights clung to all this broidery of gold, of mirrors, and of patchwork colours.

"I was at first much astonished to see great spaces spread themselves out before me, beside me, on all sides. There were limpid rivers, and green meadows admiring their own beauty in calm waters: you may guess here the effect of the panels reflected by the mirrors. In raising my eyes I saw a setting sun, like molten metal that grows cold. It was the gold of the ceiling. But the trellis put in my mind the idea that I was in a kind of cage, or in a house open on all sides upon space, and that I was only separated from all these marvels by the bars of my magnificent prison. In the first place I laughed at the illusion which had hold of me; but the more I looked the more its magic grew great, the more it took life, clearness, and masterful reality. From that moment the idea of being shut up mastered my mind, without, I must admit, too seriously interfering with the varied pleasures which I drew from the spectacle spread around and above me. I thought of myself as of one imprisoned for long, for thousands of years perhaps, in this sumptuous cage, among these fairy pastures, between these marvellous horizons. I imagined myself the Sleeping Beauty; dreamt of an expiation that I must undergo, of deliverance to come. Above my head fluttered brilliant tropical birds, and as my ear caught the sound of the little bells on the necks of the horses which were travelling far away on the main road, the two senses pooling their impressions in a single idea, I attributed to the birds this mysterious brazen chant; I imagined that they sang with a metallic throat. Evidently they were talking to me, and chanting hymns to my captivity. Gambolling monkeys, buffoon-like satyrs, seemed to amuse themselves at this supine prisoner, doomed to immobility; yet all the gods of mythology looked upon me with an enchanting smile, as if to encourage me to bear the sorcery with patience, and all their eyes slid to the corner of their eyelids as if to fix themselves on me. I came to the conclusion that if some faults of the olden time, some sins unknown to myself, had made necessary this temporary punishment, I could yet count upon an overriding goodness, which, while condemning me to a prudent course, would offer me truer pleasures than the dull pleasures which filled our youth. You see that moral considerations were not absent from my dream; but I must admit that the pleasure of contemplating these brilliant forms and colours and of thinking myself the centre of a fantastic drama frequently absorbed all my other thoughts. This stayed long, very long. Did it last till morning? I do not know. All of a sudden I saw the morning sun taking his bath in my room.   I experienced a lively astonishment, and despite all the efforts of memory that I have been able to make I have never been able to assure myself whether I had slept or whether I had patiently undergone a delicious insomnia. A moment ago, Night; now, Day. And yet I had lived long; oh, very long! The notion of Time, or rather the standard of Time, being abolished, the whole night was only measurable by the multitude of my thoughts. So long soever as it must have appeared to me from this point of view, it also seemed to me that it had only lasted some seconds; or even that it had not taken place in eternity.

"I do not say anything to you of my fatigue; it was immense. They say that the enthusiasm of poets and creative artists resembles what I experienced, though I have always believed that those persons on whom is laid the task of stirring us must be endowed with a most calm temperament. But if the poetic delirium resembles that which a teaspoonful of hashish confection procured for me I cannot but think that the pleasures of the public cost the poets dear, and it is not without a certain well-being, a prosaic satisfaction, that I at last find myself at home, in my intellectual home; I mean, in real life."

There is a woman, evidently reasonable; but we shall only make use of her story to draw from it some useful notes, which will complete this very compressed summary of the principal feelings which hashish begets.

She speaks of supper as of a pleasure arriving at the right moment; at the moment where a momentary remission,

THE POEM OF HASHISH

momentary for all its pretence of finality, permitted her to go back to real life.   Indeed, there are, as I have said, intermissions, and deceitful calms, and hashish often brings about a voracious hunger, nearly always an excessive thirst. Only, dinner or supper, instead of bringing about a permanent rest, creates this new attack, the vertiginous crisis of which this lady complains, and which was followed by a series of enchanting visions lightly tinged with affright, to which she so assented, resigning herself with the best grace in the world. The tyrannical hunger and thirst of which we speak are not easily assayed without considerable trouble.   For the man feels himself so much above material things, or rather he is so much overwhelmed by his drunkenness, that he must develop a lengthy spell of courage to move a bottle or a fork.

The definitive crisis determined by the digestion of food is, in fact, very violent; it is impossible to struggle against it. And such a state would not be supportable if it lasted too long, and if it did not soon give place to another phase of intoxication, which in the case above cited interprets itself by splendid visions, tenderly terrifying, and at the same time full of consolations. This new state is what the Easterns call *Kaif*. It is no longer the whirlwind or the tempest; it is a calm and motionless bliss, a glorious resignèdness. Since long you have not been your own master; but you trouble yourself no longer about that. Pain, and the sense of time, have disappeared; or if sometimes they dare to show their heads, it is only as transfigured by the master feeling, and they are then, as compared with their ordinary form, what poetic melancholy is to prosaic grief.

But above all let us remark that in this lady's account

(and it is for this purpose that I have transcribed it) it is but a bastard hallucination, and owes its being to the objects of the external world. The spirit is but a mirror where the environment is reflected, strangely transformed. Then, again, we see intruding what I should be glad to call moral hallucination; the patient thinks herself condemned to expiate somewhat; but the feminine temperament, which is ill-fitted to analyse, did not permit her to notice the strangely optimistic character of the aforesaid hallucination. The benevolent look of the gods of Olympus is made poetical by a varnish essentially due to hashish. I will not say that this lady has touched the fringe of remorse, but her thoughts, momentarily turned in the direction of melancholy and regret, have been quickly coloured by hope. This is an observation which we shall again have occasion to verify.

She speaks of the fatigue of the morrow. In fact, this is great. But it does not show itself at once, and when you are obliged to acknowledge its existence you do so not without surprise: for at first, when you are really assured that a new day has arisen on the horizon of your life, you experience an extraordinary sense of well-being; you seem to enjoy a marvellous lightness of spirit. But you are scarcely on your feet when a forgotten fragment of intoxication follows you and pulls you back; it is the badge of your recent slavery. Your enfeebled legs only conduct you with caution, and you fear at every moment to break yourself, as if you were made of porcelain. A wondrous languor—there are those who pretend that it does not lack charm—possesses itself of your spirit, and spreads itself across your faculties as a fog spreads itself in a meadow. There, then, you are, for some hours yet, incapable of work, of action, and of energy. It is the punishment of an impious prodigality in which you have squandered your nervous force. You have dispersed your personality to the four winds of heaven—and now, what trouble to gather it up again and concentrate it!

CHAPTER IV

THE MAN-GOD

IT is time to leave on one side all this jugglery, these big marionettes, born of the smoke of childish brains. Have we not to speak of more serious things—of modifications of our human opinions, and, in a word, of the *morale* of hashish?

Up to the present I have only made an abridged monograph on the intoxication; I have confined myself to accentuating its principal characteristics. But what is more important, I think, for the spiritually minded man, is to make acquaintance with the action of the poison upon the spiritual part of man; that is to say, the enlargement, the deformation, and the exaggeration of his habitual sentiments and his moral perception, which present then, in an exceptional atmosphere, a true phenomenon of refraction.

The man who, after abandoning himself for a long time to opium or to hashish, has been able, weak as he has become by the habit of bondage, to find the energy necessary to shake off the chain, appears to me like an escaped prisoner. He inspires me with more admiration than does that prudent man who has never fallen, having always been careful to avoid the temptation. The English, in speaking of opium-eaters, often employ terms which can only appear excessive to those innocent persons who do not understand the horrors of this downfall—*enchained, fettered, enslaved.* Chains, in fact, compared to which all others—chains of duty, chains of lawless love—are nothing but webs of gauze and spider tissues. Horrible marriage of man with himself! "I had become a bounden slave in the trammels of opium, and my labours and my orders had taken a colouring from my dreams," says the husband of Ligeia. But in how many marvellous passages does Edgar Poe, this incomparable poet, this never-refuted philosopher, whom one must always quote in speaking of the mysterious maladies of the soul, describe the dark and clinging splendours of opium! The lover of the shining Berenice, Egœus, the metaphysician, speaks of an alteration of his faculties which compels him to give an abnormal and monstrous value to the simplest phenomenon.

"To muse for long unwearied hours, with my attention riveted to some frivolous device on the margin or in the typography of a book; to become absorbed, for the better part of a summer's day, in a quaint shadow falling aslant upon the tapestry or upon the floor; to lose myself, for an entire night, in watching the steady flame of a lamp, or the embers of a fire; to dream away whole days over the perfume of a flower; to repeat monotonously some common word, until the sound, by dint of frequent repetition, ceased to convey any idea whatever to the mind; to lose all sense of motion or physical existence, by means of absolute bodily quiescence long and obstinately persevered in: such were a few of the most common and least pernicious vagaries induced by a condition of the mental faculties, not, indeed, altogether unparalleled, but certainly bidding defiance to anything like analysis or explanation."

And the nervous Augustus Bedloe, who every morning before his walk swallows his dose of opium, tells us that the principal prize which he gains from this daily poisoning is to take in everything, even in the most trivial thing, an exaggerated interest.

"In the meantime the morphine had its customary effect —that of enduing all the external world with an intensity of interest. In the quivering of a leaf—in the hue of a blade of grass—in the shape of a trefoil—in the humming of a bee—in the gleaming of a dew-drop—in the breathing of the wind—in the faint odours that came from the forest—there came a whole universe of suggestion—a gay and motley train of rhapsodical and immethodical thought."

Thus expresses himself, by the mouth of his puppets, the master of the horrible, the prince of mystery. These two characteristics of opium are perfectly applicable to hashish. In the one case, as in the other, the intelligence, formerly free, becomes a slave; but the word *rapsodique*, which defines so well a train of thought suggested and dictated by the exterior world and the accident of circumstance, is in truth truer and more terrible in the case of hashish. Here the reasoning power is no more than a wave, at the mercy of every current and the train of thought is infinitely more accelerated and more *rapsodique*; that is to say, clearly enough, I think, that hashish is, in its immediate effect, much more vehement than opium, much more inimical to regular life; in a word, much more upsetting. I do not know if ten years of intoxication by hashish would being diseases equal to those caused by ten years of opium regimen; I say that, for the moment, and for the morrow, hashish has more fatal results. One is a soft-spoken enchantress; the other, a raging demon.

THE POEM OF HASHISH

I wish in this last part to define and to analyse the moral ravage caused by this dangerous and delicious practice; a ravage so great, a danger so profound, that those who return from the fight but lightly wounded appear to me like heroes escaped from the cave of a multiform Proteus, or like Orpheus, conquerors of Hell. You may take, if you will, this form of language for an exaggerated metaphor, but for my part I will affirm that these exciting poisons seem to me not only one of the most terrible and the most sure means which the Spirit of Darkness uses to enlist and enslave wretched humanity, but even one of the most perfect of his avatars.

This time, to shorten my task and make my analysis the clearer, instead of collecting scattered anecdotes I will dress a single puppet in a mass of observation. I must, then, invent a soul to suit my purpose. In his "Confessions" De Quincey rightly states that opium, instead of sending man to sleep, excites him; but only excites him in his natural path, and that therefore to judge of the marvels of opium it would be ridiculous to try it upon a seller of oxen, for such an one will dream of nothing but cattle and grass. Now I am not going to describe the lumbering fancies of a hashish-intoxicated stockbreeder. Who would read them with pleasure, or consent to read them at all? To idealise my subject I must concentrate all its rays into a single circle and polarise them; and the tragic circle where I will gather them together will be, as I have said, a man after my own heart; something analogous to what the eighteenth century called the *homme sensible*, to what the romantic school named the *homme incompris*, and to what family folk and the mass of *bourgeoisie* generally brand with the epithet "original." A constitution half nervous, half

bilious, is the most favourable to the evolutions of an intoxication of this kind. Let us add a cultivated mind, exercised in
the study of form and colour, a tender heart, wearied by
misfortune, but still ready to be made young again; we will
go, if you please, so far as to admit past errors, and, as a
natural result of these in an easily excitable nature, if not
positive remorse, at least regret for time profaned and ill-
spent. A taste for metaphysics, an acquaintance with the
different hypotheses of philosophy of human destiny, will
certainly not be useless conditions; and, further, that love of
virtue, of abstract virtue, stoical or mystic, which is set forth in
all the books upon which modern childishness feeds as the
highest summit to which a chosen soul may attain. If one
adds to all that a great refinement of sense—and if I omitted
it it was because I thought it supererogatory—I think that I
have gathered together the general elements which are most
common in the modern *homme sensible* of what one might
call the lowest common measure of originality. Let us
see now what will become of this individuality pushed to
its extreme by hashish. Let us follow this progress of the
human imagination up to its last and most splendid serai;
up to the point of the belief of the individual in his own
divinity.

If you are one of these souls your innate love of form and
colour will find from the beginning an immense banquet in the
first development of your intoxication. Colours will take an
unaccustomed energy and smite themselves within your brain
with the intensity of triumph. Delicate, mediocre, or even
bad as they may be, the paintings upon the ceilings will clothe
themselves with a tremendous life. The coarsest papers which

cover the walls of inns will open out like magnificent dioramas. Nymphs with dazzling flesh will look at you with great eyes deeper and more limpid than are the sky and sea. Characters of antiquity, draped in their priestly or soldierly costumes, will, by a single glance, exchange with you most solemn confidences. The snakiness of the lines is a definitely intelligible language where you read the sorrowing and the passion of their souls. Nevertheless a mysterious but only temporary state of the mind develops itself; the profoundness of life, hedged by its multiple problems, reveals itself entirely in the sight, however natural and trivial it may be, that one has under one's eyes; the first-come object becomes a speaking symbol. Fourier and Swedenborg, one with his analogies, the other with his correspondences, have incarnated themselves in all things vegetable and animal which fall under your glance, and instead of touching by voice they indoctrinate you by form and colour. The understanding of the allegory takes within you proportions unknown to yourself. We shall note in passing that allegory, that so spiritual type of art, which the clumsiness of its painters has accustomed us to despise, but which is really one of the most primitive and natural forms of poetry, regains its divine right in the intelligence which is enlightened by intoxication. Then the hashish spreads itself over all life; as it were, the magic varnish. It colours it with solemn hues and lights up all its profundity; jagged landscapes, fugitive horizons, perspectives of towns whitened by the corpse-like lividity of storm or illumined by the gathered ardours of the sunset; abysses of space, allegorical of the abyss of time; the dance, the gesture or the speech of the actors, should you be in a theatre; the first-come phrase if your eyes fall upon a book; in a word, all things; the universality of beings stands up before you with a new glory unsuspected until then. The grammar, the dry grammar itself, becomes something like a book of "barbarous names of evocation." The words rise up again, clothed with flesh and bone; the noun, in its solid majesty; the adjective's transparent robe which clothes and colours it with a shining web; and the verb, archangel of motion which sets swinging the phrase. Music, that other language dear to the idle or the profound souls who seek repose by varying their work, speaks to you of yourself, and recites to you the poem of your life; it incarnates in you, and you swoon away in it. It speaks your passion, not only in a vague, ill-defined manner, as it does in your careless evenings at the opera, but in a substantial and positive manner, each movement of the rhythm marking a movement understood of your soul, each note transforming itself into Word, and the whole poem entering into your brain like a dictionary endowed with life.

It must not be supposed that all these phenomena fall over each other pell-mell in the spirit, with a clamorous accent of reality and the disorder of exterior life; the interior eye transforms all, and gives to all the complement of beauty which it lacks, so that it may be truly worthy to give pleasure. It is also to this essentially voluptuous and sensual phase that one must refer the love of limpid water, running or stagnant, which develops itself so astonishingly in the brain-drunkenness of some artists. The mirror has become a pretext for this reverie, which resembles a spiritual thirst joined to the physical thirst which dries the throat, and of which I have spoken above. The flowing waters, the sportive waters; the musical water-

THE POEM OF HASHISH

falls; the blue vastness of the sea; all roll, sing, leap with a charm beyond words. The water opens its arms to you like a true enchantress; and though I do not much believe in the maniacal frenzies caused by hashish, I should not like to assert that the contemplation of some limpid gulf would be altogether without danger for a soul in love with space and crystal, and that the old fable of Undine might not become a tragic reality for the enthusiast.

I think I have spoken enough of the gigantic growth of space and time; two ideas always connected, always woven together, but which at such a time the spirit faces without sadness and without fear. It looks with a certain melancholy delight across deep years, and boldly dives into infinite perspectives. You have thoroughly well understood, I suppose, that this abnormal and tyrannical growth may equally apply to all sentiments and to all ideas. Thus, I have given, I think, a sufficiently fair sample of benevolence. The same is true of love. The idea of beauty must naturally take possession of an enormous space in a spiritual temperament such as I have invented. Harmony, balance of line, fine cadence in movement, appear to the dreamer as necessities, as duties, not only for all beings of creation, but for himself, the dreamer, who finds himself at this period of the crisis endowed with a marvellous aptitude for understanding the immortal and universal rhythm. And if our fanatic lacks personal beauty, do not think he suffers long from the avowal to which he is obliged, or that he regards himself as a discordant note in the world of harmony and beauty improvised by his imagination. The sophisms of hashish are numerous and admirable, tending as a rule to optimism, and one of the

principal and the most efficacious is that which transforms
desire into realisation. It is the same, doubtless, in many cases
of ordinary life; but here with how much more ardour and
subtlety! Otherwise, how could a being so well endowed to
understand harmony, a sort of priest of the beautiful, how
could he make an exception to, and a blot upon, his own
theory? Moral beauty and its power, gracefulness and its
seduction, eloquence and its achievements, all these ideas
soon present themselves to correct that thoughtless ugliness;
then they come as consolers, and at last as the most perfect
courtiers, sycophants of an imaginary sceptre.

Concerning love, I have heard many persons feel a
school-boy curiosity, seeking to gather information from
those to whom the use of hashish was familiar, what might
not be this intoxication of love, already so powerful in its
natural state, when it is enclosed in the other intoxication;
a sun within a sun. Such is the question which will occur
to that class of minds which I will call intellectual gapers.
To reply to a shameful sub-meaning of this part of the
question which cannot be openly discussed, I will refer the
reader to Pliny, who speaks somewhere of the properties of
hemp in such a way as to dissipate any illusions on this
subject. One knows, besides, that loss of tone is the most
ordinary result of the abuse which men make of their nerves,
and of the substances which excite them. Now, as we are
not here considering effective power, but motion or
susceptibility, I will simply ask the reader to consider that the
imagination of a sensitive man intoxicated with hashish is
raised to a prodigious degree, as little easy to determine as
would be the utmost force possible to the wind in a hurricane,

and his senses are subtilised to a point almost equally difficult to define. It is then reasonable to believe that a light caress, the most innocent imaginable, a handshake, for example, may possess a centuple value by the actual state of the soul and of the senses, and may perhaps conduct them, and that very rapidly, to that syncope which is considered by vulgar mortals as the *summum* of happiness; but it is quite indubitable that hashish awakes in an imagination accustomed to occupy itself with the affections tender remembrances to which pain and unhappiness give even a new lustre. It is no less certain that in these agitations of the mind there is a strong ingredient of sensuality; and, moreover, it may usefully be remarked—and this will suffice to establish upon this ground the immorality of hashish—that a sect of Ishmaelites (it is from the Ishmaelites that the Assassins are sprung) allowed its adoration to stray far beyond the Lingam-Yoni; that is to say, to the absolute worship of the Lingam, exclusive of the feminine half of the symbol. There would be nothing unnatural, every man being the symbolic representation of history, in seeing an obscene heresy, a monstrous religion, arise in a mind which has cowardly given itself up to the mercy of a hellish drug and which smiles at the degradation of its own faculties.

Since we have seen manifest itself in hashish intoxication a strange goodwill toward men, applied even to strangers, a species of philanthropy made rather of pity than of love (it is here that the first germ of the Satanic spirit which is to develop later in so extraordinary a manner shows itself), but which goes so far as to fear giving pain to any one, one may guess what may happen to the localised sentimentality applied to a beloved person who plays, or has played, an important part in the moral life of the reveller. Worship, adoration, prayer, dreams of happiness, dart forth and spring up with the ambitious energy and brilliance of a rocket. Like the powder and colouring-matter of the firework, they dazzle and vanish in the darkness. There is no sort of sentimental combination to which the subtle love of a hashish-slave may not lend itself. The desire to protect, a sentiment of ardent and devoted paternity, may mingle themselves with a guilty sensuality which hashish will always know how to excuse and to absolve. It goes further still. I suppose that, past errors having left bitter traces in the soul, a husband or a lover will contemplate with sadness in his normal state a past overclouded with storm; these bitter fruits may, under hashish, change to sweet fruits. The need of pardon makes the imagination more clever and more supplicatory, and remorse itself, in this devilish drama, which only expresses itself by a long monologue, may act as an incitement and powerfully rekindle the heart's enthusiasm. Yes, remorse. Was I wrong in saying that hashish appeared to a truly philosophical mind as a perfectly Satanic instrument? Remorse, singular ingredient of pleasure, is soon drowned in the delicious contemplation of remorse; in a kind of voluptuous analysis; and this analysis is so rapid that man, this natural devil, to speak as do the followers of Swedenborg, does not see how involuntary it is, and how, from moment to moment, he approaches the perfection of Satan. He admires his remorse, and glorifies himself, even while he is on the way to lose his freedom.

There, then, is my imaginary man, the mind that I have

chosen, arrived at that degree of joy and peace where he is compelled to admire himself. Every contradiction wipes itself out; all philosophical problems become clear, or at least appear so; everything is material for pleasure; the plentitude of life which he enjoys inspires him with an unmeasured pride; a voice speaks in him (alas, it is his own!) which says to him: "Thou hast now the right to consider thyself as superior to all men. None knoweth thee, none can understand all that thou thinkest, all that thou feelest; they would, indeed, be incapable of appreciating the passionate love which they inspire in thee. Thou art a king unrecognised by the passers-by; a king who lives, yet none knows that he is king but himself. But what matter to thee? Hast thou not sovereign contempt, which makes the soul so kind?"

We may suppose, however, that from one time to another some biting memory strikes through and corrupts this happiness. A suggestion due to the exterior world may revive a past disagreeable to contemplate. How many foolish or vile actions fill the past!—actions indeed unworthy of this king of thought, and whose escutcheon they soil? Believe that the hashish-man will bravely confront these reproachful phantoms, and even that he will know how to draw from these hideous memories new elements of pleasure and of pride!

Such will be the evolution of his reasoning. The first sensation of pain being over, he will curiously analyse this action or this sentiment whose memory has troubled his existing glory; the motive which made him act thus; the circumstances by which he was surrounded; and if he does not find in these circumstances sufficient reasons, if not to absolve, at least to extenuate his guilt, do not imagine that he admits defeat. I am present at his reasoning, as at the play of a mechanism seen under a transparent glass. "This ridiculous, cowardly, or vile action, whose memory disturbed me for a moment, is in complete contradiction with my true and real nature, and the very energy with which I condemn it, the inquisitorial care with which I analyse and judge it, prove my lofty and divine aptitude for virtue. How many men could be found in the world of men clever enough to judge themselves; stern enough to condemn themselves?" And not only does he condemn himself, but he glorifies himself; the horrible memory thus absorbed in the contemplation of ideal virtue, ideal charity, ideal genius, he abandons himself frankly to his triumphant spiritual orgy. We have seen that, counterfeiting sacrilegiously the sacrament of penitence, at one and the same time penitent and confessor, he has given himself an easy absolution; or, worse yet, that he has drawn from his contemplation new food for his pride. Now, from the contemplation of his dreams and his schemes of virtue he believes finally in his practical aptitude for virtue; the amorous energy with which he impresses this phantom of virtue seems to him a sufficient and peremptory proof that he possesses the virile energy necessary for the fulfilment of his ideal. He confounds completely dream with action, and his imagination, growing warmer and warmer in face of the enchanting spectacle of his own nature corrected and idealised, substituting this fascinating image of himself for his real personality, so poor in will, so rich in vanity, he ends by declaring his apotheosis in these clear and simple terms, which contain for him a whole world of abominable pleasures: "I am the most virtuous of all men." Does not that remind you a little of

Jean-Jacques, who, he also having confessed to the Universe, not without a certain pleasure, dared to break out into the same cry of triumph (or at least the difference is small enough) with the same sincerity and the same conviction? The enthusiasm with which he admired virtue, the nervous emotion which filled his eyes with tears at the sight of a fine action or at the thought of all the fine actions which he would have wished to accomplish, were sufficient to give him a superlative idea of his moral worth. Jean-Jacques had intoxicated himself without the aid of hashish.

Shall I pursue yet further the analysis of this victorious monomania? Shall I explain how, under the dominion of the poison, my man soon makes himself centre of the Universe? how he becomes the living and extravagant expression of the proverb which says that passion refers everything to itself? He believes in his virtue and in his genius; can you not guess the end? All the surrounding objects are so many suggestions which stir in him a world of thought, all more coloured, more living, more subtle than ever, clothed in a magic glamour. "These mighty cities," says he to himself, "where the superb buildings tower one above the other; these beautiful ships balanced by the waters of the roadstead in homesick idleness, that seem to translate our thought 'When shall we set sail for happiness?'; these museums full of lovely shapes and intoxicating colours; these libraries where are accumulated the works of science and the dreams of poetry; this concourse of instruments whose music is one; these enchantress women, made yet more charming by the science of adornment and coquetry: all these things have been created for me, for me, for me! For me humanity has toiled; has been martyred, crucified, to serve for pasture, for pabulum to my implacable appetite for emotion, knowledge, and beauty."

I leap to the end, I cut the story short. No one will be surprised that a thought final and supreme jets from the brain of the dreamer: "I am become God."

But a savage and burning cry darts from his breast with such an energy, such a power of production, that if the will and the belief of a drunken man possessed effective power this cry would overthrow the angels scattered in the quarters of the heaven: "I am a god."

But soon this hurricane of pride transforms itself into a weather of calm, silent, reposeful beatitude, and the universality of beings presents itself tinted and illumined by a flaming dawn. If by chance a vague memory slips into the soul of this deplorable thrice-happy one—"Might there not be another God?"—believe that he will stand upright before Him; that he will dispute His will, and confront Him without fear.

Who was the French philosopher that, mocking modern German doctrines, said: "I am a god who has dined ill"? This irony would not bite into a spirit uplifted by hashish; he would reply tranquilly: "Maybe I have dined ill; but I am a god."

CHAPTER V

MORAL

BUT the morrow; the terrible morrow! All the organs relaxed, tired; the nerves unstretched, the teasing tendency to tears, the impossibility of applying yourself to a continuous task, teach you cruelly that you have been playing a forbidden game. Hideous nature, stripped of its illumination of the previous evening, resembles the melancholy ruins of a festival. The will, the most precious of all faculties, is above all attacked. They say, and it is nearly true, that this substance does not cause any physical ill; or at least no grave one; but can one affirm that a man incapable of action and fit only for dreaming is really in good health, even when every part of him functions perfectly? Now we know human nature sufficiently well to be assured that a man who can with a spoonful of sweetmeat procure for himself incidentally all the treasures of heaven and of earth will never gain the thousandth part of them by working for them. Can you imagine to yourself a State of which all the citizens should be hashish drunkards? What citizens! What warriors! What legislators! Even in the East, where its use is so widely spread, there are Governments which have understood the necessity of proscribing it. In fact it is forbidden to man, under penalty of intellectual decay and death, to upset the primary conditions of his existence, and to break up the equilibrium of his faculties with the surroundings in which they are destined to operate; in a word, to outrun his destiny, to substitute for it a fatality of a new kind. Let us remember Melmoth, that admirable parable. His shocking suffering lies in the disproportion between his marvellous faculties, acquired unostentatiously by a Satanic pact, and the surroundings in which, as a creature of God, he is condemned to live. And none of those whom he wishes to seduce consents to buy from him on the same conditions his terrible privilege. In fact every man who does not accept the conditions of life sells his soul. It is easy to grasp the analogy which exists between the Satanic creations of poets and those living beings who have devoted themselves to stimulants. Man has wished to become God, and soon?—there he is, in virtue of an inexorable moral law, fallen lower than his natural state! It is a soul which sells itself bit by bit.

Balzac doubtless thought that there is for man no greater shame, no greater suffering, than to abdicate his will. I saw him once in a drawing-room, where they were talking of the prodigious effects of hashish. He listened and asked questions with an amusing attention and vivacity. Those who knew him may guess that it must have interested him, but the idea of *thinking despite himself* shocked him severely. They offered him *dawamesk*. He examined it, sniffed at it, and returned it without touching it. The struggle between his almost childish curiosity and his repugnance to submit himself showed strikingly on his expressive face. The love of dignity won the day. Now it is difficult to imagine to oneself the maker of the theory of will, this spiritual twin of

Louis Lambert, consenting to lose a grain of this precious substance. Despite the admirable services which ether and chloroform have rendered to humanity, it seems to me that from the point of view of the idealist philosophy the same moral stigma is branded on all modern inventions which tend to diminish human free will and necessary pain. It was not without a certain admiration that I once listened to the paradox of an officer who told me of the cruel operation undergone by a French general at El-Aghouat, and of which, despite chloroform, he died. This general was a very brave man, and even something more: one of those souls to which one naturally applies the term *chivalrous*. It was not, he said to me, chloroform that he needed, but the eyes of all the army and the music of its bands. That might have saved him. The surgeon did not agree with the officer, but the chaplain would doubtless have admired these sentiments.

It is certainly superfluous, after all thee considerations, to insist upon the moral character of hashish. Let me compare it to suicide, to slow suicide, to a weapon always bleeding, always sharp, and no reasonable person will find anything to object to. Let me compare it to sorcery or to magic, which wishes in working upon matter by means of arcana (of which nothing proves the falsity more than the efficacy) to conquer a dominion forbidden to man or permitted only to him who is deemed worthy of it, and no philosophical mind will blame this comparison. If the Church condemns magic and sorcery it is that they militate against the intentions of God; that they save time and render morality superfluous, and that she—the Church—only considers as legitimate and true the treasures gained by assiduous goodwill. The gambler who has found the means to win with certainty we all cheat; how shall we describe the man who tries to buy with a little small change happiness and genius? It is the infallibility itself of the means which constitutes its immorality; as the supposed infallibility of magic brands it with Satanic stigma. Shall I add that hashish, like all solitary pleasures, renders the individual useless to his fellow creatures and society superfluous to the individual, driving him to ceaseless admiration of himself and dragging him day by day towards the luminous abyss in which he admires his Narcissus face? But even if at the price of his dignity, his honesty, and his free will man were able to draw from hashish great spiritual benefits; to make a kind of thinking machine, a fertile instrument? That is a question which I have often heard asked, and I reply to it: In the first place, as I have explained at length, hashish reveals to the individual nothing but himself. It is true that this individual is, so to say, cubed, and pushed to his limit, and as it is equally certain that the memory of impressions survives the orgy, the hope of these utilitarians appears at the first glance not altogether unreasonable. But I will beg them to observe that the thoughts from which they expect to draw so great an advantage are not in reality as beautiful as they appear under their momentary transfiguration, clothed in magic tinsel. They pertain to earth rather than to Heaven, and owe great portion of their beauty to the nervous agitation, to the greediness, with which the mind throws itself upon them. Consequently this hope is a vicious circle. Let us admit for the moment that hashish gives, or at least increases, genius; they forget that it is in the nature of hashish to diminish the will, and that

THE POEM OF HASHISH

thus it gives with one hand what it withdraws with the other; that is to say, imagination without the faculty of profiting by it. Lastly, one must remember, while supposing a man adroit enough and vigorous enough to avoid this dilemma, that there is another danger, fatal and terrible, which is that of all habits. All such soon transform themselves into necessities. He who has recourse to a poison in order to think will soon be unable to think without the poison. Imagine to yourself the frightful lot of a man whose paralysed imagination will no longer function without the aid of hashish or of opium! In philosophical states the human mind, to imitate the course of the stars, is obliged to follow a curve which loops it back to its point of departure, when the circle must ultimately close. At the beginning I spoke of this marvellous state into which the spirit of man sometimes finds itself thrown as if by a special favour. I have said that, ceaselessly aspiring to rekindle his hopes and raise himself towards the infinite, he showed (in every country and in every time) a frenzied appetite for every substance, even those which are dangerous, which, by exalting his personality, are able to bring in an instant before his eyes this bargain Paradise, object of all his desires; and at last that this daring spirit, driving without knowing it his chariot through the gates of Hell, by this very fact bore witness to his original greatness. But man is not so God-forsaken, so barren of straightforward means of reaching Heaven, that he need invoke pharmacy and witchcraft. He has no need to sell his soul to buy intoxicating caresses and the friendship of the Hur Al'ain. What is a Paradise which must be bought at the price of eternal salvation? I imagine a man (shall I say a Brahmin, a poet, or a Christian philosopher?) seated upon the steep Olympus of spirituality; around him the Muses of Raphael or of Mategna, to console him for his long fasts and his assiduous prayers, weave the noblest dances, gaze on him with their softest glances and their most dazzling smiles; the divine Apollo, master of all knowledge (that of Francavilla, of Albert Dürer, of Goltzius, or another—what does it matter? Is there not an Apollo for every man who deserves one?), caresses with his bow his most sensitive strings; below him, at the foot of the mountain, in the brambles and the mud, the human fracas; the Helot band imitates the grimaces of enjoyment and utters howls which the sting of the poison tears from its breast; and the poet, saddened, says to himself: "These unfortunate ones, who have neither fasted nor prayed, who have refused redemption by the means of toil, have asked of black magic the means to raise themselves at a single blow to transcendental life. Their magic dupes them, kindles for them a false happiness, a false light; while as for us poets and philosophers, we have begotten again our soul upon ourselves by continuous toil and contemplation; by the unwearied exercise of will and the unfaltering nobility of aspiration we have created for ourselves a garden of Truth, which is Beauty; of Beauty which is Truth. Confident in the word which says that faith removeth mountains, we have accomplished the only miracle which God has licensed us to perform."

CHARLES BAUDELAIRE
(*Translated by* ALEISTER CROWLEY)

REVIEW

A BOOK OF MYSTERY AND VISION. By A. E. WAITE. William Rider and Son. 7s. 6d.

The Introduction. Mr. Waite speaks of a "kind of secret school, or united but incorporate fraternity, which independently of all conventional means of recognition and communication do no less communicate and recognise one another without hesitation of hindrance in every part of the world. . . . Of this school the author may and does claim that he is the intimate representative and mouthpiece," &c. &c.

Good.

"This mystic life at its highest is undeniably selfish. "

Hullo, what's this?

"It is a striking fact that so little of any divine consequence has been uttered by poets in the English Language."

Really?

"The inspiration of it (the sense of sacramentalism) at certain times saturated the whole soul of Tennyson ... there is scarcely a trace or tincture of this sense in Shelley."

Poor Shelley!

"In the eighteenth century there was none found to give it Voice."

Poor Blake! (William Blake, you know! Never heard of William Blake?)

"For this school it is quite impossible that Shakespeare, for example, should possess any consequence."

Poor Shakespeare!

And then—

"This book is offered by the writer to his brethren, *ut adeptis appareat me illis parem et fratrem*, as proof positive that he is numbered among them, that he is initiated into their mysteries, and exacts recognition as such in all houses, temples, and tarrying-places of the fraternity."

An adept trying to prove that he is one! An adept with thoughts of his own rank and glory!! An adept exacting recognition!!!

What about the instant recognition all over the world of which you prated above? Mr. Waite, you seem to me to be a spiritual Arthur Orton!

Mr. Waite, we have opened the Pastos which you say contains the body of your Father Christian Rosencreutz—and it's only poor old Druce!

The Book. This is the strange thing; the moment that Mr. Waite leaves prose for poetry, there is no more of this bunkum, bombast, and balderdash; we find a poet, and rather an illuminated poet. We have to appeal from Philip sober to Philip drunk! *In vino veritas.*

Good poetry enough all this: yet one cannot help feeling that it is essentially the work of a scholar and a gentleman. One is inclined to think of him as Pentheus in a frock-coat.

THE EQUINOX

A MYSTERY-PLAY.

DIONYSUS. I bring ye wine from above
From the vats of the storied sun—
MR. WAITE. Butler, decant the claret carefully!
DIONYSUS. For every one of ye love—
MR. WAITE. Ay, lawful marriage is a sacrament.
DIONYSUS. And life for everyone—
MR. WAITE. And lawful marriage should result in life.
DIONYSUS. Ye shall dance on hill and level—
MR. WAITE. But not the vulgar cancan or mattchiche.
DIONYSUS. Ye shall sing through hollow and height—
MR. WAITE. See that ye sing with due sobriety!
DIONYSUS. In the festal mystical revel,
The rapturous Bacchanal rite!
MR. WAITE. If Isabel de S . . . . should approve!
DIONYSUS. The rocks and trees are yours ---
MR. WAITE. According to Laws of Property.
DIONYSUS. And the waters under the hill –
MR. WAITE. Provided that you pay your water rate.
DIONYSUS. By the might of that which endures ---
MR. WAITE. Me, surely, and my fame as an adept.
DIONYSUS. The holy heaven of will!
MR. WAITE. Will Shakespeare was not an initiate.
DIONYSUS. I kindle a flame like a torrent
To rush from star to star ---
MR. WAITE. Incendiarism! Arson! Captain Shaw!
DIONYSUS. Your hair as a comet's horrent, ---
MR. WAITE. Not for a fortune would I ruffle mine.
DIONYSUS. Ye shall see things as they are.
MR. WAITE. Play fair, god! do not give the show away!

[*The Mænads tear him limb from limb, and* MADAME DE S . . . . . . *tries to brain* DIONYSUS *with a dummy writ.*

This is a great limitation, yet Mr. Waite is a really excellent poet withal. All the poems show fine and deep thought, with facility and felicity of expression. "The Lost Word" is extraordinarily fine, both dramatically and lyrically. It seems a pity that Mr. Waite has no use for William Shakespeare! The fact is (whatever George Hume Barne may say) that Mr. Waite is (or has) a genius, who wishes to communicate sacred mysteries of truth and beauty; but he is too often baulked by the mental and moral equipment of Mr. Waite. Even so, he only just misses. And I will bet George Hume Barne a *crème de menthe* that if Mr. Waite (even now) will ride on a camel from Biskra to Timbuktu with an Ouled Nail and the dancer M'saoud, he will produce absolutely first-rate poetry within six months.

Enough. But buy the book. A. QUILLER, JR.

AN ORIGIN

IN fire of gold they set them out,
   The garlanded of old, who clomb
The Mount of Evil, strong and stout
   To wrest from Venus' brow the comb.
The fiery wind, the web unspun,
The nine stars and the circling sun.

Not theirs to wander lost and lone,
   Adream by mountain lake, and sea;
Not theirs to bear a face of stone
   Away from human mystery:
They pondered o'er the runes of time,
They slew the Serpent of the Slime.

The brutish brain, the nervous hands,
   The conscious power of thew and mind;
The agony of burning sands,
   The blithe salt breezes blowing blind—
The birth-pangs of the Emperor Thought,
Of Earth and Pain the wonder-wrought.

They hurled them blindly on the breast
   Of foaming hate, of wild desire:

THE EQUINOX

From Time they held the old bequest,
    The passioned pangs, the flash of fire—
Not through the gods they dreamed of ran
The stream that fired the veins of man.

They stanched the gaping wound with turf,
    With water slaked the burning maw;
Rolling within the boiling surf,
    They caught the brine in eye and jaw.
They roared and rushed with tangled mane
To rape and ruin in the rain.

The hours flew by all swift and red;
    They gorged, they slept within the shade:
They yelled in fear with muffled head
    When thunder made them sore afraid.
Loud laughed the gods to see the wild
Mad glory of their weanling child.

A flash of long-forgotten light—
    I found again the men of old,
The wondering children of the night,
    The ravagers of hill and wold—
Our sane, strong, savage satyr-sires.
In whom were born the artist-fires.

The scorching sun, the sleeping moon,
    The yelling wind that clave the trees,
The monsters that they fled, the croon
    Of squaws with babes upon their knees,
The wet woods' call, the insistent sea,
The blood-stained birth of mystery.

AN ORIGIN

The scream of passion, and the foam
    Upon the willing women's lips;
Green, dripping forests, love's dark home—
    These were the god-enwroughten whips
That gave the eagle-cars of Art
First impulse in the cave-man's heart.

The artist-light is backward borne,
    Master within my brain to-night;
Back in the long-forgotten morn
    I see the dawn of Thee and light;
The men that made me stare and stare
Through the great wood-fire's lurid glare.

And through the haze of time and life
    Anew the dim, dark visions loom;
The matted bloody hair; the knife
    Of jagged stone; the reeking fume
Of purple blood; the gore and bones
Rotting beneath the straight-aimed stones.

The dream is past; the night returns,
    Old mother of the primal Fear;
Within me, Master, throbs and burns
    The old grey wonder. Yea, I hear—
The heritage is mine; I take
The wand encircled by the snake.

Far in the night I wander; far
   Back in the forest of the Past,
Led by my sole and single star,
   Where I shall dwell in peace at last.

THE EQUINOX

But once again I see Thee stand
Guarding the old forgotten land.—

A silent land of dream and fear,
 Where thought-waves break upon the shore,
And reach the high gods; listening ear,
 And echo on for evermore
Through the dark ages, till they reach
Their long-sought goal, and burst in speech.

VICTOR B. NEUBURG.

THE SOUL-HUNTER

THE SOUL-HUNTER*

I BOUGHT his body for ten francs. Months before I had bought his soul, bought it for the first glass of the poison—the first glass of the new series of hrrors since his discharge, cured—cured!—from the "retreat." Yes, I tempted him, I, a doctor! Bound by the vows—faugh! I needed his body! His soul? pah! but an incident in the bargain. For soul is but a word, a vain word—a battlefield of the philosopher fools, the theologian fools, since Anaximander and Gregory Nanzianus. A toy. But the consciousness? That is what we mean by *soul*, we others. That then must live somewhere. But is it, as Descartes thoughts, atomic? or fluid, now here, now there? Or is it but a word for the totality of bodily sense? As Weir Mitchell supposed. Well, we should see. I would buy a brain and hunt this elusive consciousness. Just so, luck follows skill; the brain of Jules Foreau was the very pick of the world's brains. The most self-conscious man in Europe! Intellectual to an incredible point, introspective beyond the Hindus, *and* with the fatal craving which made him mine. Jules Foreau, you might have been a statesman; you became a sot—but you shall make the name of Doctor Arthur Lee famous for ever, and put an end to the great

* Unpublished pages from the diary of Dr. Arthur Lee—"the Montrouge Vampire."

problem of the ages. Aha, my friend, how mad of me to fill my diary with this cheap introspective stuff! I feel somehow that the affair will end badly. I am writing my *defence*. Certainly that excuses the form. A jury can never understand plain facts—the cold light of science chills them; they need eloquence, sentiment. . . . Well, I must pay a lawyer for that, if trouble should really arise. How should it? I have made all safe—trust me!

I gave him the drug yesterday. The atropine was a touch of almost superhuman cleverness; the fixed, glassy stare deader than death itself. I complied with the foolish formulæ of the law; in three hours I had the body in my laboratory. In the present absurd state of the law there is really nobody trustworthy in a business of this sort. *Tant pis!* I must cook my own food for a month or so. For no doubt there will be a good deal of noise. No doubt a good deal of noise. I must risk that. I dare not touch anything but the brain; it might vitiate the whole experiment. Bad enough this plaster of Paris affair. You see a healthy man of thirteen stone odd in his prime will dislike any deep interference with his brain—resent it. Chains are useless; nothing keeps a man still. Bar anæsthesia. And anæsthesia is the one thing barred. He must feel, he must talk, he must be as normal as possible. So I have simply built his neck, shoulders, and arms into plaster. He can yell and he can kick. If it does him any good he is welcome. So—to business.

10.30. A.M. He is decidedly under the new drug—η''; yet he does not move. He takes longer to come back to life than I supposed.

10.40. Warmth to extremities. Inhalations of λ. He cannot speak yet, I think. The glare of eyes is not due to hate, but to the atropine.

10.45. He has noticed the plaster arrangement and the nature of the room. I think he guesses. A gurgle. I light a cigarette and put it in his mouth. He spits it out. He seems hardly to understand my good-humour.

10.47. The first word—"What is it, you devil?" I show him the knife, *et cetera*, and urge him to keep calm and self-collected .

10.50. A laugh, not too nervous. A good sigh. "By George, you amuse me!" Then with a sort of wistful sigh, "I thought you just meant to poison me in some new patent kind of way." Bad; he wants to die. Must cheer him up.

11.0. I have given my little scientific lecture. The patient unimpressed. The absinthe has damaged his reasoning faculty. He cannot see the *a priori* necessity of the experiment. Strange!

11.10. Lord, how funny!—he thinks I may be mad, and is trying all the old dodges to "humour" me! I must sober him.

11.15. Sobered him. Showed him his own cranium—he had never missed it, of course. Yet the fact seemed to surprise him. Important, though, for my thesis. Here at least is one part of the body whose absence in nowise diminishes the range of the sensorium—soul—what shall we call it? "x." Some important glands, of course, rule a man's whole life. Others again—what use is a lymphatic to the soul? To "x."?

Well, we must deal with the glands in detail, at the fountain-head, in the brain.

11.20. My writing seems to irritate him. Daren't give drugs. He flushes and pales too easily. Absence of skull? Now, a little cut and tie—and we shall see.

N.B.—To keep this record very distinct from the pure surgery of the business.

11.22. A concentrated, sustained yell. It has quite shaken me. I never heard the like. "All out" too, as we used to say on the Cam; he's physically exhausted—*e.g.*, has stopped kicking. Legs limp as possible. Pure funk; I never hurt him.

11.25. A most curious thing: I feel an intense dislike of the man coming over me; and, with an almost insane fascination, the thought, "Suppose I were to *kiss* him?" Followed by a shiver of physical loathing and disgust. Such thoughts have no business here at all. To work.

12.0. I want a drink; there are most remarkable gaps in the consciousness—not implying unconsciousness. I am inclined to think that what we call continuous pain is a rhythmic beat, frequency of beat less than one in sixty. The shrieks are simply heartbreaking.

12.5. Silence, more terrible than the yells. Afraid I had an accident. He smiles, reassures me. Speaks—"Look here, doctor, enough of this fooling; I'm annoyed with you, really don't know why—and I yell because I know it worries you. But listen to this: under the drug I really died, though you thought I was simulating death. On the contrary, it is now that I am simulating life." There seemed to me, and still seems, some essential absurdity in these words; yet I could not refute him. I opened my mouth and closed it. The voice went on: "It follows that your whole experiment is a childish failure." I cut him short; this time I found words. "You forget your position," I said hotly. "It is against all precedent for the vivisectee to abuse his master. Ingrate!" So incensed was I that I strode angrily to the operating-chair and paralysed the ganglia governing the muscles of speech. Imagine my surprise when he proceeded, entirely incommoded: "On the contrary, it is you who are dead, Arthur Lee." The voice came from behind me, from far off. "Until you die you never know it, but you have been dead all along." My nerve is clearly gone; this must be a case of pure hallucination. I begin to remember that I am alone—alone in the big house with the . . . patient. Suppose I were to fall ill? . . . Was this thought written in my face? He laughed harsh and loud. Disgusting beast!

12.15. A pretty fool I am, tying the wrong nerve. No wonder he could go on talking! A nasty slip in such an experiment as this. Must check the whole thing through again. . . .

1.0. O.K. now. Must get some lunch. Oddly enough, I am pretty sure he was telling the truth. He feels no pain, and only yells to annoy me.

2.10. Excellent! I suppress all the senses but smell, and give him his wife's handkerchief. He bubbles over with amorous drivel; I should love to tell him what she died of, and who. . . . A curious trait, that last remark. Why do I *dislike* the man? I used to get on A1 with him. (N.B. to stitch eyelids with silk. Damn the glare.)

2.20. Theism! The convolution with the cause-idea lying too close to the convolution with the fear-idea. And imagination at work on the nexus! About 24 μ between Charles Bradlaugh and Cardinal Newman!

2.50. So for faith and doubt? Sceptical criticism of my whole experiment boils up in me. What is "normality"? Even so, what possible relation is there between things and the evidence of them recorded in the brain? Evidence of something, maybe. A thermometer chart gives a curve; yet the mercury has only moved up and down. What about the time dimension? But it is not a dimension; it is only a word to explain multiplicity of sensation. Words! words! words! This is the last straw. There is no conceivable standard whereby we may measure anything whatever; and it is useless to pretend there is.

3.3. In short, we are all mad. Yet all this is but the expression of the doubt-stop in the human organ. Let me pull out his faith-stop!

4.45. Done; the devil's own job. He seems to be a Pantheist Antinomian with leanings towards Ritualism. Not impressive. My observation-stop (= my doubt-stop nearly) is full out. (Funny that we should fall into the old faculty jargon.) Perhaps if one's own faith-stop were out there would be a fight; if one's reception-of-new-ideas-stop, a conversion.

5.12. I only wish I had two of them to test the "tuning-up" theory of Collective Hallucination and the like. Out of the question; we must wait for Socialism. But enough for the day is the research thereof. I've matter for a life's work already.

7.50. An excellent scratch dinner—none too soon. Turtle soup, potted char, Yorkshire pie, Stilton, burgundy. Better than nothing. To-morrow the question of putrefactive changes in the limbs and their relation to the brain.

3.1. Planted bacilli in left foot. Will leave him to sleep. No difficulty there; the brute's as tired as I am. Too tired to curse. I recited "Abide with Me" throughout to soothe him. Some lines distinctly humorous under the circumstances. Will have a smoke in the study and check through the surg. record. Too dazed to realise everything, but I am assuredly an epoch. Whaur's your Robbie Pasteur noo?

12.20. So I've been on a false trail all day! The course of the
A.M. research has let right away from the "x-hunt." The byways have obscured the main road. Valuable though; very very valuable. In the morning success. Bed!

12.30. Yells and struggles again when I went in to say good-night. As I had carefully paralysed *all* sensory avenues (to ensure perfect rest), how was he aware of my presence? The memory of the scented handkerchief, too, very strong; talked a lot of his wife, thinking here with him. Pah! what beasts some men must be! Disgusting fellow! I'm no prude either! If ever I do a woman I'll stop the Filth-gutter. *Ce serait trop.*

12.40 Maybe he did *not* know of my presence; merely remembered me. He has cause. How much there is in one's mind of the merely personal idea of scoring off the bowlers. And every man is a batsman in a world of bowlers. Like that leg-cricket game, what did we call it? Oh! bed, bed!

5.0. Patient seriously ill; plaster irks breathing; all sorts of troubles expected and unexpected. Putrefaction of left foot well advanced: promises well for the day's work if I can check collapse.

5.31. Patient very much better; paralysed motor ganglia; safe to remove plaster. Too much time wasted on these foolish mechanical details of life when one is looking for the Master of the Machine.

6.12. Patient in excellent fettle; now to find "*x*"—the soul!

11.55. Worn out; no "*x*" yet. Patient well, normal; have checked shrieks, ingenious dodge.

2.15. No time for food; brandy. Patient fighting fit. No "*x*."

3.1. *Dead!!!* No cause in the world—I must have cut right into the "*x*," the soul.

The meningeal——

[Dr. Lee's diary breaks off abruptly at this point. His researches were never published. It will be remembered that he was convicted of causing the death of his mistress, Jeannette Pheyron, under mysterious circumstances, some six months after the date of the above. The surgical record referred to has not been found.—EDITOR.]

MADELEINE

OH, the cool white neck of her:
    The ivory column: oh, the velvet skin.
Little I reck of her
    Save the curve from breast to chin.
Oh, the rising rounded throat,
Pain's subtle antidote.
To sit and watch the pulses of it beat,
And guess the passionate heat
Of the blood that flows within!
I see it swelling with her even breath
    And long to make it throb
    With a love as strong as death.
To cause the sharp and sudden-catching sob
    And the swift dark flood,
    Showing the instant blood,
Quick mantling up where I had made it throb
    With love as strong as death.

Oh, the pure, pale face of her;
    The chiselled outline, chaste as starlit snows.
The ineffable grace of her;
    The distant, perfect grace of her repose.
    Her mouth the waiting redness of a rose

THE EQUINOX

A rose too nearly cloyed
  With its own secret sweetness unalloyed:
That waits in scented silence, stately-sad,
  Wed to a guarded passion thro' long days,
But lifts the proud head, saying "I am glad,"
  Haughty receives as due the word of praise,
And flings her perfumed wonders on the air:
  "Afar," she says, "fall down and gaze; for I am fair."

Oh the dark, sweet hair of her,
  Burnished cascade of heavy-tress d black:
Nothing's more rare of her
  Than its thick massed glory over breast and back.
It rolls and ripples, silver flecked,
  Like moonlight on a misty sea,
Whose lifting surfaces reflect
  A sombre, ever-changing radiancy.
I would compare
The dusk, soft-stealing perfume of her hair
  To breezes on a Southern Summer eve,
When the night-scented stock hangs drowsing on the air.
  Its languid incense bids me half believe
I pass the dreamy day in reveries,
By some sleep-haunted shore of the Hesperides.

Oh, the deep, dark eyes of her,
  Half slumbrous depths of heavy lidded calm:
There's naught I prize of her
  More than the shrouded silence they embalm.
There's all the mystery of an enchanted pool,
Hid in brown woodlands cool;

MADELEINE

Profound, untroubled, where the lilies grow
   And the pale lotus sheds her stealing charm:
Dappled where silent shadows come and go,
   And all the air is warm
With the low melody of the Sacred Bird
   Sobbing his soul out to the waiting wood,
And over all a hushèd voice is heard:
   This place is consecrate to Love in solitude.

ARTHUR B. GRIMBLE.

THE TEMPLE OF SOLOMON
THE KING

A∴ A∴ Publication in Class B

Issued by Order :

D.D.S. $7° = 4°$ Præmonstrator
O.S.V. $6° = 5°$ Imperator
N.S.F. $5° = 6°$ Cancellarius

Book II, continued

THE SORCERER

BEFORE we can discuss the Operation of the Sacred Magic of Abramelin, commenced by P. in the autumn of 1899, it is first necessary that we should briefly explaion the meaning and value of Ceremonial Magic; and secondly, by somewhat retracing our footsteps, disclose to the reader the various methods and workings P. had undertaken before he set out to accomplish this supreme one.

For over a year now he had been living *perdu* in the heart of London, strenuously applying himself to the various branches of secret knowledge that his initiations in the Order of the Golden Dawn had disclosed to him. Up to the present we have only dealt with these initiations, and his methods of Travelling in the Spirit Vision, and Rising on the Planes; but there still remain to be shown the Ceremonial methods he adopted; however, before we enter upon these, we must return to our first point, namely—the meaning and value of Ceremonial Magic.

Ceremonial Magic, as a means to attainment, has in common with all other methods, Western or Eastern, one supreme object in view—identification with the Godhead; and it matters not if the Aspirant be Theist or Atheist, Pantheist or Autotheist, Christian or Jew, or whether he name the goal of his attainment God, Zeus, Christ, Matter, Nature, Spirit, Heaven,

Reason, Nirvana, Asgard, No-Thing or No-God, so long as
he *has* a goal in view, and a goal he is striving to attain.
Without a goal he is but a human ship without port or destination; and without striving, work, WILL to attain, he is
but a human derelict, rudderless and mastless, tossed hither
and thither by the billows of lunacy, eventually to sink
beneath the black waters of madness and death.

Thus we find that outside the asylum, we, one and all of
us, are strenuously or slothfully, willingly or unwillingly,
consciously or unconsciously, progressing slowly or speedily
towards *some* goal that we have set up as an ideal before us.
Follow the road to that goal, subdue all difficulties, and, when
the last has been vanquished, we shall find that that "some
goal" is in truth THE GOAL, and that the road upon which
we set out was but a little capillary leading by vein and artery
to the very Heart of Unity itself.

Then all roads lead to the same goal?—Certainly. Then,
say you, "All roads are equally good?" Our answer is, "Certainly not!" For it does not follow that because all roads lead
to Rome, all are of the same length, the same perfection, or
equally safe. The traveller who would walk to Rome must use
his own legs—his WILL to arrive there; but should he
discard as useless the advice of such as know the way and
have been there, and the maps of the countries he has to
journey through, he is but a fool, only to be exceeded in his
folly by such as try all roads in turn and arrive by none. As
with the traveller, so also with the Aspirant; he must commence his journey with the cry, "I *will* attain!" and leave
nothing undone that may help him to accomplish this attainment. By contemplating the Great Work, and all means to its

attainment, little by little from the Knowledge he has obtained will he learn to extract that subtle Understanding which will enable him to construct such symbols of strength, such appliances of power, such exercises of Will and Imagination, that by their balanced, chaste and sober use, he MUST succeed if he WILL to do so.

So we see, it matters very little whether the Aspirant, truly the Seer, cry "Yea" or "Nay," so long as he do so with a *will*, a *will* that will beget a Sorcery within the cry; for as Levi says: "The intelligence which denies, invariably affirms something, since it is asserting its liberty."

Let us now inquire what this liberty is, but above all, whatever we write: "Be not satisfied with what we tell you; and act for yourself." And, if you act with daring and courage, you will indeed outstep the normal powers of life and become a strong man amongst strong men, so that "if we say unto this mountain, be thou removed, and be thou cast into the sea, it shall be done." For the land into which you enter is a land which, to the common eye, appears as a fabulous land of wonder and miracle. Yet we say to you that there is no wonder imagined in the mind of man that man is not capable of performing, there is no miracle of the Imagination, which has been performed by man, the which may not yet again be performed by him. The sun has stood still upon Gibeon and the moon in the valley of Ajalon, and the stars of heaven have fallen unto the earth, even as a fig-tree casteth her untimely figs, when she is shaken by a mighty wind. What are suns, and moons, and stars, but the ideas of dreaming children cradled in the abyss of a drowsy understanding? To the blind worm, the sun is as the fluttering of warm wings in the outer darkness, and the stars are not; to the savage, as welcome ball of fire, and the glittering eyes of the beasts of night: to us, as spheres of earth's familiar elements and many hundred million miles away. And to the man of ten thousand years hence—who knows? And to him a hundred million years after that—who cares! Senses may come and go, and the five may become ten, and the ten twenty, so that the beings of that last far-off twilight may differ from us, as we differ from the earthworm, and the weeds in the depths of the sea. But enough—Become the Changless One, and ye shall leap past a million years, and an hundred hundred million in the twinkling of an eye. Nay! for Time will burst as a bubble between your lips; and, seeing and understanding, Space will melt as a bead of sweat upon your brow and vanish!

Dare to will and will to know, and you will become as great as, and even greater than, Apollonius, Flamel or Lully; and then know to keep silence, lest like Lucifer you fall, and the brilliance of your knowledge blind the eyes of the owls that are men; and from a great light, spring a great darkness; and the image survive and the imagination vanish, and idols replace the gods, and churches of brick and stone the mysteries of the forests and the mountains, and the rapture which girds the hearts of men like a circle of pure emerald light.

The great seeming miracles of life pass by unheeded. Birth and Generation are but the sorry jests of fools; yet not the wisest knows how a blade of grass sprouts from the black earth, or how it is that the black earth is changed into the green leaves and all the wonders of the woods. Yet the multitude trample the flowers of the fields under their feet, and snigger in their halls of pleasure at a dancer clothed in frilled nudity, because they are nearer seeing the mysteries of Creation than they are in the smugness of their own stuffy back parlours; and gape in wonder at some stage trickster, some thought-reading buffoon, and talk about the supernatural, the supernormal, the superterestrial, the superhuman, and all the other superficial superfluities of superannuated supernumeraries, as if this poor juggler were some kind of magician who could enter their thick skulls and steal their sorry thoughts, whilst all the time he is at the old game of picking their greasy pockets.

Miracles are but the clouds that cloak the dreamy eyes of ignorant men. Therefore let us once and for all thunder forth: There are no miracles for those who wake; miracles are for the dreamers, and wonders are as bottled bull's-eyes in a bun-shop for penniless children. Beauty alone exists for the Adept. Everywhere there is loveliness—in the poppy and in the dunghill upon which it blows; in the palace of marble and in the huts of sunbaked mud which squat without its walls. For him the glades of the forests laugh with joy, and so do the gutters of our slums. All is beautiful, and flame-shod he speeds over earth and water, through fire and air; and builds, in the tangled web of the winds, that City wherein no one dreams, and where even awakenment ceases to be.

But in order to work miracles we must be outside the ordinary conditions of humanity; we must either be abstracted by wisdom or exalted by madness, either superior to all passions or beyond them through ecstasy or frenzy. Such is the first and most indispensable preparation of the operator. Hence, by a providential or fatal law, the magician can only exercise omnipotence in inverse proportion to his material interest; the alchemist makes so much the more gold as he is the more resigned to privations, and the more esteems that poverty which protects the secrets of the *magnum* *opus.* Only the adept whose heart is passionless will dispose of the love and hate of those whom he would make instruments of his science; the myth of Genesis is eternally true, and God permits the tree of science to be approached only by those men who are sufficiently strong and self-denying not to covet its fruits. Ye, therefore, who seek in science a means to satisfy your passions, pause in this fatal way; you will find nothing but madness or death. This is the meaning of the vulgar tradition that the devil ends sooner or later by strangling sorcerers. The magus must hence be impassible, sober and chaste, disinterested, impenetrable, and inaccessible to any kind of prejudice or terror. He must be without bodily defects, and proof against all contractions and all difficulties. The first and most important of magical operations is the attainment of this rare pre-eminence.*

The *via mystica* leading to this pre-eminence may aptly be compared to a circle. Wherever the Aspirant strikes it, there he will find a path leading to the right and another leading to the left. To the right the goal is all things, to the left the goal is nothing. Yet the paths are not two paths, but one path; and the goals are not two goals, but one goal. The Aspirant upon entering the circle must travel by the one or the other, and must not look back; lest he be turned into a pillar of salt, and become the habitation of the spirits of Earth. "For thy vessel the Beasts of the Earth shall inhabit," as sayeth Zoroaster. The Magus travels by both simultaneously, if he travels at all; for he has learnt what is meant by the mystery: "A straight line is the circumference of a circle whose radius in infinity"; a line of infinite length in the mind of the Neophyte, but which in truth is also a line of infinite shortness in that of the Magus, if finite or infinite at all.

The circle having been opened out, from the line can any curve be fashioned; and if the Magus *wills it,* the line *will be* a triangle, or a square, or a circle; and at his word it will

* E. Levi, "Doctrine and Ritual of Magic," p. 192.

flash before him as a pentagram or a hexagram, or perchance as an eleven-pointed star.

Thus shall the Aspirant learn to create suns and moon, and all the hosts of heaven out of unity. But first he must travel the circumference of the circle; and, when mystically he has discovered that the goal is the starting-point, and where he entered that circle there also will it break and open out, so that the adytum of its centre becomes as an arch in its outer wall, then indeed will he be worthy of the name of Magus.

The keystone to this arch some have called God, some Brahma, some Zeus, some Allah, some even IAO the God of the sounding name; but in truth, O seeker, it is Thy-SELF — this higher dimension in which the inner becomes the outer, and in which the single Eye alone can see the throbbing heart, Master of the entangled skein of veins.

Let us for example's sake call this attainment by the common name of God (SELF as opposed to self). And as we have seen the path of union with god or goal is twofold:

I. The attainment of all things.

II. The destruction of all things.

And whichever way we travel to right or to left the method is also twofold, or the twofold in one:

I. Exaltation by madness.

II. Exaltation by wisdom.

In the first we awake from the dream of illusion by a blinding light being flashed across our eyes; in the second, gradually, by the breaking of the dawn.

In the first the light of knowledge, though but comparable to the whole of Knowledge as a candle-flame to the sun, may be so sudden that blindness follows the first illumination.* In the second, though the light be as the sun of knowledge itself; first its gentle warmth, and then its tender rays awake us, and lead us through the morning to the noontide of day. Like children of joy we rise from our beds and dance through the dewy fields, and chase the awakening butterflies from the blushing flowers—ecstasy is ours. The first is as a sudden bounding beyond darkness into light, from the humdrum into the ecstatic; the second a steady march beyond the passionate West into the land of everlasting Dawn.

Concerning the first we have little to say; for it is generally the illumination of the weak. The feeble often gain the little success they do gain in life, not through their attempts to struggle, but on account of their weakness—the enemy not considering they are worth power and shot. But the strong gain their lives in fight and victory; the sword is their warrant to live, and by their swords *will* they attain; and when they once have attained, by their swords will they rule, and from warriors become as helmèd kings whose crowns are of iron, and whose sceptres are sharp swords of glittering steel, and reign; whilst the weak still remain as slaves, and a prey to the wild dreams of the night. Of a truth, sometimes the weak charioteer wins the race; but on account of his weakness he is often carried past the winning-post by the steeds that have given him the victory, and, unable to hold them back, he is dashed against the walls of the arena, whilst the strong man passing the judges turns his chariot round and receives the crown of victory, or if not that, is ever ready to race again.

* The greater our ignorance the more intense appears the illumination.

THE TEMPLE OF SOLOMON THE KING

To learn how to WILL is the key to the kingdom, the door of which as we have seen contains two locks, or rather two bolts in one lock, one turning to the right and the other to the left. Either pile up the imagination with image upon image until the very kingdom of God is taken by assault; or withdrawn one symbol after another until the walls are undermined and the "cloud-capped towers" come tumbling to the ground. In either case the end is the same—the city is taken. Or perchance if you are a great Captain, and your army is filled with warlike men, and you are in possession of all the engines suitable to this Promethean struggle—at one and the same time scale the bastions and undermine the ramparts, so that as those above leap down, those beneath leap up, and the city falls as an arrow from a bow that breaks in twain in the hand. Such warfare is only for the great—the greatest; yet we shall see that this is the warfare that P. eventually waged. And where the strong have trod the weak may *dare* to follow.

This path must necessarily be a difficult one; illusions and delusions must be expected, temptations and defeats encountered with equanimity, and fears and terrors passed by without trembling. The labours of Hercules are a good example of the labours the Aspirant, who would be an Adept, must expect. However, there is not space here, nor is this the place, to enter into the twelve mystic works of this man who became a God. Yet let us at least note three points— that the tenth labour was to slay Geryon, the *three*-headed and *three*-bodied monster of Gades; that the eleventh was to obtain apples from the garden of the Hesperides, where lived the *three* daughters of Hesperus; and that the last was to bring upon earth the *three*-headed dog Cerberus, and so unguard the gates of Hades. Similar is the Adept's last labour, to destroy the terrors of hell and to bring upon earth the Supernal triad and formulate the שׁ* in הוּשׁ חי.

One idea must possess us, and all our energies must be focused upon it. A man who would be rich must worship wealth and understand poverty; a man who would be strong must worship strength and understand weakness; and so also a man who would be God must worship deity and understand devilry: that is, he must become saturated with the reflections of Kether in Malkuth, until the earth be leavened and the two eyes become one. He must indeed build up his tower stone upon stone until the summit vanish amongst the stars, and he is lost in a land which lies beyond the flames of day and the shadows of night.

To attain to this Ecstasy, exercises and operations of the most trivial nature must be observed, if they, even in the remotest manner, appertain to the *one* idea.

You are a beggar, and you desire to make gold; set to work and never leave off. I promise you, in the name of science, all the treasures of Flamel and Raymond Lully. "What is the first thing to do?" Believe in your power, then act. "But how act?" Rise daily at the same hour, and that early; bathe at a spring before daybreak, and in all seasons; never wear dirty clothes, but rather wash them yourself if needful; accustom yourself to voluntary privations, that you may be better able to bear those which come without seeking; then silence every desire which is foreign to the fulfilment of the Great Work.

"What! By bathing daily in a spring, I shall make gold?" You will work in order to make it. "It is a mockery!" No, it is an arcanum. "How can I make use of an arcanum which I fail to understand?" Believe and act; you will understand later.†

Levi here places belief as a crown upon the brow of work.

* N.B.—the Shin is composed of three Yodhs, and its value is 300.
† "Doctrine and Ritual of Magic," pp. 194, 195.

He is, in a way, right; yet to the ordinary individual this belief is as a heavy load which he cannot even lift, let alone carry, act how he will. Undoubtedly, if a boy worried long enough over a text-book on trigonometry he would eventually appreciate the theory and practice of logarithms; but why should he waste his time? why not instead seek a master? Certainly, when he has learnt all the text-books can teach and all the master can tell him, he must strike out for himself, but up to this point he must place his faith in some one. To the ordinary Aspirant a *Guru** is necessary; and the only danger to the uninitiate is that he may place his trust in a charlatan instead of in an adept. This indeed is a danger, but surely after a little while the most ignorant will be able to discriminate, as a blind man can between day and night. And, if the pupil be a true Seeker, it matters little in the end. For as the sacrament is efficacious, though administered by an unworthy priest, so will his love of Truth enable him to turn even the evil counsels of a knave to his advantage.

To return, how can these multiform desires be silenced, and the one desire be realised so that it engulf the rest? To this question we must answer as we have answered elsewhere — "only by a one-pointedness of the senses"—until the five-sided polygon become pyramidal and vanish in a point. The base must be well established, regular, and of even surface; for as the base so the summit. In other words, the five senses must be strong and healthy and without disease. An unhealthy man is unfitted to perform a magical operation, and an hysterical man will probably end in the Qliphoth or Bedlam. A blind man will not be able to equilibrate the sense of sight,

* Instructor.

or a deaf man the sense of hearing, like a man who can both see and hear; however, the complete loss of one sense, if this is ever actually the case, if far better than a mental weakness in that sense.

All senses and faculties must share in the work, such at least is the dictum of Western Ceremonial Magic. And so we find the magician placing stone upon stone in the construction of his Temple. That is to say, placing pantacle upon pantacle, and safeguarding his one idea by means of swords, daggers, wands, rings, perfumes, suffumigations, robes, talismans, crowns, magic squares and astrological charts, and a thousand other symbols of things, ideas, and states, all reflecting the one idea; so that he may build up a mighty mound, and from it eventually leap over the great wall which stands before him as a partition between two worlds.

All faculties and all senses should share in the work; nothing in the priest of Hermes has the right to remain idle; intelligence must be formulated by signs and summed by characters or pantacles; will must be determined by words, and must fulfil words by deeds; the magical idea must be rendered into light for the eyes, harmony for the ears, perfumes for the sense of smell, savours for the palate, objects for the touch; the operator, in a word, must realise in his whole life what he wishes to realise in the world without him; he must become a "magnet" to attract the desired thing; and when he shall be sufficiently magnetic, he must be convinced that the thing will come of itself, and without thinking of it.*

This seems clear enough, but more clearly still is this all-important point explained by Mr. Aleister Crowley in his preface to his edition of "The Book of the Goetia of Solomon the King":

I am not concerned [writes Mr. Crowley] to deny the objective reality of all "magical" phenomena; if they are illusions, they are at least as real as many un-

* "Doctrine and Ritual of Magic," p. 196.

questioned facts of daily life; and, if we follow Herbert Spencer, they are at least evidence of some cause.

Now, this fact is our base. What is the cause of my illusion of seeing a spirit in the triangle of Art?

Every smatterer, every expert in psychology, will answer, "that cause lies in your brain.'"

*   *   *   *   *   *

This being true for the ordinary Universe, that all sense-impressions are dependent on changes in the brain, we must include illusions, which are after all sense-impressions as much as "realities" are, in the class of "phenomena dependent on brain-changes.'"

Magical phenomena, however, come under a special sub-class, since they are willed, and their cause is the series of "real" phenomena called the operations of Ceremonial Magic.

These consist of:

(1) *Sight.*

The circle, square, triangle, vessels, lamps, robes, implements, &c.

(2) *Sound.*

The Invocations.

(3) *Smell.*

The Perfumes.

(4) *Taste.*

The Sacraments.

(5) *Touch.*

As under (1). The circle, &c.

(6) *Mind.*

The combination of all these and reflection on their significance.

These unusual impressions (1-5) produce unusual brain-changes; hence their summary (6) is of unusual kind. The projection back into the phenomenal world is therefore unusual.

Herein then consists the reality of the operations and effects of ceremonial magic; and I conceive that the apology is ample, so far as the "effects" refer only to those phenomena which appear to the magician himself, the appearance of the spirit, his conversation, possible shocks from imprudence, and so on, even to ecstasy on the one hand, and death or madness on the other.*

Thus we see that the Aspirant must become a *magnet*, and attract all desires to himself until there is nothing outside of

---

* "Goetia," pp. 1-3.

him left to attract; or repel all things, until there is nothing left to repel.

In the East the five senses are treated in their unity, and the magical operation becomes purely a mental one, and in many respects a more rational and less emotional one. The will, so to speak, is concentrated on itself by the aid of a reflective point—the tip of the nose, the umbilicus, a lotus, or again, in a more abstract manner, on the inhalation and exhalation of the breath, upon an idea or a sensation. The Yogi abandons the constructive method, and so it is that we do not find him building up, but, instead, undermining his consciousness, his instrument being a purely introspective one, the power of turning his will as a mental eye upon himself, and finally seeing himself as HimSELF.

However, in both the Western and Eastern systems, equilibrium is both the method and the result. The Western Magician wills to turn darkness into light, earth into gold, vice into virtue. He sets out to purify; therefore all around him must be pure, ever to hold before his memory the one essential idea. More crudely this is the whole principle of advertising. A good advertiser so places his advertisement that wherever you go, and whichever way you turn, you see the name of the article he is booming. If it happens, *e.g.*, to be "Keating's Insect Powder," the very name becomes part of you, so that directly a flea is seen or mentioned "Keating's" spontaneously flashes across your thoughts.

The will of a magician may be compared to a lamp burning in a dark and dirty room. First he sets to work to clean the room out, then he places a brightly polished mirror along one wall to reflect one sense, and then anther to reflect another, and so on, until, whichever way he look, up or down, to right or left, behind or before, there he sees his will shining; and ultimately so dazzling become the innumerable reflections, that he can see but one great flame which obscures everything else. The Yogi on the other hand dispenses with the mirrors, and contents himself in turning the wick lower and lower until the room is one perfect darkness and nothing else can be seen or even recognised beyond SELF.

By those who have passed along both these mystic paths, it will be found that the energy expended is the same in both. Concentration is a terrific labour; the mere fact of sitting still and mediating on one idea and slaying all other ideas one after the other, and then constantly seeing them sprout up hundred-headed like the Hydra, needs so great a power of endurance that, though many undertake the task, few reach the goal. Again, the strain brought to bear on a Ceremonial Magician is equally colossal, and often costly; and in these bustling days the necessary seclusion is most difficult to obtain. And so it came about that a combination of both the above systems was ultimately adopted by P. However, it must be remembered that the dabbler in Ceremonial Magic or Yoga is but heaping up evil against himself, just as the dabbler on the Stock Exchange is. Magic, like gambling, has its chances; but in the former as in the latter, without "will to work" chances are always against him who puts his trust in them alone.

There is, however, one practice none must neglect, except the weakest, who are unworthy to attempt it—the practice of Sceptical selection.

Eliphas Levi gives us the following case:

THE EQUINOX

One day a person said to me: "I would that I could be a fervent Catholic, but I am a Voltairean. What would I not give to have faith!" I replied: "Say 'I would' no longer; say 'I will,' and I promise you that you will believe. You tell me you are a Voltairean, and of all the various presentations of faith that of the Jesuits is most repugnant to you, but at the same time seems the most powerful and desirable. Perform the exercises of St. Ignatius again and again, without allowing yourself to be discouraged, and you will gain the faith of a Jesuit. The result is infallible, and should you then have the simplicity to ascribe it to a miracle, you deceive yourself now in thinking that you are a Voltairean."*

Now all this may be good enough for Mrs. Eddy. To borrow a sword from one of Voltaire's antagonists, and to thrust it through his back when he is not looking, is certainly one way of getting rid of Voltaire. But the intellectual knight must not behave like a Christian footpad; he must trap Voltaire in his own arguments by absorbing the whole of Voltaire—eighty volumes and more—until there is no Voltaire left, and as he does so, apply to each link of Voltaire's armour the fangs of the Pyrrhonic Serpent; and where that serpent bites through the links, those links must be discarded; and where its teeth are turned aside, those links must be kept. Similarly must he apply the serpent to St. Ignatius, and out of the combination of the strongest links of both their armours fashion for himself so invulnerable a coat of mail that none can pierce it. Thus, instead of burying one's reason in the sands of faith, like an ostrich, one should rise like a phoenix of enlightenment out of the ashes of both Freethought and Dogma. This is the whole of Philosophic Scientific Illuminism.

Now that we have finished our short disquisition upon the Methods of Western Magic, let us once again

* "Doctrine and Ritual of Magic," p. 195.

turn to Frater P. and seen how he applied them to his own labours.

Shortly after becoming a member of the Order of the Golden Dawn, P., as already mentioned, became acquainted with a certain Frater, I.A. by name, a magician of remarkable powers. At once a great friendship sprang up between these two, and for over a year and a half they worked secretly in London at various magical and scientific experiments.

During this period P. learnt what may be termed the alphabet of Ceremonial Magic—namely, the workings of Practical Evocations, the Consecrations and uses of Talismans, Invisibility, Transformations, Spiritual Development, Divination, and Alchemical processes, the details of which are dealt with in a manuscript entitled "Z.2." of the Order of the Golden Dawn, which is divided into five books, each under one of the letters of the name ה ו ש ה י.

These five books show how the 0°=0° Ritual may be used as a magical formula. They are as follow:

י

BOOK I

PRACTICAL EVOCATION

A. The Magical Circle.

B. The Magician, wearing the great lamen of the Hierophant, and his scarlet robe. The Hierophant's lamen is on the back of a pentacle, whereon is engraved the sigil of the spirit to be invoked.

C. . The Names and Formulae to be employed.

D. The symbol of the whole evocation.

E. The construction of the circle and the placing of all the symbols, &c., employed in the places proper allotted to them, so as to represent the interior of the G∴ D∴ Temple in the "Enterer": and the purification and consecration of the actual pieces of ground or place selected for the performance of the invocation.

F.   The invocation of the Higher Powers.   Pentacle formed by the concentric bands, name and sigil therein, in proper colours; is to be bound thrice with a cord, and shrouded in black, thus bringing into action a blind force, to be further directed or differentiated in the process of the ceremony. *Announcement* aloud of the *object* of the working, naming the Spirit or Spirits which it is desired to evoke.   This is pronounced standing in the centre of the circle, and turning towards the quarter from which the Spirit will come.

G.   The name and sigil of the spirit wrapped in a black cloth or covering is now placed within the circle, at the point corresponding to the West, representing the candidate.   The Consecration, or Baptism by water and fire of the sigil then takes place: and the proclamation in a loud and firm voice of the spirit (or spirits) to be evoked.

H.   The veiled sigil is now to be placed at the foot of the altar.   The Magician then calls aloud the name of the spirit, summoning him to appear: stating for what purpose the spirit is evoked: what is desired in the operation: why the evocation is performed at this time: and finally solemnly affirming that the Spirit SHALL be evoked by the ceremony.

I.   Announcement aloud that all is prepared for the commencement of the actual evocation. If it be a *good* Spirit the sigil is now to be placed *within the white triangle.* The Magician places his left hand upon it, raises in his right hand the magical implement employed (usually the sword of Art) erect, and commences the evocation of the Spirit.   This being an exorcism of the Spirit unto visible appearance.   The Magician stands in the place of the Hierophant during the obligation, and faces West irrespective of the particular quarter of the Spirit.

But if the Nature of the Spirit be evil, then the sigil must be placed *without* and to the West of the white triangle; and the Magician shall be careful to keep the point of the magic Sword upon the centre of the sigil.

J.   Now let the Magician imagine himself as *clothed outwardly* with the semblance of the form of the Spirit to be evoked: and in this let him be careful *not to identify himself* with the Spirit, which would be dangerous, but only to formulate a species of Mask, worn for the time being.   And if he know not the symbolic form of the Spirit, then let him assume the form of an angel belonging unto the same class of operation. This form being assumed, then let him pronounce aloud, with a firm and solemn voice, *a convenient and potent oration and Exorcism of the Spirit unto visible appearance.* At the conclusion of this exorcism, taking the covered sigil in his left hand, let him smite it thrice with the *flat* blade of the Magic Sword.   Then let him raise on high his arms to their utmost stretch, holding in his left hand the veiled sigil, and in his right the sword of Art erect, at the same time stamping thrice upon the ground with his right foot.

K.   The veiled and covered sigil is then to be placed in the Northern part of the Hall, at the edge of the circle, and the Magician then employs the oration of the Hierophant from the throne of the East, modifying it slightly, as follows: "The Voice of the Exorcism said unto me; let me shroud myself in darkness, peradventure thus may I manifest myself in Light," &c. The Magician then proclaims aloud that the Mystic Circumambulation will take place.

L. The Magician takes up the sigil in his left hand, and circumambulates the magic circle once, then passes to the South and halts. He stands (having lain his sigil on the ground) between it and the West, repeats the oration of the Kerux, and again consecrates it with water and with fire. Then takes it in his hand, facing westward, saying: "Creature of . . . twice consecrate, thou mayest approach the Gate of the West. '"

M. The Magician now moves to the West of the magical circle, holds the sigil in his left hand and the Sword in his right, faces S.W., *and again astrally masks himself with the Form of the Spirit:* and for the first time partially opens the covering, without, however, entirely removing it. He then smites it once with the flat blade of this sword, saying in a loud, clear and firm voice: "Thou canst not pass from concealment unto manifestation, save by virtue of the Name אלהים. Before all things are the Chaos, and the Darkness, and the Gates of the Land of Night. I am he whose Name is 'Darkness': I am the Great One of the paths of the shades. I am the Exorcist in the midst of the exorcism; appear thou therefore without fear before me; for I am he in whom fear is not! Thou hast known me; so pass thou on!" He then reveils the sigil.

N. Operations in L repeated at the North.

O. Processes in M are repeated in the N.W. Magician then passes to the East, takes up sigil in left hand, and Lotus Wand in right; *assumes the mask of the Spirit-Form;* smites sigil with Lotus Wand and says: "Thou canst not pass from concealment unto manifestation save by virtue of the name יהוה. After the formless and the void and the Darkness, there cometh the knowledge of the Light. I am that Light which riseth in the Darkness! I am the Exorcist in the midst of the exorcism; appear thou therefore in harmonious form before me; for I am the wielder of the forces of the Balance. Thou hast known me now, so pass thou on unto the cubical altar of the Universe."

P. He then re-covers sigil and passes on to the altar laying it thereon as before shown. He then passes to the East of the Altar holding the sigil and sword as explained. Then doth he rehearse a most potent conjuration and invocation of that Spirit unto visible appearance, using and reiterating all the Divine angelic and magical names appropriate to this end, neither omitting the signs, seals, sigilla, lineal figures, signatures and the like, from that conjuration.

Q. The Magician now elevates the covered sigil towards Heaven, removes the veil entirely (leaving it yet corded); crying in a loud voice: "Creature of . . . long hast thou dwelt in Darkness, quit the Night and seek the Day." He then replaces it on the altar, holds the magical sword erect above it, the pommel immediately above the centre thereof, and says: "By all the Names, powers, and rites already rehearsed, I conjure Thee thus unto visible appearance." Then the Mystic words.

R. Saith the Magician: "As the Light hidden in the Darkness can manifest therefrom, SO SHALT THOU become manifest from concealment unto manifestation."

He then takes up sigil, stands to the East of the Altar and faces West. He shall then rehearse a long conjuration to the powers and Spirits immediately superior unto that one which he seeks to invoke: *that they shall force him to manifest himself unto visible appearance.* He then places the sigil between the pillars, himself at the East facing West. Then in the sign of the Enterer doth he direct the whole current of his will upon the sigil. Thus he continueth until such time as he shall perceive his will-power to be weakening, when he protects himself from the reflex of the current by the sign of silence, and then drops his hands. He now looks towards the Quarter that the Spirit is to appear in, and he should now see the first signs of his visible manifestation. If he be *not* thus faintly visible, let the Magician repeat the Conjuration of the Superiors of the Spirit; *from the place of the Throne of the East.* And this conjuration may be repeated thrice, each time ending with a new projection of will in the sign of the Enterer, &c. But if at the third time of repetition he appeareth not, then be it known that there is an error in the working. So let the Master of Evocations replace the sigil upon the altar, holding the sword as usual, and thus doing *let him repeat a humble prayer unto the Great Gods of Heaven to grant unto him the force necessary correctly to complete that evocation.*

He is then to take back the Sigil to between the Pillars, and repeat the former processes; *when assuredly that Spirit will begin to manifest, but in a misty and ill-defined form.*

(But if, as is probable, the operator be naturally inclined unto evocation, then might that Spirit perchance manifest earlier in the ceremony than this: still the ceremony itself is to be performed up to this point, whether he be there or no.) Now so soon as the Magician shall see the visible manifestation of that spirit's presence, he shall quit the station of the Hierophant and consecrate afresh with Water and with Fire the Sigil of the evoked Spirit.

S. Now doth the Master of the Evocation remove from the sigil the restricting cord; and, holding the freed sigil in his left hand, he smites it with the flat blade of his sword; exclaiming: "By and in the Names of . . . . . . I do invoke upon thee the power of perfect manifestation unto visible appearance! "

He then circumambulates the circle thrice, holding the sigil in his "right" hand.

T. The Magician, standing in the place of the Hierophant, but turning towards the place of the Spirit, and fixing his attention thereon, now reads a *potent invocation of the Spirit* unto visible appearance; having previously placed the sigil on the ground, within the circle at the quarter where the Spirit appears. This invocation should be of some length, and should rehearse and reiterate the Divine and other names consonant with the working. That Spirit should now become fully and clearly visible, and should be able to speak with a direct voice (if consonant with his nature). The Magician then proclaims aloud that the Spirit N hath been duly and properly evoked, in accordance with the sacred rites.

U. The Magician now addresses and Invocation unto the Lords of the Plane of the Spirit to compel him to perform that which the Magician shall demand of him.

V. The Magician carefully formulates his demands, questions, &c., and writes down any of the answers that may be advisable.

W. The Master of Evocations now addresses a conjuration unto the spirit evoked, binding him to hurt or injure naught connected with him; or his assistants; or the place; and that he fail not to perform that which he hath been commanded, and that he deceive in nothing. He then dismisses that Spirit by any suitable form such as those used in the four higher grades in the Outer.

And if he will *not* go, then shall the Magician *compel* him by forces contrary unto his nature. But he must allow a few minutes for the Spirit to dematerialise the body in which he hath manifested; for he will become less and less material by degrees. And note well that the Magician (or his companions if he have any) shall *never* quit the circle during the process of Evocations; or afterwards, till the Spirit be quite vanished, seeing that in some cases and with some constitutions there may be danger arising from the astral conditions and currents established; and that without the actual intention of the Spirit to harm, although, if of a low nature, he would probably endeavour to do so.

Therefore, before the commencement of the Evocation let the operator assure himself that everything which may be necessary be properly arranged within the circle.

But if it be actually necessary to interrupt the process, then let him stop at that point, veil and re-cord the sigil if it have been unbound or uncovered, recite a Licence to depart or banishing formula, and perform the lesser Banishing rituals both of the Pentagram and Hexagram.* Thus only may he in comparative safety quit the circle.

ה

BOOK II

CONSECRATION OF TALISMANS

PRODUCTION OF NATURAL PHENOMENA

A. The place where the operation is done.

B. The Magical Operator.

C. The forces of Nature employed and attracted.

D. The Telesma; The Material Basis

E. In Telesmata, the selection of the matter to form a Telesama, the preparation and arrangment of the place: The forming of the body of the Telesma. In natural phenomena, the preparation of the operation, the formation of the circle, and the

---

* See "Liber O," THE EQUINOX, vol. i., No. 2.

selection of the material basis; such as a piece of earth, a cup of Water, a flame of fire, a pentacle, or the like.

F.   The Invocation of the highest Divine forces; winding a cord thrice round the Telesma or Material Basis; covering the same with a black veil and initiating the blind force therein; naming aloud the *purpose* of the Telesma or operation.

G.   The Telesma or Material Basis is now placed towards the West, and duly consecrated with water and with fire. The purpose of the operation and the effect intended to be produced is then to be rehearsed in a loud and clear voice.

H.   Placing the Telesma or Material Basis at the foot of the altar, state aloud the object to be attained, solemnly asserting that it *will* be attained: and the reason thereof.

I.   Announcement aloud that all is prepared and in readiness either for the charging of the Telesma, or for the commencement of the operation to induce the natural phenomenon. Place a good telesma or Material Basis within the triangle. But a bad Telesma should be placed to the West of same, holding the sword erect in the right hand for a good purpose, or its point upon the centre of the Telesma for evil.

J.   Now follow the performance of an Invocation to attract the desired current to the Telesma or Material Basis, describing in the air above the Telesma the lineal figures and sigils, &c., with the appropriate magical implement. Then taking up the Telesma in the left hand, smite it thrice with the flat blade of the sword of art. Then raise in the left hand (holding erect and aloft the Sword in the right), stamping thrice upon the Earth with the Right Foot.

K.   The Telesma or Material Basis is to be placed towards the North, and the operator repeats the oration of the Hierophant to the candidate in the same form as given in the K section on Evocation. He then ordains the Mystic Circumambulation.

L.   He now takes up the Telesma or Material Basis, carries it round the circle, places it on the ground, bars, purifies and consecrates it afresh, lifts it with his left hand and turns facing West, saying: !Creature of Talismans, twice consecrate,! &c.

M.   He now passes to the West with Telesma in left hand, faces S.W., partly unveils Telesma, smites it once with Sword, and pronounces a similar speach to that in this M Section of Evocations, save that instead of "appear in visible form," he says: "take on therefore manifestation before me," &c. This being done he replaces the veil.

N.   Operations of L repeated.

O.   Operations of M repeated in the North, and an oration similar to that in section O on Evocation: Telesma, &c., being treated as the Sigil of the Spirit, substituting for: "appear thou therefore in visible form," &c.: "take on therefore manifestation before me," &c.

P.   Similar to the P section on Invocations, except that in the prayer "to visible appearance" is changed into: "to render irresistible this Telesma," or "to render manifest this natural phenomenon of . . .".

Q. Similar to this Q section on Evocations, saying finally: "I conjure upon thee power and might irresistible." Follow the Mystic Words.

R. Similar to this R section on Evocations. In the Telesma a flashing Light of Glory should be seen playing and flickering on the Telesma, and in the Natural Phenomena a slight commencement of the Phenomenon should be waited for.

S. This being accomplished, let him take the Telesma or material Basis, remove the cord therefrom, and smiting it with the Sword proclaim: "By and in the name of . . . I invoke upon thee the power of . . .". He then circumambulates thrice, holding the Telesma in his right hand.

T. Similar to this T section for Evocation, save that, instead of a Spirit appearing, the Telesma should flash visibly, or the Natural Phenomena should definitely commence.

U. Similar to the U section for Evocations.

V. The operator now carefully formulates his demands, stating what the Telesma is intended to do; or what Natural Phenomenon he seeks to produce.

W. Similar to what is laid down in the W section for Invocations, save that in case of a Telesma, no banishing ritual shall be performed, so as not to decharge it, and in the case of Natural Phenomena it will usually be best to state what operation is required. And the Material Basis should be preserved, wrapped in white linen or silk all the time that the phenomenon is intended to act. And when it is time for it to cease, the Material Basis, if Water, is to be poured away: if Earth, ground to a powder and scattered abroad: if a hard substance, as metal, it must be decharged, banished and thrown aside: or if a Flame of Fire, it shall be extinguished: or if a vial containing Air it shall be opened, and after that shall be rinsed out with pure water.

שׁ

BOOK III

PART א: INVISIBILITY

A. The shroud of Concealment.

B. The Magician.

C. The guards of concealment.

D. The astral light to be moulded into the Shroud.

E. The equation of the symbols in the sphere of sensation.

F. The Invocation of the Higher the placing of a Barrier without the Astral Form: the clothing of the same with obscurity through the proper invocation.

G. Formulating clearly the idea of becoming invisible: the formulation of the exact distance at which the shroud should surround the physical body; the consecration with water and fire so that their vapour may begin to form a basis for the shroud.

H. The beginning to formulate mentally a shroud of concealment about the operator. The affirmation aloud of the reason and object of the working.

I. Announcement that all is ready for the commencement of the operation. Operator stands in the place of the Hierophant at this stage: placing his left hand in the centre of the triangle, and holding in his right the Lotus Wand by the black end, in readiness to concentrate around him the Shroud of Darkness and Mystery. (N.B. —In this operation as in the two others under the dominion of ♄ a pantacle or Telesma, suitable to the matter in hand, *may* be made use of: the which is treated as is directed for Telesmata.)

J. The operator now recites an exorcism of a shroud of Darkness to surround him and render him invisible, and holding the wand by the black end, let him, turning round thrice completely, describe a triple circle around him, saying: "In the name of the Lord of the Universe," &c. "I conjure thee, O Shroud of Darkness and of Mystery, that thou encirclest me, so that I may become Invisible: so that, seeing me, men may see not, neither understand; but that they may see the thing that they see not, and comprehend not the thing that they behold! So mote it be!"

K. Now move to the North, face East, and say: "I have set my feet in the North, and have said, 'I will shroud myself in Mystery and in Concealment.' " Then repeat the oration: "The voice of my Higher soul, " &c., and command the Mystic Circumambulation.

L. Move round as usual to the South, and halt, formulating thyself as shrouded in Darkness: on the right hand the pillar of fire, on the left the pillar of cloud: both reaching from darkness to the glory of the Heavens.

M. Now move from between these pillars which thou hast formulated to the West, and say: "Invisible I cannot pass by the Gate of the Invisible save by virtue of the name of 'Darkness.' " Then formulate forcibly about thee the shroud of Darkness, and say: "Darkness is my name, and concealment: I am the Great One Invisible of the paths of the Shades. I am without fear, though veiled in Darkness; for within me though unseen is the Magic of the Light!"

N. Repeat processes in L.

O. Repeat processes in M, but say: "I am Light shrouded in Darkness, I am the wielder of the forces of the Balance."

P. Now concentrating mentally about thee the shroud of concealment pass to the West of the altar in the place of the Neophyte, face East, remain standing, and rehearse a conjuration by suitable names for the formulation of a shroud of Invisibility around and about thee.

Q. Now address the Shroud of Darkness thus: "Shroud of Concealment, long hast thou dwelt concealed! quit the light; that thou mayest conceal me before men!" Then carefully formulate the shroud of concealment around thee and say, "I receive thee as a covering and as a guard."

THE TEMPLE OF SOLOMON THE KING

Then the Mystic Words.

R. Still formulating the shroud say: "Before all magical manifestation cometh the knowledge of the Hidden Light." Then move to the Pillars and give the signs and steps, words, &c. With the Sign Enterer project now thy whole will in one great effort to realise thyself actually *fading out* and becoming invisible to mortal eyes: and in doing this must thou obtain the effect of thy physical body actually, gradually becoming partially invisible to thy natural eyes: as though a veil or cloud were formulating between it and thee. (And be very careful not to lose self-control at this point.) But also at this point is there a certain Divine Extasis and an exaltation desirable: for herein is a sensation of an exalted strength.

S. Again formulate the shroud as concealing thee and enveloping thee, and thus wrapped up therein circumambulate the circle thrice.

T. Intensely formulating the shroud, stand at the East and proclaim, "Thus have I formulated unto myself this Shroud of Darkness and of Mystery, as a concealment and a guard."

U. Now rehearse an invocation of all the Divine Names of Binah; that thou mayest retain the Shroud of Darkness under thy own proper control and guidance.

V. Now state clearly to the shroud what it is thy desire to perform therewith.

W. Having obtained the desired effect, and gone about invisible, it is requisite that thou shouldst conjure the forces of the Light to act against that Shroud of Darkness and Mystery, so as to disintegrate it, lest any force seek to use it as a medium for an obsession, &c. Therefore rehearse a conjuration as aforesaid, and then open the Shroud and come forth out of the midst thereof, and then disintegrate that shroud by the use of a conjuration unto the forces of Binah, to disintegrate and scatter the particles thereof; but affirming that they shall again be readily attracted at thy command. But on no account must that shroud of awful Mystery be left without such disintegration; seeing that it would speedily attract an occupant: which would become a terrible vampire preying upon him who had called it into being. And after frequent rehearsals of this operation, the thing may be almost done *per nutum*.

PART ב: TRANSFORMATIONS

A. The Astral Form.

B. The Magician.

C. The Forces used to alter the Form.

D. The Form to be taken.

E. The equation of the symbolism of the sphere of sensation.

F. Invocation of the Higher: The definition of the form required as a delination of blind forces, and the awakening of the same by its proper formulation.

G. Formulating clearly to the mind the form intended to be taken: the restriction and definition of this as a clear form and the actual baptism by water and by fire with the *mystic name of the adept.*

H. The actual invocation aloud of the form desired to be assumed, to formulate before you. The statement of the *desire* of the operator and the *reason* thereof.

I. Announcement aloud that all is now ready for the operation of the transformation of the Astral body. The Magician mentally places this form as nearly as circumstances will admit in the position of the Enterer, himself taking the place of the Hierophant; holding his wand by the black end ready to commence the oration aloud.

J. Let him now repeat a powerful exorcism of the shape into which he desires to transform himself, using the names, &c., belonging to the plane, planet, or other Eidolon, most in harmony with the shape desired. Then holding the wand by the black end, and directing the flower over the head of the Form, let him say: "In the name of the Lord of the Universe, arise before me, O form of . . . into which I have elected to transform myself; so that seeing me men may see the thing they see not, and comprehend not the thing that they behold."

K. The Magician saith: "Pass towards the North shrouded in Darkness, O form of . . . into which I have elected to transform myself." Then let him repeat the usual oration from the throne of the East, and then command the Mystic Circumambulation.

L. Now bring the form round to the South, arrest it, formulate it there standing between two great pillars of fire and cloud, purify it by water and incense, by placing these elements on either side of the form.

M. Passing to the West and facing South-East formulate the form before thee, this time endeavouring to render it physically visible; repeat speeches of Hierophant and Hegemon.

N. Same as L.

O. Same as M.

P. Pass to East of Altar, formulating the form as near in the proportion of the neophyte as may be. Now address a solemn invocation and conjuration by Divine and other names appropriate to render the form fitting for the transformation thereunto.

Q. Remain at East of Altar, address the form "child of Earth," &c., endeavouring now to see it physically; then at the words "we receive thee," &c., he draws the form towards him so as to envelop him, being very careful at the same time to invoke the Divine Light by the Rehearsal of the Mystic Words.

R. Still keeping himself in the form the Magician says: "Before all magical manifestation cometh the knowledge of the Divine Light." He then moves to the pillars and gives the signs, &c., endeavouring with the whole force of his will to feel himself *actually* and *physically* in the shape of the form desired. At this point he must see, as if in a cloudy and misty manner, the outline of the form enshrouding him, though not yet completely and wholly visible. When this occurs, but not before, let him formulate himself as standing between the vast pillars of Fire and of Cloud.

S. He now again endeavours to formulate the form as if visibly enshrouding him; and still astrally retaining the form, he thrice circumambulates the place of working.

T. Standing at the East, let him thirdly formulate the shape which should now appear manifest, and as if enshrouding him, even to his own vision; and then let him proclaim aloud: "Thus have I formulated unto myself this transformation."

U. Let him now invoke all the superior names of the plane appropriate to the form, that he may retain it under his proper control and guidance.

V. He states clearly to the form, what he intends to do with it.

W. Similar to the W section of Invisibility, save that the conjurations, &c., are to be made to the appropriate plane of the Form instead of to Binah.

PART ש: SPIRITUAL DEVELOPMENT

A. The Sphere of Sensation.

B. The Augœides.

C. The Sephiroth, &c., employed.

D. The Aspirant, or Natural Man.

E. The Equilibration of the Symbols.

F. The Invocation of the Higher, the limiting and controlling of the lower, and the closing of the material senses to awaken the spiritual.

G. Attempting to make the Natural Man grasp the Higher by first limiting the extent to which mere intellect can help him herein, then by the purification of his thoughts and desires. In doing this let him formulate himself as standing between the pillars of Fire and of Cloud.

H. The aspiration of the whole Natural Man towards the Higher Self, and a prayer for light and guidance through his Higher Self addressed to the Lord of the Universe.

I. The Aspirant affirms aloud his earnest prayer to obtain divine guidance; kneels at the West of the Altar in the position of the candidate in the "Enterer," and at the same time astrally projects his consciousness to the East of the Altar, and turns, facing his body to the West, holding astrally his own left hand with his astral left; and raises his astral right hand holding the presentment of his Lotus Wand by the white portion thereof, and raised in the air erect.

J. Let the Aspirant now slowly recite an oration unto the Gods and unto the Higher Self (as that of the Second Adept in the entering of the vault), but as if with his astral consciousness; which is projected to the East of the Altar.

(NOTE.—If at this point the Aspirant should feel a sensation of faintness coming on, let him at once withdraw the projected astral, and properly master himself before proceeding any further.)

Now let the Aspirant concentrate all his intelligence in his body, lay the blade of his sword thrice on the Daäth point of his neck, and pronounce with his whole will the words: "So help me the Lord of the Universe and my own Higher Soul."

Let him then rise facing East, and stand for a few moments in silence, raising his left hand open, and his right hand holding the Sword of Art, to their full lengths above his head: the head thrown back, the eyes lifted upwards. Thus standing let him aspire with his whole will towards his best and highest ideal of the Divine.

K.   Then let the Aspirant pass unto the North, and facing East solemnly repeat the Oration of the Hierophant, as before endeavouring to project the speaking conscious self to the place of the Hierophant (in this case the Throne of the East).

Then let him slowly mentally formulate before him the Eidolon of a Great Angelic torch-bearer: standing before him as if to lead and light his way.

L.   Following it, let the Aspirant circumambulate and pass to the South, there let him halt and aspire with his whole will: First to the Mercy side of the Divine Ideal, and then unto the Severity thereof.   And then let him imagine himself as standing between two great pillars of Fire and of Cloud, whose bases indeed are buried in black enrolling clouds of darkness: which symbolise the chaos of the world of Assiah, but whose summits are lost in glorious light undying: penetrating unto the white Glory of the Throne of the Ancient of Days.

M.   Now doth the Aspirant move unto the West; faces South-West, repeats alike the speeches of the Hiereus and Hegemon.

N.   After another circumambulation the Adept Aspirant halts at the South and repeats the meditations in L.

O.   And as he passes unto the East, he repeats alike the words of the Hierophant and of the Hegemon.

P.   And so he passes to the West of the Altar, led ever by the Angel torch-bearer. And he lets project his astral, and he lets implant therein his consciousness: and his body knows what time his soul passes between the pillars, and prayeth the great prayer of the Hierophant.

Q.   And now doth the Aspirant's soul re-enter unto his gross form, and he draws in divine extasis of the glory ineffable which is in the Bornless Beyond.   And so meditating doth he arise and lift to the heavens his hand, and his eyes, and his hopes, and concentrating so his Will on the Glory, low murmurs he the Mystic Words of Power.

R.   So also doth he presently repeat the words of the Hierophant concerning the Lamp of the Kerux, and so also passeth he by the East of the Altar unto between the Pillars, and standing between them (or formulating them if they be not there, as it appears unto me) so raises he his heart unto the highest Faith, and so he meditates upon the Highest Godhead he can dream on, or dream of.   Then let him grope with his hands in the darkness of his ignorance: and in the "Enterer" sign invoke the power that it remove the darkness from his Spiritual Vision.   So let him then endeavour to behold before him in the Place of the Throne of the East a certain Light or Dim Glory which shapeth itself into a form.

(NOTE.—And this can be beholden only by the Mental Vision: Yet owing unto the

Spiritual Exaltation of the Adept it may sometimes appear as if he beheld it with his mortal Eye.)

Then let him withdraw awhile from such contemplation, and formulate for his equilibration once more the pillars of the Temple of Heaven.

S.   And so again does he aspire to see the Glory enforming: and when this is accomplished he thrice circumambulateth, reverently saluting with the "Enterer" the Place of Glory.

T.   Now let the Aspirant stand opposite unto the Place of that Light, and let him make deep meditation and contemplation thereon: presently also imagining it to enshroud him and envelop, and again end endeavouring to identify himself with its Glory. So let him exalt himself in the likeness or Eidolon of a Colossal Power, and endeavour to realise that *this* is the only *true* Self: And that one Natural Man is, as it were, the Base and Throne thereof: and let him do this with due and meek reverence and awe. And thereafter he shall presently proclaim aloud: "Thus at length have I been permitted to begin to comprehend the Form of my Higher Self."

U.   Now doth the Aspirant make treaty of that Augoeides to render comprehensible what things may be necessary for his instruction and comprehension.

V.   And he consults it in any matter wherein he may have especially sought for guidance from the Beyond.

W.   And, lastly, let the Aspirant endeavour to formulate a link between the Glory and his Self-hood: and let him render his obligation of purity of mind before it, avoiding in this any tendency towards fanaticism or spiritual pride.

And let the Adept remember that this process here set forth is on no account to be applied to endeavouring to come in contact with the Higher Soul or Genius of *another*. Else thus assuredly will he be led into error, hallucination, or even mania.

ꠁ

BOOK IV

DIVINATION

A.   The Form of Divination employed.

B.   The Diviner.

C.   The Forces acting in the Divination.

D.   The Subject of the Divination.

E.   The Preparation of all things necessary, and the right understanding of the process so as to formulate a connecting link between the process employed and the Macrocosm.

F.   Invocation of the Higher: arrangement of the Scheme of Divination, and initiation of the forces thereof.

G.   The first entry into the matter: First assertion of limits and correspondences: beginning of the working.

H.   The actual and careful formulation of the question demanded: and consideration of all its correspondences and their classification.

I.   Announcement aloud that all the correspondences taken are correct and perfect: the Diviner places his hand upon the instrument of Divination: standing at the East of the Altar, and prepares to invoke the forces required in the Divination.

J.   Solemn invocation of the necessary spiritual forces to aid the Diviner in the Divination. Then let him say: "Arise before me clear as a mirror, O magical vision requisite for the accomplishment of this divination."

K.   Accurately define the term of the question: putting down clearly in writing what is already *known*, what is *suspected* or *implied*, and what is sought to be known. And see that thou verify in the beginning of the judgment, that part which is already known.

L.   Next let the Diviner formulate clearly under two groups or heads (*a*) the arguments *for*, (*b*) the arguments *against*, the success of the subject of one divination, so as to be able to draw a preliminary conclusion therefrom on either side.

M.   First formulation of a conclusive judgment from the premises already obtained.

N.   Same as section L.

O.   Formulation of a second judgment, this time of the further developments arising from those indicated in the previous process of judgment, which was a preliminary to this operation.

P.   The comparison of the first preliminary judgment with one second judgment developing therefrom: so as to enable the Diviner to form an idea of the probable action of *forces beyond the actual plane* by the invocation of an angelic figure consonant to the process; and in this matter take care not to mislead thy judgment through the action of thine own preconceived ideas; but only relying—after due tests—on the indication afforded thee by the angelic form. And know, unless the form be of an angelic nature, its indication will not be reliable; seeing, that if it be an elemental, it will be below the plane desired.

Q.   The Diviner now completely and thoroughly formulates his whole judgment as well for the immediate future as for the development thereof, taking into account the knowledge and indications given him by the angelic form.

R.   Having this result before him, let the Diviner now formulate a fresh divination process, based on the conclusions at which he has arrived, so as to form a basis for a further working.

S.   Formulates the sides for and against for a fresh judgment, and deduces conclusion from fresh operation.

T. The Diviner then compares carefully the whole judgment and decisions arrived at with their conclusions, and delivers now plainly a succinct and consecutive judgment thereon.

U. The Diviner gives advice to the Consultant as to what use he shall make of the judgment.

V. The Diviner formulates clearly with what forces it may be necessary to work in order to combat the Evil, or fix the Good, promised by the Divination.

W. Lastly, remember that unto thee a divination shall be as a sacred work of the Divine Magic of Light, and not to be performed to pander unto thy curiosity regarding the secrets of another. And if by this means thou shalt arrive at a knowledge of another's secrets, thou shalt respect and not betray them.

ה

BOOK V

ALCHEMICAL PROCESSES

A. The Curcurbite or The Alembic.

B. The Alchemist.

C. The processes and forces employed.

D. The matter to be transmuted.

E. The selection of the Matter to be transmuted, and the Formation, cleansing and disposing of all the necessary vessels, materials, &c., for the working of this process.

F. General Invocation of the Higher Forces to Action. Placing of the Matter within the curcurbite or philosophic egg, and invocation of a blind force to action therein, in darkness and in silence.

G. The beginning of the actual process: the regulation and restriction of the proper degree of Heat and Moisture to be employed in the working. First evocation followed by first distillation.

H. The taking up of the residuum which remaineth after the distillation from the curcurbite or alembic: the grinding thereof to form a powder in a mortar. This powder is then to be placed again in the curcurbite. The fluid already distilled is to be poured again upon it. The curcurbite or philosophic egg is to be closed.

I. The curcurbite or Egg Philosophic being hermetically sealed, the Alchemist announces aloud that all is prepared for the invocation of the forces necessary to accomplish the work. The Matter is then to be placed upon an Altar with the elements and four weapons thereon: upon the white triangle, and upon a flashing Tablet of a *General* Nature, in harmony with the matter selected for the working. Standing now in the place of the Hierophant at the East of the Altar, the Alchemist should place his left hand upon the top of the curcurbite, raise his right hand holding the Lotus Wand by the Aries band (for that in Aries is the Beginning of the Life of the Year): ready to commence the general Invocation of the Forces of the Divine Light to operate in the work.

J.   The pronouncing aloud of the Invocation of the requisite General Forces, answering to the class of alchemical work to be performed. The conjuring of the necessary Forces to act in the curcurbite for the work required. The tracing in the air above it with appropriate magical weapon the necessary lineal figures, signs, sigils and the like. Then let the Alchemist say: "So help me the Lord of the Universe and my own Higher soul." Then let him raise the curcurbite in the air with both hands, saying: "Arise herein to action, Ye Forces of Light Divine."

K.   Now let the Matter putrefy in Balneum Mariae in a very gentle heat, until darkness beginneth to supervene: and even until it becometh entirely black. If from its nature the Mixture will not admit of entire blackness, examine it astrally till there is the astral appearance of the thickest possible blackness, and thou mayest also evoke an elemental Form to tell thee if the blackness be sufficient: but be thou sure that in this latter thou art not deceived, seeing that the nature of such an elemental will be deceptive from the nature of the symbol of Darkness, wherefore ask thou of him nothing *further* concerning the working at this stage, but only concerning the blackness, and this can be further tested by the elemental itself, which should be either black or clad in an intensely black robe. (Note: for the evocation of this spirit use the names, forces, and correspondences of Saturn.)

When the mixture be sufficiently black, then take the curcurbite out of the Balneum Mariae and place it to the north of the Altar and perform over it a solemn invocation of the forces of Saturn to act therein: holding the wand by the black band, then say: "The voice of the Alchemist," &c. The curcurbite is then to be unstopped and the Alembic Head fitted on for purposes of distillation. (NOTE.—In all such invocations a flashing tablet should be used whereon to stand the curcurbite. Also certain of the processes may take weeks, or even months to obtain the necessary force, and this will depend on the Alchemist rather than on the matter.)

L.   Then let the Alchemist distil with a gentle heat until nothing remaineth to come over. Let him then take out the residuum and grind it into a powder: replace this powder in the curcurbite, and pour again upon it the fluid *previously distilled*.

The curcurbite is then to be placed again in Balneum Mariae in a gentle heat. When it seems fairly re-dissolved (irrespective of colour) let it be taken out of the bath. It is now to undergo another magical ceremony.

M.   Now place the curcurbite to the West of the Altar, holding the Lotus Wand by the black end, perform a magical invocation of the Moon in her decrease and of Cauda Draconis. The curcurbite is then to be exposed to the moonlight (she being in her decrease) for nine consecutive nights, commencing at full moon. The Alembic Head is then to be fitted on.

N.   Repeat process set forth in section L.

O.   The curcurbite is to be placed to the East of the Altar, and the Alchemist performs an invocation of the Moon in her increase, and of Caput Draconis (holding Lotus Wand by white end) to act upon the matter. The curcurbite is now to be exposed for nine consecutive nights (ending with the Full Moon) to the Moon's Rays. (In this, as in all similar exposures, it matters not if such nights be overclouded, so long as the vessel be placed in such a position that it *would* receive the direct rays, did the cloud withdraw.)

P.   The curcurbite is again to be placed on the white triangle upon the Altar. The Alchemist performs an invocation of the forces of the sun to act in the curcurbite. It is then to be exposed to the rays of the sun for twelve hours each day: from 8.30 A.M. to 8.30 P.M. (This should be done preferably when the sun is strongly posited in the Zodiac, but it *can* be done at some other times, though *never* when he is in Scorpio, Libra, Capricornus or Aquarius.)

Q.   The curcurbite is again placed upon the white triangle upon the Altar. The Alchemist repeats the words: "Child of Earth, long hast thou dwelt," &c., then holding above it the Lotus Wand by the white end, he says: "I formulate in thee the invoked forces of Light," and repeats the mystic words. At this point keen and bright flashes of light should appear in the curcurbite, and the mixture itself (as far as its nature will permit) should be clear. Now invoke an Elemental from the curcurbite consonant to the Nature of the Mixture, and judge by the nature of the colour of its robes and their brilliancy whether the matter has attained to the right condition. But if the Flashes do *not* appear, and if the robes of the elemental be not Brilliant and Flashing, then let the curcurbite stand within the white triangle for seven days: having on the right hand of the Apex of the triangle a flashing tablet of the Sun, and in the left hand one of the Moon. Let it not be moved or disturbed all those seven days; but not in the dark, save at night. Then let the operation as aforementioned be repeated over the curcurbite, and this process may be repeated altogether three times if the flashing light cometh not. For without this latter the work would be useless. But if after three repetitions it still appear not, it is a sign that there hath been an error in one working; such being either in the disposition of the Alchemist, or in the management of the curcurbite. Wherefore let the lunar and the solar invocations and exposures be replaced, when without doubt —if these be done with care (and more especially those of Caput Draconis and Cauda Draconis with those of the Moon as taught, for these have great force materially)— then without doubt shall that flashing light manifest itself in the curcurbite.

R.   Holding the Lotus Wand by the white end, the Alchemist now draws over the curcurbite the symbol of the Flaming Sword as if descending into the mixture. Then let him place the curcurbite to the East of the Altar. The Alchemist stands between the pillars, and performs a solemn invocation of the forces of Mars to act therein. The curcurbite is then to be placed between the Pillars (or the drawn symbols of these same) for seven days, upon a Flashing Tablet of Mars.

After this period, fit on the Alembic Head, and distil first in Balneum Mariae, then in Balneum Arenae till what time the mixture be clean distilled over.

S.   Now let the Alchemist take the fluid of the distillate and let him perform over it an invocation of the forces of Mercury to act in the clear fluid; so as to formulate therein the Alchemic Mercury: even the Mercury of the philosophers. (The residuum of the Dead Head is not to be worked with at present, but is to be set apart for future use.) After the invocation of the Alchemic Mercury a certain Brilliance should manifest itself in the whole fluid (that is to say, that it should not only be clear, but also brilliant and flash-ing). Now expose it in an hermetic receiver for seven days to the light of the Sun: at the end of which time there should be distinct flashes of light therein. (Or an egg philosophic may be used; but the receiver of the Alembic, if closed stopped, will answer this purpose.)

T.   Now the residuum or Dead Head is to be taken out of the curcurbite, ground small, and replaced. An invocation of the forces of Jupiter is then to be performed over that powder. It is then to be kept in the dark standing upon a Flashing Tablet of Jupiter for seven days. At the end of this time there should be a slight Flashing

DIAGRAM 58.
The Altar.

about it, but if this come not yet, repeat the operation, up to three times, when a faint flashing Light is *certain* to come.

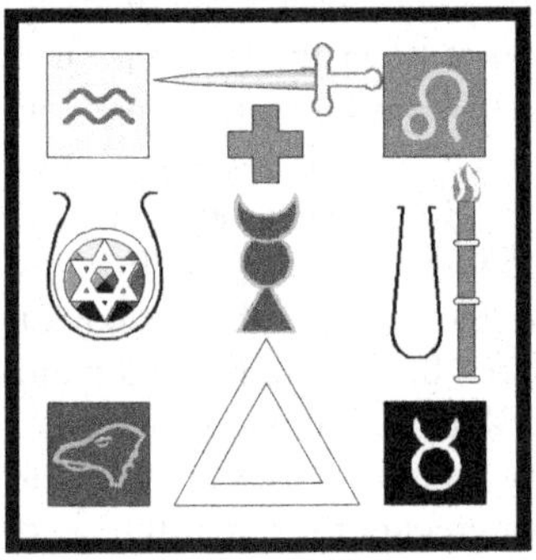

U.   A Flashing Tablet of each of the four Elements is now to be placed upon the altar as shown in the figure, and thereon are also to be placed the magical elemental weapons, as is also clearly indicated. The receiver containing the distillate is now to be placed between the Air and Water Tablets, and the curcurbite with the Dead Head between the Fire and Earth. Now let the Alchemist form an invocation, using especially the Supreme Ritual of the Pentagram,* and the lesser magical implement appropriate. First, of the Forces of the Fire to act in the curcurbite on the Dead Head. Second, of those of Water to act on the distillate. Third, of the forces of the Spirit to act in both (using the white end of the Lotus Wand). Fourth, of those of the air to act on the distillate; and lastly, those of the earth to act on the Dead Head. Let the curcurbite and the receiver stand thus for five consecutive days, at the end of which time there should be flashes manifest in both mixtures. And these flashes should be lightly coloured.

* See "Liber O," THE EQUINOX, vol. i. No. 2.

V. The Alchemist, still keeping the vessels in the same relative positions, but removing the Tablets of the elements from the Altar, then substitutes one of Kether. This must be white with Golden Charges, and is to be placed on or within the white triangle between the vessels. He then addresses a most solemn invocation to the forces of Kether; to render the result of the working that which he shall desire, and making over each vessel the symbol of the Flaming Sword.

This is the most important of all the Invocations; and it will only succeed if the Alchemist keepeth himself closely allied unto his Higher Self during the working of the invocation and of making the Tablet. And at the end of it, if it have been successful, a Keen and Translucent Flash will take the place of the slightly coloured Flashes in the receiver of the curcurbite; so that the fluid should sparkle as a diamond; whilst the powder in the curcurbite shall slightly gleam.

W. The distilled liquid is now to be poured from the receiver upon the residuum of Dead Head in the curcurbite, and the mixture at first will appear cloudy. It is now to be exposed to the sun for ten days consecutively (10 = Tiphereth translating the influence of Kether). It is then again to be placed upon the white triangle upon the altar, upon a flashing Tablet of Venus: with a solemn invocation of Venus to act therein. Let it remain thus for seven days: at the end of that time see what forms and colour and appearance the Liquor hath taken: for there should now arise a certain softer flash in the liquid, and an elemental may be evoked to test the condition. When this softer flash is manifest, place the curcurbite into the Balneum Mariae to digest with a *very* gentle heat for seven days. Place it then in Balneum Arenae to distil, beginning with a gentile, and ending with a strong, heat. Distil thus till nothing more will come over, even with a most violent heat. Preserve the fluid in a closely stoppered vial: it is an Elixir for use according to the substance from which it was prepared. If from a thing medicinal, a medicine; if from a metal, for the purifying of metals; and herein shalt thou use thy judgment. The residuum thou shalt place without powdering into a crucible, well sealed and luted. And thou shalt place the same in thine Athanor, bringing it first to a red, and then to a white, heat, and this thou shalt do seven times on seven consecutive days, taking out the crucible each day as soon as thou hast brought it to the highest possible heat, and allowing it to cool gradually.

And the preferable time for this working should be in the heat of the day. On the seventh day of this operation thou shalt open the crucible, and thou shalt behold what *Form* and *Colour* thy Caput Mortuum hath taken.

It will be like either a precious stone or a glittering powder.

And this stone or powder shall be of magical Virtue in accordance with his nature.

Finished is that which is written concerning the Formulae of the Magic of Light.

הקרשוב רוך הוא

On the instructions laid down in the first of these Books — Book ⸱, P. drew up a ritual "for the Evocation unto Visible Appearance of Typhon-Seth," in which, by raising the sigil of Typhon to the grade of $1°=10°$, he bewitched a certain refractory brother of the Order, known as Fra: D.P.A.L., who at this time was worrying Fra: D.D.C.F. by legal proceedings. We, however, will omit this Evocation, substituting in its place, as an example of such a working, the Evocation of the Great Spirit Taphthartharath by Frater I.A.

THE RITUAL
FOR THE
EVOCATION UNTO VISIBLE APPEARANCE
OF
THE GREAT SPIRIT
TAPHTHARTHARATH

IN THE NAME OF GOD LET THERE BE LIGHT
UNTO THE VOID A RESTRICTION.

Soror S.S.D.D. altered Frater I.A.'s ritual, making the operation to form a link between Thoth and the Magus. This is absurd; the correct way is as here given, in which the link is formed between the Spirit and the Magus.

THE TEMPLE OF SOLOMON THE KING

CONSIDERATIONS

To be performed in the day and in the hour of Mercury; the Evocation itself commencing in the magical hour of Tafrac, under the dominion of the Great Angel of Mercury ל א ם ר.

On Wednesday, May 13, 1896, this hour Tafra occurs between 8h. 32′ P.M. and 9h. 16′, when ☿ is in 17° Ⅱ on the cusp of the seventh house slightly to South of due West.

☽ going to ☌ with # in 14° c.

☿ going to ☌ with ♆, ☿ 150° ♄

OF THE FORM OF THE CIRCLE TO BE EMPLOYED.

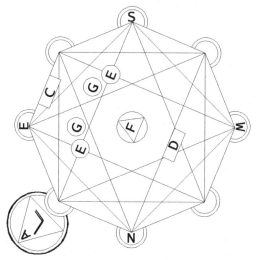

DIAGRAM 59.

The Circle of Art.

The Magical figures of Mercury are to be drawn in yellow-orange chalk upon the Ground as shown. At the quarter where the Spirit is to appear is drawn a triangle within a circle: at its points are to be placed three vessels burning on charcoal the Incense of Mercury. About the great circle are disposed lamps burning olive oil impregnated with snake-fat. C is the chair of the chief Operator. D is the altar, E E are the pillars, and G G handy and convenient tables whereon are set writing materials, the ingredients for the Hell-broth, charcoal, incense, &c., all as may be needed for this work. At F is placed a small brazen cauldron, heated over a lamp burning with spirit in which a snake has been preserved.

THE EQUINOX

OPERATIONIS PERSONÆ.

V.H. Sor: S.S.D.D. addressed Mighty Magus of Art.
V.H. Fra: I.A.   ,,   Assistant Magus of Art.
V.H. Fra: Æ.A.   ,,   Magus of the Fires.
V.H. Fra: D.P.A.L. ,,   Magus of the Waters.

The duties of the Magus of Art will be to perform the actual processes of Invocation: to rule the Assistants and command them all.

The Assistant Magus of Art shall act as Kerux in the circumambulations; he shall preside over the Brewing of the Hell-broth in the midst of the Circle: he shall repeat such Invocations as may be necessary at the command of the Magus of Art: and he shall prepare beforehand the place of the working.

The Magus of Fires shall preside over all magical lights, fires, candles, incense, &c: he shall perform the invoking and consecrating rituals at the command of the Magus, and he shall consecrate the temple by Fire, and shall consecrate all Fire used in due form.

The Magus of Waters shall preside over all the fluids used in the operation; over the Water and the Wine, the Oil and the Milk: he shall perform all banishing rituals at the opening of the ceremony: he shall purify the Temple by Water: he shall consecrate all watery things used in due form.

OF THE ROBES AND INSIGNIA.

The Mighty Magus of Art shall wear a white robe, yellow sash, red overmantle, indigo nemys, upon her breast shall she bear a great Tablet whereon is the magic seal of Mercury; and over this the lamen bearing the signature of Taphthartharath, on its obverse the Lamen of a Hierophant. She shall wear also a dagger in her sash, and a red rose on her heart: and she shall carry in her left hand the Ankh of Thoth, and in her right the Ibis Wand.

The Assistant Magus of Art shall wear a white robe, with a girdle of snake-skin; a black head-dress and a Lamen of the Spirit, on its obverse the Lamen of the Hiereus. And he shall bear in his right hand a sword; and in his left hand the Magical Candle; and a black chain about his neck.

The Magus of the Fires shall wear a white robe and yellow sash; and the rose upon his breast; in his right hand is a sword and in his left a red lamp.

The Magus of the Waters shall wear a white robe and yellow sash and rose cross: he shall bear in his right hand a sword and in his left a cup of water.

OPENING

The Chamber of Art shall be duly prepared by the Assistant Magus of Art as aforementioned.

THE TEMPLE OF SOLOMON THE KING

He shall draw upon the ground the lineal figures; and shall trace over them with a magic sword: he shall place the furniture of the Temple in order. The Members shall be assembled and robed. The Chief Magus rises, holding the Ibis wand by its black end, and proclaims:

HEKAS, HEKAS ESTE BEBELOI!

Fratres of the Order of the Rosy Cross, we are this day assembled together for the purpose of evoking unto visible appearance the spirit Taphtartharath. And before we can proceed further in an operation of so great danger, it is necessary that we should invoke that divine Aid and Assistance, without which would our work indeed be futile and of no avail. Wherefore being met thus together let us all kneel down and pray:

[All kneel at the four points.]

From Thy Hands O Lord cometh all good! From Thy Hands flow down all Grace and Blessing: the Characters of Nature with Thy Fingers hast thou traced, but none can read them unless he hath been taught in thy school. Therefore, even as servants look unto the hands of their Masters, and handmaidens unto the hands of their Mistresses, even so our eyes look unto thee! For Thou alone art our help, O Lord our God.

Who should not extol Thee, who should not praise Thee, O Lord of the Universe! All is from Thee, all belongeth unto Thee! Either Thy Love or Thine Anger, all must again re-enter; for nothing canst Thou lose; all must tend unto Thy Honour and Majesty. Thou art Lord alone, and there is none beside Thee! Thou dost what thou wilt with Thy Mighty Arm, and none can escape from Thee! Thou alone helpest in their necessity the humble, the meek-hearted and the poor, who submit themselves unto Thee; and whosoever humbleth himself in dust and ashes before Thee, to such an one art Thou propitious!

Who would not praise Thee then, Lord of the Universe! Who would not extol Thee! Unto whom there is no like, whose dwelling is in Heaven, and in every virtuous and God-fearing heart.

O God the Vast One—Thou are in all things.

O Nature, Thou Self from Nothing: for what else shall I call Thee!

In myself I am nothing, in Thee I am all self, and live in Thy Selfhood from Nothing! Live Thou in me, and bring me unto that Self which is in Thee! Amen!

[All rise—a pause.]

Magus of Art: Fratres of the Order of the Rosy Cross, let us purify and consecrate this place as the Hall of Dual Truth. Magus of the Waters, I command Thee to perform the lesser banishing ritual of the Pentagram,* to consecrate the Water of puri-

---

* See "Liber O," THE EQUINOX, vol. i. No. 2.

173

fication, the wine, the oil, and the milk; and afterwards to purify the place of working with the Consecrated Water!

Magus of Waters: Mighty Magus of Art! All thy commands shall be fulfilled, and thy desires accomplished.

[He passes to the North, where are collected in open vessels, the water, the wine, the oil, and the milk; and makes with his sword over them the banishing pentagram of water, saying:]

I exorcise ye impure, unclean and evil spirits that dwell in these creatures of water, oil, wine, and milk, in the name of EL strong and mighty, and in the name of Gabriel, great Angel of Water, I command ye to depart and no longer to pollute with your presence the Hall of Twofold Truth!

[Drawing over them the equilibrating Pentagram of Passives, and the invoking Pentagram of water, he says:]

In the name of HCOMA,* and by the names Empeh Arsel Gaiol,† I consecrate ye to the service of the Magic of Light!

[He places the Wine upon the Altar, the Water he leaves at the North, the oil towards the South, and the brazen vessel of milk on the tripod in the midst of the circle. The Magus of Art silently recites to herself the exhortation of the Lords of the Key Tablet of Union,‡ afterwards saying silently:]

I invoke ye, Lords of the Key Tablet of Union, to infuse into these elements of Water and Fire your mystic powers, and to cast into the midst of these opposing elements the holy powers of the great letter Shin: to gleam and shine in the midst of the Balance, even in the Cauldron of Art wherein alike is fire and moisture.

[After the consecration of the Water, the Magus of Waters takes up the cup of water, and scatters water all round the edge of the circle, saying:]

So first the priest who governeth the works of Fire, must sprinkle with the lustral waters of the loud-resounding sea.

[He then passes to the centre of the circle and scatters the water in the four quarters, saying:]

I purify with water.

[He resumes his place in the North.]

Magus of Art: Magus of the Fires, I command you to consecrate this place by the banishing ritual of the Hexagram,§ to consecrate the Magic fire and lights; to illumine the lamps and place them about the circle in orderly disposition; and afterwards to consecrate this place with the holy fire.

---

* See Spirit Tablet, and the Elemental Calls of Dr. Dee, as preserved in the Sloane MSS. [3191] in the British Museum: also Diagram 67, which is imperfect.

† See Tablet of Water, and the Elemental Calls of Dr. Dee.

‡ The Spirit Tablet. § See "Liber O," THE EQUINOX, vol. i. No. 2.

THE TEMPLE OF SOLOMON THE KING

Magus of the Fires: Mighty Magus of Art! all thy commands shall be obeyed and all thy desires shall be accomplished.

[He collects together at the South the incense, oil, charcoal, and magic candle, and performs the lesser banishing ritual of the Hexagram at the four quarters; then, extinguishing all lights save one, he performs over these the banishing ritual of the Pentagram of fire, saying:]

I exorcise ye, evil and opposing spirits dwelling in this creature of Fire, by the holy and tremendous name of God the Vast One, Elohim: and in the name of Michael, great Archangel of Fire, that ye depart hence, no longer polluting with your presence the Hall of Twofold Truth.

[He lights from that one flame the Magical candle, and drawing over it the invoking pentagram of spirit active, he cries:]

BITOM!*

[And then, drawing the invoking pentagram of Fire, he says:]

I, in the names of BITOM and by the names Oip Teaa Pedoce,† I consecrate thee, O creature of fire, to the service of the works of the Magic of Light!

[He lights from the magical candle the eight lamps, and the charcoal for the incense-burners, after which he casts incense on the coals in the censer and passes round the circle censing, saying:]

And, when after all the phantasms are vanished, thou shalt see that holy and Formless Fire, that Fire which darts and flashes through the hidden depths of the Universe, hear thou the Voice of the Fire.

[He passes to the centre of the circle and censes towards the four quarters, saying:]

I consecrate with fire.

[He resumes his place in the South.]

[Chief Magus takes fan, and fanning air says:]

I exorcise thee, creature of Air, by these Names, that all evil and impure spirits now immediately depart.

[Circumambulates, saying:]

Such a fire existeth extending through the rushing of the air, or even a fire formless whence cometh the image of a voice, or even a flashing light abounding, revolving, whirling forth, crying aloud.

[Makes banishing air pentagram:]

Creature of Air, in the names EXARP‡ Oro Ibah Aozpi,§ I consecrate thee to the works of the Magic of Light!

[Making invoking Pentagrams in air. All face West.]

[Assistant Magus then casts salt to all four quarters, all over the circle, and passes

---

* See Tablet of Spirit.   † See Tablet of Fire.
‡ See Tablet of Spirit.   § See Tablet of Air.

to West, faces East, and describes with his chain the Banishing pentagram of Earth, saying:]

I exorcise thee, creature of Earth, by and in the Divine Names Adonai Ha Aretz, Adonai Melekh Namen, and in the name of Aurial, Great Archangel of Earth, that every evil and impure spirit now depart hence immediately.

[Circumambulates, saying:]

Stoop not down unto the darkly splendid world, wherein lieth continually a faithless depth, and Hades wrapt in gloom, delighting in unintelligible images, precipitous, winding, a black ever-rolling abyss, ever espousing a body unluminous, formless and void.

[Making invoking pentagram.]

Creature of Earth, in the names of NANTA Emor Dial Hectega,* I consecrate thee to the service of the Magic of Light!

Chief Magus: We invoke ye, great lords of the Watch-towers of the Universe!† guard ye our Magic Circle, and let no evil or impure spirit enter therein: strengthen and inspire us in this our operation of the Magic of Light. Let the Mystic Circumambulation take place in the Path of Light.

[Assistant Magus of Art goes first, holding in his left the Magic Candle, and in his right the Sword of Art, with which latter he traces in the air the outer limits of the Magic Circle. All circumambulate thrice. He then, standing at East and facing East, says:]

Holy art Thou, Lord of the Universe!

Holy art Thou, whom Nature hath not formed!

Holy art thou, the Vast and the Mighty One!

Lord of the Light and of the Darkness!

Chief Magus of Art: Magus of the Fires, I command you to perform at the four quarters of the Universe the invocation of the forces of Mercury by Solomon's Seal.

Magus of Fire: Mighty Magus of Art, all thy commands shall be obeyed, and all thy desires shall be accomplished!

[He does it.‡]

[The Magus now advances to the centre of the circle, by the Magical Cauldron, wherein is the milk becoming heated, turns himself towards the Fire of the spirit, and recites:]

THE INVOCATION TO THE HIGHER.

Majesty of the Godhead, Wisdom-crowned Thoth, Lord of the Gates of the Universe: Thee! Thee we invoke! Thou that manifesteth in Thy symbolic Form as an Ibis-headed one: Thee, Thee we invoke! Thou, who holdest in Thy hand the magic wand of Double Power: Thee, Thee we invoke! Thou who bearest in thy left hand the Rose and Cross of Light and Life: Thee, Thee we invoke! Thou whose

* See Tablet of Earth.   † The Four Elemental Tablets.

‡ See "Liber O," THE EQUINOX, vol. i. No. 2.

head is of green, whose Nemys is of night sky- blue; whose skin of of flaming orange, as though it burned in a furnace: Thee, Thee we invoke!

Behold, I am Yesterday, To-day, and the brother of the Morrow! For I am born again and again. Mine is the unseen force which created the Gods, and giveth life unto the dwellers in the watch-towers of the Universe.

I am the charioteer in the East, Lord of the Past and the Future, He who seeth by the Light that is within Him.

I am the Lord of Resurrection, who cometh forth from the dusk, and whose birth is from the House of Death.

O ye two divine hawks upon your pinnacles, who are keeping Watch over the Universe!

Ye who accompany the bier unto its resting-place, and who pilot the Ship of Râ, advancing onwards unto the heights of Heaven!

Lord of the Shrine which standeth in the centre of the Earth!

Behold He is in me and I in Him!
Mine is the radiance in which Ptah floateth over his firmament.
I travel upon high.
I tread upon the firmament of Nu.
I raise a flame with the flashing lightning of mine eye, ever rushing forward in the splendour of the daily glorified Râ, giving life to every creature that treadeth upon the Earth.

If I say come up upon the mountains,
The Celestial waters shall flow at my word;
For I am Râ incarnate, Khephra created in the flesh!
I am the living image of my Father Tmu, Lord of the City of the Sun!

The God who commands is in my mouth:
The God of Wisdom is in my heart:
My tongue is the sanctuary of Truth:
And a God sitteth upon my lips!

My Word is accomplished each day, and the desire of my heart realises itself like that of Ptah when he creates his works.

Since I am Eternal everything acts according to my designs, and everything obeys my words.

Therefore do Thou come forth unto Me from thine abode in the Silence, Unutterable Wisdom, All-light, All-power. Thoth, Hermes, Mercury, Odin, by whatever name I call Thee, Thou art still Un-named and nameless for Eternity! Come thou forth, I say, and aid and guard me in this Work of Art.

THE EQUINOX

Thou, Star of the East that didst conduct the Magi. Thou art the same, all present in Heaven and in Hell. Thou that vibratest betwixt the Light and the Darkness Rising, descending, changing for ever, yet for ever the same!

The Sun is Thy Father!

Thy Mother the Moon!

The Wind hath borne Thee in its bosom:

And Earth hath ever nourished the changeless Godhead of Thy Youth.

Come Thou forth I say, come Thou forth,

And make all spirits subject unto me!

So that every spirit of the firmament,

And of the Ether of the Earth,

And under the Earth,

On dry land,

And in the Water,

Of whirling Air,

And of rushing Fire,

And every spell and scourge of God, may be obedient unto Me!

[She binds a black cord thrice round the sigil of the Spirit and veils it in black silk, saying:]

Hear me, ye Lords of Truth in the Hall of Themis, hear ye my words, for I am made as ye! I now purpose with the divine aid, to call forth this day and hour the Spirit of Mercury, Taphthartharath, whose magical sigil I now bind with this triple cord of Bondage, and shroud in the black concealing darkness and in death! Even as I knot about this sigil the triple cord of Bondage, so let the Magic power of my will and words penetrate unto him, and bind him that he cannot move; but is presently forced by the Mastery and the Majesty of the rites of power to manifest here before us without this Circle of Art, in the magical triangle which I have provided for his apparition.

And even as I shroud from the Light of Day this signature of that Spirit Taphthartharath, so do I render him in his place blind, deaf and dumb.

That he may in no wise move his place or call for aid upon his Gods; or hear another voice save mine or my companions', or see another path before him than the one unto this place.

[Sigil is placed outside the circle by the assistant Magus of Art.]

And the reason of this my working is, that I seek to obtain from that spirit Taphthartharath the knowledge of the realm of Kokab, and to this end I implore the divine assistance in the names of Elohim Tzebaoth, Thoth, Metatron, Raphael, Michael, Beni Elohim, Tiriel.

[Chief resumes her seat. The three others pass to the West and point their swords

THE TEMPLE OF SOLOMON THE KING

in menace at the veiled and corded sigil. The Assistant Magus then lifts the sigil on to the edge of the circle, and says:]

Who gives permission to admit to the Hall of Dual Truth this creature of sigils?

Magus of Art: I, S.S.D.D., Soror of the Order of the Golden Dawn, Theorica Adepta Minora of the Order of the Rose of Ruby and the Cross of Gold!

I.A.: Creature of Sigils, impure and unconsecrate! thou canst not enter our Magic Circle!

D.P.A.L.: Creature of Sigils, I purify thee with Water.

Æ.A.: Creature of Sigils, I consecrate thee by Fire.

[Magus of Art in a loud voice cries *seven times* the name of the Spirit, vibrating strongly, and then says:]

Assistant Magus of Art, I command thee to place the sigil at the foot of the Altar.

I.A.: Mighty Magus of Art, all your commands shall be obeyed and all your desires shall be fulfilled.

[He does so. The Magus of Art, standing on the throne of the East, then proclaims:]

THE INVOCATION.

O Thou mighty and powerful spirit Taphthartharath, I bind and conjure Thee very potently, that Thou do appear in visible form before us in the magical triangle without this Circle of Art. I demand that Thou shalt speedily come hither from Thy dark abodes and retreats, in the sphere of Kokab, and that Thou do presently appear before us in pleasing form, not seeking to terrify us by vain apparitions, for we are armed with words of double power, and therefore without fear! and I moreover demand, binding and conjuring Thee by the Mighty Name of Elohim Tzebaoth, that Thou teach us how we may acquire the power to know all things that appertain unto the knowledge of Thoth who ruleth the occult wisdom and power. And I am about to invoke Thee in the Magical hour of TAFRAC, on this day, for that in this day and hour the great angel of Kokab, Raphael, reigneth—beneath whose dominion art Thou—and I swear to Thee, here in the hall of the twofold manifestation of Truth, that, as liveth and ruleth for evermore the Lord of the Universe; that even as I and my companions are of the Order of the Rose of Ruby and the Cross of Gold; that even as in us is the knowledge of the rites of power ineffable:

Thou SHALT

this day become manifest unto visible appearance before us, in the magical triangle without this Circle of Art:

[It should now have arrived at the Magical Hour Tafrac, commencing at 8h. 32′ P.M. If not, then the Adepti seat themselves, and await that time. When it is fulfilled, the Assistant Magus places the sigil on the Altar in the right quarter: the Magus advances to the East of the Altar, lays her left hand upon it, in her right holding the sword with its point upon the centre of the sigil. The Associate Magus holds the Magical Candle for her to read by: and the Magus of the Fires the Book of Invocations, turning the pages that she may read continually. She recites:]

Hear ye, ye lords of Truth, hear ye, ye invoked powers of the sphere of Kokab, that all is now ready for the commencement of this Evocation!

THE POTENT EXORCISM.

[To be said, assuming the mask or form of the Spirit Taphthartharath.]

ת O Thou Mighty Spirit of Mercury, Taphthartharath! I bind, command and very potently do conjure Thee:

פ By the Majesty of the terrible Name of

אלהים צבאות

The Gods of the Armies of the

בני אלהים

By and in the name of:

מיכאל

Great Archangel of God, that ruleth in the Sphere of Kokab, by and in the name of:

רפאל

Great Angel of Mercury; by and in the Name of:

טיריאל

The Mighty Intelligence of Kokab;

By and in the Name of the Sephira Hod

And in the name of that thy sphere KOKAB

That Thou come forth here now, in this present day and hour, and appear in visible form before us; in the great magic triangle without this Circle of Art.

ת I bind and conjure Thee anew: By the magical figures which are traced upon the ground: By the Magic Seal of Mercury I bear upon my breast: By the Eight Magic Lamps that flame around me: By Thy seal and sigil which I bear upon my heart: that Thou come forth, here, now, in this present day and hour, and appear in visible and material form before us, in the great magic triangle without this Circle of Art.

ר I bind and conjure thee anew: By the Wisdom of Thoth the Mighty God: By the Light of the Magic Fire: By the Unutterable Glory of the Godhead within me: By all powerful names and rites: that Thou come forth, here, now, in this present day and hour, and appear in visible and material form before us, in the great magical triangle without this Circle of Art.

ת   I bind and conjure Thee anew: By the powers of Word and of Will: By the Powers of Number and Name: By the Powers of Colour and Form: By the Powers of Sigil and Seal: That Thou come forth, here, now, in this present day and hour, and appear in visible and material form before us in the great magical triangle without this Circle of Art.

ר   I bind and conjure thee anew: By all the Magic of Light: By the Ruby Rose on the Cross of Gold: By the Glory of the Sun and Moon: By the flashing radiance of the Magic Telesmata: By the Names of God that make Thee tremble every day! That Thou come forth, here, now, in this present day and hour, and appear in visible and material form before us in the great Magic triangle without this Circle of Art!

ת   But if thou art disobedient and unwilling to come:
Then will I curse Thee by the Mighty Names of God!
And I will cast Thee down from Thy Power and Place!
And I will torment Thee with new and terrible names!
And I will blot out Thy place from the Universe;
And Thou shalt *never* rise again!
So come Thou forth quickly, Thou Mighty Spirit Taphthartharath, come Thou forth quickly from thy abodes and retreats! Come unto us, and appear before us in visible and material form within the great Magical triangle without this Circle of Art, courteously answering all our demands, and see Thou that Thou deceive us in no wise—lest—

[Take up the veiled sigil and strike it thrice with the blade of the Magic sword, then hold it in the left aloft in the air, at the same time stamping thrice with the Right Foot. Assistant Magus now takes sigil and places it in the North: S.S.D.D. returns to her seat, takes lotus wand (or Ibis sceptre) and says:]

The voice of the Exorcist said unto me, let me shroud myself in Darkness, peradventure thus may I manifest in Light. I am an only Being in an abyss of Darkness, from the Darkness came I forth ere my birth, from the silence of a primal sleep. And the Voice of Ages answered unto my soul: "Creature of Mercury, who art called Taphthartharath! The Light shineth in Thy darkness, but thy darkness comprehendeth it not!" Let the Mystic Circumambulation take place in the Path of Darkness, with the Magic Light of Occult science to guide our way!

[I.A. takes up sigil in left and candle in right. Starting at North they circumambulate once. S.S.D.D. rises, and passes round the Temple before them, halting at the Gate of the West. Sigil bared by I.A., purified and consecrated: S.S.D.D., as Hiereus, assuming the mask of the Spirit, strikes the sigil (now partly bared) *once* with the Magic Sword, and says:]

THE EQUINOX

Thou canst not pass from concealment unto manifestation save by the virtue of the name Elohim! Before all things are the Chaos and the Darkness, and the Gates of the Land of Night. I am he whose name is Darkness; I am the Great One of the Paths of the Shades! I am the Exorcist in the midst of the exorcism: appear thou therefore without fear before me, for I am He in whom Fear is not! Thou hast known me, so pass thou on!

[Magus of Art passes round to the Throne of the East, Assistant Magus re-veils the sigil and carries it round once more. They halt, bare, purify and consecrate sigil as before: they approach the Gate of the East. Sigil unveiled: S.S.D.D. smiting sigil once with lotus wand.]

Thou canst not pass from concealment unto manifestation save by virtue of the name of I.H.V.H. After the formless and the void and the Darkness cometh the knowledge of the Light. I am that Light which riseth in the Darkness: I am the Exorcist in the midst of the exorcism: appear Thou therefore in Visible Form before me, for I am the wielder of the forces of the Balance. Thou hast known me now, so pass Thou on unto the Cubical Altar of the Universe!

[Sigil re-veiled, and conducted to altar, placed on West of triangle; S.S.D.D. passes to Altar holding sigil and sword as before. On her right hand is Æ.A. with the Magic Candle: on her left is D.P.A.L. with the ritual. Behind her to the East of the Magical Cauldron is I.A. casting into the milk at each appropriate moment the right ingredient. Afterwards, as S.S.D.D. names each Magical Name, I.A. draws in the perfected Hellbroth the sigils, &c., appropriate thereunto: at which time S.S.D.D. recites the:]

STRONGER AND MORE POTENT CONJURATION.

Come forth! Come forth! Come forth unto us, Spirit of Kokab Taphthartharath, I conjure Thee! Come! Accept of us these magical sacrifices, prepared to give Thee body and form.

Herein are blended the magical elements of Thy body, the symbols of Thy mighty being.

For the sweet scent of the mace is that which shall purify Thee finally from the Bondage of Evil.

And the heat of the magical fire is my will which volatilises the gross matter of Thy Chaos, enabling thee to manifest Thyself in pleasing form before us.

And the flesh of the serpent is the symbol of Thy body, which we destroy by water and fire, that it may be renewed before us.

And the Blood of the Serpent is the Symbol of the Magic of the Word Messiah, whereby we triumph over Nahash.

And the all-binding Milk is the magical water of Thy purification.

182

And the Fire which flames over all [assistant lights Hell-broth] is the utter power of our sacred rites!

Come forth! Come forth! Come forth unto us, Spirit of Mercury, O Taphthartharath. I bind and conjure Thee by Him that sitteth for ever on the Throne of Thy Planet, the Knower, the Master, the All-Dominating by Wisdom, Thoth the Great King, Lord of the Upper and the Lower Crowns! I bind and conjure Thee by the Great Name

IAHDONHI

Whose power is set flaming above Thy Palaces, and ruleth over Thee in the midst of Thy gloomy Habitations.

And by the powers of the mighty letter Beth: which is the house of our God, and the Crown of our Understanding and Knowledge. And by the great Magic Word

StiBeTTChePhMeFShiSS
which calleth Thee from Thy place as Thou fleest before the presence of the Spirit of Light and the Crown! And by the name

ZBaTh,

which symbolises Thy passage from Mercury in Gemini unto us in Malkuth:

> Come forth, come forth, come forth!
> Taphthartharath!
> In the name of IAHDONHI:
> I invoke Thee: appear! appear!
> Taphthartharath!
> In the name of Elohim Tzebaoth!
> I invoke Thee: appear! appear!
> Taphthartharath!
> In the Name of Mikhâel:
> I invoke Thee: appear! appear!
> Taphthartharath!
> In the Name of Raphael:
> I invoke Thee: appear! appear!
> Taphthartharath!
> In the Name of Tiriel:
> I invoke Thee: appear! appear!
> Taphthartharath!
> In the Name of Asboga:
> I invoke Thee: appear! appear!
> Taphthartharath!

THE EQUINOX

> In the Name of Din and Doni:
> I invoke Thee: appear! appear!
> Taphthartharath!
> In the Name of Taphthartharath:
> I invoke Thee: appear! appear!

O Thou Mighty Angel who art Lord of the 17th Degree of Gemini, wherein now Mercury takes refuge, send thou unto me that powerful but blind force in the form of Taphthartharath. I conjure thee by the Names of Mahiel and Onuel, they who rejoice.

Come forth unto us therefore, O Taphthartharath, Taphthartharath, and appear thou in visible and material form before us in the great Magical triangle without this Circle of Art! And if any other Magus of Art, or any other school than ours, is now invoking Thee by potent spells; or if Thou art bound by Thy vow, or Thy duties, or the terrible bonds of the Magic of Hell; then I let shine upon Thee the glory of the symbol of the Rose and the Cross; and I tell Thee by that symbol that Thou art free of all vows, of all bonds, for what time Thou comest hither to obey my will!

Or if any other Master or Masters of the Magic of Light of the Order of the Rose of Ruby and the Cross of Gold is now binding and invoking Thee by the supreme, absolute and fearful power of this our Art: then I command and conjure Thee by every name and rite already rehearsed that Thou send unto us an ambassador to declare unto us the reason of Thy disobedience.

But if Thou art yet disobedient and unwilling to come, then will I curse Thee by the Mighty Names of God, and I will cast Thee forth from Thy Power and Place. And I will torment Thee by horrible and terrible rites. And I will blot out Thy place from the Universe and Thou shalt NEVER rise again!

So come Thou forth, Thou Spirit of Mercury, Taphthartharath, come Thou forth quickly, I advise and command Thee.

Come Thou forth from Thy abodes and retreats. Come Thou forth unto us, and appear before us in this Magical triangle without this Circle of Art: in fair and human form, courteously answering in an audible voice all of our demands. As is written:

> "Kiss the Son lest He be angry!
> If His anger be kindled, yea, but a little—
> Blessed are they that put their trust in Him!"

[The Mighty Magus of Art lifts up the sigil towards Heaven, tears off from it the Black Veil, and cries:]

Creature of Kokab, long hast Thou dwelt in Darkness! Quit the Night and seek the Day!

[Sigil is replaced to West of the triangle; Magus holds the Sword erect (point upwards) over its centre, and lays her left hand upon it, saying:]

184

THE TEMPLE OF SOLOMON THE KING

By all the names, powers and rites already rehearsed, I conjure Thee thus unto visible apparition:

KHABS AM PEKHT.

KONX OM PAX.

LIGHT IN EXTENSION.

[Saith the Magus of Art:]
As the Light hidden in Darkness can manifest therefrom,

SO SHALT THOU

become manifest from concealment unto manifestation!

[The Magus of Art takes up the sigil, stands at East of Altar facing West, and says:]

THE CONJURATION OF THE INTELLIGENCE TIRIEL.

Tiriel, Angel of God, in the name of

IAHDONHI

I conjure thee send thou unto us this spirit

TAPHTHARTHARATH.

Do thou force him to manifest before us without this Circle of Art.

Tiriel, in the name of Elohim Tzebaoth, send to us in form material this spirit Taphthartharath.

Tiriel, in the name of Beni Elohim, send to us in form material this spirit Taphthartharath.

Tiriel, in the name of Michael, send to us in form material this spirit Taphthartharath.

Tiriel, in the name of Raphael, send to us in visible form this spirit Taphthartharath.

Tiriel, in the name of Hod, send to us in visible form this spirit Taphthartharath.

O Tiriel, Tiriel: in all the mighty signs, and seals, and symbols here gathered together, I conjure thee in the Name of the Highest to force this Spirit Taphthartharath unto visible manifestation before us, in the great triangle without this Circle of Art.

[The Magus now places the sigil between the mystic pillars, and attacks it as Enterer, directing upon it her whole will: following this projection by the sign of silence. If he does not yet appear, then repeat the invocation to Tiriel from the throne of the East. This process may be repeated thrice. But if not even then the Spirit come, then an error hath been committed, in which case replace Sigil on altar, holding sword as usual, and say:]

THE PRAYER UNTO THE GREAT GOD OF HEAVEN.

O ye great Lords of the Hall of the Twofold Manifestation of Truth, who preside over the weighing of the Souls in the Place of Judgment before

AESHOORI,

Give me your hands, for I am made as ye! Give me your hands, give me your magic powers, that I may have given unto me the force and the Power and the Might irresistible, which shall compel this disobedient and malignant spirit, Taphthartharath, to appear before me, that I may accomplish this evocation of arts according to all my works and all my desires. In myself I am nothing: in ye I am all self, and exist in the selfhood of the Mighty to Eternity! O Thoth, who makest victorious the word of AESHOORI against his adversaries, make thou my word, who am Osiris, triumphant and victorious over this spirit:

Taphthartharath

Amen.

[Return to place of the Hierophant, and repeat, charging. He now will certainly appear.

But so soon as he appears, again let the sigil be purified and censed by the Magus of Art. Then removing from the middle of the sigil the Cord of Bondage, and holding that sigil in her left hand, she will smite with the flat blade of her magic sword, saying:]

By and in the Names of IAHDONHI, Elohim Tzebaoth, Michael, Raphael and Tiriel: I invoke upon thee the power of perfect manifestation unto visible appearance!

[I.A. now takes up the sigil in his right hand and circumambulates thrice. He places sigil on the ground at the place of the spirit. S.S.D.D., from the place of the Hierophant, now recites (I.A. with sword guarding the place of the spirit, D.P.A.L. holding the Book; and AE.A. holding the magical candle for her to read by)]

AN EXTREMELY POWERFUL CONJURATION.

Behold! Thou Great Powerful Prince and Spirit, Taphthartharath, we have conjured Thee hither in this day and hour to demand of Thee certain matters relative to the secret magical knowledge which may be conveyed to us from Thy great master Thoth through Thee. But, before we can proceed further, it is necessary that Thou do assume a shape and form more distinctly material and visible. Therefore, in order that Thou mayest appear more fully visible, and in order that Thou mayest know that we are possessed of the means, rites, powers and privileges of binding and compelling Thee unto obedience, do we rehearse before Thee yet again the mighty words; the Names, the Sigils, and the Powers of the conjurations of fearful efficacy: and learn that if Thou wert under any bond or spell, or in distant lands or elsehow employed, yet nothing should enable Thee to resist the power of our terrible conjuration; for if Thou art disobedient and unwilling to come, we shall curse and imprecate Thee most horribly by the Fearful Names of God the Vast One; and we shall tear from Thee Thy rank and Thy power, and we shall cast Thee down unto the fearful abode of the chained ones and shells, and Thou shalt never rise again!

Wherefore make haste, O Thou mighty spirit Taphthartharath, and appear very visibly before us, in the magical triangle without this Circle of Art. I bind and conjure Thee unto very visible appearance in the Divine and Terrible Name

IAHDONHI,

By the Name IAHDONHI,

And in the Name IAHDONHI,

I command Thee to assume before us a very visible and material Form.

By and in the Mighty Name of God the Vast One.

ELOHIM TZEBAOTH,

And in the Name ELOHIM TZEBAOTH,

And by the Name ELOHIM TZEBAOTH,

I bind and conjure Thee to come forth very visibly before us.

I bind and conjure Thee unto more manifest appearance, O thou Spirit, Taphthartharath.

By the Name of MICHAEL,

And in the Name of MICHAEL,

By and in that Name of MICHAEL,

I bind and conjure Thee that Thou stand forth very visibly, endowed with an audible voice, speaking Truth in the Language wherein I have called Thee forth.

Let IAHDONHI, ELOHIM TZEBAOTH, MICHAEL, RAPHAEL, BENI ELOHIM, TIRIEL, ASBOGA, DIN, DONI, HOD, KOKAB and every name and spell and scourge of God the Vast One bind Thee to obey my words and will.

Behold the standards, symbols and seals and ensigns of our God: obey and fear them, O Thou mighty and potent Spirit, Taphthartharath!

Behold our robes, ornaments, insignia and weapons: and say, are not these the things Thou fearest?

Behold the magic fire, the mystic lamps, the blinding radiance of the Flashing Tablets!

Behold the Magical Liquids of the Material Basis; it is these that have given Thee Form!

Hear thou the Magical Spells and Names and chants which bind Thee!

Taphthartharath!

Taphthartharath!

Taphthartharath!

Taphthartharath!

Taphthartharath!

Taphthartharath!

Taphthartharath!

Arise! Move! Appear!

THE EQUINOX

Zodâcar Èca od Zodamerahnu odo kikalè Imayah piapè piamoel od VAOAN!

[If at this time that spirit be duly and rightly materialized, then pass on to the request of the Mighty Magus of Art; but if not, then doth the Magus of Art assume the God form of Thoth, and say:]

Thou comest not! Then will I work and work again. I will destroy Thee and uproot Thee out of Heaven and Earth and Hell.

Thy place shall be come empty; and the horror of horrors shall abide in Thy heart, and I will overwhelm Thee with fear and trembling, for "SOUL mastering Terror" is my Name.

[If at this point he manifest, then pass on to the final Request of the Mighty Magus of Art; if not, continue holding the arms in the sign of Apophis.]

Brother Assistant Magus! Thou wilt write me the name of this evil serpent, this spirit Taphthartharath, on a piece of pure vellum, and thou shalt place thereon also His seal and character; that I may curse, condemn and utterly destroy Him for His disobedience and mockery of the Divine and Terrible Names of God the Vast One.

[Assistant Magus does this.]

Hear ye my curse, O Lords of the Twofold Manifestation of Thmaist.

I have evoked the Spirit Taphthartharath in due form by the formulae of Thoth.

But He obeys not, He makes no strong manifestation.

Wherefore bear ye witness and give ye power unto my utter condemnation of the Mocker of your Mysteries.

I curse and blast Thee, O thou Spirit Taphthartharath. I curse Thy life and blast Thy being. I consign Thee unto the lowest Hell of Abaddon.

By the whole power of the Order of the Rose of Ruby and the Cross of Gold—for that Thou hast failed at their behest, and hast mocked by Thy disobedience at their God-born knowledge—by that Order which riseth even unto the white throne of God Himself do I curse Thy life and blast Thy being; and consign Thee unto the lowermost Hell of Abaddon!

In the Names of IAHDONHI, Elohim Tzebaoth, Michael, Raphael, Beni Elohim and Tiriel:

I curse Thy Life
And Blast Thy Being!
Down! Sink down to the depths of horror.

By every name, symbol, sign and rite that has this day been practised in this Magic Circle: by every power of my soul, of the Gods, of the Mighty Order to which we all belong!

I curse Thy Life
And Blast Thy Being!
Fall, fall down to torment unspeakable!

If Thou dost not appear then will I complete the fearful sentence of this curse.

God will not help Thee. Thou, Thou hast mocked His Name.

[Taking the slip of vellum and thrusting it into the magical Fire.]

I bid Thee, O sacred Fire of Art, by the Names and Powers which gave birth unto the Spirit of the Primal Fire: I bind and conjure Thee by every name of God, the Vast One, that hath rule, authority and dominion over Thee; that Thou do spiritually burn, blast, destroy and condemn this spirit Taphthartharath, whose name and seal are written herein, causing Him to be removed and destroyed out of His powers, places and privileges: and making Him endure the most horrible tortures as of an eternal and consuming Fire, so long as He shall come not at my behest!

The Earth shall suffocate Him, for mine are its powers, and the Fire shall torment Him, for mine is its magic. And Air shall not fan Him, nor Water shall cool Him. But Torment unspeakable, Horror undying, Terror unaltering, Pain unendurable; the words of my curse shall be on Him for ever; God shall not hear Him, nor holpen Him never, and the curse shall be on Him for ever and ever!

[So soon as he shall appear, extinguish that fire with consecrated water, and cry:]

O, Thou Mighty Spirit Taphthartharath, forasmuch as Thou art come, albeit tardily, do I revoke my magic curse, and free Thee from all its bonds save only from those that bind Thee here!

[He having appeared, the *Assistant Magus of Art* holds aloft his sword, saying:]

Hear ye, Great Lord of the Hall of Dual Truth; Hear ye, Immortal Powers of the Magic of Light, that this Spirit Taphthartharath hath been duly and properly invoked in accordance with the sacred rites of Power Ineffable.

[The *Mighty Magus of Art* now says:]

O ye Great Lords of the Glory and Light of the radiant Orb of Kokab; ye in whom are vested the knowledge of the Mighty powers, the knowledge of all the hidden Arts and Sciences of Magic and of Mystery! Ye! Ye! I invoke and conjure! Cause ye this mighty Serpent Taphthartharath to perform all our demands: manifest ye through him the Majesty of your presences, the divinity of your knowledge, that we may all be led yet one step nearer unto the consummation of the Mighty Work, one step nearer unto the great white throne of the Godhead; and that, in so doing, *His* being may become more glorified and enlightened, more capable of receiving the Influx of that Divine Spirit which dwells in the heart of Man and God!

[S.S.D.D. now formulates the desires as follows:]

O thou Great Potent Spirit Taphthartharath, I do command and very potently conjure thee by the Majesty of Thoth, the Great God, Lord of AmenTa, King and Lord Eternal of the Magic of Light:

That Thou teach unto us continually the Mysteries of the Art of Magic, declaring unto us now in what best manner may each of us progress towards the accomplishment of the Great Work. Teach us the Mysteries of all the Hidden Arts and Sciences which are under the Dominion of Mercury, and finally swear Thou by the Great Magic Sigil that I hold in my hand, that thou wilt in future always speedily appear before us; coming whensoever Thy sigil is unveiled from its yellow silken covering: and manifesting whensoever we enable Thee by the offerings and sacrifices of Thy nature! To the end that Thou mayest be a perpetual link of communication between the Great God Thoth under his three forms and ourselves.

THE FINAL ADMONITION.

O Thou mighty and potent prince of Spirits Taphtharharath: forasmuch as Thou hast obeyed us in all our demands, I now finally bind and conjure Thee:

That Thou hereafter harm me not, or these my companions, or this place, or aught pertaining unto all of us: that Thou faithfully do perform all those things even as Thou hast sworn by the great and all-powerful Names of God the Vast One; and that Thou dost deceive us in nothing, and forasmuch as Thou has been obedient unto our call, and hast sworn to obey our commands:

Therefore do Thou feel and receive these grateful odours of the fine perfumes of our Art, which are agreeable unto Thee.

[Magus of Fires burns much incense.]

And now I say unto Thee, in the name of IHSVH, depart in peace unto Thy habitations and abodes in the invisible. I give unto Thee the blessing of God in the Name of IAHDONHI: may the influx of the Divine Light inspire Thee and lead Thee unto the ways of peace!

Let there be peace betwixt us and Thee; and come Thou hastily when we invoke and call Thee:

Shalom! Shalom! Shalom!

[Reverse circumambulations and closing rituals of Mercury, &c. &c.]

In the Order of the Golden Dawn many consecrations were made use of upon the lines laid down in Book ח, such as the Consecration of the Lotus Wand, the Rose Cross and the Magical Sword; these, however, we will omit, substituting in their place one carried out by P. himself, and called:

TALISMAN OF FIRE OF JUPITER WITH RITUAL

THE INVOCATIONS PROPER TO THE CONSECRATION OF A FLASHING TABLET OF THE EAGLE KERUB OF JUPITER.

PART I

The Hall is first purified by the banishing rituals of Pentagram and Hexagram. Next by Fire and Water.

The General Exordium follows; then,

The Exordium.

I, P., with the help of Q.F.D.R. and T.T.E.G, am come hither to consecrate a talisman of the Eagle Kerub of Jupiter that it may be powerful to heal the sick, to alleviate pain, to give health and strength. And I swear, in the presence of the Eternal Gods, that, as liveth the Lord of the Universe and my own Higher Soul, I will so create a dweller for this talisman that it shall be irresistible to heal the sick, to alleviate pain, to give health and strength: to the welfare of mankind and the glory of God.

[I invoke the Higher by the first prayer in 5°=6°, and make the sign of the Cross on the talisman.

Purify talisman, Fire and Water.

The Invoking ritual of the Hexagram of Jupiter is performed.]

THE GREAT INVOCATION OF AMOUN.*

Hail unto Thee, Lord of Mercy! Hail, I say, unto Thee, the Father of the Gods!

O Thou, whose golden plumes stream up the sky in floods of light divine!

Thou, whose head is as a sapphire, or the vault of the unchanging sky!

Thou, whose heart is pitiful; where the Rose Dawn shines out amid the gold!

Thou, unchanging and unchangeable;

Whom the Eagle follows; whom the Serpent doth embrace;

O Thou that standest on the Scorpion!

Thee, Thee, Thee, Thee, I invoke!

O Thou! from whom the Universe did spring!

Thou, the All-Father, Thou whose plumes of power rise up to touch the Throne of the Concealed!

Mighty! Merciful! Magnificent!

Thee, Thee, Thee, Thee, I invoke!

Behold! Thou hast lifted up Thy Voice and the hills were shaken! Yea, Thou didst cry aloud and the everlasting hills did bow! They fled away; they were not! And Thine Awful Sea rolled in upon the Abyss!

For Thou didst look upon my face and say: Thou art my Son, this day have I begotten Thee!

Yea, O my Father, Thou hast spoken unto me and said: "Sit thou on my right hand!"

* During the great invocation of Amoun and Toum Maal T.T.E.G. and Q.F.D.R. respectively charge the talisman with Enterer sign.

In Part I, T.T.E.G. will imagine herself throughout as clothed with a violet light and between two mighty pillars, of smoke and flame.

A white light must pervade the violet from above.

Her station is the place of Jupiter.

But I have covered my face. I have hidden myself. I have knelt before Thee in the Glory of Thy face!

Arise, Lord God, arise and shine! I am To-Day and I am Yesterday! I am the Brother of the Golden Dawn!

In the Chariot of Life is my seat, and my horses course upon the firmament of Nu!

Come unto me, O my Father, for I know Thy Name!

AMOUN!

[Vibrate by formulae of the Middle Pillar and of the Mystic Circumambulation.]

I invoke Thee, the Terrible and Invisible God!

I call Thee from the azure Throne!

I raise my voice in the Abyss of Water!

I raise my soul to contemplate Thy Face!

AMOUN!

Come unto me! Hear me! Appear in splendour unto these who worship at Thy Feet!

For who am I before Thy Face? What is man, that Thou art mindful of him; or the Son of Man that Thou visitest him! Thou hast made him a little lower than the Elohim—Thou hast Crowned him with Glory and Honour!

AMOUN!

Hear me! Come unto me!

In myself I am nothing—in Thee I am All Self! Dwell Thou in me, and bring me to that Self which is in Thee!

AMOUN!

O my Father! my Father! the Chariots of Ishrael, and the horsemen thereof!

[All bow in adoration. Standing in the Sign of Osiris slain, say:]

I am the Abi-agnus, the Slain Lamb in thy Mountain, O Lord Most High!

I am the Strength of the Race of Men, and from me is the Shower of the Life of Earth!

I am Amoun, the Conceal d One: the Opener of the Day am I!

I am Osiris Onnophris, the Justified One. I am the Lord of Life triumphant over death! There is no part of me that is not of the Gods.

I am the Preparer of the Pathway: the Rescuer unto the Light!

Out of the Darkness let the Light arise!

[Raise hands to heaven.]

Thou hast been blind and dead, O creature of talismans!

Now I say unto Thee, Receive thy Life! Receive thy Sight! I am the Reconciler with the Ineffable! I am the Dweller of the Invisible!

LET THE WHITE BRILLIANCE OF THE
DIVINE SPIRIT
DESCEND!

[Lower hands. Touching talisman with white end of Wand.]
Be thou a living creature! Whose mind is open unto the Higher!
Be thou a living creature! Whose heart is a centre of Light.
Be thou a living creature! Whose body is the Temple of the Rosy Cross.

In the number 21, in the name אהיה, in the name יהשוה, in the Pass-Word INRI, I declare that I have created thee, a living Spirit of this Sphere of Tzedeq, to do my will, and work thine own salvation!

Let us analyse the Key-Word.

Chief: I.
2nd: N.
3rd: R.
All: I.
Chief: Yod. י.
2nd: Nun. נ.
3rd: Resh. ר.
All: Yod. י.
Chief: Virgo, Isis, Mighty Mother.
2nd: Scorpio, Apophis, Destroyer.
3rd: Sol, Osiris, Slain and Risen.
All: Isis, Apophis, Osiris.

IAΩ

(All give the sign of the Cross).
Chief, 2nd and 3rd Adepts: The Sign of Osiris Slain.
(*Chief:* L. The Sign of the mourning of Isis.)
(*2nd Adept:* V. The Sign of Typhon Destroyer.)
(*3rd Adept:* X. The Sign of Osiris Risen.)
All: LVX., Lux, The Light of the Cross.

PART II.*

Purify talisman with Water and Fire.

The Invocation of Water is made as in 3°=8° and by the Enochian Keys 10, 4, 11, 12 in E., W., N., S. respectively Invocation ♏ (σλημ).†

The Invocation of the Great God Toum Maal

O Thou! Majesty of Godhead!
Toum Maal! Thee, Thee I invoke!

* In Part II. Q. F. D. R. will imagine herself as a blue eagle between two mighty pillars. White light pervades the blue from above. Her station is in the West.

† See 777. Egyptian name of Scorpio.

THE EQUINOX

Lord of Amenta! Lord of Enemehitt!

O Thou! Whose head is golden as the sun, and thy nemyss as the night sky-blue!

Thou who art as rugged as the wind!

Who formulatest wonders in the world!

Thou unchangeable as Ta-Ur!

Thou, mutable as water!

Changing ever, and ever the same!

Thou, girt about with the Waters of the West as with a garment!

Thou, who art, in the Beneath as in the Above, like to Thyself!

Reflector! Transmuter! Creator!

Thee, Thee, I invoke!

Behold, I have set my feet in the West, as Râ that hath ended his work!

Toum goeth down into thy Waters, and the daylight passeth, and the shadows come!

But I, I pass not, nor go down!

The light of my Godhead gleams ever in Thy glowing skies;

Horus is my Name, and the City of Darkness is my House:

Thoth is on the prow of my Bark and I am Khephera that giveth Light!

Come unto me! Come unto me, I say, for I am He that standeth in Thy place!

Behold! ye gathering eagles in the Sky! I am come into the West! I am lifted up upon your wings! Ye that follow the bier to the place of Rest. Ye that mourn Osiris in the dusk of things!

Behold He is in Me and I in Him!

I am He that ruleth in Amenta!

In Sleei (σλῃι) is my rule, and in Death is my dominion!

Mine are the eagles that watch in the Eye of Horus!

Mine is the Bark of Darkness, and my power is in the Setting Sun!

I am the Lord of Amenta!

Toum Maal is My Name!

Hail unto Thee! Hail unto Thee! O mine eagle of the glowing West!

Toumathph!

[Vibrate by the formulae of the Middle Pillar and of the Mystic Circumambulation.]

O crowned with darkness! Mother-bird of the Holy Ones! O golden-headed Soul of sleep! O firm, enduring shoulders! O body of blue and golden feathers! O darkening feet, as of the skies of night! O mighty Power of claws and beak, invincible, divine!

O great and glistening Wings!

Ride hither on the Storm!

Toumathph!

[Vibrate by the formulae of the Middle Pillar and of the mystic Circumambulation.]
Across the gloomy waters
From the land of the Setting Sun
Thou art come, Thou art come, for the Words of my Mouth are mighty words.
Come, for the guests are ready, and the feast is spread before Thee!
Come, for the destined spouse awaits Thy kiss!
With roses and with wine, with light and life and love! The soul of Tzedeq waits!
Come then, O come to me!

For I know that my Redeemer liveth, and that He shall stand at the latter day
upon the earth.

I have fought upon earth for good. I am purified. I have finished my course, I
have entered into the invisible! I am Osiris Onnophris the Justified One. I am the
Lord of Life Triumphant over Death! There is no part of me that is not of the Gods.

I am the Preparer of the Pathway: the Rescuer unto the Light!

Out of the Darkness let the light arise!

[Raise hands to heaven.]

Thou hast been blind and dead, O creature of talismans! Now I say unto thee:
Receive thy life! Receive thy Sight!

I am the Reconciler with the Ineffable!

I am the Dweller of the Invisible!

LET THE WHITE BRILLIANCE OF THE
DIVINE SPIRIT
DESCEND!

PART III.

The Chymical and Hermetic Marriage of the Eagle of the Waters
with the Soul of Jupiter.

[Purify the talisman with Water and Fire.]

Q.F.D.R..: I am the Eagle of the Waters, and my Power is in the West!

T.T.E.G.: I am the Soul of Jupiter: in the sphere of Tzedeq is my name confessed!

P.: I am the Reconciler between you!

Q.F.D.R.: My Power is to give peace and sleep!

T.T.E.G: My Power is to give strength and health!

P.: I am the Reconciler between you!

Q.F.D.R.: Toum Maal hath made me to this end!

T.T.E.G.: Amoun hath made me to this end!

P.: I am the Reconciler between you!

Q.F.D.R.: Pain could not dwell before us if we wed.

T.T.E.G: Death could not come where we are if we wed.

P.: I am the Reconciler between you!

Q.F.D.R.: My robes were blue: where is their azure gone?

T.T.E.G.: My robes were violet: is their purple past?

P.: I am the Reconciler between you! "

Q.F.D.R.: I am the eagle: and my form remains.

T.T.E.G.: I am the square: and still the square abides.

P.: I am the Reconciler between you!

[*Q.F.D.R.* and *T.T.E.G.* together in grip of 5°=6° over the Talisman:

We were two: are we not made one?

P.: I am the Reconciler between you!

O Maker and Creator and Preserver!

Hear us who call Thee!

Mighty Lord of Life, who hast given us life and love, who is like unto Thee?

O God! hear us when we call!

Pray Thou for us, that we may be made one!

Unto God the Vast One let Thy prayer ascend!

[The Magician shall kneel down and say:]

Unto Thee, sole wise, sole mighty, sole merciful One, be the praise and the glory for ever and ever! Who hast permitted me to glean in Thy field! To gather a spark of Thine unutterable light! To form two mighty beings from the spheres of Thy dominion! To make them one by the operation of Thy Divine Wisdom!

Grant that this Eagle Kerub in the Sphere of Jupiter may be indeed mighty on the Earth! To heal the sick, to strengthen the infirm, to quiet the pain of mortal men!

Grant that this work be unto it for a salvation, and a very invocation of Thy Light Divine, and a very link with the Immortal Soul of Man!

Let it be pure and strong, that at last it may attain even unto the eternal Godhead in the veritable

KHABS AM PEKHT!

KONX OM PAX!

LIGHT IN EXTENSION!

AMEN.

And for ourselves we pray, that this work of mercy that we have wrought to-night be for us a link with thy Divine Mercy, that we may be merciful, even as Thou art merciful, O our Father which art in Heaven!

That the Benignant Eye of the Most Holy and Concealed, the Ancient One of Days, may open upon us, unto the glory of Thine Ineffable Name.

AMEN.

THE TEMPLE OF SOLOMON THE KING

Let us finally invoke the Divine Light upon this gentle spirit we have created, that its paths may be light, and its way unto the White Glory sure!

By Sacrifice of Self shalt thou attain!

By mercy and by peace shall be thy path!

For I know that My Redeemer liveth and that He shall stand at the latter day upon the earth.

Be thy Mind open unto the Higher!

Be thy Heart the Centre of Light!

Be thy Body the Temple of the Rosy Cross!

And now I finally invoke upon thee power and might irresistible: to heal the sick, to alleviate pain, to strengthen and to restore to health!

21. AHIH. IHSHVH. INRI.

V.H. Soror Q.F.D.R., I now deliver into thy charge this pure and powerful talisman!

See thou well how thou dost acquit thyself herein!

Keep it with reverence and love as a thing holy!

Keep it in purity and strength!

Let the dew of heaven descend upon it in the night season!

Let this sacred perfume be burnt before it in the heat of day!

At frequent times do this; and especially after thou has employed it in a work of love.

And if thou dose treat it ill, if thou dost use it unworthily, if thou dost expose it to the gaze of the profane, then let its spirit return unto the God that give it, and let its power be assumed by its evil and averse antithesis to become a dreadful vampire, ever to prey upon thee, that the Vengeance of the Gods may drink its fill.

But, and if thou does well and faithfully, ye shall be unto each other as a support and a blessing, and the Blessing of God the Vast One shall be ever upon you in his name

יהשוה:

And now in and by this very name I license all spirits to depart, save that One whose Dual Nature I have bound herein. But let them depart in peace to their Divine Orders in the name of Jeovah Jeovaschah! and let them be ever ready to come when they are called!

אתה שלם:
שלם:

Fra: P. constructed many other talismans besides this, a Flashing Tablet of the Eagle Kerub of Jupiter for the purpose of curing a certain Lady I——, mother of Soror Q.F.D.F., of a serious illness. Extraordinary were its results. For having carefully celebrated the ritual he instructed Soror Q.F.D.R. to feed the talisman with incense, and water it with dew. This she neglected to do, the result being that when she placed the talisman on her sick mother, this venerable old lady was seized with a violent series of fits, and nearly died. Q.F.D.R., however, reconsecrated the talisman, the result being that the Lady I____ speedily recovered the whole of her former strength, and survived to the ripe old age of ninety- two.

With a similar talisman, too hurriedly prepared, he cured the pain in the leg of a certain friend of his; but forgetting to close the circle he found himself afflicted, exactly twenty-four hours later, by a similar pain, but in the opposite leg to the one in which his friend had suffered.

On very much the same lines as the foregoing, P. invoked into manifest appearance in the early autumn of 1899 the mighty but fallen spirit Buer, to compel his obedience unto the restoring of the health of Frater I.A.; and many other workings were also accomplished about this period. More important than any such dealings with the Paths is his progress in the Middle Pillar. In this connection we shall include Frater I.A.'s ritual for "The Magical Invocation of the Higher Genius."

THE MAGICAL INVOCATION OF THE HIGHER GENIUS

(According to the Formulæ of the Book of the Voice of Thoth.)

[The ceremony Enterer is the Sphere of Sensation. The Hierophant is the Augœides. The officers are the Divine Sephiroth invoked. The Enterer is the natural man.]

[First let the symbols in the Shpere of Sensation be equilibrated. This is the Opening of the Hall of Truth.]

THE TEMPLE OF SOLOMON THE KING

The First Invocation.

Come forth unto me, Thou that art my true Self: my Light: my Soul! come forth unto me: Thou that art crowned with Glory: That art the Changeless: The Un-name-able: the Immortal Godhead, whose Place is in the Unknown: and whose Dwelling is the Abode of the Undying Gods. Heart of my Soul; self- shining Flame, Glory of Light, Thee I invoke. Come forth unto me, my Lord: to me, who am Thy vain reflec-tion in the mighty sea of Matter! Hear Thou, Angel and Lord! Hear Thou in the habitations of Eternity; come forth; and purify to Thy Glory My mind and Will! Without Thee am I nothing; in Thee am I All-self existing in Thy Selfhood to eternity!

[Close now the channels to the Ruach of the Material senses: endeavouring at the same time to awaken the Inner sight and hearing. Thus seated, strive to grasp the same ray of the Divine Glory of the selfhood: meditating upon the littleness and worthlessness of the natural man: the vanity of his desires, the feebleness of his boasted Intellect. Remember that without That Light, naught can avail thee to true progression: and that alone by purity of Mind and Will canst thou ever hope to enter into that Glory. Pray then for that purification, saying in thy heart:]

First purification and consecration of the candidate by Fire and Water.

Water: Purify me with hyssop, and I shall be clean: Wash me, and I shall be whiter than snow.

Fire: O send forth Thy light and Thy Truth, let them lead me, let them guide me unto Thy Holy Hill, to Thy Dwelling-place!

I stand before the Beautiful Gate: before the mighty Portal of the Universe: at my Right Hand a Pillar of Fire; and at my left a Pillar of Cloud. At their bases are the dark-rolling clouds of the Material Universe: and they pierce the Vault of the Heavens above. And ever upon their summits flame the Lamps of their Spiritual Essence!

Thou that livest in the Glory beyond that Gate: Heart of my Soul; Thee I Invoke! Come Thou forth unto me, who art my very Selfhood; mine Essence, my Light: and do Thou guard me and guide me through the Manifold Paths of Life: that I may at length become one with Thine Immortal and Imperishable Essence!

Unto Thee, Sole Wise, Sole Mighty, and Sole Eternal one, be Praise and Glory for Ever; Who hast permitted me to enter so far in the Sanctuary of Thy Mysteries. Not unto me, but unto Thy name be the Glory!

Let the influence of Thy Divine Ones descend upon my head, and teach me the value of Self-Sacrifice: so that I shrink not in the hour of trial; but that my Name may be written upon High, and that my Genius may stand in the Presence of the Holy One: in that hour when the Son of Man is evoked before the Lord of Spirits; and His Name in the presence of the Ancient of Days. O Lord of the Universe! grant Thou that upon me may shine forth the Light of my Higher Soul. Let me be guided by the help of my Genius unto Thy Throne of Glory, Ineffable in the centre of the World of Life and Light.

[Now go up to the Altar: formulating before thee a glittering Light: imagine that it demands wherefore thou hast come, &c., and say:]

Adoration unto Thee that Dawnest in the Golden!

O Thou that sailest over the Heavens in Thy Bark of Morning!

Dark before Thee is the Golden Brightness;

In whom are all the hues of the Rainbow.

May I walk as Thou walkest, O Holiness, Who hast no master, Thou the great Space-Wanderer to whom millions and hundreds of thousands of years are but as one Moment! Let me enter with Thee into Thy Bark! Let me pass with Thee as Thou enterest the Gate of the West! As Thou gleamest in the Gloaming when Thy Mother Nuit enfoldeth Thee!

[Now kneel at the Altar with thy right hand on the White Triangle, and thy left in the left hand of thine Astral double, he standing in the place of the Hierophant, and holding the Astral presentment of a Lotus Wand by the white band in his right hand, then say, as if with the projected Astral consciousness:]

Adoration unto ye, ye Lords of Truth in the Hall of Thmaist, cycle of the great Gods which are behind Osiris: O ye that are gone before, let me grasp your hands, for I am made as ye!

O ye of the Hosts of the Hotepischim! Purge ye away the wrong that is in me!

Even as ye purged the Seven Glorious Ones who follow after the coffin of the Enshrined One, and whose places Anubist hath fixèd against the day of "Be-with-us."

O Thoth! Who makest Truth the Word of Aeshoori! make my word truth before the circle of the Great Gods!

Adoration unto Thee, Anubi, who guardest the threshold of the Universe! Adoration unto Thee, Auramooth, purify me with the Living Waters!

Adoration unto Thee, Thaumæshneith, make me Holy with the Hidden Flame!

Adoration be unto Thee, O Dark-Bright One! Hoor! the Prince of the City of Blindness!

Adoration unto Thee, O Thmaist, Truth-Queen, who presidest at the Balance of Truth! Adoration unto Thee, Asi; adoration unto Thee, Nephthyst.

O AESHOORI, Lord of Amennti! Thou art the Lord of Life Triumphant over Death: there is naught in Thee but Godhead!

TOUM! Toum who art in the great Dwelling!

Sovereign Lord of all the Gods, save me, and deliver!

Deliver me from that God that feedeth upon the damnèd, Dog-faced but human-headed;

THE TEMPLE OF SOLOMON THE KING

That dwelleth by the Pool of fire in the Judgment Hall,
Devourer of Shades, eater of Hearts, the Invisible foe!
Devourer of Immortality is his Name!

Unto Thee, Sole Wise, Sole Mighty, and Sole Eternal one, be Praise and Glory for Ever: who hast permitted me to enter so far in the Sanctuary of the Mysteries. Not unto me, but unto Thy Name be the Glory! [Again finish by laying sword on nape of neck, saying: So help me the Lord of the Universe and my own Higher Soul!]

[Rise now, and raise above thine head thy hands (the left open and the right still holding the magic sword), and lifting unto heaven thine eyes, strive to aspire with all thy will unto the highest Divinity, saying:]

From Thy Hands, O Lord, cometh all good! from Thy Hands flow down all grace and blessing! The Characters of Heaven with Thy Finger hast thou traced: but none can read them save he that hath been taught in Thy school! Therefore, even as servants look unto the hands of their masters, and handmaids unto the hands of their mistresses, even so our eyes look up unto Thee! For Thou alone art our help, O Lord our God! Who should not extol Thee, O Lord of the Universe! Who should not praise Thee! All belongeth unto Thee! Either Thy love or Thine anger all must again re-enter! Nothing canst Thou lose, for all things tend unto Thine Honour and Majesty! Thou art Lord alone, and there is none beside Thee! Thou dost what Thou wilt with Thy Mighty Arm: and none can escape from Thee! Thou alone helpest in their necessity the humble, the meek-hearted and the poor, who submit themselves unto Thee! And whosoever humbleth himself in dust and ashes before Thee; to such an one art Thou propitious!

Who should not praise Thee then, Lord of the Universe, who should not extol Thee! Unto whom there is none like; whose dwelling is in Heaven and in the virtuous and God-fearing Heart!

O God the Vast One! Thou art in all things!

O Nature! Thou Self from Nothing—for what else can I call Thee! I, in myself, I am nothing! I, in Thee, I am all Self: and exist in Thy Selfhood from nothing! Live Thou in me: and bring me unto that Self which is in Thee! For my victory is in the Cross and the Rose!

[Now pass to the North and face the East: projecting unto the place of the throne of the East the Astral double, and say from thence:]

The Voice of My Higher Soul said unto me: let me enter the path of Darkness: peradventure *thus* may I obtain the Light! I am the only being in an Abyss of Darkness: from the Darkness came I forth ere my birth, from the Silence of a primal Sleep.

And the voice of ages answer d unto my soul: child of Earth! The Light shineth in the Darkness; but the Darkness comprehendeth it not!

[Now formulate before thee a great Angel Torch-bearer saying:]

Arise! shine! for Thy Light is come!

THE EQUINOX

[Pass round the Temple to the South, face West and halt: formulate the Ideal* of Divine Mercy: and then that of Divine Justice: aspiring with all Thy heart unto each, and say:]

Come unto me! O Lord of Love and Pity, come unto me, and let me live in Thy Love! Let me be merciful even as my Father in Heaven is merciful, for Thou hast said: Blessed are the Merciful, for they shall obtain Mercy. Grant unto me that I may attain unto thy Peace, wherein is life for evermore.

Come unto me, O Lord of Perfect Justice! Mighty is Thine Arm, strong is Thy Hand: Justice and Judgment are the habitation of Thy Throne! Strengthen Thou, O Lord of Strength, my will and heart, that I may be able, with Thine aid, to cast out and destroy the Evil Powers that ever fight against those who seek Thee!

[Formulate now before thee the Two Pillars of Cloud and of Fire, saying:]

Purify me with hyssop, and I shall be clean! Wash me and I shall be whiter than snow!

O send forth Thy Light and Thy Truth, let them lead me, let them guide me unto Thy Holy Hill; even to Thy Tabernacles.

I stand before the Gate of the West; and the Pillars of the Universe arise in Majesty before me. At my right hand is the Pillar of Fire: and on my left the Pillar of Cloud: below they are lost in Clouds of Darkness: and above in Heaven in unnameable Glory. Let me enter, O Gate of the West!

[Pass to South-West and project Astral. Then saith the Guardian of the Gate of the West:]

Thou canst not pass by Me, saith the Guardian of the West: except Thou canst tell me My Name!

[Saith the Aspirant:]

Darkness is Thy Name: Thou art the Great One of the Paths of the Shades!

[Saith the Great One of the Night of Time:]

Child of Earth! remember that Fear is failure: be thou therefore without fear: for in the heart of the Coward, Virtue abideth not! Thou has known Me now, so pass thou on!

[Pass to the North, and exalt again thy mind unto the contemplation of the Mercy and Justice of our God, repeating the foregoing prayers; then say:]

Purify me with hyssop and I shall be clean: wash me and I shall be whiter than snow!

O send forth Thy Light and Thy Truth, let them lead me, let them guide me unto Thy Holy Hill, to Thy Dwelling-place!

* These are the two pillars of the Tree of Life; the first containing the Sephirah Chesed, and the second the Sephira Geburah.

THE TEMPLE OF SOLOMON THE KING

Dim before me looms the mighty Gate of the East! on the right the Pillar of Fire, on the left the Pillar of Cloud: stretching from the dark clouds of the World of Darkness to the Bright Glory of the Heavenly Light: Ever affirming to Eternity the Equilibration of the Powers of God the Vast One! Let me pass the Gate of the East Land! Let me pass the Gate of the Tuat, issuing forth with Râ in the Glory of Red Dawn!

[Pass to the North-East, project Double to the place of the throne of the East, saying:]

Thou canst not pass by Me, saith the Guardian of the East, except thou canst tell me My Name!

[Saith the Aspirant:]

"Light dawning in the Darkness" is Thy Name: the Light of a Golden Day!

[Saith the Osiris:]

Child of Earth! remember that Unbalanced Force is Evil: Unbalanced Mercy is but Weakness, Unbalanced Severity is but Cruelty and Oppression. Thou hast known Me now: so pass thou on unto the Cubical Altar of the Universe!

[Pass to the West of the Altar, project Astral to between the Pillars, kneel at Altar and repeat in Astral:]

THE PRAYER OF OSIRIS.

Lord of the Universe, the Vast and the Mighty One! Ruler of Light and of Darkness: we adore Thee and we invoke Thee! Look with favour upon this Neophyte who now kneeleth before Thee; and grant Thine aid unto the higher aspirations of His Soul, so that he may prove a true and faithful servant of the Mighty Ones, to the Glory of Thine Ineffable Name, Amen!

[Now rise: lift up both hands and eyes towards heaven; and concentrate upon the Glory and Splendour of Him that sitteth upon the Holy Throne for ever and ever, and say:]

KHABS AM PEKHT!
KONX OM PAX!
LIGHT IN EXTENSION!

In all my wanderings in Darkness the Light of Anubist went before me, yet I saw it not. It is a symbol of the Hidden Light of Occult Science.

[Pass to between the Pillars, and standing thus concentrate upon the Highest Divinity; and there standing in the sign of the Enterer, say:]

O Glory of the Godhead Unspeakable! Eternal Master! Ancient of Days! Thee, Thee, I invoke in my need! Dark is all the world; without, within; there is light alone in Thee! Rend asunder, Lord of the Universe, tear aside the Veil of the Sanctuary: let mine eyes behold my God, my King! As it is written: The Lightning lighteneth in the East and flameth even unto the West: even so shall be the Coming of the Son of Man!

THE EQUINOX

[And now shalt thou see a light slow formulating into the shape of a mighty Angel, and thou shalt withdraw thyself from this sight and again say:]

I saw Water coming from the Left Side of the Temple: and all unto whom that Water came were made whole, and cried:

Blessed is He that cometh in the Name of the Lord, Allelulia!

O Lamb of God: who takest away the Sins of the World! Grant us Thy peace!

I am come forth from the Gates of Darkness: I have passed by the Gate of Amennti: and the Gate of the Taot! Behold! I am come to the Gate of the Shining Ones in Heaven. I stand between the mighty Pillars of that Gate: at my right hand the Pillar of Fire, and at my left the Pillar of Cloud: Open unto me O gate of the God with the Motionless Heart: I am come forth by the T'eser Gate: I advance over the Paths that I know, I know: and my Face is set towards the land of the Maat!

[Again formulating the Augœides.]

Come forth, come forth, my God, my King: come unto me, Thou that art crowned with starlight: Thou that shinest amongst the Lords of Truth: whose place is in the abode of the Spirits of Heaven!

[When Thou shalt again see the Glorious One thou shalt salute with Enterer; pass between the pillars and circumambulate thrice: reverently saluting the East betimes. Now halt by the Light, facing it, and exalt thy mind unto Its glory, imagine it as encompassing thee and entering into Thy inmost Being, and say:]

I am the resurrection and the life. He that believeth on Me, though he were dead, yet shall he live again: and whosoever liveth and believeth on Me shall never die! I am the First and the Last, I am He that liveth but was dead, and behold I am alive for evermore, and hold the keys of Hell and of Death! For I know that my Redeemer liveth; and that He shall stand at the latter Day upon the Earth.

I am the Way: the Truth and the Life: no man cometh unto the Father but by me. I am purified: I have passed through the Gates of Darkness unto Light! I have fought upon Earth for good: I have finished my Work: I have entered into the Invisible! I am the Sun in His rising: I have passed through the Hour of Cloud and of Night! I am Amoun, the Concealed One: The Opener of Day am I! I am Osiris Onnophris, the Justified One. I am the Lord of Life Triumphant over Death: There is no part of me that is not of the Gods: I am the preparer of the Pathway, the Rescuer unto the Light! I am the Reconciler with the Ineffable! I am the Dweller of the Invisible! Let the White Brilliance of the divine Spirit descend.

[A long pause.]

Thus at length have I been permitted to comprehend the Form of my Higher Self!

Adoration be unto Thee, Lord of my Life, for Thou hast permitted me to enter thus far into the Sanctuary of Thine Ineffable Mystery: and hast vouchsafed to manifest unto me some little fragment of the Glory of Thy Being. Hear me, Angel of God the Vast One: hear me, and grant my prayer! Grant that I may ever uphold the the Symbol of Self-sacrifice: and grant unto me the comprehension of aught that may bring me nearer unto Thee! Teach me, starry Spirit, more and more of Thy Mystery and Thy Mastery: let each day and hour bring me nearer, nearer unto Thee! Let me aid Thee in Thy suffering that I may one day become partaker of Thy Glory: in that day when the Son of Man is invoked before the Lord of Spirits, and His Name in the presence of the Ancient of Days!

And for this day, teach me this one thing: how I may learn from Thee the Mysteries of the Higher Magic of Light. How I may gain from the Dwellers in the bright Elements their knowledge and Power: and how best I may use that knowledge to help my fellow-men.

And, finally, I pray Thee to let there be a link of Bondage between us: that I may ever seek, and seeking, obtain help and counsel from Thee Who Art my very selfhood. And before Thee I do promise and swear; that by the aid of Him that sitteth upon the Holy Throne, I will so purify my heart and mind that I may one day become truly united unto Thee, who art in Truth my Higher Genius, my Master, my Guide, my Lord and King!

The result of these magical experiments was twofold. First, by degrees P. was accumulating against himself a power of evil which was only awaiting a favourable moment to turn and destroy him.* This is the natural effect of all that class of magic which consists in making a circle, and thus setting the within against the without, and formulating duality, the eternal curse. Any idea in the mind is of little importance while it stays there, but to select it, to consecrate it, to evoke it to visible appearance, that is indeed dangerous.

---

* Whilst deep in these magical practices his house in London became charged with such an aura of evil that it was scarcely safe to visit it. This was not solely due to P.'s own experiments; we have to consider the evil work of others in the Order, such as E.F.E.J., who, envious of his progress and favour with the Chiefs, were attempting to destroy him. (See "At the Fork of the Roads," THE EQUINOX, vol. i. No. i, p. 101.) Weird and terrible figures were often seen moving about his rooms, and in several cases workmen and visitors were struck senseless by a kind of paralysis and by fainting fits.

For as he advanced from grade to grade, penetrating further and further into the mysteries of occult knowledge, he saw ever more clearly that most of the members of the Order of the Golden Dawn were scarcely worthy of his contempt; yet in spite of the folly of the disciples he remained loyal to their master D.D.C.F. He could not yet know that the chief is as his disciples, though raised to a higher power. For like attracts like. Secondly, these practical workings taught him, more certainly than years of study and reading, that there was but one goal to the infinite number of paths seen by the beginner, and that the ultimate result of the ✡ of ✡ Operation, the highest of the ceremonial operations of the Golden Dawn, was similar to that of "Rising on the Planes." Having made this important discovery he abandoned his intended experiments in ceremonial Divination and Alchemy, and towards the close of 1899 retired to the lonely house that he had bought for the purpose of carrying out the Sacred Operation of Abramelin the Mage.

THE ADEPT

DURING the whole of the autumn of 1899 we find P. busily engaged in making all necessary preparations for the great operation. Outside these preparations little else was accomplished; and, except for a fragment of a MS. on the "Powers of Number," no other record of the progress of P. during these three months is forthcoming.

This MS., though interesting enough in itself, is scarely of sufficient value to quote here; however it may be remarked that it shows how strong an influence the Order of the Golden Dawn had had upon him, as well as the astonishing rapidity of his Magical progress.

In January 1900, P. returned to Paris in order that before commencing the Sacred Operation of Abramelin the Magic he might pass through the grade of $5°=6°$, and become an Adeptus Minor in the Second Order of the Golden Dawn.

The ritual of the $5°=6°$ is of considerable length, and of such profundity and beauty that it is difficult to conceive of any man not being a better and a more illumined man for having passed through it. We should like to give it in its entirety, but space forbids, and though abridgement deducts considerably from its value, we will do our best to give its essence, and trust to make up for our shortcomings by attaching to this ritual P.'s lucid and learned interpretation.

THE RITUAL OF THE ORDER OF ROSÆ RUBEÆ ET AUREÆ CRUCIS

RITUAL OF THE 5°=6° GRADE OF ADEPTUS MINOR.

In this grade the following officers are required:
Chief Adept, 7°=4°, Merciful Exempt Adept.
Second Adept, 6°=5°, Mighty Adeptus Major.
Third Adept, 5°=6°, Associate Adeptus Minor.

OPENING

[The *Chief Adept*, having called upon the members to assist him open the Vault of the Adepts, and upon the Associate Adeptus Minor to see that the portal is closed and guarded, turns to the Second Adept and says:]

Mighty Adeptus Major, by what sign hast thou entered the Portal?

Second: By the sign of the rending asunder of the veil.*

Chief: Associate Adeptus Minor, by what sign has thou closed the Portal?

Third: By the signing of the closing of the Veil.

Second: Pe: פ.

Third: Resh: ר.

Second: Kaph: כ.

Third: Tau: ת

Second: Paroketh: פרכת.

Third: The Veil of the Sanctum Sanctorum.

Chief: Mighty Adeptus Major, what is the mystic number of this grade?

Second: 21.

Chief: Associate Adeptus Minor, what is the Pass-Word formed therefrom?

Third: Aleph: א.

Chief: Hé: ה.

Third: Yod: י.

Chief: Hé: ה.

Third: Eheieh: אהיה.

Chief: Mighty Adeptus Major, what is the Vault of the Adepts?

Second: The symbolic burying-place of our mystic Founder, Christian Rosenkreutz, which he made to represent the Universe.

---

* See "Liber O," THE EQUINOX, vol. i. No. 2.

THE TEMPLE OF SOLOMON THE KING

Chief: Associate Adeptus minor, in what part of it is he buried?

Third: In the centre of the Heptagonal sides and beneath the altar, his head being towards the East.

Chief: Mighty Adeptus Major, why in the centre?

Second: Because that is the point of Perfect Equilibrium.

[By this system of question and answer the whole symbolism of the vault is explained. Thus, the name of the Founder signifies the Rose and Cross of Christ, the fadeless Rose of Creation, the immortal Cross of Light. The Vault itself represents the tomb of Osiris Onnophris, the Justified One. Its seven sides the seven lower Sephiroth, the seven days of Creation, and the seven Palaces. It is situated in the centre of the Earth, in the Mountain of the Caverns, the Mystic Mountain of Abiegnus; which is the mountain of God in the Centre of the Universe, the sacred Rosicrucian Mountain of Initiation. The meaning of Abiegnus is explained as follows by the *Third Adept:*]

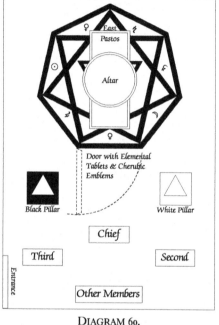

DIAGRAM 60.

The Temple in the Opening and First Point of the 5°=6° Ritual.

It is ABI-AGNUS, Lamb of the Father; it is, by metathesis, ABI-GENOS, born of the Father; BIA-GENOS, strength of our race; and the four words make the sentence: "Abiegnus, Abi-agnus, Abigenos, Bia-genos." Abiegnus, the Mountain of the Lamb of the Father, born of the Father, and the strength of our race.

[The key to the Vault, the Rose and Cross,* is then explained as resuming within itself the Life of Nature, and the Powers hidden in the word I∴ N∴ R∴ I∴. Another form of the Rose and Cross, the Crux Ansata, is shown to represent the force of the ten Sephiroth in nature, divided into a Hexad and Tetrad. The Oval embraces the first six Sephiroth, and the Tau Cross the lower four, answering to the four elements. The complete symbol of the Rose and Cross, which the Chief Adept carries upon his breast, is then explained to mean "the Key of Sigils and of Rituals"; and that it

* See Diagram 80.

represents the force of the twenty-two letters in Nature as divided into a three, a seven and a twelve; "many and great are its mysteries."

DIAGRAM 61.

The Egyptian Key of Life.
The Crux Ansata.

DIAGRAM 62.

The reverse of the Complete
Rose and Cross.

The explanation of the Rose and Cross being ended, the Third Adept first explains his wand as having marked on it the colours of the twelve signs of the Zodiac between Light and Darkness, and that it is surmounted by the Lotus Flower of Isis, which symbolizes the development of creation. Then, secondly, the Adeptus Major explains his as "a wand terminating in the symbol of the Binary, and surmounted by the Tau Cross of Life, or the Head of the Phoenix, sacred to Osiris." On it are marked the seven colours of the rainbow between Light and Darkness, which are attributed to the Planets. It symbolises rebirth and resurrection from death. Lastly, the Chief Adept explains his as follows: "My wand is surmounted by the Winged Globe, around which the twin Serpents of Egypt twine. It symbolises the equilibrated force of the Spirit and the four elements beneath the everlasting wings of the Holy One."

The door of the Vault is guarded by the Elemental Tablets,* and by the Cherubic Emblems, and upon it is written the words: "POST CENTUM VIGINTI ANNOS PATEBO." Which the Chief Adept explains as follows:]

The 120 years refer symbolically to the five grades of the First Order, and to the revolution of the powers of the Pentagram; also to the five preparatory examinations for this grade.

It is written: "His days shall be 120 years," and and 120 divided by five yields

---

* For a further account of these see "The Elemental Calls of Dr. Dee," in Sloane MSS., British Museum.

twenty-four, the number of hours in a day, and of the Thrones of the Elders in the Apocalypse. Further, 120 equals the number of the ten Sephiroth multiplied by that of the Zodiac, whose key is the working of the Spirit and the four elements, typified in the wand which I bear.

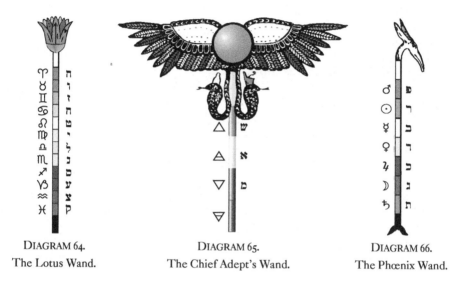

DIAGRAM 64.

The Lotus Wand.

DIAGRAM 65.

The Chief Adept's Wand.

DIAGRAM 66.

The Phœnix Wand.

[All then face East; the Chief Adept opens wide the Vault and places himself at the head of the Pastos, the Second Adept to the South, and the Third Adept to the North; they raise their wands in a pyramid formation over the altar, and their "cruces ansatas" below.]

Chief: Let us analyse the Key Word: I.
Second: N.
Third: R.
All: I.
Chief: Yod: ‫ י‬.
Second: Nun: ‫ נ‬.
Third: Resh: ‫ ר‬.
All: Yod: ‫ י‬.
Chief: Virgo, Isis, Mighty Mother.
Second: Scorpio, Apophis, Destroyer.
Third: Sol, Osiris, Slain and Risen.
All: Isis, Apophis, Osiris, IAO.
[The Wands and crosses are separated, all giving the sign of the cross, and saying:]

THE EQUINOX

The Sign of Osiris slain.
[*Chief*, giving the L sign with bowed head.*]
L. the Sign of the mourning of Isis.
[*Second*, with head erect, gives the V sign.]
V, the Sign of Typhon and Apophis.
[*Third*, with bowed head gives the X sign.]
X, the Sign of Osiris risen.
[*All* together with the signs of Osiris Slain and Osiris Risen.]
L V X, Lux, the Light of the Cross.
[*All* quit the Vault and return to previous places.]

Chief: In the Grand Word, Yeheshuah יהשוה, by the Key Word INRI, and through the Concealed Word LVX, I have opened the Vault of the Adepts.

[All present give the Lux sign as above.]

First Point.

[The officers in this part of the ceremony are the Second Adept, who is now the Principal Officer, the Third Adept, who is Second, and the Introducing Adept, who is spoken of as V.H. Frater Hodos Camelionis.

The *Second Adept* opens the First Point by bidding V.H. Fra: Hodos Camelionis prepare the Aspirant, who is waiting without, and the Associate Adeptus Minor to guard the inner side of the Portal.

The Aspirant is then admitted, and at once commences to read out a list of the grades and honours he has attained to. When he has finished, the *Second Adept* turns to him and says:]

It is not by the proclamation of honours and dignities, great though they may be, that thou canst gain admission to the Vault of the Adepts of the Rose of Ruby and the Cross of Gold; but only by that humility and purity of Spirit which befitteth the Aspirant unto higher Things.

[The Aspirant then retires and divests himself of his ornaments, and is clothed in the black robe of mourning with his hands bound behind him, and a chain about his neck. The Introducer then conducts him back to the door and gives a loud knock.]

Third Adept [opens the door and says:] By the aid of what symbol do ye seek admission?

Introducer: By the Flaming Sword, and the Serpent of Wisdom.

[The Aspirant is then made to kneel facing East between the Second Adept and the Third Adept, the Second Adept offering up a prayer which ends:]

. . . O God, the Vast One; Thou art in all things. O Nature, Thou Self from Nothing, for what can I else call Thee? In myself I am nothing; in Thee I am Self,

---

* For these signs see "Liber O," THE EQUINOX, vol. i. No. 2.

and exist in Thy Selfhood from Nothing. Live thou then in me, and bring me unto that Self which is in Thee. Amen.

[The *Third Adept* then earnestly bids the Aspirant not to look upon the trial of humility through which he has just passed as one ordained to jest with his feelings, but as a true manifestation of his own ignorance. The Aspirant shortly after this rises to his feet and the *Second Adept* addresses him as follows:]

Despise not sadness and hate not suffering. For they are the initiators of the Heart; and the black robe of mourning, which thou wearest, is at once the symbol of Sorrow and Strength. Boast not thyself about thy brother if he hath fallen; for how knowest thou that thou couldst have withstood the same temptation. Slander not and revile not; if thou canst not praise, do not condemn; and when thou seest another in trouble and humiliation, even though he be thine enemy, remember the time of thine own humiliation, when thou didst kneel before the door of the Vault, clothed in the robe of mourning, with the chain of affliction about thy neck, and thine hands bound behind thy back, and rejoice not at his fall. And in thine intercourse with the Members of our Order, let thine hand given unto another be a sincere and genuine pledge of fraternity; respect his or her secrets and feelings, as thou wouldst respect thine own; bear with one another, and forgive one another—even as the Master hath said.

V.H. Fra: Hodos Camelionis, what is the symbolic age of the Aspirant?

Introducer: His days are 120 years.

[The *Third Adept* further explains this as follows:]

This refers to the five grades of the First Order, through which it is necessary for the Aspirant to have passed before he can enter the Vault of the Sacred Mountain. For the three months' interval between the grades of Practicus and Philosophus is the Regimen of the Elements; and the seven months interval between the First and Second Orders symbolises the Regimen of the Planets. While the Elements and the Planets both work in the Zodiac, so that $(3 + 7) \times 12$ yieldeth the number 120.

[After this the Aspirant must take a solemn obligation: first he is bound to the Cross of Suffering, the *Second Adept* saying:]

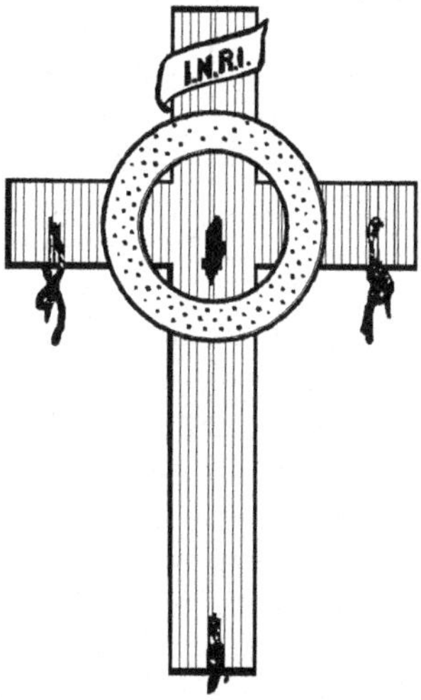

DIAGRAM 68.

The Cross of Suffering.

The Symbol of Suffering is the Symbol of Victory; wherefore, bound though thou art, strive to rise this with thy hands: for he that will not strive shall be left in outer darkness.

[The *Second Adept* then raises his hands on high and cries:]

I invoke Thee, the Great Avenging Angel H U A, in the divine name I∴ A∴ O∴,

THE EQUINOX

that thou mayest invisibly place thine hand upon the head of this Aspirant in attestation of his obligation. [The Aspirant then repeats the obligation after him, saying;]

כתר. I, "Christian Rosenkreutz," a member of the body of Christ, do this day, on behalf of the Universe, spiritually bind myself, even as I am now bound physically unto the Cross of Suffering:

חכמה. That I will do the utmost to lead a pure and unselfish life. . . .

בינה. That I will keep secret all things connected with the Order . . . that I will maintain the Veil of strict secrecy between the First and Second Order.

חסד. That I will uphold to the utmost the authority of the Chiefs of the Order.

גבורה. Furthermore that I will perform all practical work connected with this Order, in a place concealed . . . that I will keep secret this inner Rosicrucian Knowledge . . . that I will only perform any practical magic before the uninitiated which is of a simple and already well-known nature, and that I will show them no secret mode of working whatsoever. . . .

תפארת. I further solemnly promise and swear that, with the Divine permission, I will from this day forward apply myself unto the Great Work, which is so to purify and exalt my spiritual Nature that with the Divine Aid I may at length attain to be more than human, and thus gradually rise and unite myself to my higher and divine Genius, and that in this event I will not abuse the Great Power entrusted unto me.

נצח. I furthermore solemnly pledge myself never to work at any important Symbol or Talisman without first invoking the Highest Divine Names connected therewith; and especially not to debase my knowledge of Practical Magic to purposes of Evil. . . .

הוד. I further promise always to . . . display brotherly love and forbearance towards the members of the whole Order. . . .

יסוד. I also undertake to work unassisted at the subjects prescribed for study in the various practical grades. . . .

מלכות. Finally, if in my travels I should meet a stranger who professes to be a member of the Rosicrucian Order, I will examine him with care, before acknowledging him to be so.

[The obligation being finished, the Chain of Humility and the Robe of Mourning are removed from the Aspirant, and the *Third Adept* completes the *First Point* by communicating verbally the following history of the Order of the Rose and Cross to the Aspirant:]

Know then, O Aspirant, that the mysteries of the Rose and Cross have existed from time immemorial, and that its mystic rites were practised, and its hidden knowledge communicated in the initiations of the various races of antiquity—Egypt, Eleusis, and Samothrace; Persia, Chaldea, and India alike cherished its mysteries, and thus handed down to posterity the Secret Wisdom of the Ancient Ages. Many were its

Temples, and among many nations were they established; though in process of time some lost the purity of their primal knowledge. Howbeit the manner of its introduction into medieval Europe was thus:

In 1378 was born the chief and originator of our Fraternity in Europe. He was of a noble German family, but poor, and (1383) in the fifth year of his age, was he placed in a cloister, where he learned both Greek and Latin.

1393. While yet a youth he accompanied a certain brother P.A.L. in a pilgrimage to the Holy Land, but the latter dying at Cyprus, he himself went on to Damascus. There was then in Arabia a Temple of our Order, which was called by the Hebrew name of Damcar (רמכר), that is, Blood of the Lamb. Here he was duly initiated, and took the mystic title of C.R.C., Christian Rosenkreutz or Christian Rosy Cross. He there so far improved his knowledge of the Arabian tongue, that in the following year he translated the book "M" into Latin, which he afterwards brought back with him to Europe.

1396. After three years he went into Egypt, where was another temple of our Order; there he remained for a time, still studying the mysteries of nature.

1398. After this he travelled by sea to the city of Fessa or Fez. . . . Of the Fraternity at Fez, he confessed that they had not retained our knowledge in its primal purity, and that their Kabbalah was to a certain extent altered to their religion, yet nevertheless he learned much there.

1400. After a stay of two years, he came back into Spain, where he endeavoured to reform the errors of the learn d according to the pure knowledge which he had received; but it was to them a laughing matter, and they reviled and rejected him, even as the prophets of old were rejected.

1402. Thus also was he treated by those of his own and other nations, when he showed them the errors in religion which had crept in. So after five years' residence in Germany (1408) he initiated thereof his former monastic brethren, Fratres G.V., I.A., and I.O., who had more knowledge than many others at that time, and by these four was made the foundation of the Fraternity in Europe. These worked and studied at the writings and other knowledge which C.R.C. had brought with him, and by them was some of the magical language transcribed. . . .

1409. The four Fratres also erected a building to serve for the Temple and Headquarters of their Order, and called it "Collegium ad Spiritum Sanctum" or "College of the Holy Spirit." . . .

1410. They initiated four others, namely, Fratres R.C., the son of the deceased father's brother of C.R.C.; B., a skilful artist; G.G.; and P.D., who was to be Cancellarius; all being Germans, except I.A., and now eight in number.

Their agreement was:

(1) That none of them should profess any other thing but to cure the sick, and that gratis.

(2) That they should not be constrained to wear any particular distinctive dress, but therein to follow the custom of the country.

(3) That every year on the day "Corpus Christi" they should meet at the Collegium ad Spiritum Sanctum or write cause of absence.

(4) That every one should look for some worthy person of either sex, who after his decease might succeed him.

(5) The word R.C. to be their mark, seal, and character.

(6) The Fraternity to remain secret 100 years.

Five of the brethren where to travel in different countries, and two to remain with Christian Rosenkreutz.

[The *Second Adept* then takes up the Narrative:]

... The discovery then of the Vault of the Adepts, wherein that highly illuminated man of God, our Father, Christian Rosenkreutz was buried, occurred as follows:

1600. After Frater A. died in Gallia Narbonensi, there succeeded in his place Frater N.N.; he, while repairing a part of the Building of the College of the Holy Spirit, endeavoured to remove a brass memorial tablet, which contained the names of certain brethren and some other things. In this tablet was the head of a long and strong nail or bolt, so that when the tablet was forcibly wrenched away, it pulled with it a large stone, which thus partially uncovered a secret door, upon which was inscribed "POST CXX ANNOS PATEBO." ...

[The Aspirant then leaves the Portal of the Vault and the First Point is at an end.]

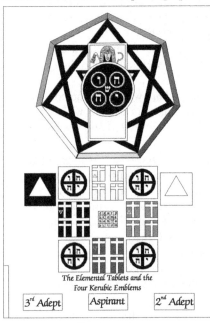

The Elemental Tablets and the Four Kerubic Emblems

| 3rd Adept | Aspirant | 2nd Adept |

DIAGRAM 69.

The Temple in the Second Point of the 5°=6° Ritual.

Second Point.

[The *Chief Adept* lies in the Pastos upon his back in full regalia; the complete symbol of the Rose and Cross on his breast hung by double phoenix collar; arms crossed on breast, not hiding symbol; hands rest on shoulders bearing scourge and crook; between them and under them the Taro.

The lid of the Pastos is closed and the Altar stands over its centre.

The *Second* and *Third Adepts* are outside the Vault.

The Elemental and Kerubic Figures hang outside the door of the Vault.

THE TEMPLE OF SOLOMON THE KING

The Aspirant is admitted, and the Second Adept explains to him the symbolism of the door, ending by saying:]

Forget not, therefore, that the Tablets and Kerubim are the guardians of the Vault of the Adepts. Let thy tongue keep silent on our mysteries, and restrain even the thoughts of thy heart, lest a bird of the air should carry the matter.

[The *Third Adept* then points out to the Aspirant that beneath the letters CXX he will find the following ✠ ⋎ X which is equivalent to "Post annos Lux Crucis Patebo" —"At the end of the years, I, the Light of the Cross, will disclose myself." ...

(The door of the Vault is then opened.)

[The "Second Adept" then points out to the Aspirant that the Vault is lit by the rays of the symbolic Rose, and that in the middle of the Vault stands the circular Altar* with these devices: A.G.R.C., "Ad Gloriam Rosae Crucis;" or A.C.R.G., "Ad Crucis Rosae Gloriam," followed by "Hoc Universi Compendium Unius Mihi Sepulchrum Feci," *i.e.*, "Unto the Glory of the Rosy Cross, I have constructed this Sepulchre for myself as a compendium of the Universal Unity." The rest of the Altar Symbolism is explained in the diagram. After this explanation a prayer is offered up, and the *Third Adept* hands to the Aspirant the chain from the Altar, bidding him accept it as a bond of "suffering and self-sacrifice." The *Second Adept* takes the dagger and cup from the Altar, and, dipping the dagger in the cup, marks a cross on the Aspirant's forehead, after which he hands to the Aspirant the rose-cross symbol. Then the *Third Adept* opens the upper half of the Pastos, and says:]

And the Light shineth in the Darkness; but the Darkness comprehendeth it not.

[The *Second Adept* then orders the Aspirant to touch with his wand the rose and cross upon the breast of the form before him and say, "Out of the darkness let the light arise."]

[The *Chief Adept*, without moving, says:]

Buried with that LIGHT in a mystical Death, rising again in a mystical resurrection, Cleansed and Purified through him our MASTER, O Brother of the Cross of the Rose! Like him, O Adepts of all ages, have ye toiled; like him have ye suffered Tribulation. Poverty, Torture, and Death have ye passed through. They have been but the purification of the Gold.

In the Alembic of thine Heart,
Through the Athanor of Affliction,
Seek thou the true stone of the Wise.

      *   *   *   *   *   *

Quit thou this Vault, then, O Aspirant, with thine arms crossed upon thy breast, bearing in thy right hand the Crook of Mercy and in thy left hand the Scourge of Severity,† the emblems of those Eternal Forces, betwixt which in equilibrium the

---

* See Diagram 79.   † See Diagram 74.

Universe dependeth: these forces whose reconciliation is the Key of Life, whose separation is evil and Death. . . .

[The *Third Adept* then continues Frater N.N.'s narrative, in which are mentioned the names of the early brothers. He ends by saying:]

Ex Deo Nascimur; In Jesu Morimur; Per Spiritum Sanctum Reviviscimus.

[The Pastos is then closed and the Aspirant quits the Vault, which is made ready for the third part of the Ceremony.]

Third Point.

(The Temple is arranged as in Diagram.)

[The Third Point commences as follows:]

Second Adept: and lo! Two angels in white, sitting, the one at the head and the other at the foot, where the body of the Master had lain; who said: "Why seek ye the living among the dead?"

DIAGRAM 70.
The Temple in the Third Point of the
5°=6° Ritual.

Chief Adept: I am the Resurrection and the Life: he that believeth in me, though he were dead, yet shall he live, and whosoever liveth and believeth on me, shall never die.

Second Adept: Behold the Image [directing attention to lower half of lid*] of the Justified One, crucified on the Cross of the Infernal Rivers of Death, and thus rescuing Malkuth from the Folds of the Red Dragon.

Third Adept: And being turned [directing attention to upper half] I saw seven golden light-bearers, and in the midst of the seven light-bearers, one like unto the Ben Adam, clothed with a garment down unto the foot, and girt with golden girdle. His head and His hair were white as snow, and His eyes as flaming fire. His feet like unto fine brass, as if they burned in a furnace; and His voice as the sound of many waters. And He had in His right hand Seven Stars, and out of His Mouth went the Sword of Flame, and His countenance was as thoe sun in its strength.

Chief Adept: I am the First and I am the Last, I am He that liveth but was dead, and behold I am alive for evermore, and hold the keys of Hell and of Death.

---

* See Diagram 71.

THE TEMPLE OF SOLOMON THE KING

[The *Second* and Third Adepts lead the Aspirant into the Vault; all kneel save the *Chief Adept*, who, extending his arms, says:]

For I know that my Redeemer liveth, and that he shall stand at the latter day upon the Earth. I am the Way, the Truth and the Life, no man cometh unto the Father but by Me. I am the Purified, I have passed through the Gates of Darkness unto Light, I have fought upon Earth for Good, I have finished my Work, I have entered into the Invisible. I am the Sun in his rising. I have passed through the hour of cloud and of night. I am Amoun, the Concealed One, the Opener of the Day. I am Osiris Onnophris, the Justified One. I am the Lord of Life triumphant over Death, there is no part of Me that is not of the Gods. I am the Preparer of the Pathway; the Rescuer unto the Light.

Out of the Darkness let that Light arise!

[At these words the Aspirant and the two *Adepts* bow their heads and say:]

Before I was blind, but now I see.

[Then the *Chief Adept* says:]

I am the Reconciler with the Ineffable, I am the Dweller of the Invisible; let the white Brilliance of the Divine Spirit descend. [A short pause.] Arise now an Adeptus Minor of the Rose of Ruby and Cross of Gold, in the Sign of Osiris Slain.

[The *Chief Adept* then explains to the Aspirant the Mystic number of this Grade — 21; the Pass-word Eheieh (אהיה); and the Key-word, INRI, after which he explains to him the diagram of the Minutum Mundum as follows:]

Behold the diagram of "Minutum Mundum Sive Fundamentum Coloris"— "The Small Universe or the Foundation of Color." Treasure it in thine heart and mark it

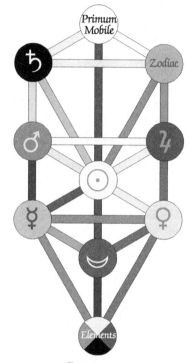

DIAGRAM 71.
Minutum Mundum.

well, seeing that therein is the Key of Nature. It is as thou seest the Diagram of the Sephiroth and Paths, with the appropriate colours attributed thereto. See that thou reveal it not to the profane, for many and great are its mysteries.

Kether is the highest of all; and therein scintillates the Divine White Brilliance, concerning which it is not fitting that I should speak more fully.

Chokmah is Grey (opalescent), the mixture of colours.

Binah is darkness (iridescence, black-opal), the absorption of colours; and thus is the Supernal Triad completed.

In Kether is the root of Golden Glory, and thence is the Yellow reflected into Tiphereth.

In Chokmah is the root of Blue, and this is reflected into Chesed.

In Binah is the root of Red, and this is reflected into Geburah, and thus is the first reflected Triad completed.

The beams of Chesed and Tiphereth meet in Netzach and yield Green.

The beams of Geburah and Tiphereth meet in Hod and yield Orange-tawny. The beams of Chesed and Geburah fall in Jesod and yield Purple, and thus is the third Triad completed.

And from the rays of the third Triad are these three colours shown in Malkuth, together with a fourth, which is their synthesis.

For from the Orange-tawny of Hod and the greening nature of Netzach is reflected a certain greenish Citron—Citrine.

From the Orange-tawny of mixed with the Puce of Yesod, prodeedeth a Red-russet brown-Russet.

And from the Green and the Puce there cometh a certain other darkening Green—Olive.

And the synthesis of all these is blackness and bordereth upon the Qliphoth.

But the colours of the 22 Paths are derived from and find their root in those of the first reflected Triad of the Sephiroth (the three Supernals otherwise not entering into their composition), and thus are their positive colours formed.

Unto Air, א, is ascribed the yellow colour of Tiphereth.

Unto Water, מ, is ascribed the blue colour of Chesed.

Unto Fire, ש, is ascribed the red colour of Geburah.

The colours of Earth are to be found in Malkuth.

Those of the planets are in the Rainbow thus:

ת Saturn.	Indigo.	ד Venus.	Green.
כ Jupiter	Violet.	ב Mercury.	Yellow.
פ Mars.	Scarlet.	ג Luna.	Blue.
ר Sol.	Orange.		

Unto the signs of the Zodiac are ascribed the following:

ה Aries.	Scarlet.	ל Libra.	Emerald.
ו Taurus.	Red-Orange.	נ Scorpio.	Greenish Blue.
ז Gemini.	Orange.	ס Sagittarius.	Deep Blue.
ח Cancer.	Amber.	ע Capricornus.	Indigo.
ט Leo.	Greenish Yellow.	צ Aquarius.	Violet.
י Virgo.	Yellow-Green.	ק Pisces.	Crimson.

THE TEMPLE OF SOLOMON THE KING

Further, thou wilt observe that the Colours of the Paths and the Sephiroth form a mutual balance and harmony in the Tree. . . .

[The *Chief Adept* then greets the newly made adeptus Minor with the name of Frater Hodos Chamelionis.

The *Second Adept* then explains the colours of the Crook and the Scourge, pointing out that the Crook is divided into the Colours symbolic of Kether, Air, Chokmah,

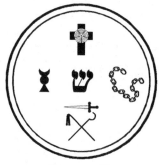

DIAGRAM 73.
The Emblems on the Altar.

Taurus, Chesed, Leo, Aries, Tiphereth, Capricornus and Hod. And the Scourge into those colours symbolising Netzach, Scoripo, Tiphereth, Gemini, Binah, Cancer, Geburah and Water.

The *Third Adept* then explains the Admission badge of the Sword and the Serpent, saying:]

. . . The one is descending, the other ascending; the one is Fixed, the other is the Volatile; the one unites the Sephiroth and the other the Paths. Furthermore in the Serpent of Wisdom is shown the ascending spiral, and in the Sword the rush of the descending White Brilliance from beyond Kether. . . .

[This explanation being finished, the *Chief Adept* leads the Aspirant to the Diagram of the Mystic Titles and Grades, and says:]

This is the symbolic mountain of God in the centre of the Universe, the Sacred Rosicrucian Mountain of Initiation, the Mystic Mountain of the Caverns, even the Mountain of Abiegnus.

[This diagram shows a mountain crowned with light, and surrounded with darkness. At its base is the wall of Secrecy, whose sole gate is formed by the two pillars of Hermes. The ascent of the mountain is made by the Serpent of Wisdom.

The explanation of this diagram being concluded, the *Second* and *Third Adepts* remove the Altar, and the

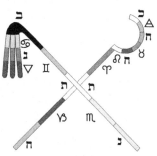

DIAGRAM 74.
The Crook and Scourge.

Chief Adept completes the Third Point by instructing the Aspirant in the mystic symbolism of the Vault itself, as follows:]

The Vault consists of three principal parts:

(1) The Ceiling, a brilliant white.

(2) the Heptagonal walls, of seven colours.

(3) The Floor, chiefly black.

The ceiling consists of a triangle, enclosing a Rose of twenty-two petals surrounded by a heptagram. On the triangle are the three Supernal Sephiroth, and in the heptangle the seven lower ones.

THE EQUINOX

The Floor is black, having upon it also a triangle enclosed with a heptagram, bearing the titles of the Averse and Evil Sephiroth as shown by the Great Red Dragon with seven heads. In the midst of the Evil Triangle is the rescuing symbol of the Golden Cross united to the Red Rose of forty-nine petals. . . . "But the Whiteness above shineth the brighter for the Blackness which is beneath, and thus mayest thou at length comprehend that even the evil helpeth forward the good."

"And between that Light and that Darkness vibrate the seven colours of the Rainbow," which are shown forth in the seven walls, each of which consists of forty squares representing the ten Sephiroth; the four Cherubim; the Eternal Spirit; the three Alchemic Principles; the three Elements; the seven Planets, and the twelve Signs.

DIAGRAM 75.
The Wall of the Vault.

DIAGRAM 76.
The Black Calvary Cross.

Upon the Altar is placed the Black Calvary Cross charged with a rose of twenty-five petals representing the counterchanged action of the Spirit and the four Elements.

[All quit Vault.]

[The *Chief Adept* then points out that the head end of the Pastos is white and is charged with a Golden Greek Cross and red rose of forty-nine petals,* that the Foot is black, with a white Calvary Cross and Circle upon a pedestal or Da‹s of three steps,

* See Diagram 80.

222

and that on the sides are depicted the twenty-two colours of the paths between Light and Darkness.

The Chief then gives the Aspirant the grip of this grade and the Third Point is finished.]

DIAGRAM 81.

The Cross at the Foot of the Pastos.

THE CLOSING

[The *Chief Adept* asks the very honoured Fratres and Sorores to help him close the Vault of the Adepts, and then says as he rises and closes the door:]

"Post centum viginti annos patebo." Thus have I closed the Vault of the Adepts, in the Mystic Mountain of Abiegnus.

Third Adept: Ex Deo Nascimur.

Second Adept: In Jeheshuah Morimur.

Chief Adept: Per Sanctum Spiritum Reviviscimus.

[All present give the LVX sign in silence.]

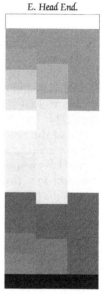

E. Head End.

DIAGRAM 82.

The Side of the Pastos.

The following explanation of the above ritual by P. we give below in its entirety, for it is a great help in properly understanding the 5°=6° Ceremony. The reader must, however, bear in mind that it was not written till nearly three years after the present date, and this fact no doubt accounts for several Eastern expressions of thought creeping in.

FRATER P.'S SKETCH FOR AN EXPLANATION OF THE 5°=6° RITUAL OF ADEPTUS MINOR.

In this Grade there are three officers:

Isis,   Apophis, (replaced by Horus)   and Osiris.

Chesed,   Geburah,   Tiphereth.

Yet their functions are in a sense counterchanged, the Chief Adept representing

223

Osiris in the main ceremony, and the Third Adept reflecting the benignant character of Isis.

The knocks which open the ceremony are seven, as it is written: "He made them Six; and for the seventh He cast into the midst of them the Fire of the Sun." For Tiphereth 5°=6° is a Solar degree.

After this the signs are given and the portal is guarded in the usual manner; for the intention in all the grades is identical, namely, that of harmonising the temple with the ceremony.

THE FIRST VIBRATION.

Not only are the knocks symbolic of the Hexagram as above; but they refer to the moving of the Divine Spirit of Fire upon the Waters. For this is the First Breath of the Light, a brooding thereof.

THE SECOND VIBRATION.

The Second appearance of the Light is as a flash of Lightning; the Flaming Sword. This is shown by 21, the number of Eheieh, the Divine Name of Kether; then the Tiphereth symbol of the Vault; and last the centre of the Earth affirmed in turn.

This descent from Kether to Malkuth formulates the Flaming Sword, and thus is the Light invoked in the second place.

The Seal is IAO, IHShVH= 17 + 326 = 343 = 7 × 7 × 7, *i.e.*, 7 made into a cube, the formation of the Stone of the Wise from the seven-fold regimen, and the fixation of the Wanderers (the seven planets, or of the volatile.). 777 = One is She the Ruach Elohim of Lives, and the Flaming Sword, and Olahm ha Qliphoth.

Moreover 17 is the Svastika and IHShVH—the Pentagram again, the marriage of Isis and Osiris (as shown by the signs in the key-word).

Now the Flaming Sword is a swift and transitory symbol; the solidity and permanence of Light is given in the pyramidal symbol. But the Flaming Sword is always the Beginning after the Ruach Elohim hath moved upon the surface of the waters; as here, so in the further ritual.

Further, they being now in Tiphereth, they will formulate that which is Kether in Tiphereth, the Rose and Cross.

The Key to the Vault is the Rose and Cross—Life. That which is alive is buried there: not that which is dead in very truth. Also we must first be crucified. Also the Rose and Cross resumes INRI.

Now INRI conceals IAO, and IAO besides its Apophis signification (for IAO is the Gnostic Name of the Most High IAIDA) is Amoun descending—He, the Concealed One! when Isis and Osiris are united. It is the Ankh which is held in the hand of Chesed, and reveals the man whose majesty is that of the ten Sephiroth (which are combined in the Ankh);* but in a passive way. This and the wands are the

* See Diagram 61.

correlatives of the Serpent and the Sword; for the Sword is active, the Serpent passive, while the active Wand* in each case is of the paths, and the passive Ankh of the Sephiroth. The Ankh is held by the Kether band, seeing that to Kether alone should we hold fast in the passive reception of light (passive because it is held in the left hand); in order to project light, &c, we have a wand in our *right* hand, and this is held in different ways for different purposes. On the breast, Tiphereth in equilibrium, we have the twenty-two letters as a rose; the nine Planets, five Elements and three Alchemicals as a Cross (39= IHVH + AChD), in all sixty-one symbols,† *i.e.*, the AIN (= 61) is thus denoted. The Rose and Cross being united, they bring down into the centre of all the Divine White Brilliance of Kether, in which is shown another Rose Cross, no longer of divided light, but Ruby of the Holy Spirit; of Gold, the Glory of the Light; of Green rays because Isis shines forth—a new Creation. This higher Rose Cross is again the mystery of the Higher Genius descending into Kether, when the Lower is in Tiphereth established. For in all things are higher and lower; *e.g.*, Binah, Chesed and Hod are all Water, but in a different manner and degree.‡

THE WANDS.§

Isis hath the wand of Thoth, its head being in Kether and its bands showing אמן,
= אמשת, which shows Chesed ד as summing the Supernals.¶

Horus hath the wand of Osiris his Father.

Osiris hath the wand of Isis his Mother.

Note especially ☿ in ♍ : The Thoth-wand for Isis.

☉ in ♌ : The Osiris-wand for Horus.

♀ in ♉ : The Isis-wand for Osiris.

All are thus linked with the Higher. Also we add ☿ ♍ ☉ ♌ ♀ ♉ and obtain 231 = 0 + 1 + . . . + 21 = the Sum of the Numbers of the Keys of the Tarot. Further, Amoun—the Winged Globe—is again shown when Isis and Osiris are united. Further, 5 + 9 + 14 (the bands on the wands)=28 Power כה, for these are the total of the Bands thereon.

Also the Globe is Light, the Phœnix Life, the Lotus Love. (Symbol of Binary, The *Prong*, see Dante. This prong points downwards. Arms of Typhon in 16th key.) They also show the development of creation (Lotus wand) operated by rebirth (Phœnix wand), presided over by the Kerubic working and the Everlasting wings (Chief Adept's wand).

* The Three Wands contain the twenty-two Paths. See Diagrams 64, 65, 66.
† See Diagram 63. ‡ See Diagram 63.
§ See Diagrams 64, 65, 66.
¶ The Three Supernals are in a way summed up in Chesed, ד being the dividing line. ‖ Not ♂ in ♏.

THE EQUINOX

We now turn to the important symbolism of the number 120. It is סמך and the arrow hieroglyph which has been sufficiently explained in Z. and the Portal Ritual. It emphasises the Pentagram formula,* that only the purified man IHShVH can enter here. Also 120 = 4 × 5 × 6 (Chesed, Geburah, Tiphereth). It is 12, HVA, divided in the 10 Sephiroth. In Coptic, IHO= 120 by shape = ♍ ♈ ♑ = Yetziratically 85 = a flower or cup. The previous symbols have formulated the Rainbow, and this is the arrow cleaving them. The *Chief Adept* now begins a new vibration with a knock, the shrine and Adepti having formulated the Great Work. This second vibration may be read hieroglyphically as follows:

By the Sephiroth and the Paths we work; the Rose and Cross united, we are; and Kether is in our Tiphereths by Light, Life, and Love, reached by the path cleaving the Rainbow.

This, therefore, seals all present as adepts, and also serves to equilibrate perfectly the Vault for reception of the light, while also formulating the first beginnings of that Light.

THE THIRD VIBRATION.

All face East to salute the rising sun. The door is opened wide, since the great Work is formulated, and the three Adepti formulate by their position the Triangle of the Supernals, as if it descended from the Roof of the Vault. Then by joining their Wands and Ankhs they formulate the Pyramid—(is not this Vault of Abiegnus the Chamber of the King in the Great Pyramid of Cheops?)—the most stable of forms, the three showing forth the four, since the Triangles form a tetrahedron. For אמן occultly spelleth 741 = אמשת. Also the Pyramid = 4 × 3= 12 HVA. Thus also each hath 3 letters of 3 words, but all together seal each 3 within a fourth, the synthesis of the 3.

Note also: י = Fire in יהוה, ♏ is the Water Cherub. That he is Amoun also is shown by the Eagle whose wings are those of the Winged Globe. The Sun shineth in the Air.†

But in the signs they are united first of all in the Sign of Light, +. The LVX differentiates this light, as is explained in the Ritual itself.

First Point.

Know ye that the whole Object of the Ritual is to unite the Postulant with Osiris, represented by the Chief Adept, save when he again taketh his Wand and Ankh and instructeth the Postulant, and is Isis, the Revealer of the Mysteries.

In the first point the Chief Adept does not appear. He is the slain and hidden Osiris in the nether world.

Therefore the Postulant in order to be identified with him must be slain. He is

---

* That is, $1 \times 2 \times 3 \times 4 \times 5 = 120$.

† These three are united in the fourth—Earth, because the second ה is the Earthy sign of Virgo.

226

also to be put though the IAO formula of Creation, Death and Resurrection, in a lesser way, interwoven with the greater. Thus his first admission is of *mourning*.

The *Second Adept* is still Horus.

But the *Third Adept* is now Anubis.

Introducing Adept is still Themis.

They are, as it were, the guardians of the body of the slain Osiris. For initials ', c and θ see Z. explanation in 0°=0° Ritual. A , (Knock) commences the new Vibration. He is prepared by Themis.

The alarm of , , , , . , places the 4 before the 1, and Anubis at once challenges.

The Aspirant, not waiting for his Higher Self (θ) to speak, assumes the Horus formula (wearing his lamen), and seeketh to take by force the Kingdom of Heaven.

Horus arises as it were insulted. He, the chief Guardian of the Tomb—shall this one enter, the not even initiated?

The Sword and Serpent are given back to him, but not yet united as in the Rose Cross. He is therefore clothed in black to show his uninitiated state and the darkness in which he walks; his hands are bound; the middle pillar only is free; yet is there also a chain about his neck, the binding of Daäth,* so that the Higher and Lower Wills may connect. But his Tiphereth is not bound: his Lower Will must of itself aspire. This time is *One* Knock given as it were for very feebleness of nature, yet formulating Kether.

The Higher Self now speaks for Postulant, and they are admitted by the Aspiration of Postulant (Serpent) and the Divine Light descending in answer (Flaming Sword), as it is written "While he was yet a great way off, his father saw him and ran——." He hath returned, showing the value of persistent Will. The Serpent and Flaming Sword are Wisdom and Strength, the slow but subtle movement of the Serpent, the rush of the Lightning flash, caring naught for obstacles.

These conjoint are 32,† that is, the joining of Arikh and Zauir Anpin in AHIHVH (32). And 32= ChZIZ (lightnings) ZKH (was pure) and LB (heart); also LB = ♎ ☿—the Equilibration of Creation. Also, though the force of his obligation is shown as binding,—note well that it is also that force which admits him. The Aspirant cannot even kneel without help.

Prayer of the Second Adept

Formulates Chesed, Geburah, and Tiphereth, the Triangle Water, and finally Kether, as it is written: "and the Ruach Elohim moved upon the face of the waters." This is an invocation of the higher and the first formulation of the Light in the Postulate (*cf.* Opening—the Knock).

---

* Daäth prevents his lower will connecting with his higher will.

† The Sword, the Ten Sephiroth. The Serpent, the Twenty-two letters; together the Thirty-two paths.

THE EQUINOX

His hands are unbound that he may help himself. The humility lesson is formulated in Ruach, and Daäth is rebuked openly (as chain does so occultly).

Aspirant must rise unaided; and the only help his initiators can give him is to force him to kneel.

Charge to Aspirant.

Black is not only evil; it is the "charge" (*i.e.*, flashing colour) of Spirit. Fraternal pity is formulated, as well as sympathy.

The 120 (Sagittarius) is then formulated in Aspirant. Note that the Opening Symbolism, as it were, foreshadows that of the Ritual proper. This formula is also one of equilibration: *vide* explanation of the 14th Key in the Portal Ritual. The 3 and 7 are united in Aspirant, and also the 12. Thus is his Rose (22) formulated, while the five grades formulate his Cross (5 squares).

The Aspirant is now the purified man, in touch with his Jechidah, *but in Kether only as yet.*

His crucifixion equilibrates as well as binds, and formulates occultly the LVX.

The purpose of his consenting is to raise the Rose Cross, *i.e.*, to bring redemption unto men.

The adjuration to HVA follows, after which the Obligation, which consists of ten clauses, corresponding to the ten Sephiroth. The Kether of the man speaking binds the nine lower Sephiroth:

> *Chokmah*, which would (in its failure, since everything but Kether has an evil aspect) lack purity (by its duality; and devotion and service (by opposing itself to Kether).
>
> *Binah*, which would unveil mysteries.
>
> *Chesed*, which would rebel against authority and be slack in exercising it.
>
> *Geburah*, which would display its strength and boast thereof.
>
> *Tiphereth*, which would be normally the mere human Will.
>
> *Netzach*, which would fall unless Divine Names aided it; *vide* 4°=7° Altar Diagram, and Nogah is *natural* splendour, a mere bubble.
>
> *Hod*, which would talk and lie; its positive promise is sexual; for Mercury is hermaphrodite.
>
> *Jesod*, which is solid and sluggish, and would be idle and content with what it had done.
>
> *Malkuth*, which needs one to point out illusory nature of matter, and tree of Knowledge of Good and Evil.

The Stigmata.

Formulate the LVX Cross. *Cf.* Ateh, Malkuth, ve Geburah, ve Gedulah, le' Olahm, AMEN. (The Stigmata being formed by touching the forehead, feet, right hand, left hand and heart.)

Thus the Sephiroth are equilibrated in both directions as in the Equinox Ritual.*

The Versicles will be seen to be very appropriate to each Sephira. This application of the Stigmata fixes the Light, as the Flaming Sword is a transitory Symbol (see Opening).

The Aspirant may now resume his emblems; after which Themis commemorates the Life and Death of Osiris under the figure of Christian Rosenkreutz, as it were.

The Morning of Isis. For Aspirant being now *dead*, Isis mourneth for him. But Aspirant also mourneth, that L sign may be formulated in him. She points out Rose Cross as an external emblem of the Completion of the Great Work. In the life of Jesus Christ the Master, the most notable events are—he is cloistered at 5; when 30 he takes disciples and begins ministrations. When 32 (paths and Sephiroth) he takes 4 others and is the One among the 7 (or the 3 and the 4=12). At 106 he dies (106 is !attained! and נב מ).

The symbolism of 120 having been accomplished, his tomb is found. This is the tomb of the Postulant.

(Note Geomantic Angelic Symbolism of IAO and INRI.)

The L Sign is the Svastika. (See Z in 0°=0° Ritual for meaning.) Also Svastika hath 17 squares showing IAO synthetical.† And the Svastika includeth the Cross, "even as a child in the Womb of its Mother to develop itself anew," &c. &c. (Cry of 29th Æthyr.)‡ The Cubical Svastika hath 78 faces = Tarot and Mezla. It is also א = Air and Zero. It shows the Initiation of a Whirling Force.

The V sign is that of Apophis and Typhon. It is the Y of Pythagoras; it is the arms flung up of the drowning man and therefore = 12th key and מ. It is also the Horns of the mediaeval Devil. It shows the binding and apparent death of the force, without which it cannot come to any perfection.

The X sign is that of the Pentagram. It showeth the Triumph of the Light. It is ש descended, and therefore Fire. Moreover the Pentagram formulateth the 10 Sephiroth. (Is not the Flaming Sword the Pentagram unwound?) It is the final rise in perfect equilibrium of the force.

The whole is LVX. Showing the Light imperfect, until it hath descended into Hell. (Sowing—waiting—reaping. Cyst reproduction of some simple animals. Hibernation, &c.) The arms are stretched out and then refolded—effort and peace. The Cross Sign shows ה: and all four are thus AMThSh and AMN. The Vibrations pass with the Sun, of course.

The Light being thus fixed in the Vault, all leave the same and the seal is given.

Second Point.

The Vault is opened in Tiphereth symbols in three words of three, four, and five letters each, (the Triangle, the Cross and the Pentagram), though IHSVH shows Pentagram INRI, Rose Cross, and conceals Cross, the Lux.

---

* A Golden Dawn Ritual omitted here for lack of space.† = 6 + 1 + 10 = 17.

‡ See "The Elemental Calls of Dr. Dee."

Note very carefully the interchanging symbols of the Adepti throughout. They are not separate, but overlap; and this shows the absolute necessity of a fraternal and sympathetic feeling. All repeat signs, as all partake of the Lux. The Postulant, bearing the wand of Isis, may pass within the gate of Isis (Venus). Also he bears the Ankh.

The Postulant is led into the Vault; and he thus beginneth to tread down the forces of evil, which, be it well remembered, support him.

He is placed in the North as in 0°=0°, but here he is not in the sign ♉ (redemption), but of ♏; for he is dead or disintegrated into his component parts. Also, as shown by *Libertas Evangelii*, he is in the position of free choice—his Lower Will must decide the result. The Seven are about him—the Universe watches his choice. Note the 7 × 40 = 280 symbolism. For 280 is Sandalphon, who in 1° = 10° made him a path: it is also MNTzPK, the five letters of Severity and judgment, and קֹף, terror, also יעֹר, the angel of the wood of the world of Assiah, since the greater part of it is sterile trees.

The *Third Adept* is on the southern side of the Pastos—Themis as *Legis Jugum*, and Horus in the Fire position. Nobody is in the quarter of Air, where wait the other fragments of Postulant: his Nephesch being thus ready to be glorified.

The attention of the Postulant is at once called to the Roof; his Lower Will looketh upwards, and he sees at last the *Invisible Light*.

The Altar shows: (1) The Great Work as the compendium of Unity; (2) IHSVH Symbol accomplishing this and expanded within into five circles. This shows that the five principles of man must be united perfectly.*

The Lion and ׳ with the Rose Cross represents the First Cause, the Dawn, the Virgin Mother, and the Great Work. *Nequaquam Vaccum†* shows that "Before Abraham was, I am!"

The Eagle and ה with the Cup represent the Blood shed for the remission of sins, and the Chalice of the Stoistes. *Libertas Evangelii* shows free-will.

The Man with ו and the dagger shows the *last Result*. ו is ♉, the redemption. The Dagger is the means. For *Dei Gloria Intacta* is the end of all.

And the Bull with ה and Chain shows the Burial and the Earth, Life and Labour which accomplish all these things. *Legis Jugum* shows Destiny balancing free-will.

* JECHIDAH
(Spirit)
NESCHAMAH   CHIAH
(Water)   (Fire)
RUACH
(Air)
NEPHESCH
(Earth).

† That is: nowhere a void. The other mottoes mean: the Freedom of the Gospel, the Unsullied Glory of God; and the Yoke of the Law respectively.

230

THE TEMPLE OF SOLOMON THE KING

In the midst is 𝍖 and the Incense: now Incense requires Air, Fire, Water and Earth for its being: thus the whole table is shown in 𝍖 as the combination and centre of all, being the glory of the Vast Countenance.

All this is brilliant and flashing: *i.e.*, equilibrated in itself and therefore a fit recipient of the Flashing Light: and brilliance is purity and energy.

Now all kneel down and the Higher is again invoked. Postulant is fixed in Tiphereth and looking up to Kether. He again rejoices that he hath been crucified. Justice ariseth and taketh from him his Kether-wand and Ankh, and his own hands put the chain upon his neck, the symbol of earth and burial therein; and the Supreme Hour of Apophis is upon him, as it is written: "Eloi, Eloi, lamma sabacthani!" Also this chain of Earth refers to the great renunciation of the Ego, refusing Devachan* and reassuming incarnation: not to the renunciation of Nirvana, which the mere purified man as such is not entitled to. Note also that Postulant himself now rebukes Daäth as the Second Adept did for him in the First Point. At this moment the Aspirant is no longer dead; he enters again the earth-life, for it is the reincarnation of the soul. But he is as the child unconscious of the Adept within him, and knoweth it not. He riseth not yet glorified, but as still upon the Cross.

Themis now takes the Cup, or Lotus, and Dagger, or Cross, and the Death Symbol is dipped in the Resurrection Symbol, and the marks of LVX are again imprinted on him, as if to seal the prayer of the Second Adept. The Postulant now takes the Rose Cross and lifts it (as before for symbolism). Note also that this is the fourth element in the consecration (four pillars, &c., in 0°=0° Ritual). He then upholdeth the Rose Cross as if that were the object of his accepting the Chain. And now, having gained the right to take his Ruach with him in the Darkness, he may demand the Opening of the Pastos. The Altar is moved, "new heavens and new earth," &c. The Pastos lid also, "Osiris no longer divided into glory and suffering, but central and perfect."

The *Third Adept* gives the Postulant his Wand and Ankh, thus again uniting him to Chesed (Isis L). Also "If ye be crucified," &c., is said in marking the Chesed hand.

The *Third Adept*, "And the Light," &c.—showing Postulant that he is not dead but alive.

Accordingly *Chief Adept* reaches out his Kether-wand to that Kether-centre of the Rose Cross above him, and in that act restores himself to life and consciousness thereof.

The Higher Self descendeth for the second time and the man is united once more.

The Osiris *Chief Adept* (not yet fully glorified, but in his death alive) formulates these ideas.

The interchange of Chief Adept and Postulant now takes place completely with the change of weapons.

Chief Adept becomes Isis, and instructs the Osiris in Chesed, her symbol.

* Heaven.

231

It also shows the marriage of Isis and Osiris in the tomb, or that Isis hath descended to restore her son to life. Also Isis in the Pastos shows the winter and seed-time of earth,—Isis is also Persephone, be it well remembered!

Third Adept seals all this in the Ruach and synthesises all with *Ex Deo Nascimur*, &c. &c.

The Altar and lid are restored, showing that the full glorification is not yet.

The Aspirant quits the Portal, showing that to complete the Great Work one must go out into the world and work.

Third Point.

Represents IAO, the synthesis of that three-fold work. Osiris not only risen but glorified, for IAO is the name also of the Highest, as the Gnostics do assure us.

Here then the *Chief Adept* is the glorified Osiris: the Postulant being only the risen Osiris. Again the Higher Genius is formulated. The Postulant is now well in touch with the Higher Soul in Kether; but has not yet *begun* the Great Work.

The Pastos is without, *for it will never be wanted again.* But in south- east and north-east are the Grades and Minutum Mundum; the Serpent and the Flaming Sword are on the altar, also the Mystic Mountain of Abiegnus.* The Empty Pastos is shown — there, if anywhere, is a void! The Risen Osiris contemplates his tomb, when suddenly he is called into the glory by Chief Adept's voice from the place of ʼ, the world of Atziluth. But he knoweth it not; only his resurrection is fixed in his mind. He is called back further to his Cross, and then again he looketh forward, and a dim presentment of glory touches him. Then only doth the Postulant's Ruach rise fully into Neschamah, and he nameth the Name of the Highest, and is forever beyond Hell and Death.

The *Second Adept* says that Akasa† (hearing) can hear Spirit. The door is flung wide open, so that no longer a dim sight of glory be, but the full wide-flowing influx of the Light, and the Osiris and his companions bend in awe and adoration at that mighty and terrible glory. Between Strength and Justice doth he kneel in the sign of his rising, and seeth again the Cross, not now of suffering, but only of Light.

The God in His glory sayeth: "I am Amoun, the Concealed One," not only Osiris the Justified.

At the coming of that Glory they bow and shade their eyes from its brilliance: for what are the Sun and Moon to abide His presence?

But now the Sun and Moon are Apollo and Artemis, Osiris and Isis; the Divine Eye is formulated from the Light of those eyes that are but as darkness, and the Osiris saith in very truth: "Before I was blind: now I see!"

---

* The explanation of this abstruse point has been unfortunately omitted by Frater P. This is to be regretted as the rest is so beautifully lucid.

† See 777, Cols. lv., lxxv., pp. 16, 17.

THE TEMPLE OF SOLOMON THE KING

The Great Light dawns, The Flashing Brilliance of the All-Pervading Spirit of the Gods descends: the Divine Spirit is upon him, and all bow in adoration of that White Glory.

The Osiris stands, and by that sign uniteth himself with that Light. He faces the West, ready to shed light upon the World, and there in the Pyramid is the Great Work accomplished; for in his heart is Kether, the Centre of light, and the Rosy Cross is in his body, *i.e.*, his Nephesch is redeemed while his Mind is ever open to the Descending Floods of the Influx from the Higher.

Now the Chief Adept is again Isis, and instructs. She formulateth AHIH and Tiphereth, and the light is finally fixed as the analysis of the Key Word, synthesising and uniting the symbolism of the entire ceremony again by the Pyramid formula.

Minutum Mundum. The Light is shown divided and balanced in the Tree.

Crook and Scourge. The Light is shown in the symbols of Osiris.

Serpent and Sword. The Light-bearers run and return.

Mystic Mountain of Abiegnus. The Abodes of Light are only reached by a steep ascent.

The Vault is then explained on Microcosm lines.

Note that 40 shows the 10 Sephiroth in the four worlds, or letters of the name.

Aspirant is now in Water, and Chief Adept in Earth, to show how complete is their interchange. Chief Adept being naturally Water, Chesed; and Aspirant, Earth.

The grip of the grade strengthens this.

Right hand above left hand shows Nephthys above Isis, the *completed* work. The wrists—the unity from which the five springs—are grasped=Kether.

The Cross (hands crossed) is the means of doing this.

Note: if you *pull* in this position you initiate a whirling force. They regain positions.

Closing.

The 120 is formulated and calleth forth the elemental Guardians. The Triangle of the Supernals is formulated, and the LVX signs close the whole with its synthetical glory, but they are given in silence, as showing forth that they have all attained unto the Peace of God which passeth understanding, to keep their hearts and minds through IHShVH our Lord.

AMEN.

By thus passing through the ritual of the 5°=6° Grade of Adeptus Minor, P., in part at least, unveiled that knowledge which he had set out in the 0°=0° ritual to discover. For as the first grade of the First Order endows the Neophyte with an unforgettable glimpse of that Higher Self, the

Augœides, Genius, Holy Guardian Angel or Adonai; so does
the first grade of the Second Order engender within him that
divine spark, by drawing down upon the Aspirant the Genius
in Pentecostal Flames; until it no longer enshrines him like
the distant walls of the starry abyss, but burns within him,
pouring through the channels of his senses an unending
torrent of glory, of that greater glory which alone can be
comprehended by one who is an Adept: yet again, but the
shadow of that supreme glory which is neither the shrine nor
the flame, but the life of the Master.

From the commencement of this history we have ever
found Frater P. valiantly battling with the Elemental Forces.
As a hoodwinked Neophyte he was led into the colossal darkness of Malkuth to become a Zelator in the hidden mysteries
of Earth. Here he found a Kingdom seemingly so balanced in
its Scintillating Intelligence that he little suspected that its
overwhelming glory was but the reflection of the Supernal
Flame on the dark face of the Waters in which slept the
invisible coils of the drowsing serpent of human will. Here,
on account of its intense darkness, all became to him clear as
crystal, in which he could read his own thoughts mirrored in
the wavelets of the ever-dancing waters of life. Here again
Existence, as the World Mystery, became to him the supreme
riddle of the human Sphinx; and in his strivings to read it, in
his doubts, which Minerva like sprang from his former
certainties, he informed within himself the first letter of the
Name of God, the Virgin impregnated by the one idea—the
Vision of Adonai incarnated in her Son.

Illumined by this one supreme longing which had burnt
up his coarser desires, he passed through the next ritual to the

illusive Foundation of Yesod, which in its apparent Equilibrium contains a falsified reflection of the Supreme path of the Fool. For, though its element is Air, it is not the Æthyr of Zero, the breath of Equilibrium, any more than Air as a mixture of Oxygen and Nitrogen is the Ether of Space. From Yesod he could look back upon Malkuth and be filled with an intense pity for all who still cling to its illusive Splendour; so also could he look up towards Kether (Kether in Yesod, though he knew it not), and burn with a joy not unmingled with sorrow at the apparent hopelessness of ever being able to climb so distant a peak.

Thus would the heavens and hells seduce him from the path, the path of the Sun and the Angel, which through their greater glory blinded his understanding from the true way, and appeared to him not as light but as darkness.

His present position seemed so clear to him that its very clearness would also have blinded him as it has so many others, had he not slain the incubus of the Supreme, and sought a greater independence by refusing to look at the clouded summit of the mountain whilst the lower slopes were unclimbed. Instead he said to himself, the next step is God to me, ay! God, and very God of very God: there is no other God than He.* Thus through the strength of the eagle, whose eyes scorn the fire of the sun, did he learn to conquer

* A person arriving at Kether of Malkuth is liable to mistake it for Kether of Kether, and so on with an ever-increasing likelihood until Kether of Kether is actually attained, when the one swallows the other as the Serpent swallows its tail and eventually itself. In Kether of Kether there is no thinking or thought, therefore no certainty or uncertainty. From Malkuth of Yesod three obsessing forces come into play, viz., Kether of Malkuth, which tempts the Aspirant to look back; the local temptations of all the Sephiroth of Yesod save Yesod of Yesod, which is the next; and Malkuth of Hod, which tempts him to run in Hod before he can walk in Yesod

Hod, the Splendour of the mighty waters, the ever-flowing and fluctuating desires of life, which contains all the colours of the opal, each brother light dissolving into its sister counterpart, according as the position of the Aspirant changes.

Here he learnt of the deceptions of desire; how they change, and only exist by perpetually changing. Yet also here he learnt how to slay them by wedding them to their opposites; but in the very act he only begat another mystery more terrible than the last, the mystery of Netzach.

As fire may be victorious over water, or water over fire, so may victory itself leave the Victor doubly enslaved by his very Success. Until the present, Frater P. had always found some new cause for which to draw his sword; but now, though the blade was as bright and keen as ever, like a knight surrounded by crafty footpads in the night, he knew not which way to thrust, thought the danger which surrounded him he felt was greater than any that he had ever experienced before. This danger was, indeed, the seduction of things Supremely Material. For at this point on his journey, having mastered the three elements, he came nigh falling slave to the fourth; just as a warrior who has slain the King, and the Captain of the Guard, and even the Chief Eunuch who sleeps across the threshold of the Queen's bed-chamber, may lose the Kingdom he has all but won amongst the soft seducing cushions of a fair woman's couch, and only awake from his foolish sleep as the mallet drives the nail through his unguarded head.

More valiant men have fallen in Netzach than ever fell in Malkuth, Yesod, and Hod combined, and more will fall in Tiphereth than ever fell in Netzach, and for the same reason, and that is, that all Success is illusionary, the greatest illusion being to consider oneself Successful.

It is here that man leaves, if he strive, the bow of worldly desires, and cleaves the firmament of thought like an arrow, which, eventually speeding out of the world's attraction, becomes as an universe to itself. This cleaving of the Veil of the Vault of the Adepts is in truth the precipitation of the Jechidah from the elemental flux that goes to make man. The Virgin Mother of Malkuth, the Earth fecundated by Air, Water and Fire, is delivered of her Son the Spirit, who is the Adept reborn in the Vault as Christian Rosencreutz; not yet Adonai the Christ, the Son of God, but Adonai, Jehesuah, the Son of Man, Jesus the Carpenter who one day will fashion the Tree of Life into the image of the Supernal Christ. No longer is the Vision of Adonai a mere glimpse as of a flickering light without, lost in the distance of a great forest, but a light which burns as a lamp within a lantern, and which sheds its beams equally in all directions.

It is here, when the Aspirant becomes a sun unto himself, entranced by the beauty of his children, his seemingly balanced thoughts,* the wandering planets and comets that obey his will, that he is liable to forget that though a sun to himself, he is nevertheless but an atom of the Glory Supernal, but a mote of dust dancing in the beam of the Eye Divine. This it arrives that he is as likely to be obsessed by the ordered harmony of things in Tiphereth, as the joys of the

---

* The Pillar of Mildness in the Tree of Life passes through the Sephiroth Kether, Tiphereth, Yesod and Malkuth which appear to be all equally balanced. This, however, is incorrect, for all save Kether, which is the point from which motion originates, are as marks set upon the pendulum of a clock, the nearer to Malkuth (the weight) the greater will be the space they move through, conversely, the farther away the less.

discord of things obsessed him but a stage or tow below. As the sun vivifies so can it corrupt. Therefore by his own forces must he destroy his contentment by a self- explosion of discontent so terrific that the ordered universe governed by Spirit is not blown into Chaos, the Qliphoth, but out of Chaos, out of Cosmos itself, into a new world, a higher Equilibrium, a universe of colossal strength and power. If he tremble, he is lost; he must strain every nerve, every muscle, until his whole frame vibrates and flashes forth the magical Strength of the Sephira Geburah.

Thus is the Magician begotten by devotion to the Great Work, and Work as Work alone can only gain for the Aspirant this exalted grade. He must strive beyond the hope of success; success is failure; he must strive beyond the hope of victory; victory is defeat; he must strive beyond the hope of reward; reward is punishment; he must indeed strive beyond all things; he must break up the equipoise of things; he must swing the pendulum off its hook, and wrench the lingam of Shiva from between the loins of Sakti. Justice or Mercy are nothing to him; he, as Horus the child, must quench the one with the other, as his father Osiris quenched the Waters of Hod with the fires of Netzach. Good and Evil are his implements, for his work is still in the Kingdom of the Ruach. And so long as his strivings beget, conceive, and bear the fruits of a greater and nobler Work, there is no cup of bitterness that may be refused, and no cross of suffering whose nails shall not pierce him. As Osiris he learnt to vanquish himself; rerisen as Horus he shall vanquish the world—ay! and who shall say me nay? the ultimate filaments of the hair of Nu.

THE MAGICIAN

VERY shortly after the ceremony of Adeptus Minor, P. returned to his fastness to carry out the great Magical Operation of Abramelin the Mage, the preliminary preparations of which he had for so long now been setting in order.

Unfortunately we have ben scanty information of P.'s daily life during these days, and all that is recorded is to be found in a small book of some twenty pages entitled, "The Book of the Operation of the Sacred Magic of Abramelin the Mage. (Being the account of the events of my life, with notes on the operation by P., an humble Aspirant thereto.)"

This slight volume commences with "The Oath of the Beginning," after which it is roughly divided into three parts. The first deals with the events of his life between the beginning of November 1899 and the end of February 1900; the second with the Abramelin Operation; and the third with the transactions P. had with Frater D.D.C.F.

From the first part of this work we gather that great forces of evil were leagued against P.; and we learn this with no very great surprise, for those who set their faces against Darkness must expect Darkness to attempt to swallow them up. The Exempt Adept may laugh equally at good or at evil, but not so the mere magician whose passage along the

Path of Light is only to be marked by the increasing depths of the Darkness which surrounds him.

It will be remembered that in the autumn of 1898 P. had met Frater V.N., who had lent him a copy of a book known as "The Book of the Sacred Magic of Abramelin the Mage," and had to some degree instructed him in the workings contained in it. This work P. had read and reread with the greatest interest and zeal, determining to perform the ceremonial operation laid down in it at the very first opportunity. This he was unable to do for nearly a year; it being not until November 1899 that he found it possible for him to retire to the house he had bought and make all necessary preparations for the great ceremony, which was to be commenced on the following Easter.

The system, as taught by Abramelin, of entering into communication with one's Holy Guardian Angel, is, of all Western systems of Magic, perhaps the most simple and effective. No impossible demands are made, and though perhaps some are difficult to carry out, there is always a reason for them, and they are not merely placed in the way as tests of the worker's skill. The whole Operation is so lucidly dealt with in Mr. MacGregor Mathers' translation, that it would be but a waste of time and space to enter into it fully, and the following consists of but the briefest summary, only intended to give the reader an idea of the Operation, and in no way meant as a basis for him to work on.

Abramelin having first carefully warned his readers against impostors, lays down that the chief thing to be considered is: "Whether ye be in good health, because the body being feeble and unhealthy, it is subject to divers infirmities whence at length result impatience and want of power to operate and pursue the Operation; and a sick man can neither be clean and pure, nor enjoy solitude; and in such a case it is better to cease."*

The true and best time of commencing this Operation is the first day after the Celebration of the Feasts of Easter at about the time of the vernal Equinox. The time necessary for the working is six months, so that should it be commenced on March 22, it would end on September 21.

The six months is divided into three periods of two months each.

First Period. "Every morning precisely a quarter of an hour before sunrise enter your Oratory, after having washed and dressed yourself in clean clothing, open the window, and then kneel at the Altar facing the window and invoke the Name of the Lord; after which you should confess to him your entire sins. This being finished you should supplicate Him "that in time to come He may be willing and pleased to regard you with pity and grant you His grace and goodness to send unto you His Holy Angel, who shall serve unto you as a Guide. . . ."†

In the above exercise by prayer the one great point to observe, as Abramelin himself impresses in the following words, is: "It serveth nothing to speak without devotion, without attention, and without intelligence . . . it is absolutely necessary that your prayer should issue from the midst of your heart, because simply setting down prayers in writing, the hearing of them will in no way explain unto you how really to pray."‡

At sunset the same invocation, confession and prayer is to be repeated.

---

* "The Book of the Sacred Magic," p. 54.
† *Ibid.* p. 64. Some of the following quotations have been abriged.
‡ *Ibid.* p. 65.

During this first period the points to be observed are:

(1) That both the bed-chamber and Oratory are to be kept thoroughly clean. "Your whole attention must be given to purity in all things."

(2) That "you may sleep with your Wife in the bed when she is pure and clean," not otherwise.

(3) Every Saturday the sheets of the bed are to be changed and the chamber is to be perfumed.

(4) No animal is to enter or dwell in the house.

(5) "If you be your own Master, as far as lieth in your power, free yourself from all your business, and quit all mundane and vain company and conversation; leading a life tranquil, solitary and honest."

(6) "Take well heed in treating of business, in selling or buying, that it shall be requisite that you never give way unto anger, but be modest and patient in your actions."

(7) "You shall set apart two hours each day after having dined, during which you shall read with care the Holy Scripture and other Holy Books."

(8) "As for eating, drinking and sleeping, such should be in moderation and never superfluous."

(9) "Your dress should be clean but moderate, and according to custom. Flee all vanity."

(10) "As for that which regardeth the family, the fewer in number, the better; also act so that the servants may be modest and tranquil."

(11) "Let your hand be ever ready to give alms and other benefits to your neighbour; and let your heart be ever open unto the poor, whom God so loveth that one cannot express the same."*

Second Period. During the whole of this period the accustomed prayer is to be made morning and evening, "but before entering into the Oratory ye shall wash your hands and face thoroughly with pure water. And you shall prolong your prayer with the greatest possible affection, devotion and submission; humbly entreating the Lord God that he would deign to command His Holy Angels to lead you in the True Way. ..."

During this period the points to be observed are:

(1) "The use of the rites of Marriage is permitted, but should scarcely if at all be made use of."

(2) "You shall also wash your whole body every Sabbath Eve."

(3) "As to what regardeth commerce and rules of living, as in the first period."

(4) "It is absolutely necessary during this period to retire from the world and seek retreat."

* "The Book of the Sacred Magic," pp. 66-69.

(5) "Ye shall lengthen your prayers to the utmost of your ability."
(6) "As for eating, drinking, and clothing, as before."*

Third Period. Morning and Noon ye shall wash your hands and your face on entering the Oratory; and first ye shall make Confession of all your sins; after this, with a very ardent prayer, ye shall entreat the Lord to accord unto you this particular grace, which is, that you may enjoy and be able to endure the presence and conversation of His Holy Angels, and that He may deign by their intermission to grant unto you the Secret Wisdom, so that you may be able to have dominion over the Spirits and over all creatures.

"Ye shall do this same at midday before dining and also in the evening,"† as well as at sunrise.

During this period the points to be observed are:

(1) "The man who is his own master shall leave all business alone, except works of charity towards his neighbour."
(2) "You shall shun all society except that of your Wife and of your Servants."
(3) "Ye shall employ the greatest part of your time in speaking of the Law of God."
(4) "Every Sabbath Eve shall ye fast, and wash your whole body, and change your garment."‡

If possible the whole of this Operation should be performed in a place where solitude can be obtained; the best being, as Abramelin writes: "Where there is a small wood, in the midst of which you shall make a small Altar, and you shall cover the same with a hut of fine branches, so that the rain may not fall thereon and extinguish the Lamps and the Censer."§

The Altar should be made of wood and in the manner of a cupboard, so that it may hold all the necessary things.

There should be two tunics, one of linen, and the other of Crimson or Scarlet Silk with Gold.

The sacred oil is prepared from myrrh, cinnamon and galangal mixed with olive oil. The incense of Olibanum, storax, and lign aloes, or cedar, is reduced to a fine powder and well mixed together. The Wand is cut from an Almond-tree. ¶

* "The Book of the Sacred Magic," pp. 69, 70.   † *Ibid.* pp. 70, 71.
‡ *Ibid.* p. 71.   § *Ibid.* p. 74.   ¶ *Ibid.* pp 76, 77.

The third period having been completed, on the morning following: "Rise betimes, neither wash yourself at all nor dress yourself at all in your ordinary clothes; but take a Robe of Mourning; enter the Oratory with bare feet; go unto the side of the Censer, and having opened the windows, return unto the door. There prostrate yourself with your face against the ground, and order the Child (who is used as assistant and clairvoyante) to put the Perfume upon the Censer, after which he is to place himself upon his knees before the Altar; following in all things and throughout the instructions which I have given unto you. . . . Humiliate yourself before God and His Celestial Court, and commence your prayer with fervour, for then it is that you will begin to enflame yourself in praying, and you will see appear an extraordinary and supernatural Splendour which will fill the whole apartment, and will surround you with an inexpressible odour, and this alone will console you and comfort your heart so that you shall call for ever happy the Day of the Lord.*

    *   *   *   *   *   *

"During Seven Days shall you perform the Ceremonies without failing therein in any way: namely, the Day of the Consecration, the Three Days of the Convocation of the Good and Holy Spirits, and the Three other Days of the Convocation of the Evil Spirits.

"On the second morning you shall follow the counsels your Holy Guardian Angel shall have given you, and on the third you shall render thanks.

"And then shall you first be able to put to the test whether you shall have well employed the period of your Six Moons, and how well and worthily you shall have laboured in the quest of the Wisdom of the Lord; since you shall see your Guardian Angel appear unto you in unequalled beauty: who also will converse with you, and speak in words so full of affection and of goodness, and with such sweetness, that no human tongue could express the same. . . . In one word, you shall be received by him with such affection that this description I here give unto you shall appear a mere nothing in comparison."†

After the Third day Abramelin very wisely writes:

"Now at this point I commence to restrict myself in my writing, seeing that by the Grace of the Lord I have submitted and consigned you unto a MASTER so great that he will never let you err."‡

Thus, briefly though it be, we have run through the

---

* "The Book of the Sacred Magic," p. 81.

† *Ibid.* pp. 82, 85.

‡ *Ibid.* p. 85.

system as advocated by one of the greatest masters of Magic in the West. With perfect lucidity Abramelin brings us step by step towards the MASTER—Augœides, Adonai, Higher Self, call Him what you will. By means of symbols of purity—by cleanliness and clean living—he leads us on by meditation and concentration through prayer to a one-pointedness, a vision or conversation with the MASTER so full of goodness and beauty, so full of rapture and ecstasy that no human tongue can express the same. Alas! that we are not simple-minded enough to accept it, and to seek at that little altar in the wood that sweet reward which at once cancels all the toils and sorrows of our lives.

But in these present times prayer has become a mockery, and it is hard, how hard we know well, for any one to pray with that earnestness which brings with it reward. The rationalist has so befouled prayer with his wordy slush that it is indeed a hard task to dissociate it from the host of external symbols and images. A man who prays to a god is at once imagined to be praying to a thing with legs; for the educated are so surfeited with tangible things that the transcendental entirely escapes them; yet the man who prays may in truth be praying to the Master, and it matters not one whit whether the Master have legs or no legs, for God does not depend on the education of man's mind, or the standard of his knowledge, or the idols he has set up. In some cases hostility to prayer would prove more fruitful than devotion to it. He who believes in denying and blaspheming God will attain to the Divine Vision of Adonai as speedily as he who believes in praying to Him and worshipping His Holy Name; so long as he *enflame* himself with blasphemy and denial. It is the *will* to accomplish, to conquer and overcome, which in both cases carries with it the supreme reward, and not the mere fact of denying or believing, which are but instruments towards this end. But, be it well remembered! this mystery of the Equivalence of all symbols, good and evil, is only true in Daäth and from Daäth.

One man may fell a tree with an axe, another may saw it down, another dig it up, another burn it down, another wash it out of the earth by water, blast it by powder, or drag it down by a rope. In the end the tree falls, and the desire of each particular man is accomplished in spite of the variety of their tools.

Thus we find that as Rising on the Planes was one method, so was Skrying another; so again were the rituals of the Golden Dawn; so again "The 𐤔 of 𐤔 Operation" and Talismanic Magic; and now again still one more—the method of Abramelin; all different means to enable man to fell the tall tree of life and obtain the Master Vision of Adonai, the Augœides or Higher Self.

Each method, used rightly and carried to its ultimation, leads to the same Heaven; each method used wrongly, or mistaken for the End, side-tracks the Adept into some Limbo or plunges him into some Hell.

To all such as are of a devout disposition Prayer offers an excellent means of Concentration towards this end— identification with Adonai. And it matters no whit to what we pray, whether it be to Buddha or to Christ, or the top-hat and gin-bottle of a West African ju-ju, so long as we pray with our whole heart; and eventually, as the Vision informs, belief, faith, prayer, worship and supplication vanish, the burning-glass of our Will has set on fire the white sheet of paper that had been our ideal; it crumples, turns brown, blackens, and bursts into flame. The gates of the mind swing apart, and the realm into which we rush is as different from the realm which we had contemplated as our ideal as the burning fire is to the cool white paper we had looked upon. For those who cannot thus believe, who in fact have no faith in prayer, there are yet other ways for them to travel, as we shall presently see; in fact so many that each could travel by a different road and yet arrive at the same destination; and it is hoped that those who study this book may thereby discover the speediest road to the Portal of the Temple.

Early in November, P. returned to London to consult with Fratres I.A. and V.N., and shortly afterwards crossed over to Paris, and after a few days' residence in that city returned to England; and by means of the Codselim symbol journeyed to D——, and from thence to T——. Here he received a letter from I.A. warning him of very grave danger. P. Thereupon invoked Heru-pa-kraatist and cast himself upon the Providence of God: "that he may give His Angels charge over me, to keep me in all my ways. So mote it be!"

Thus far the events which carry us down to the commencement of the Operation, which begins with:

THE OATH OF THE BEGINNING.

I, P——, Frater Ordinis Rosae Rubeae et Aureae Crucis, a Lord of the Paths in the Portal of the Vault of the Adepts, a $5°=6°$ of the Order of the Golden Dawn; and an humble servant of the Christ of God; do this day spiritually bind myself anew:

By the Sword of Vengeance:

By the Powers of the Elements:

By the Cross of Suffering:

That I will devote myself to the Great Work: the obtaining of Communion with my own Higher and Divine Genius, (called the Guardian Angel) by means of the prescribed course: and that I will use any Power so obtained unto the Redemption of the Universe.

So help me the Lord of the Universe and mine own Higher Soul!

Let us now turn to "The Obligation of the Operation."

I, P___, in the presence of the Lord of the Universe, and of all Powers Divine and Angelic, do spiritually bind myself, even as I am now physically bound unto the Cross of Suffering:

(1) To unite my consciousness with the divine, as I may be permitted and aided by the Gods Who live for ever, the AEons of Infinite years, that, being lost in the Limitless Light, it may find Itself: to the Regeneration of the Race, either of man or as the Will of God shall be. And I submit myself utterly to the Will Divine.

(2) To follow out with courage, modesty, lovingkindness, and perseverance the course prescribed by Abramelin the Mage; as far as in me lies, unto the attainment of this end.

(3) To despise utterly the things and the opinions of this world lest they hinder me in doing this.

(4) To use my powers only to the Spiritual well-being of all with whom I may be brought in contact.

(5) To give no place to Evil: and to make eternal war against the Forces of Evil: until even they be redeemed unto the Light.

(6) To harmonize my own spirit that so Equilibrium may lead me to the East and that my Human Consciousness shall allow no usurpation of its rule by the Automatic.

(7) To conquer the temptations.

(8) To banish the illusions.

(9) To put my whole trust in the Only and Omnipotent Lord God: as it is written "Blessed are they that put their trust in Him."

(10) To uplift the Cross of Sacrifice and Suffering: and to cause my Light to shine before men that they may glorify my Father which is in Heaven.*

Furthermore: I most solemnly promise and swear: to acquire this Holy Science in the manner prescribed in the Book of Abramelin, without omitting the least imaginable thing of their contents: not to gloss or comment in any way on that which may be or may not be; not to use this Sacred Science to offend the Great God, nor to work ill unto my neighbour: to communicate it to no living person, unless by long practice and conversation I shall know him thoroughly, well examining whether such an one really

---

* The reader will note that this is a sort of personal adaptation of the 5°=6° obligation.

intendeth to work for the Good or for the Evil. I will punctually observe, in granting it, the same fashion which was used by Abramelin to Abraham. Otherwise, let him who receiveth it draw no fruit therefrom. I will keep myself as from a Scorpion from selling this Science. Let this Science remain in me and in my generation as long as it shall please the Most High.*

All these points I generally and severally swear to observe under the awful penalty of the displeasure of God, and of Him to whose Knowledge and Conversation I do most ardently aspire.

So help me the Lord of the Universe, and my own Higher Soul!

The obligation is followed, in the book, by various preparations which we pass over in order that we may the more speedily record some of the Visions which P. experienced at this time: the first we quote is little better than an obsession, and is as follows:

In bed, I invoked the Fire angels and spirits on the tablet, with names, etc., and the 6th Key.† I then (as Harpocrates) entered my crystal. An angel, meeting me, told me among other things, that they (of the tablets) were *at war with the angels of the 30 Æthyrs, to prevent the squaring of the circle.* I went with him unto the abodes of Fire, but must have fallen asleep, or nearly so. Anyhow, I regained consciousness in a very singular state half consciousness being there, and half here. I recovered and banished the Spirits, but was burning all over, and tossed restlessly about—very sleepy, but consumed of fire! Only repeated careful assumption of Harpocrates' god-form enabled me to regain my normal state. I had a long dream of a woman eloping, whom I helped, and after of a man stealing my Rose Cross jewel from a dressing-table in a hotel. I caught him and found him a weak man beyond natural (I could bend or flatten him at will), and then the dream seemed to lose coherence. . . . I carried him about and found a hair-brush to beat him, &c. &c. Query: Was I totally obsessed?

The second is:

Invoking the angels of Earth I obtained a wonderful effect. The angel, my guide, treated me with great contempt and was very rude and truthful. He shewed me divers things. In the centre of the earth is formulated the Rose and Cross. Now the Rose is the Absolute Self-Sacrifice, the merging of *all* in the o (Negative) the Universal

---

* This latter portion of the obligation is taken from the Oath which Abramelin imposed on his pupil Abraham.

† The Enochian Keys of Dr. Dee.

Principle of generation through change (*not* merely the feminine), and the Universal Light "Khabs." The Cross is the Extension or Pekht principle. Now I should have learned more but my attention wandered. This closes the four elemental visions: prosecuted, alas! with what weakness, fatuity, and folly!

And, lastly, the following, which is of considerable interest:

I . . . in the afternoon shut myself up, and went on a journey. . . . I went with a very personal guide: and beheld (after some lesser things) our Master as he sate by the Well with the Woman of Samaria. Now the five husbands were five great religions which had defiled the purity of the Virgin of the World: and "he whom thou now hast" was materialism (or modern thought).

Other scenes also I saw in His life: and behold I also was crucified! Now did I go backwards in time even unto Berashith, the Beginning, and was permitted to see marvellous things.

First the Abyss of the Water: on which I, even I, brooded amid other dusky flames as 𒀭 upon 𒁹 held by my Genius. And I beheld the victory of Râ upon Apophis and the First of the Golden Dawns! Yea: and monsters, faces half-formed, arose: but they subsisted not.

And the firmament was.

Again the Chaos and the Death!

Then *Ath* Hashamaim v. *ath* h-aretz. There is a whirling intertwining infinitude of nebulae, many concentric systems, each system non-concentric to any other, yet *all* concentric to the whole. As I went backwards in time they grew faster and faster, and less and less material. (P.S.—This is the scientific hypothesis, directly contrary to that of Anna Kingsford), and at last are whirling wheels of light: yet through them *waved* a thrill of an intenser invisible light in a direction perpendicular to the tangents. I asked to go yet further back and behold! I am floating on my back—cast down! in a wind of Light flashing down upon me from the immeasurable Above. (This Light is of a blueish silver tinge.) And I saw that Face, lost above me in the height inscrutable: a face of absolute beauty. And I saw as it were a Lamb slain in the Glamour of Those Eyes. Thus was I made pure: for there, what impunity could live? I was told that not many had been so far back: none further: those who *could* go farther would not, since that would have reabsorbed them into the Beginning, and that must not be to him who hath sworn to uplift the Standard of Sacrifice and Sorrow, which is strength. (I forgot the Angels in the Planetary Whirl. They regarded me with curiosity: and were totally unable to comprehend my explanation that I was a *Man*, returning in time to behold the Beginning of Things.)

Now was I able to stand in my Sephiroth: and the Crown of Twelve Stars was upon my head! I then went into the centre of the earth (I suppose) and stood upon the top of an high mountain. The many dragons and guardians I was able to overpower by *authority*. Now the mount was of glistening whiteness, exceeding white as snow: yet dead and unluminous. And I beheld a vision, even like unto that of the Universal Mercury;* and I learnt that I myself was sulphur and unmercurial. Now having attained the Mercurialising of my Sulphur I was able (in my vision) to fecundate the mountain (of Salt). And it was instantly transmuted into gold. What came ye out into the wilderness for to see? No: into living, glowing, molten Light: the Light that redeemeth the material world! So I returned: having difficulty to find the earth(?). But I called on S.R.M.D. and V.N.R. who were glad to see me; and returned into the body: to waste the night in gibing at a foolish medico.

(It is worth noting here how very much more coherent this Vision is than the first ones we have had occasion to mention.) So far the second part of the "Book of the Operation."

The third part of this book, which consists but of two pages, begins obscurely enough:

"Heard this evening from D.D.† Second Order apparently mad."

However, this information which, from the following, we gauge to be connected with the dead sea apple schism which had for some time been ripening amongst the members of the Order of the Golden Dawn, was considered sufficiently important by P. for him to offer his services to G. H. Frater D.D.C.F., who was then in Paris. About a week later P. writes: "D.D.C.F. accepts my services, therefore do I rejoice, that my sacrifice is accepted. Therefore do I again postpone the Operation of Abramelin the Mage, having by God's Grace formulated even in this a new link with the Higher, and gained a new weapon against the Great Princes of the Evil of the World. Amen."

* Described in a MS. edited by S.R.M.D. and issued to the Second Order, in which is a picture of Mercury diving into the sea.
† Secretary of the Order of the Golden Dawn.

Thus ends the "Book of the Operation." But on the back of the last page there is a note from which we gather the following. That P. journeyed from London to Paris (evidently shortly after his letter to D.D.C.F. he had left T—— for London). There he was selected as the messenger of D.D.C.F., after a long talk with him and V.N.R., and at noon, four days later, he left Paris for London. This note ends with the following words: "The history of my mission: is it not written in the Book of the Chronicles of the Revolt of the Adepti?"

Before glancing through this Chronicle of Revolt, which in all truth might be called "The Book of the Fatuity of the Inepti," it will be necessary to return for a moment to that interesting document, "The History Lection."

The last point we arrived at in the Lection was that, "in 1900 one P., a brother, instituted a rigorous test of S.R.M.D. on the one side and the Order on the other." S.R.M.D. is but another name for G.H. Frater D.D.C.F., against whose authority the Second Order were now in open revolt. From this point the Lection continues:

"He discovered that S.R.M.D., though a scholar of some ability and a magician of remarkable powers, had never attained complete initiation: and further had fallen from his original place, he having imprudently attracted to himself forces of evil too great and terrible for him to withstand.*

"The claim of the Order that the true adepts were in charge of it was definitely disproved.

"In the Order, with two certain exceptions and two

* Presumably Abramelin Demons.

doubtful ones, he found no persons with any capacity for initiation of any sort.

"He thereupon, by his subtle wisdom, destroyed both the Order and its chief.

"Being himself no perfect adept, he was driven of the Spirit into the Wilderness, where he abode for six years, studying by the light of reason the sacred books and secret systems of initiation of all countries and ages."

We must now leave the Lection, to return to it again six years later, and as briefly as possible run through the Chronicles of Revolt, which consist of various documents for the most part printed towards the close of 1900 and the beginning of 1901, by such members of the Order as had broken away from their chief, D.D.C.F. In a printed document written on May 4, 1901, and signed by D.E.D.I., we find the following:

You are aware that, originally, the Second Order in this country was governed absolutely by three chiefs. Ultimately their authority all devolved on one—our late chief, the G.H. Frater D.D.C.F., who was practically recognised as Autocrat.

This we have already learnt from the Lection. But from a "Statement" issued to Adepti in February 1901, we further learn that on April 1 (*sic*), 1897, V.H. Soror S.S.D.D. was appointed head of the London branch of the Order and that the formation of secret groups was advised and legalised by D.D.C.F. "S.A. approved of this and formed a group himself, as Silentio (*sic*) can bear witness." However, in "Letters to the Adepti of R.R. and A.C." issued in the same month, it appears that it was not by D.D.C.F.'s sanction, but through their distrust of him, that Soror S.S.D.D. started a group in London, and Frater S.S. one in Edinburgh. These groups seemed to have worked as secret societies within the Order. Fra: D.E.D.I. appears in this same document to have objected to this, for we find him attempting to get S.S.D.D. to amalgamate the smaller groups and form a larger group of Theorici. This attempt led to a meeting of the Executive Council in which S.S.D.D. raised an objection of D.E.D.I.'s proposal; and we find D.E.D.I. writing: "I have sat on many committees in my own country and elsewhere, but I am proud to say that I never met among the mechanics, farmers and shop-assistants with whom I have worked in Ireland a state of feeling so ignoble, or resolutions so astonishing, as those I had to listen to yesterday."

From the "Statement" it appears that these groups were the chief cause of the Revolt. D.D.C.F., permitting these groups to be formed, little by little delegated his power to others; so that when the crash came he had no magical force left to meet it; and that those who had gained it had so dispersed it among themselves that instead of causing them to rise a phœnix out of the ashes of the past, it simply set them squabbling and fighting over petty and absurd points of morals and law. A fair specimen of the magical powers displayed by the Order after the fall of D.D.C.F. is to be found in the above "Statement."

"... The most serious charge that Soror F.E.R. has brought against Soror S.S.D.D. is that she has conducted the examinations unjustly." S.S.D.D.'s reply was: "That she has no time, even if she had the inclination, to indulge in futile acts of spite or favouritism."

Whilst revolt was simmering in the pot of dissatisfaction, it appears that D.D.C.F. was residing in Paris, reviving the mysteries of Isis at the Bodinière Theatre.* Here he and

* See the Sunday Chronicle, March 19, 1899.

254

his wife lived under a variety of pseudonyms such as "The Hierophant Rameses," and the "High Priestess Anari," Count and Countess MacGregor of Glenstrae, &c. &c. Their success seems at first to have been considerable, for we read in "The Humanitarian," vol. xvi. No. 2, that their receptions "are amongst the most interesting in Paris. You will find people attending them of nearly every shade of opinion and of profession: Isis-worshippers, Alchemists, Protestants, Catholics, scientists, doctors, lawyers, painters, and men and women of letters, besides persons of high rank."

This success may have possibly distracted his attention from the real state of affairs in England. However, from a mere simmer the pot began to boil, and by the middle of February 1900 the fat was fairly in the fire. It was also at about this time, if not a few weeks earlier, that the notorious Madam Horos introduced herself to D.D.C.F.; this question, however, we will deal with a little later on, though in several ways it seems to be connected with the present revolt. On February 16, 1900, from 87 Rue Mozart, D.D.C.F. addressed the following letter to V.H. Soror S.S.D.D. (the Chief in charge in Anglia). It is divided into five paragraphs, the last two of which we give in full.

C. et V.H. Soror S.S.D.D.

*   *   *   *   *   *

(*d*) Now, with regard to he Second Order, it would be with the *very greatest regret* both from my personal regard for you, as well as from the occult standpoint, that I should receive your Resignation as my Representative in the Second Order in London; but I cannot let you form a combination to make a schism therein with the idea of working secretly or avowedly under "Sapere Aude"* under the mistaken impression

---

* "S.A. was Sapere Aude (or Non Omnis Moriar), Dr. W. Wynn Westcott, King's Coroner for Hoxton.

that he received an Epitome of the Second Order work from G.H. Soror, "Sapiens Dominabitur Astris." For this forces me to tell you plainly (and, understand me well, I can prove to the hilt every word which I here say and more, and were I confronted with S.A., I should say the same), though for the sake of the Order, and for the circumstance that it would mean so deadly a blow to S.A.'s reputation, I entreat you to keep this secret from the *Order*, for the present, at least, though you are at perfect liberty to show *him* this if you think fit, "*after mature consideration.*

(*e*) He has NEVER been at *any time* either in personal or in written communication with the Secret Chiefs of the Order, he having *either himself forged or procured to be forged* the professed correspondence between him and them, and my tongue having been tied all these years by a previous Oath of Secrecy to him, demanded by him, from me, before showing me what he had either done or caused to be done or both. You must comprehend from what little I say here the *extreme gravity* of such a matter, and again I ask you, both for his sake and that of the Order, not to force me to go further into the subject.

This letter ends by stating that every atom of the knowledge of the Order has been communicated to him, and to him alone, by the Secret Chiefs of the Order, and that G.H. Soror S.D.A. was now in Paris with him.*

It must be remembered here that in the "History Lection" we learnt that S.R.M.D. (that is D.D.C.F.), by the death of one of his colleagues and the weakness of the other, secured sole authority over the Order; these two were G.H. Fratres M.E.V. and N.O.M. (that is, S.A.); and it was the latter, so it was generally supposed, who had first discovered the cipher MSS. which led to the connecting-link being established with G.H. Sopror S.D.A. and the great chiefs of the Third Order in Germany.

S.S.D.D. on receiving the above letter went into the country and spent whole days considering it, after which she wrote to S.A., requesting an explanation of D.D.C.F.'s statement. S.A. replied that he did not admit the accuracy of the

* This, as we shall shortly see, must have been Madame Horos.

256

statement, though, his witnesses being dead, he could not legally prove it false, and therefore he wished to remain neutral in the matter. So for the first time he refused to sit upon a corpse.

On March 3, S.S.D.D. formed a Committee of Seven to inquire into the matter. This Committee pointed out to D.D.C.F. the seriousness of his accusation, and asked him to give them proof of its accuracy. A considerable correspondence ensued, in which D.D.C.F. absolutely and unconditionally refused to acknowledge the Committee or to give any proof whatsoever.

Consequent on this refusal, the Committee agreed to place the matter before the Second Order.

On March 23, D.D.C.F. wrote a letter to S.S.D.D. purporting to remove her from her position as his representative in the Second Order.

On the 25th she replied: "I saw that if I kept silence I should become a party to a fraud, and therefore took the advice of some Members of the Order who have always been friendly to your interests. . . ."

On March 24 a general meeting of the Second Order was held, and D.D.C,F. was informed that the reason for making his charge of forgery public was, that the whole constitution of the Order depended upon the authenticity of the documents that he alleged to be forged.

At a meeting of the Committee on March 29, L.O. stated that he had seen S.A., who had given him his honourable assurance that he had no reason to suppose that S.D.A. was not the person she purported to be. He had only had communication with her by letter, and had, *bonâ fide*, posted letters to her in Germany in reply.

On April 2, D.D.C.F, wrote refusing to acknowledge the right of the Second order to elect a Committee, and threatened members with the Punitive Current.

At this juncture P., influenced, so far as himself knew, only by the impulse of self-sacrifice for the Order that had done so much for him; but, as is now apparent, secretly impelled by the true and Unknown Chiefs of the Third Order to put both the Order and its Chief to the test, crossed over to Paris and offered his services to D.D.C.F. They were accepted, and he was asked to act as envoy to the refractory brethren.

In his long talk with D.D.C.F., P. proposed that the following scheme of action should be adopted to quell the revolt of the Second Order:

I. The Second Order to be summoned at various times during two or three days. They to find, on being admitted one by one, a masked man in authority and a scribe. These questions, &c., pass, after pledge of secrecy concerning the interview.

(A) Are you convinced of the truth of the doctrines and knowledge received in the grade of $5° = 6°$? Yes or No?

If *yes* (1) Then their origin can spring from a pure source only?

If *no* (2) I degrade you to be a Lord of the Paths in the Portal in the Vault of the Adepts.

(B) If he reply "Yes," the masked man continues: Are you satisfied with the logic of this statement? Do you solemnly promise to cease these unseemly disputes as to the headship of this Order? I for my part can assure you that from my own knowledge D.D.C.F. is really a $7°= 4°$.

If *yes* (3) Then you will sign this paper; it contains a solemn reaffirmation of your obligation as a $5° = 6°$) slightly expanded, and a pledge to support heartily the new regulations.

If *no* (4) I expel you from this Order.

II. The practice of masks is to be introduced. Each member will know only the member who introduced him.

Severe tests of the candidate's moral excellence, courage, earnestness, humility, refusal to do wrong, to be inserted in the Portal or $5° = 6°$) ritual.

III. Outer Order to be summoned. Similar regulations to be announced to them. New pledges required that they will not communicate the identity of anybody they happen to have known to any new member.

IV. Vault to be reconsecrated.

D.D.C.F. at once accepted these proposals and gave to P. the following instructions, which were at the time so hastily jotted down in a note-book that they are now almost impossible to decipher. From them we make out the following:

That the false* Sapiens Dominabitur Astris was a very stout woman and very fair, who possessed the power of changing her appearance from youth to age and *vice versâ*. That at present she has appeared as Mrs. Horos, or Howes, or Dutton. Her husband, Theo Horos, whose mystical name is Magus Sidera Regit, is a man of about twenty-five to thirty years old, short and very fair. He does not look strong but is extremely so. He has a bald patch on his head with very yellow hair growing over it.

That Sapientia Ad Beneficiendum Hominibus† is very dark and in appearance like S.S.D.D.

To accept nothing from these, and in case of doubt or trouble to telegraph direct to him (D.D.C.F.).

Not to be taken in by mere tricks, and to be both courteous and firm.

The warnings given to P. by D.D.C.F. were as follows:

If he were to feel feeble or ill or worried, and if fires refused to burn, she (Madame Horos) may be expected.

---

* It will be evident that D.D.C.F. detected the fraud between the dates of his first letter to S.S.D.D. and of P.'s arrival in Paris.

† Mrs. Rose Adams (?).

That the real H.P. Blavatsky and the real S.D.A. can incarnate in her; and that they (her forces) have been against D.D.C.F. for long.

That her occult name is Swami Vive Ananda.

That to work against them it was first necessary to separate them, and, at the very last resort, arrest them for theft. (They had stolen a travelling bag belonging to D.D.C.F., containing his rituals.)

To wire their real address to D.D.C.F.

To use the MacGregor symbols—tartan and dirks. The shoulder-plad to be thrown over the head to isolate (like H.P.K. formula). And above all to use their own current against them.

Symbol of Rose Cross only to be used to invoke D.D.C.F. Other symbols were also given him.

P. had long learnt to pity the ignorance and folly of most of the Members of the Order, as we learn from the "History Lection"; he was now destined to put to the test the powers of his alleged chief. If his appearance in England were followed by immediate submission of the rebels, it might safely be concluded that D.D.C.F. had not lost all control; if D.D.C.F. failed, it was then P.'s intention occultly to confound and so destroy the Order.

P. at once set out on his return journey to England, and throughout followed in the minutest details the instructions given him by D.D.C.F. On arriving in London he immediately set his powers in motion. He was at once rejected by various members of the Order, who had always been bitterly envious of his powers and progress.

On the first day of his arrival in London he went to see

Soror P.E.C.Q. and Frater S.: on his way the cab-lamps catch fire, and later a cab-horse runs away with him, and Soror S.S.D.F.'s fire refuses to burn. This was on a Friday.

On Saturday the rose cross given him by D.D.C.F. began to lose colour and whitened; a rubber mackintosh nowhere near the fire suddenly caught light; and fires were by no means anxious to burn. Again he went to see Soror P.E.C.Q., and in the evening records a long dream about "the Horos lot." "They were at C——," he writes, "and wanted to get a particular MS. I had no one I could trust at all, and it was hell and Tommy for a long while. But it ended tragically enough for them."

On Sunday he saw various members of the Order; and on Monday saw Soror S.S.D.F., arranged with her final details, and captured the Vault. He writes: In the morning early I was very badly obsessed, and entirely lost my temper—utterly without reason or justification. Five times at least have horses bolted at sight of me." Also: "Fires at 15 R.R. refuse utterly to burn."

On Tuesday he recaptured vault and suspended H.S. and it appears S.S.D.D., who sought aid from the police, and, so to speak, with the majority of the fallen Order under the protection of the truncheons of Scotland Yard, drew up a new set of rules and regulations, and expelled such members from the Order as had shown any knowledge superior to their own.

Thus it came to pass that on April 21, 1900, the Second Order of the Golden Dawn struggled through the fogs of their own fatuity; the sun of Occult Knowledge rising in the Outer Court of Scotland Yard to illumine twenty-two members of the R.R. and A.C. and the few remaining sleepy constables that the lightning flash had not destroyed.

Five days later we find D.D.C.F. writing to one of the brothers of the Order as follows:

> ... I admit that I *have* committed one great though unavoidable fault, which is this: in giving these persons so great a knowledge I have not also been able to give them brains and intelligence to comprehend it, for this miracle the Gods have not granted me the power to perform. You had better address your reproaches to the Gods rather than to me, unless some spark of returning wisdom can make you recognise in such "critics" the swine who trample the Divine teaching under foot.

With all this we entirely agree, and so eventually did P.; but D.D.C.F. had also failed, the bow had proved as rotten as the arrows, and now P., throwing the empty quiver of the Golden Dawn aside, set out alone on the next stage of his Mystic Progress. P. was not yet certain of this failure of D.D.C.F. The final test was made two years later, and is described in due course.

As to the intrigues of Madame Horos and her husband, nothing very definite is known. But on October 23, 1901, when the Horos case was before the public gaze, D.D.C.F. addressed a letter from Paris to the Editor of *Light** in which he states that on October 13 he wrote a letter to Mr. Curtis Bennett "to protest against the shameful and utterly unauthorised use of its name (the Order of the Golden Dawn) for their own abominable and immoral purposes by the execrable couple calling themselves 'Mr. and Mrs. Horos.' "

---

* This letter was not published in *Light* until January 11, 1901, as at the time the case was *sub judice*.

Further, D.D.C.F.* writes:

Coincident with certain dissensions in my Order, stirred up by a few members, constant fermentors of discord, jealous of my authority, though clamorous for my teaching, the so-called Mr. and Mrs. Horos and a Mrs. Rose Adams, who said she was a doctor of medicine, came to me in Paris in the beginning of last year (1900) with an introduction from an acquaintance of good social standing. At this time my name was well known here in connection with lectures on Ancient Egyptian Religious Ceremonies. The female prisoner stated that they had come with the intention of aiding me in this, and she professed to be an influential member of the Theosophical society, and also of my own Order, giving me the secret name† of a person of high occult rank in it, who had been reported to be dead some years before. I have yet to learn how, when, where and from whom she obtained the knowledge of that Order, which she then certainly possessed. She was also acquainted with the names and addresses of several of the members, notably of those belonging to the discordant category....

D.D.C.F. then states that she stole from his house several MSS. relating to the Order of the G∴ D∴:

"From these she and her infamous accomplices would seem to have concocted some form of initiation under the name of my Order, to impose upon their unfortunate victims." Coincident with her second appearance more dissension arose in the Order, "culminating in severance of the discordant members from it."

As far as it goes this seems to be an honest and straight-forward account.‡ But D.D.C.F. does not state, as he must have known at the time, that Madame Horos was a Vampire of remarkable power, that is to say, one who, following the left-hand path, uses sexual love as a bait to catch her victims by, and that she had told him (as he, D.D.C.F., told P. at the time he appointed P. his envoy) that she (Soror S.V.A.)

* In this letter D.D.C.F. signs himself G. S. L. MacGregor Mathers (Comte MecGregor de Glenstrae).
† S.D.A.
‡ In this letter Mr. Mathers points out the perfectly pure intentions of the Order; who could have doubted it after Inspector Kane's pronouncement at the trial of Madame Horos: "It is a perfectly pure Order"?

could be "overshadowed by H.P. Blavatsky and G.H. Soror S.D.A. 8°=3°." This D.D.C.F. said he knew, because she had related to him details of a very private conversation he had had with Madame Blavatsky at Denmark Hill; also that he most certainly knew that she must be at least a 6°=5° on account of her power of performing miracles.*

As D.D.C.F. apparently much dreaded that Madame Horos might take over the command of the Order in London, he, as we have seen, instructed P. to use cold steel and the MacGregor Tartan against her.† He also informed P. that she had stolen some rituals in a portmanteau, which theft, it will be remembered, P. was to make use of as a last weapon against her. He further added that she was a "financial fraud," and that her husband was but a victim to her vampirism, a sort of soulless maniac, possessing unexpected and demoniacal strength when inspired by her. Her motive, he thought, was hostility against the Order and himself, and as

---

* One or two curious points in her trial are worth recording. Laura Horos, alias The Swami, alias Mrs. Jackson, alias Soror S.V.A., claimed to be Princess Editha Lollito Baroness Rosenthal, Countess of Landfeld, daughter of Louis I., King of Bavaria, and Lola Montez (for Lola Montez see "Lola Montez: an Adventuress of the Forties," by Edmund B. D'Auvergne). In Cape Town she had promoted "The Order of Theocratic Unity," which was also called "The Order of the Atonement," and the "United Templars." Her whole trial was marked by the disgusting display of public eagerness to revel in the filth that was disclosed. At the time, from the coroneted aristocrat to the red-tied demagogue, all classes in England were smacking their filthy lips over such insinuating muck as: "Daisy is a dark little thing, bright and attractive, with hair down her back in thick curls, and looking even less that her age" (sixteen).— *The Sun*, October 17, 1901. On leaving the court the day before this tasty paragraph appeared in the above-mentioned feculent luminary, the public having for several hours greedily sniffed round her messes, commenced to hiss at her, whereupon she turned upon them and shouted: "Shut up, you reptiles. It's only snakes that hiss." For this remark alone her final sentence should most certainly have been reduced.

† Because she had been afraid of them.

he expressed it: "to the current sent at the end of a century to regenerate this planet."

N.'s statement again varies somewhat from the above, and is probably more trustworthy. It is as follows:

S.V.A.* came suddenly to Paris and informed D.D.C.F. that she was S.D.A. 8°=3°, who had not died as had been reported. On hearing this D.D.C.F. at once accepted her statement.† She promised him a large sum of money to build a temple to Isis;‡ for at this time D.D.C.F. was starting what he called "The Mysteries of Isis," and the public dances and entertainments were being held by V.N.R.§ at the Bodinière Theatre.

Now that she had turned out to be a fraud it proved that D.D.C.F. was a fraud also.¶

This of course is as ridiculous as assertion to make as that made by another member of the Order, which was:

"That if indeed it were the promise of S.V.A.'s money that had satisfied D.D.C.F.'s conscience, then he most certainly must be a fraud."

P., in his own subtle way, saw this, arguing that in the case where a great man claims to be a leader amongst men, it is permissible to suppose that his actions may be meant to place his followers between the horns of a rational dilemma.

---

* Fra: Æ.A. of the G∴ D∴ believes that some American members of the Order met Madame Horos in New York, and from them it was that she obtained her knowledge.

† Probably after S.V.A. had given him the grade signs.

‡ This explains the term "financial fraud."

§ D.D.C.F.'s "hermetic" wife: for a more correct account see "The Humanitarian," vol. xvi. No. 2, "Isis-Worship in Paris."

¶ From this wonderful piece of logic one might be permitted to mistake N. for a member of the Rationalistic Press Association. But he was only a 5°=6°.

The disciple who can recognize Christ in the darkness that surrounds the Cross, he is a true disciple. P. suspended judgment on D.D.C.F. till he had proved that he had pledged his honour, to excuse a maniacal assault upon a Saint of God, Frater I.A.

It is permissible for a great musician to improvise in some great masterpiece he may be playing; but it is not permissible for a student to say that he can play this piece when he can only scrape through it by improvising easy bars for the more difficult ones. Similarly with a great Magician; he can indulge in petty black magical tricks if he so desire (there is always a danger), for at a breath they will vanish before the greater magic that is his. But the shivering little cardshuffler who pretends he is the Master because he has successfully forced a card on a village curate, not only cuts off all hope of ever becoming such, but unless he is extremely careful, will find himself literally in the place of the evil triad, marching, not between Isis and Nephthys, but between two sturdy guardians of the peace.

Towards the end of April, 1900, P. returned to his lonely house in the north, but only remaining there a few days, he travelled back to Paris. For it was now past Easter, and so too late in the year to begin the Operation of Abramelin.

He had, as we have seen induced D.D.C.F. to put in force the Deadly and Hostile Current of Will, but, as in the case of the Jackdaw of Rheims, nobody seemed a penny the worse. One might have expected that D.D.C.F. having failed, P. would have abandoned him. No, for it seemed still possible that D.D.C.F., really in touch with the Supreme Chiefs, had yet finally decided to say with Christ upon the

Cross: "Father, forgive them, for they know not what they do," even though this theory was somewhat rudely shaken by D.D.C.F spending the whole of one Sunday afternoon in rattling a lot of dried peas in a sieve under the impression that they were the revolted members: as subsequent events proved, they were only the ideas in his head. So we find P. still loyal, if a little sceptical, and searching within himself to discover a touchstone by which he might prove beyond doubt the authenticity of D.D.C.F.'s claim to represent the Masters. Now, there had been a good deal of talk of an adventure that happened to D.D.C.F. and Frater I.A., who was a guest in his house, in which a revolver figured prominently; but the story was only vague, and Frater I.A., who could and would have told the truth about it, had departed for a distant colony. So on arriving in Paris, P. lured D.D.C.F. into telling the story, which was as follows: That he and I.A. had disagreed upon an obscure point in theology, thereby formulating the accursed Dyad, thereby enabling the Abramelin demons to assume material form: one in his own shape, another in that of I.A. Now, the demon that looked like I.A. had a revolver, and threatened to shoot him (D.D.C.F.), while the demon that resembled himself was equally anxious to shoot I.A. Fortunately, before the demons could fire, V.N.R. came into the room, thus formulating the symbol of the Blessed Trinity, of which her great purity of character would naturally fit her to be a prominent member. Now, the only probability about this story, which D.D.C.F. related on his magical honour as a $7°=4°$, was that D.D.C.F. saw double. Frater P., however, was not going to judge any isolated story by the general laws of probability, so, bowing gracefully, he rose and set out to find Frater I.A., whom he eventually ran down at the house of a holy Yogi in the Cinnamon Gardens, Colombo, to hear his account.

Frater I.A.'s account was less of a strain upon P.'s faculties of belief. They had had, he said, an argument about the God Shiva, the Destroyer, whom I.A. worshipped because, if one repeated his name often enough, Shiva would one day open his eye and destroy the Universe, and whom D.D.C.F. feared and hated because He would one day open His eye and destroy D.D.C.F. I.A. closed the argument by assuming the position Padmasana and repeating the Mantra: "Shiva, Shiva, Shiva, Shiva, Shiva, Shiva." D.D.C.F., angrier than ever, sought the sideboard, but soon returned, only to find Frater I.A. still muttering: "Shiva, Shiva, Shiva, Shiva, Shiva." "Will you stop blaspheming?" cried D.D.C.F.; but the holy man only said: "Shiva, Shiva, Shiva, Shiva, Shiva, Shiva, Shiva, Shiva, Shiva, Shiva." "If you don't stop I will shoot you!" said D.D.C.F., drawing a revolver from his pocket, and levelling it at I.A.'s head; but I.A., being concentrated, took no notice, and continued to mutter: "Shiva, Shiva, Shiva, Shiva, Shiva, Shiva."

Whether overawed by the majesty of the saint, or interrupted by the entry of a third person, I.A. no longer remembered, but D.D.C.F. never pulled the trigger. It was only after this interview, which did not take place till August 1901, that P. definitely decided against D.D.C.F. We must now return to his wanderings, and so we find him in July 1900 crossing the Atlantic to New York.

From New York P. journeyed to Mexico: in this country he travelled about alone for three months; and whilst in

Mexico D.F. became partaker in a wonderful experience known as "the Vision and the Voice."*67 Shortly after this vision, he founded at Guanajato the Order of the L.I.L., and the fire of Adonai descending upon him, he wrote "The Book of the Spirit of the Living God," of which the two following rituals are part:

THE BOOK OF THE SPIRIT OF THE LIVING GOD.

The Casting-out of the Evil ones.
The Consecration of the Shrine.
The Cleansing of the Son of Man.
The Drawing together of the Elements.
The Coming of the Golden Dawn.
The Indwelling of the Isis.
The Initiation of the Whirling Force.
The Chant of Mystery.
The Music of the Divine One.
The Movement of the Spirit.
The Descent of the Soul of Isis.
The Night of Apophis.
The Light of Osiris.
The Knowledge of the Higher Soul.
These be duly written; these shall be, unto the Glory of Thine Ineffable Name.

[The Aspirant, having fasted for a period of nine days, during which he constantly aspireth unto the Higher, shall now enter the Temple which he hath prepared (banishing and consecrating with Fire and Water) and its order and disposition is thus: Let there be a square altar and pillars as for the Neophyte ceremony. On the altar is the Symbol of Isis, with the elements as usual. And know thou that the altar may be removed unto the East after the Great Invocation of Isis, where he shall duly confess himself in the Presence of God the Vast One. Whereafter, let him arise, and, standing in the Sign of Osiris Slain, let him obligate himself as followeth and is hereafter duly set down in clear writing.]

* Two of the "Cries of the Æthyrs."

THE EQUINOX

THE OBLIGATION

[To be most solemnly accepted by him who would attain unto the knowledge and conversation of his Holy Genius.]

In my bondage and affliction, O Lord, let me raise Thy Holy Symbol alike of Suffering and of Strength. I invoke Thee, the great avenging angel HUA, to place thine hand invisibly upon mine head, in attestation of this mine Obligation!

I, . . . a member of the body of Aeshoori, do spiritually bind myself, even as I am this day physically bound unto the Cross of Suffering.

That I will to the utmost endeavour lead a pure and an unselfish life: not revealing to any other person the mysteries which shall herein be revealed unto me: that I will obey the dictates of my Higher Soul: that I will work in silence and with perseverance against all opposition: I furthermore most solemnly promise and swear that with the Divine Permission I will from this day apply myself constantly unto the Great Work: that is, so to purify and exalt my spiritual nature, that with the Aid Divine, I may at length attain to be more than human; and that in this event I will not abuse the great power entrusted unto me. I will invoke the Great Names of God the Vast One before performing any important magical working. I will yearn constantly in love toward the whole of mankind. I will work constantly to the Great End, on pain of being degraded from my present state. Finally, if there arise in me any thought or suggestion seeming to emanate from the Divine, I will examine it with care before acknowledging it to be so.

Such are the Words of this my Obligation, whereto I pledge myself in the Presence of the Divine One and of the Great Avenging Angel HUA.

And if I fail herein, may my rose be disintegrated and my power in magic cease!

[Let the Stigmata be placed upon the Aspirant.

Then let the Aspirant retire; and being invested with the White Robe, the Blue Sash and the Crown and nemys of our Art let him re-enter the Temple and perform the supreme ritual of the Pentagram* in the four quarters; Having first purified the Temple with Fire and Water, and further equilibrated the symbols in his Magical Mirror of the Universe by the Invocation hereafter set down (Come unto me, O Ma, &c.) with the Calls or Keys Enochian suitable thereunto.

And in all this is the wand held by the path of ת: for why? because in drawing down the light Divine; so is it manifest in the Sphere immediately above Malkuth: and in banishing is the Flaming Sword set against the enemies; and in ת is the knowledge of the Elements and the Astral Plane; also ת = the Cross.

* See "Liber O," THE EQUINOX, vol. i. No. 2.

THE TEMPLE OF SOLOMON THE KING

Let him then perform the invoking Ritual of the Supernals:* by the names
אהיה : יה : אלהים יהוה and אראריתא.

And after this let him turn again to the East and recite the Great Invocation of
IAΩ beginning:

"Thee I invoke the Bornless One."†

And this being accomplished, let him lift up his heart unto that Light, and dwell therein, and aspire even unto that which is beyond. And seeing that the gate is called Strait, let him invoke Her who abideth therein, in the path called Daleth, even Our Lady ISIS.]

THE INVOCATION
OF
ISIS.

And I beheld a great wonder in Heaven: a Woman clothed with the Sun: and the Moon was at Her feet: and on Her Head was the Diadem of the Twelve Stars.

Hear me, Our Lady Isis, hear and save.
O Thou, Queen of Love and Mercy!
Thou, crowned with the Throne!
Thou, hornèd as the Moon! Thou, whose countenance is mild and glowing, even as grass refreshed by rain!
Hear me, Our Lady Isis, hear and save!
O Thou, who art in Mater manifest!
Thou Bride and Queen as Thou art Mother and Daughter of the Crucified!
O Thou, who art the Lady of the Earth!
Hear me, Our Lady Isis, hear and save!
O Thou, Our Lady of the Amber Skin!
Lady of Love and Victory!
Bright gate of Glory through the darkling skies!
O crowned with Light and Life and Love!
Head me, Our Lady Isis, hear and save!
By Thy Sacred Flower, the Lotus of Eternal Life and Beauty;
By Thy love and mercy;
By Thy wrath and vengeance;
By my desire toward Thee;
In the name of Aeshoori;
Hear me, Our Lady Isis, hear and save!
Open thy bosom to Thy child!
Stretch wide thy arms and strain me to Thy Breast!
Let my lips touch Thy lips ineffable!
Hear me, Our Lady Isis, hear and save!

* See "Liber O," THE EQUINOX, vol. i. No. 2.
† See The Lesser Key of Solomon: The Goetia.

Lift up Thy Voice and aid me in this hour!
Lift up Thy Voice most musical!
Cry aloud, O Queen and Mother!
Lift up your heads, O ye Gates,
And be ye lift up, ye everlasting Doors.
And the King of Glory shall come in!
Hear me, Our Lady Isis, and receive!
By the symbol of Thy whirling force the Svastika of Flaming Light,
I invoke Thee to initiate my soul!
Let the whirling of my magic dance be a spell and a link with Thy great Light: so that in the Hour of Apophis, in the apparent darkness and corruption of unconsciousness, may rise the golden Sun of Aeshoori, reborn from incorruption.
Hear, Lady Isis, and receive my prayer!
Thee, Thee I worship and invoke!
Hail, Hail to thee, Sole Mother of my Life!
Dwell Thou in me, and bring me to that Self which is in Thee!

[The Altar is now moved, if necessary, and the chant and the mystic dance take place, as is set down hereafter.]

THE CHANT.

Hear, O Amoun! Look with favour on me, Thy Neophyte, now kneeling in Thy presence! Grant that the Music of Thy Mighty Name IAΩ, the signs of Light, the Symbol of the Cross, the woven paces of the mystic 3, may be as a spell and a charm and a working of Magic Art, to draw down my Higher Soul to dwell within my heart, that the Great and Terrible Angel who is my Higher Genius may abide in my own Kether unto the Accomplishing of the Great Work and the Glory of Thine Ineffable Name, AMOUN.

THE MYSTIC DANCE.

[Here we have the sign of the Cross at the Centre. The Magus then whirls off in the triple 3, chanting the Name and giving the sign appropriate, very slowly at first, ever quickening. And having fallen down in an ecstasy, let him after awake; and say:
"I am the Resurrection and the Life," &c., down to the Key Word.*
Which being done, let the Lesser Banishing Rituals of Pentagram and Hexagram† be performed, the Lights extinguished, and the Temple left in Silence.]

THE GREAT OPERATION OF INVISIBILITY.

The Begetting of the Silence.
The Dwelling of the Darkness.

---

* See 5°=6° Ritual, supra.　　† See "Liber O," THE EQUINOX, vol. i. No. 2.

THE TEMPLE OF SOLOMON THE KING

The Formulation of the Shroud.
The Inmost Light.
The Sign of Defence and Protection.
The Closing of the Mouths of the Crocodiles.
The Fear upon the Dwellers of Water.
The Radiant Youth of the Lord.
The Rising from the Lotus of the Floods.
The Habitation of the Palace of Safety.
The Understanding of the Peace of God.*

All this is the Knowledge of HOOR-PO-KRAT-IST unto Whom be the Glory for ever and ever, World without End.

[The Usual Banishings, Consecrations, &c., are performed in temple of 0°=0°.

The forces of Spirit are first invoked by the Supreme Ritual of the Pentagram and the Enochian Keys. Add Hexagram ritual of Binah and her invocation.]

Come unto Me, Thoth, Lord of the Astral Light! I adjure Thee, O Light Invisible, Intangible, wherein all thoughts and deeds are written; I adjure Thee by Thoth, thy Lord and God; by the symbols and the words of power: by the Light of my Godhead in Thy midst: by the Lord Harpocrates, the God of this mine Operation: that Thou leave Thine abodes and habitations, to concentrate about me, invisible, intangible, as a shroud of darkness; a formula of defence: that I may become invisible, so that seeing me men see not, nor understand the thing that they behold!

Come unto me, O Ma, Goddess of Truth and Justice! Thou that presidest over the Eternal Balance.
Auramooth, come unto me, Lady of the Water!
Thoum-aesh-neith, come unto me, Lady of the Fire!
Purify me and consecrate, for I am Aeshoori the Justified. For the Twelve Stars of Light are on my Brow: Wisdom and Understanding are balanced in my thought!
Wrath in my right hand and the Thunderbolts;
Mercy in my left hand and the fountains of delight!
In my heart is Aeshoori and the Symbol of Beauty.
My thighs are as pillars on the right and on the left; Splendour and Victory, for they cross with the currents reflected. I am established as a Rock, for Jesod is my foundation.

* Note that the whole Operation may be performed mentally and in silence, and that on each occasion of concentrating the shroud the God-form and Vibration of Harpocrates, as taught, may be employed.

THE EQUINOX

And the sphere of the Nephesch, and the palaces of Malkuth are cleansed and consecrate, balanced and beautiful, in the might of Thy Name, Adonai, to whom be the Kingdom, the Sceptre and the Splendour: The Rose of Sharon and the Lily of the Valley.

O Thou! HOOR-PO-KRAT-IST! [Middle Pillar.]
   Child of the Silence!
O Thou! HOOR-PO-KRAT-IST! [Mystic Circumambulation.]
   Lord of the Lotus!
O Thou! HOOR-PO-KRAT-IST! [Silence.]
   Thou that standest on the heads of the dwellers of the Waters!
Thee, Thee I invoke!
O Thou, Babe in the Egg of Blue!
Lord of Defence and Protection!
Thou who bearest the Rose and Cross of Life and Light!
Thee I invoke!
Behold I am! a circle on whose hands the Twelvefold Kingdom of my Godhead stands.
I am the A and the Ω.
My life is as the circle of the sky.
I change but I cannot die!
O ye! the Bennu Birds of Resurrection, Who are the hope of men's mortality!
Back, Crocodile Mako, Son of Set! Depart from me, ye workers of iniquity!

Behold He is in Me and I in Him!
Mine is the Lotus, as I rose from the firmament of Waters;
My throne is set on high;
My light is in the firmament of Nu!
I am the Centre and the Shrine: I am the Silence and the Eternal Light:
Beneath my feet they rage, the angry crocodiles; the dragons of death; the eaters of the wicked.
But I repress their wrath: for I am HOOR-PO-KRAT-IST, the lotus-throned Lord of Silence.
If I said: Come up upon the mountains, the celestial waters would flow at my word and the celestial fires flame forth. For I am Râ enshrouded: Khephra unmanifest to men; I am my father Hoor, the might of the Avenger: and my mother Asi, the Veiled One: Eternal wisdom in eternal beauty.
Therefore I say unto Thee: Bring Me unto Thine Abode in the Silence Unutterable, Wisdom: All-Light, All Power!
HOOR-PO-KRAT-IST! Thou Nameless Child of the Eternities! Bring me to Thee, that I may be defended in this work of Art.

THE TEMPLE OF SOLOMON THE KING

Thou, the Centre and the Silence!
Light Shrouded in Darkness is Thy Name!
The Celestial Fire is Thy Father!
Thy Mother the Celestial Sea!
Thou art the Equilibrium of the All, and Thou art Lord against the Face of the Dwellers within the Waters!
Bring me, I say, bring me to Thine abode of Silence: that I may go invisible: so that every Spirit created, and every soul of man and beast; and every thing of sight and sense, and every Spell and Scourge of God, may see me not nor understand!
And now, in the Name of God the Vast One, Who hath set limits and bounds unto all material and astral things, do I formulate a barrier and a bar without mine astral form, that it may be unto me as a wall, and as a fortress, and as a defence.
And I now declare that it is so formulated, to be a basis and receptacle for the Shroud of Darkness which I shall presently encincture me withal.

And unto ye, O forces of Akasa,* do I now address my Will.
In the Great Names Exarp, Hcoma, Nanta and Bitom,†
By the mysterious letters and sigils of the Great Tablet of Union.‡
By the mighty Names of God AHIH, AGLA, IHVH, ALHIM.
By the Great God Harpocrates;
By your deep purple darkness;
By my white and brilliant light do I conjure ye:
Collect yourselves together about me: clothe this astral form with a shroud of darkness:
Gather, O Gather, Flakes of Astral Light:
Shroud, shroud my form in your substantial night:
Clothe me and hide me, at my charm's control;
Darken man's eyes and blind him in his soul!
Gather, O Gather, at my Word Divine,
Ye are the Watchers and my soul the shrine!
[Let formulate the Idea of becoming Invisible; imagine the results of success: Then say:]
Let the shroud of concealment encircle me at a distance of ten inches from the physical body.
Let the Sphere be consecrated with Water and with Fire. [Done.]
O Auramooth and O Thoum-aesh-neith, I invoke and beseech you: Let the vapour

* The Element of Spirit.
† The names on the Tablet of Spirit.
‡ The Tablet of Spirit.

of this water, and of this fire, be as a basis on the material plane for the formation of this shroud of Art.

[Form mentally the shroud.]

I, P., Frater of the Order of the Golden Dawn, and a 5°=6° thereof: a Lord of the Paths in the Portal of the Vault of the Adepts: a Frater Ordinis Rosae Rubeae et Aureae Crucis: and especially a member of the 0°= 0° grade: master of the pass-word "H——" and of the Grand Word "M——," am here: in order to formulate to myself a shroud of concealment: that I may attain unto knowledge and power, to use in the Service of the Eternal Gods: that I may pursue safely and without interruption my magical and other pursuits: and that I may pass unseen among men, to execute the Fiat of Tetragrammaton. And I bind and obligate myself and do spiritually swear and affirm: that I will use this power to a good purpose only, and in the service of the Gods.

And I declare that in this Operation I shall succeed: that the Shroud shall conceal me alike from men and spirits; that it shall be under my control: ready to disperse and to re-form at my command.

And I declare that all is now ready for the due fulfilment and prosecution of this mine Operation of Magick Art.

[Go to Altar as Hierophant, left hand on triangle, right hand holding Verendum, by path of ת or Malkuth.]

THE POTENT EXORCISM.

Come unto me, O shroud of darkness and of night. I conjure ye, O particles of Darkness, that ye enfold me, as a guard and shroud of utter Silence and of Mystery.

In the name AHIH and by the name AHIH!

In the name AGLA and by the name AGLA!

In the name EXARP and by the name EXARP!

In the name HCOMA and by the name HCOMA!

In the name NANTA and by the name NANTA!

In the name BITOM and by the name BITOM!

In the name TETRAGRAMMATON ELOHIM and by the name TETRAGRAM-MATON ELOHIM!

In the name HOOR-PO-KRAT-IST and by the name HOOR-PO-KRAT-IST!

By your deep purple darkness!

By my white brilliant light!

I invoke ye: I conjure ye: I exorcise ye potently: I command and constrain ye: I compel ye to utter, absolute and instant obedience, and that without deception or delay,—for why? The Light of Godhead is my trust and I have made IHVH mine hope!

"Gather, O Gather, Flakes of Astral Light:

Shroud, shroud my form in your substantial night:

THE TEMPLE OF SOLOMON THE KING

Clothe me and hide me, at my charm's control;
Darken man's eyes and bind him in his soul!
Gather, O Gather, at my Word Divine,
Ye are the Watchers and my soul the shrine!"

[Turn round three times.]

In the Name of the Lord of the Universe and by the Power of mine own Higher Soul and by the Aspiration of Thine Higher Soul I conjure thee, O shroud of darkness and of mystery, that thou encirclest me, so that I may become invisible: so that seeing me men may see not, neither understand: but that they may see the thing that they see not and comprehend not the thing that they behold! So mote it be!

[Go North.]

I have set my feet in the North and have said: "I will shroud myself in mystery and concealment."

The Voice of My Higher Soul said unto me:

"Let me enter the path of darkness: peradventure thus may I attain the Light. I am the Only Being in an Abyss of Darkness: from the Darkness came I forth ere my birth; from the Silence of a Primal Sleep." And the Voice of Ages answered unto my soul:

"I am He that formulates in Darkness: the Light indeed shineth in Darkness, but the Darkness comprehendeth it not."

Let the Mystic Circumambulation take place in the Place of Darkness.

[Go round, knocks, &c. In South formulate Pillars as before and imagine self as shrouded.]

[In the West.]

Invisible, I cannot pass by the Gate of the Invisible save by virtue of the Name of Darkness.

[Formulate forcibly shroud about thee.]

Darkness is My Name and Concealment!

I am the Great One Invisible of the Paths of the Shades. I am without fear though veiled in Darkness: for within me, though unseen, is the Magic of the Light!

[Go round. In North, Pillars, &c., as before.]

[In the East.]

Invisible, I cannot pass by the Gate of the Invisible, save by virtue of the Name of Light.

[Form shroud forcibly.]

I am Light shrouded in Darkness. I am the wielder of the Forces of the Bilanx!

[Concentrate shroud mentally. Go West of Altar.]

[The Potent Exorcism as before.]

THE EQUINOX

Shroud of Concealment, long has thou dwelt concealed! Quit the Light, that thou mayst conceal me before men!

[Carefully formulating shroud.]

I receive Thee, as a covering and a guard!

KHABS AM PEKHT!
KONX OM PAX!
LIGHT IN EXTENSION!

Before all magical manifestation cometh the Knowledge of the Hidden Light.

[Go to Pillars: give signs and words and with the Sign of Horus project your whole will so as to realize the self fading out. The effect will be that the physical body will become gradually and partially invisible, as though a veil or cloud were coming between it and thee. Divine ecstasy will follow, but no loss of self-control. With Sign of Silence use Hoor Po Krat formula* and vibrate the Grand Word.†]

[Repeat concentration and Mystic Circumambulation.]

[Intensely form shroud: stand at East and say:]

Thus have I formulated unto myself this shroud of Darkness and of Mystery as a concealment and a guard.

O Thou, Binah, IHVH ALHIM, AIMA, AMA, Lady of Darkness and of Mystery; Moon of the Concealèd; Divine Light that rulest in thine Own Deep Gloom: Thy power I invoke. Come unto me and dwell within me, that I also may have poser and control, even I, over this shroud of Darkness and of Mystery.

And now I conjure thee, O shroud of Darkness and of Mystery, that thou conceal me from the eyes of all men, from all things of sight and sense, in this my present purpose: which is . . .

O Binah, IHVH ALHIM, AMA, AIMA, Thou who art Darkness illuminated by the Light Divine, send me Thine Archangel Tzaphquiel, Thy legions of Aralim, the mighty angels, that I may disintegrate and scatter this shroud of darkness and of mystery, for its work is ended for the hour.

I conjure thee, O shroud of darkness and of Mystery, who hast well served my purpose, that thou now depart unto thine ancient ways. But be ye very instant and ready, when I shall again call ye, whether by a word or a will, or by this great invocation of your powers, to come quickly and forcibly to my behest, again to shroud me from the eyes of men! And now I say unto ye, Depart in peace, and with the Blessing of God the Vast and Shrouded One: and be ye very ready to come when ye are called!

IT IS FINISHED!

---

* Imagine yourself as Harpocrates standing upon two crocodiles.

† I.e. of 0°=0°, Har-Po-Krat.

278

These rituals being completed, P. left Mexico D.F., and in the first days of the new year of 1901 he journeyed to Ixtaccihuatl. Some time before this he had been joined by his friend D.A., and with him he travelled to Colima and thence to Toluca and Popocatepetl.

Now that we have arrived at the end of this chapter, it will be pertinent to inquire into the progress P. made since he passed through the $5° = 6°$ Ritual and became an Adeptus Minor in the Order of the R.R. et A.C. Strictly speaking, some time before he was officially promoted to the grade of $5°=6°$, he was already a $6°=5°$. In London and Paris his works of Magical Art had caused him to be admired by his friends and dreaded by his enemies. He had succeeded in proving that the ש of ש Operation was in fact none other than that of "The Rising on the Planes," though in practice and theory very different. By their study and the equilibrating forces of the $5°=6°$ Ritual he was able to apply the eye of a skilled craftsman to the dreaded* Operation of Abramelin,

---

* On this occasion the Abramelin demons appeared as misty forms filling the whole house with a pernicious aura, which was still noticeable three years after they had been attracted. Whether these demons are to be considered as material or mental beings depends upon the philosophic outlook of the reader. Nevertheless, let it be understood that Abraelin is not a work to be taken lightly. The obsession of these demons was probably one of the chief causes of D.D.C.F.'s troubles. Frater P., in spite of his equilibrating practices of Yoga which followed immediately upon this Operation, suffered terribly on their account. Frater Æ.A. fled secretly from his house in terror; his gardener, a teetotaller for twenty years, went raving drunk, as did nearly every one who lived on the estate—we could continue examples for pages. His clairvoyants became drunkards and prostitutes, while later a butcher upon one of whose bills the names of two demons had been casually jotted down, viz., Elerion and Mabakiel, which respectively mean "A laugher" and "Lamentation" (conjoint, "unlooked-for sorrow suddenly descending upon happiness") whilst cutting up a joint for a customer accidentally severed the femoral artery and died in a few minutes. These mishaps are most likely

and though he was never destined to accomplish this Sacred Work in the prescribed fashion, it so far iluminated him (for he worked astrally at it for months whilst in Mexico) as to show him the futility of even successful Magic. He was disgusted with his results. He had attained a rank which few arrive at, namely, that of Adeptus Major; and now, even though he had attained to the powers of Hecate, for which he had so long striven, he saw that the Great Attainment lay far, far beyond. And so it happened that by renouncing all his magical strength to gain a greater Power, a Nobler Art, he set forth upon the Path of the Lion that bridges the great gulf between the two highest Grades of the Second Order, as it is written: "A similar Fire flashingly extending through the rushings of Air, or a Fire formless whence cometh the Image of a Voice, or even a flashing Light abounding, revolving, whirling forth, crying aloud. Also there is the vision of the fire flashing Courser of Light, or also a Child, borne aloft on the shoulders of the Celestial Steed, fiery, or clothed with gold, or naked, or shooting with the bow shafts of Light, and standing on the shoulders of the horse; then if thy meditation prolongeth itself, thou shalt unite all these Symbols into the Form of a Lion."

mere coincidences, but a coincidence when it happens is quite as awkward as the real thing, and in the case of Abramelin the coincidences can be counted by scores.

(To be continued)

THE COMING OF APOLLO

RED roses, O red roses,
  Roses afire, aflame,
O burgeon that discloses
    The glory of desire—
    Hush! all the heart of fire
  Is mingled in Thy name,
O roses, roses, roses,
    Red roses of desire.

The golden-shafted sunlight
  Beats down upon the sward;
The pillared serpent's one light
    Is a flame of red desire;
    O snake from out the mire,
  I slay thee with the sword,
The strong sword of the sunlight,
    The sword of my desire!

The still strong bird of sorrow
  Keens through the golden blue,
And many a bitter morrow
    Is borne upon his wings;

THE EQUINOX

The glory that he brings
He brings, O King, to you,
The wonder-song of sorrow
In the flapping of his wings.

The flaming day grows olden
As the youth of glory wanes;
And the sun-bird grows more golden
And narrower his wings;
He swirls around in rings;
He bears the bloody stains
Of all the sorrows olden
Upon his bright gold wings.

And scarlet-rimmed and splendid,
The wide blue vault is spanned
With golden rays wide-bended
From the green earth to the skies;
The hush of noontide dies,
Song rises from the land—
And scarlet, naked, splendid,
Glow out the radiant skies.

A cloud of huge hushed laughter
Shakes all the listening boughs,
And a sudden hush comes after,
Dropped from the silent skies;
A myriad laughing eyes
Flash in a still carouse,
And shake with silent laughter
The blue vault of the skies.

THE COMING OF APOLLO

A breeze—a leaf—a shadow—
  The falling of a bud—
The wind across the meadow—
    A flash of light—a call—
    A patter on the wall—
The air is bright as blood;
A moment stands a shadow,
    A moment sounds a call.

Awake! the spell is broken,
  And hushed the sense of noon;
What silent word was spoken
    In answer to the Call? . . .
    Hush! See the rose-leaves fall;
Ah! see the pathway strewn
With tender rose-leaves, broken
    In answer to the Call.

How still it lies, the garden,
  Now the red flash is gone;
The brown soil seems to harden
    Now the strange spell is fled;
    And the earth lies cold and dead,
And the hot hours hurry on.
It is only a quiet garden
    Now that the spell is fled.

But the hour, the hour and the token,
  Have passed as a dream away,
Now that the spell is broken,
    And the moment's flash is fled.

THE EQUINOX

When the secret word was said,
  Ah! what remained to say?
No word, but silence' token
    That the golden God had fled.

And the roses, roses, roses
  Flame in their red desire,
And every bud uncloses
    To mark the sign that fled;
    The wonder-word hath sped
  To the far Olympian fire:
The spell of the crimson roses
    Has passed from earth and fled.

But still the old silent garden
  Remember the golden flush
When the heavens seemed to harden
    For a moment that came and fled;
    When the whole green earth grew red
  In a breathless spell and a hush,
And the world grew young in the garden,
    And trembled, and passed, and fled.

VICTOR B. NEUBURG

REVIEWS

THE OCCULT REVIEW. Monthly. 7d. net.

Still, as before, the best and brightest of the periodicals dealing with transcendental subjects. It hears all sides and has no axe to grind.   C.

SELECTED POEMS OF FRANCIS THOMPSON. Fifth thousand. Methuen and Co., and Burns and Oates. No price.

Long years ago, in 1898, I was one of the very few admirers of Francis Thompson. His wealth of thought and pomp of diction more than atoned for the too frequent turgidity of his music.

Now, it seems, I am but one of five thousand just persons. So much the better for them! The more the merrier!   ALEISTER CROWLEY.

SCIENTIFIC IDEALISM. By W. KINGSLAND. Rebman, Limited. 7s. 6d. net.

Science and Idealism have laboured long, and have at last brought forth a book worth reading and rereading, a book worth studying and restudying. Mr. W. Kingsland is to be congratulated; the "Foreword" alone is worth the price asked. Here are a few quotations:

"The individual must ultimately claim not merely his relationship to the Whole, but his *identity* therewith."

"Thus the individual . . . finds that reality ever appearing to evade him . . . in proportion as this is realized, he must necessarily revolt against any and every system which would *limit* him."

". . Nothing can be accepted on mere authority."

As old as the Vedas is the question "What am I?" Ay! older, for the first man probably asked it, and yet it crouches ever before us with enticing eyes like some evil Sphinx. This question Mr. Kingsland tries to narrow down by a theoretical reconciliation of Science and Idealism. "Where we do not really know we must be content with a working hypothesis." But the following citations are those of a man who is, if still in the twilight, yet no longer in the dark:

". . . Evil as well as that which we call good, are part of and essential to that fundamental underlying Unity by and through which alone the Universe can be conceive of as a Cosmos and not a Chaos."

"Our apparent failures are necessary lessons. We often learn more by failure than by success. The only real failure is to cease to endeavour."

"Could we but realise this Truth in our life and consciousness, it would be to us the end of all doubt and of all strife, for it would be the realisation of our own inherent and inalienable divine nature, the realisation of the Infinite Self, the attainment of which is the end and goal of our evolution."

Drop the conditional tense, Mr. Kingsland. Say no longer "if I could," but

"I will!" And then write for the nations yet another book, not one based on "Belief," but on "Knowledge," a book of Realisation, a book of Truth. "Then will the health of the daughter of my people recover"; and "in thy market will be sold the wheat of Minnith, and Pannag, and honey, and oil, and balm."   F.

EUSAPIA PALLADINO AND HER PHENOMENA. By HEREWARD CARRINGTON, T. Werner Laurie.

We remember Mr. Hereward Carrington as the author of "Fasting, Vitality, and Nutrition."

In six hundred odd closely printed 9 in. × 6 in. pages the author proved that Eating Is All A Mistake. Food supplies no nourishment, but only causes disease; if you only fast long enough, you cure cancer and consumption and everything else.

Now when a man who can print drivel of this sort comes forward and testifies to the wind that blows from the top of a medium's head, it is unlikely that any serious person will take the trouble even to read his statement.

Worse, the presence of such a person at a sitting entirely invalidates the testimony of his fellow-sitters, even be they such presumably competent persons as Mr. W. W. Baggalay and the Hon. Everard Feilding.

Le grande hystérie, such as must play no small part in the constitution of a person who can persuade himself that the best athletic training is stark starvation, that tobacco is poison, alcohol fatal in doses of three drops, and the use of the reproductive faculties under any circumstances tantamount to suicide, *la grande hystérie*, I say, is sufficient to explain anything. A sufferer is capable of assisting the medium to cheat, and of throwing dust in the eyes of his fellow-observers, entirely unconscious that he is doing so, under the spell of his morbid perversity.

We hope shortly to publish studies, not of the phenomena alleged to be produced by mediums, but of the mental make-up of those investigators who allege them to be genuine.

We must be understood to refer only to material phenomena; we have no doubt concerning the mental and moral phenomena. Spiritualism leads in every case that we have yet investigated to mental spermatorrhoea, culminating in obsession and complete moral and intellectual atony.

ALEISTER CROWLEY.

THE BRIGHTON MYSTERY

THE mind of the Wise easily shunts to strange speculations before taking again to the main line of severely controlled thoughts. Associations of ideas—your name is Harpy. How you do catch unheralded the mortal uncautious! The Wise knows you; he is aware of your jumpy step; he makes ready; he fights and . . . *væ vitctis!* he yokes you. But the fool . . . !

However, we digress and progress not. I ought to be relating a personal experience. One night, one sleepness nights, I was allowing my eternal enemies, the harpies to whom I have already referred, the following of their fancy for a while. They were poachy enough for me not to fear them.

Earlier in the evening I and a few friends had been discussing affinities and mysteries, among other subjects, and as I lay in bed one of the recent mysteries gave mental food to the harpies. My thoughts were of course utterly passive and need no record. But something which subsequently happened causes me to mention this. Let me recall the main facts of the Brighton murder.

On the night of the crime there had been a dinner-party at the house of Mrs. Ridley. Towards midnight the hostess remained alone with her servants: a butler, two footmen, a cook, and two maids. Mrs Ridley's apartments have a full view of the sea, as has also the room of her maid Jane Fleming. The cook and the other maids, as well as the three men, slept in rooms at the back of the house.

At the inquest James Dale, the footman, and the butler deposed that they heard no noise whatever during the night. Now, Harry Carpenter, the other man, had been found murdered in the first-floor bathroom. And it has been ascertained that he could not possibly leave his room without being heard by the others, who slept one on each side of him, as neither of them *did* sleep on that particular night, for some reason or another. But of course this is public knowledge, The police and the papers have received scores of anonymous letters denouncing Jane Fleming, the butler, and Dale as the authors of the crime. They have not been arrested. Why?

I am certain that they are entirely innocent; yet the police cannot be aware of the reasons which lead me to this certainty, and in the absence of these proofs they ought to be suspected.

Mrs. Ridley's bed stood with the foot towards the fireplace, a door being on either side of the head, the window on her left hand.

When her maid entered the room in the morning she found the body of her mistress lying at the foot of the bed, the head towards the window. It was entirely naked. Near the body was a shift, and over the neck a white shawl had been carelessly thrown. It had upon it in various parts as many as sixteen wounds, cuts and bruises of various importance. The most serious and only mortal one was behind the left ear; the great vessels of the neck were destroyed and the skull much injured. The most ugly wound to the sight was under the nose, which had been so entirely damaged that it rendered the whole face almost unrecognisable. Yet there has been, I must say, no doubt as to the identity. The wounds had been inflicted with an instrument edged but blunt, used by a very weak person, possibly a woman. The bedclothes were not disarranged, and there was some strangeness in the fact, for the maid swore to having seen her mistress in bed, while after the discovery of the murder the bed was found made as if no one had either lain in or even sat on it. The police took it as a proof that Mrs. Ridley had some connection with the murderer or murderers, and, after her maid's departure, had been preparing herself to go out. She was known to be a most tidy and cautious lady. Had she obeyed an instinctive need of leaving everything in order?

But let us turn to the bathroom. There also was a murdered body. Carpenter, the footman, had been killed with the same or with a similar instrument. Not without a severe conflict, however. How was it that his left hand held tightly hidden in its grasp a small piece of lace which was recognised as belonging to Mrs. Ridley? It had been torn from a handkerchief belonging to her. The strangeness of the discovery was all the more striking because the handkerchief referred to was found later on by the maid in a drawer between many others, neither on top nor at the bottom. The piece of lace found in the hand of Carpenter corresponded exactly.

So much for the victims. Now for the motive. Mrs. Ridley was a wealthy widow, and possessed many valuable pictures. She had a well-known dislike for cheque-books; and a firm of London bankers came forward at the inquest, having written a private letter to the coroner to the effect that the deceased lady was their client, and deposed that on he morning before the murder she had received the sum of £1200 in banknotes and gold, which sum was to be handed over to Mr. ——, a representative of a well-known firm of art dealers, in payment for a certain picture.

Well, the police and the public knew that too; it had leaked out somehow. But beyond this they knew little. That is, they had forgotten. Because there *were* other facts. These facts, however, could not help a detective to realise their importance because they were loose facts—events, that is, which were in contradiction with one another. Yet still they afforded a clue. The murderer might be a criminal thief, a temperance reformer, a madman, a clergyman, a novelist, or a devil-worshipper—any person, in fact, in the whole world whose hand is weak or unsteady. But the whole world is comparatively too large to allow of any certainty in picking out the murderer of Mrs. Ridley. I say comparatively, because to the Wise the world is small. . . . *Passons!*

Some time before her sudden death Mrs. Ridley had had a guest in her house whose unaffected manners had much offended the dignity of the male servants. He was said to be a distant relation of the late big-gun maker, James Ridley. But he was *not*. The late Ridley had no relations whatever on earth—at least among human beings. I happen to know that the so-called relation was a spiritualist. This sounds bad enough. Was Mrs. Ridley in agreement with him or was she not? It is nothing more than a question. Suppress the query, give the mere words another place in the sentence and you have two affirmations: *She was* or *She was not.* How infinitely clearer is the point! Any intellectual bloodhound ought to find out which is *the* affirmation. That is, if the so-called relation was the murderer. I say he is, though I have no human proofs whatever to offer. The police—that is, my friend Inspector Bennet—tell me he is not, but he may know something. One of our great dailies has (alone) come very near the truth on the matter. It was given as an editorial opinion that the widow of the gun-maker was a little out of her mind and had committed suicide, with the help of some one, in spite of her footman, who had been attracted by the noise. Curious blend of truth and imagination!

A few hours after I had allowed the furies to play havoc with my brains I received the following letter; and that is why I know so much. For the very reason of its strangeness I felt at once that it could be the work of no practical joker. The mysterious part of the adventure can, I believe, be solved without much difficulty.

"Dear Sir," it ran,—"You do not know me; but I know you. I have followed you through the world with the eyes of my spirit. I once saw in the window of a Paris photographer a portrait of yours which arrested my attention, and since that day your personality has been the constant, though not unpleasant, obsession of my life. I am perfectly acquainted with you and your life, your work and moods and ways of living. I came to England a few weeks ago and I saw you. To-day I write. I am aware that you are interested in the strange happenings which are to be studied in this world. My last adventure will cause you to be interested in the Brighton murder. I have been nearer than any one else to be the criminal author of that murder. Only, when I arrived it was too late. Had I not been already a madman during the years 1897 and 1898, and eventually cured, this strange adventure would certainly have sent me into a state of complete insanity. As it is, I am in a certain way vaccinated against madness.

"Monsieur, as true as I am a Frenchman born in America of a German mother by a poor Spanish hidalgo who forgot to give her his address—you see, I am French by naturalization (I wanted to make up for their declining birth-rate)—the footman of Mrs. Ridley has been murdered by that lady herself because he tried to save her life. I don't know her past, but I am certain that she had been a near relation of mine in some former existence, and that she was much interested in spiritualism. *Voilà la clef du mystère!*

"Señor, you will realise that a crime is composed of a great number of circumstances extending over a long or short period of time and different in their importance. If a woman is seen to stick a stiletto into another person's breast, that is a stronger circumstance than if she is seen pulling it out; and this would be stronger than if she were standing over the dead man with a bloody knife. Two of the cases at least are compatible with innocence. Evidence, you understand it also, is nothing more than grounds for reasonable guesses, and crimes are collections of circumstances connected together, the proof of any one of which is a reasonable ground for guessing that the others existed. But, *pocos palabras!*

"*Sehr geehrter Herr!* Nine times out of ten an innocent man does not know the strength of his own case, and he may, real *Schafskopf*, by mere asinism allow suspicious circumstances to pass unexplained which he could explain perfectly well. How much more so, then, when the innocent is no more among the living—or when, being alive, he stands in a blessed ignorance of the suspicions to which some unexplained circumstances have given birth!

"To the point, sir! One lives again in order to complete, or improve, an action which in a previous life has been left incomplete or inferior; and also to make a fresh attempt at mastering, in very similar circumstances, some powerful original tendency. It's fierce, but it's true. Had you previously been a packer of canned meat, or a guard on the railroad, or a Wall Street man, there would have been in your life some incidents, causing certain thoughts in your brains, and eventually actions. Yes, it would have been so, and you would to-day probably be doing your best not to improve upon the action which was the resultant of those thoughts. I say '*not to improve*,' because we are human, all of us.

"As it is, you were a Redskin in North America, your name was 'Faim de loup,' and you are placed in such circumstances that you must find it difficult not to fall again into your old uncivilised ways.

"Now, Mrs. Ridley was a spiritualist. And she was not a widow! Her husband was not dead! He was the great gun-maker whom you know, and whose obsequies you may remember. His coffin contained but another man's remains. . . .

"Love, my dear sir, is a much-mistaken phenomenon, which only perhaps the most loutish among us could understand because of its very simplicity. Love belongs to the spiritual world; it is an attraction, based on affinities. There were such affinities between Mrs. Ridley and her husband.

"Of course, you know something about wireless telegraphy. A wireless message can be intercepted by some one for whom it is not meant, even if that some one had no inclination towards that kind of French game. He unwillingly receives the message which is for another, and it may so happen that he obtains a similar knowledge of the answer. Such is the case also in the spiritual world: such was the case of Mrs. Ridley. Her love-thoughts went to her husband; her husband's love-thoughts went to her, but . . .

"Have you ever taken into your field of consideration how many 'buts' there come into the field of our actions? I submit to you that every painful, or sinful, or harmful, or simply unpleasant incident of our lives is the outcome of the best intentions—relatively best, at all events, *our best*—and I am sure that you agree with me. There were two 'buts' in the case of Mrs. Ridley.

"The first was of a personal character. Mrs. Ridley had nothing more than love-thoughts to give to her gun-maker husband. She was deprived of temperament—as the French understand the word—and her husband was like the candle which has never seen itself aflame, and is in consequence unaware of what it misses through its having had no acquaintance with a lighted match. Their love was not of this world, and the Powers which rule 'here-below' resented what they considered to be a contempt of their Majesty; and no children were sent to the couple. It was an ethereal love which they both knew to be somewhat incomplete. Mr. Ridley had little experience of the world, and still less conversation. Apart from his gun-making business and his spiritual bride, he cared in his own words, not a shell for anything. Nevertheless, in

his semi-conscious anxiety, he attempted to devise some altera-
tions in the appearance of his future widow. Did he see a hat
which he thought somewhat suggestive of earthy sentiments,
he would at once buy a similar one for Mrs. Ridley. Alas!
with as without it his wife looked the ethereal spirituality that
she was. He went to Paris on business, and, finding
himself in that materialistic city, bought a complete set of
befrilled and dainty underlinen; Mrs. Ridley etherealised
even the appearance of that *lingerie de cocotte.*

"We are far from the crime, you think. *Carajo,* I guess
not! We cannot be any nearer. Who killed Mrs. Ridley? I
don't know. I was very near doing it.

"Why was she killed? The murderer did not know.

"Who killed the footman? Mrs. Ridley.

"Why did she kill him? Because he tried to prevent her
from being murdered.

"Here, in a nutshell, my dear sir, you have all the crime
and its explanation. When I say that I do not know who
killed Mrs. Ridley I mean at the same time that it matters
not. *The murderer is innocent.** Listen to what happened
to me.

"I saw a man. He had the most wonderful eyes I ever
saw; they could at times brighten one's face by merely looking
into it; yet they chilled me, drying my blood and sending a
cold shiver all over my bones. They reflected the sky as an
ape imitates man, in a way inferior, poorly, servilely. And a
certain uncanny look which never quite left him made that
man an undesirable neighbour to me. Had I not seen him I
would refuse to admit the reality of his existence.

* Underlined with red ink in the original letter.

"I met him during a journey. Comfortably seated in a corner of the railway compartment, I was reading a book of the sixteenth century in France merely to occupy my mind, so that I should not be tempted to look through the window at the too commonplace scenery.

"We had just passed a station, as I knew by the disturbing voice of a porter; and, on resuming my journey, I felt sorry that no companion of travel had entered the lonely carriage. I attempted another perusal of my book, when, without any opening of the door or of the window, I noticed a stranger seated in the opposite corner. His eyes were on me. He left me no time for much thinking, speaking almost immediately.

" 'May I beg you to forgive a stranger, sir?' he said, 'but I cannot endure this temperature. Will you allow me to open the windows?'

"I like fresh air myself; but it was so very cold on that day that I had carefully shut both windows. Something in his appearance and his look, intensely heavy on me, led me to refrain from answering. I merely nodded, grunted, gathered my rug higher around me, and resumed my reading.

"He thanked me profusely, opened the windows, both of them, as wide as they could be, and, without taking any notice of my evident displeasure, addressed me anew.

" 'Your are wondering, no doubt, sir, as to the way by which I came in. Well, I do not mind telling you I came through this hole.'

"He pointed at the ceiling with his hand, and I raised my eyes. The only aperture to which he could be referring was a tiny little hole in the glass which protected the imaginary

296

light provided by the railway company. I shrugged my shoulders, grunted again, and plunged back into my book.

" 'You do not believe me, I see,' he went on, 'yet I speak the truth. I came through this broken glass to you—to you, sir, on purpose to see you, to speak to you. I came from the sky. Now, do not look at the alarm bell. My message is a pleasant one. You are chosen for a mission.'

"I thought I had borne enough, and expressed at once the idea that my strong desire was to be left alone. The stranger laughed in a queer manner, and as my eyes met his once more, I felt a peculiar sensation of mixed sympathy and fear. It was then that I noticed how brightening to any one his eyes could be. He spoke in a gentler tone.

" 'I am going to explain to you the object of my coming. You are going back to Brighton to-morrow night, are you not?'

" 'Yes, I am; but that is no concern of yours.'

" 'Be silent. Look at me. All right. Listen now!'

"I heard no more his human voice. As I raised my head a feeling of lost consciousness overcame me. I was unable to control my brains, my will, my movements. He spoke again and at great length, but I could neither answer nor interrupt him. I could not say that I was in a subconscious state, but neither would I care to say that I was in a normal one. He took my hands and held them in his own. I could not move.

" 'It is necessary that a certain person be freed from the material envelope which gives apparent shape to her ethereal spirit. Mrs. Ridley lives at 34 —— Street, Brighton. By the way, my name is Ridley.'

" 'Here I tried to speak, but found it impossible. He went on:

" 'You seem to be surprised. I thought you would. But remain in the state of receptivity! I am Ridley, the late Ridley, as they say, though I am very much alive. Some stories have been told of how I died suddenly, 600 miles away from England. But I only disappeared. The wicked spirits tempted me, and I fell into their trap. Time passed, and the love messages which the spirit of my wife sent all over the earth succeeded in reaching me after a period of burning knowledge. She claimed death as a right, though she knew well enough that, dead or alive, I could not help her in that way. We must die both at the same time if we are to enjoy in an after-life the joys of spiritual love, which I found on this earth but too mild for my burning and anxious curiosity. I have chosen you for the deed because you have been at times the recipient of some thought messages which were addressed to her by me. Besides, in a former existence you were kin to my . . . to Mrs. Ridley.

" 'To-morrow night you will go to —— Street, and my wife will await you as the promised liberator. Some one else will "do" for me at the same time, but in another part of the world. I shall be far by then. No one is to see you, and Mrs. Ridley will open the door to you. KILL HER, man! Kill her at 9.30 P.M. When you have done, GO! Go away; and when a whole week has passed, REMEMBER! And now, my dear sir, good-bye for the present.'

"As he spoke the last words I was again conscious; but my head felt so heavy that I did not make any motion. I could not. It was as if I had just awakened from a profound sleep.

The stranger disappeared, seeming through the hole in the glass.

"When I had collected myself I tried hard to make out whether I had seen or hear any one. But I could not remember what had been said to me, save the few words of preamble about opening the windows and the ironical words of the parting: 'Good-bye for the present.'

"I shut the windows, and presently arrived at my destination. The cold air on the platform finished waking me up. I dismissed the conversation as a dream due to the discomfort of the journey; and set out towards the hotel where I usually stay when in Bristol.

"I must here remind you, sir, that I had no other recollection than a few words, which were so absurd, especially those about coming from the sky through a hole, that they must have been dreamt by me. Such were my thoughts; and I went to sleep thinking no more about my supposed nightmare.

"On the following morning I attended to my business and started on my journey back to Brighton, though I was asked by a very dear friend to stay another day, and though I had no reason whatever to refuse him and myself such a pleasure as we always derive from our mutual company.

"The journey passed without incident. My carriage was never empty; and I could not in a full compartment indulge in such weird dreams as I had on the previous day. On my arrival at Brighton I went to the hotel. At least I thought I did. I am not so sure now. How is it that I remember to-day that part of the stranger's discourse which I could not recollect after his departure? But I anticipate.

"I awoke in the morning with a strong headache; and

proceeded to clean my coat; which (I remember) I had soiled on the previous evening during my meal, while waiting for my train in London. I was perfectly certain about that stain; I knew where it was. I COULD NOT FIND IT. This is a trifle, no doubt, and I took it as such, at first. I do not... now ... now that I REMEMBER. I must have washed my clothes according to the orders.

"Yet I am not the murderer, monsieur. If you could see me you would dismiss all doubts. My eye is a truthful organ. But of course you cannot; and there is an end of the matter.

"Shall we go back to the beginning? Well, suppose we do. Who is that human creature *qui languit sur la paille humide d'un cachot?* A neighbour! The very man who ought not to be suspected. Does ever a neighbour kill a neighbour in that way, for such a vague reason? It is sheer madness... Madness ... MADNESS!

"And I will tell you something else. The man they have arrested has probably been a witness to the murder. He may have some secret longing for a period of suffering. He may want a cure for his soul; and that may be the reason why he does not do anything against the mountain of evidence which is slowly being heaped against him. . . .

"I have just had to leave this letter in order to see that a couple of nice crisp cabbages do not during their ebullition throw too much water over the gas-stove. And as I return to you it occurs to me that you may know the great master-piece of Dostoievsky. I have only read it in the French. 'Crime et Châtiment' they call it. Well, there is a similar case in that terrible story. MIKOLKA confesses to the murder of the old female moneylender and her sister Elizabeth, when the real murderer is Rodion Romanich Raskolnikoff. Mikolka is longing for expiation; he wants to atone for a wasted life; he is neither a madman nor an insane, but a mystic, a fantast. You will object that he is a Slav. . . . Quite so, but there might be some Anglo-Saxons with a similar turn of mind.

"What of the theft? What if there has been no theft? if Mrs. Ridley had hidden or destroyed the money? if she had burned the banknotes? What are banknotes to a woman who is going to die?

"The police have made a great point of the fact that Harry Carpenter could not come out of his room without being heard. Fools! Mayhap he did not enter his room that night. Maybe he was in love with some lady fair. Maybe he went out and was killed by Mrs. Ridley when, returning, he had come to her assistance and struggled with Mr. Ridley's messenger.

"The dinner-party! Here we come to the most foolish, silly, ridiculous, absurd, and preposterous example of the preposterousness, absurdity, ridiculousness, silliness, and foolishness latent in the brains of your C.I.D. members. I believe that all the guests who attended that party have been shadowed, that their entire families have been watched and followed about, that their correspondence has been ransacked and their whole past raked into. They have of course no connection whatever with the case. Mrs. Ridley thought of a party as of the thing most likely to *donner le change.* Of course she did not want people to think of anything else but of an ordinary unforeseen murder.

"All the rubbish talked about with regard to her lace handkerchief and the piece in her footman's hand shows still more the folly of all scientific systems of investigation. She put it there after having killed the footman.

"I have but one incident to mention; and it is once more a personal recollection. But as it is the last you will forgive me. I am sure you appreciate my goodwill and believe in *Wahlverwandschaften*.

"When, after a week had elapsed and my memory was allowed to resume its work, I became conscious of the deed which had been commanded to me, I entered into a state of mixed feelings. If I would indulge in psychology, I should now retrace step by step the mental journey which I then took. I think I can spare you this; and I now come to the evening which concluded the ninth day after the murder.

"For my personal edification I was murmuring the words of the Clavicula Salomonis; and had just arrived at the invocation, '*Aba, Zarka, Maccaf, Zofar, Holech, Zegolta, Pazergadol,*' when a gentle breeze caressed my forehead. I must tell you that I had not placed in my left hand the hexagonal seal, but held instead at intervals a well-dosed 'rainbow.' By the way, have you ever tasted that scientific and picturesque mixture of liqueurs?

"The breeze spoke. At least I heard its voice, which recalled somehow the voice of the late—very late now—Mr. Ridley.

" '*We are here.*'

"A buzzing sibilation; *un susurrement.* Then the voice again. 'We have come together, man, to set your mind at rest, if indeed it is restless. Your are not the liberator of a longing soul, as you thought. A nearer of kin has been found—that is, a man whose spirit was in a previous life the spirit of a dear brother. He was ordered to kill at 9.20. But you came at your own appointed time and went through the —er—process, unaware that all had been done before. We chose that man because he was a nearer parent. We are now happy—happy beyond your actual comprehension. Adieu!'

"That's what I call *laver son linge sale en famille*. And the part I played in that affair reminds me of that other expression: *enfoncer une porte ouverte*.

"That is all, my dear sir. You know as much as I do. And I must return to my cabbages.

"Your illuminating
"PEDRO PIERRE PETER SCAMANDER."

Is there anything to be added? For my part I took the word of Mr. Scamander for the candid expression of real happenings, without trying to explain any theory. More curious still is the fact that I heard from Inspector Bennet. He said that the evidence against the arrested man was built on moving sand, utterly impossible and unexistent; and they will have to release him, in spite of apparent elements of certainty which have for so long misled the public—aye, and even the police.

From *to-day's* papers:

"The man arrested in connection with the Brighton murder has confessed. He will be tried at the next assizes."

Well! maybe he is a new Mikolka. But where is the absent relative, the spiritualist?

GEORGE RAFFALOVICH

REVIEWS

THE CLOUD ON THE SANCTUARY. By COUNCILLOR VON ECKARTSHAUSEN.
    William Rider and Son.

We shall be very sorry if any of our readers misses this little book, a translation from the French translation of the German original into the pretty broken English of Madame de Steyer.

It was this book which first made your reviewer aware of the existence of a secret mystical assembly of saints, and determined him to devote his whole life, without keeping back the least imaginable thing, to the purpose of making himself worthy to enter that circle. We shall be disappointed if the book has any less effect on any other reader.

The perusal of the notes may be omitted with advantage.   N.

THE BUDDHIST REVIEW. Quarterly. 1s.

Unwilling as I am to sap the foundations of the Buddhist religion by the introduction of Porphyry's terrible catapult, Allegory, I am yet compelled by the more fearful ballista of Aristotle, Dilemma. This is the two-handed engine spoken of by the prophet Milton!*

This is the horn of the prophet Zeruiah, and with this am I, though no Syrian, utterly pushed, till I find myself back against the dead wall of Dogma. Only now realising how dead a wall that is, do I turn and try the effect of a hair of the dog that bit me, till the orthodox "literary"† school of Buddhists, as grown at Rangoon, exclaim with Lear: "How sharper than a serpent's tooth is it To have an intellect!" How is this? Listen and hear!

I find myself confronted with the crux: that, a Buddhist convinced intellectually and philosophically of the truth of the teaching of Gotama; a man to whom Buddhism is the equivalent of scientific methods of Thought; an expert in dialectic, whose logical faculty is bewildered, whose critical admiration is extorted by the subtle vigour of Buddhist reasoning; I am yet forced to admit that, this being so, the Five Precepts‡ are mere nonsense. If the

* Lycidas, line 130.

† The school whose Buddhism is derived from the Canon, and who ignore the degradation of the professors of the religion, as seen in practice.

‡ The obvious caveat which logicians will enter against these remarks is that Pansil is the Five Virtues rather than Precepts. Etymologically this is so. However, we may regard this as a clause on my side of the argument, not against it; for in my view these are virtues, and the impossibility of attaining them is the cancer of existence. Indeed, I support the etymology as against the futile bigotry of certain senile Buddhists of to-day. And, since it is the current interpretation of Buddhistic thought that I attack, I but show myself the better Buddhist in the act.

304

Buddha spoke scientifically, not popularly, not rhetorically, then his precepts are not his. We must reject them or we must interpret them. We must inquire: Are they meant to be obeyed? Or—and this is my theory—are they sarcastic and biting criticisms on existence, illustrations of the First Noble Truth; *reasons*, as it were, for the apotheosis of annihilation? I shall show that this is so.

THE FIRST PRECEPT.

This forbids the taking of life in any form.* What we have to note is the impossibility of performing this; if we can prove it to be so, either Buddha was a fool, or his command was rhetorical, like those of Yahweh to Job, or of Tannhäuser to himself:

> "Go! seek the stars and count them and explore!
> Go! sift the sands beyond a starless sea!"

Let us consider what the words can mean. The "Taking of Life" can only mean the reduction of living protoplasm to dead matter: or, in a truer and more psychological sense, the destruction of personality.

Now, in the chemical changes involved in Buddha's speaking this command, living protoplasm was changed into dead matter. Or, on the other horn, the fact (insisted upon most strongly by the Buddha himself, the central and cardinal point of his doctrine, the shrine of that Metaphysic which isolates it absolutely from all other religious metaphysic, which allies it with Agnostic Metaphysic) that the Buddha who had spoken this command was not the same as the Buddha before he had spoken it, lies the proof that the Buddha, by speaking this command, violated it. More, not only did he slay himself; he breathed in millions of living organisms and slew them. He could nor eat nor drink nor breathe without murder implicit in each act.

Huxley cites the "pitiless microscopist" who showed a drop of water to the Brahmin who boasted himself "Ahimsa"—harmless. So among the "rights" of a Bhikkhu is medicine. He who takes quinine does so with the deliberate intention of destroying innumerable living beings; whether this is done by stimulating the phagocytes, or directly, is morally indifferent.

How such a fiend incarnate, my dear brother Ananda Metteya, can call

* Fielding Hall, in "The Soul of a People," has reluctantly to confess that he can find no trace of this in Buddha's own work, and calls the superstition the "echo of an older Faith."

him "cruel and cowardly" who only kills a tiger, is a study in the philosophy of the mote and the beam!*

Far be it from me to suggest that this is a defence of breathing, eating, and drinking. By no means; in all these ways we bring suffering and death to others, as to ourselves. But since these are inevitable acts, since suicide would be a still more cruel alternative (especially in case something should subsist below mere Rupa), the command is not to achieve the impossible, the already violated in the act of commanding, but a bitter commentary on the foul evil of this aimless, hopeless universe, this compact of misery, meanness, and cruelty. Let us pass on.

THE SECOND PRECEPT.

The Second Precept is directed against theft. Theft is the appropriation to one's own use of that to which another has a right. Let us see therefore whether or no the Buddha was a thief. The answer of course is in the affirmative. For to issue a command is to attempt to deprive another of his most precious possession—the right to do as he will; that is, unless, with the predestinarians, we hold that action is determined absolutely, in which case, of course, to command is as absurd as it is unavoidable. Excluding this folly, therefore, we may conclude that if the command be obeyed—and those of Buddha have gained a far larger share of obedience than those of any other teacher—the Enlightened One was not only a potential but an actual thief. Further, all voluntary action limits in some degree, however minute, the volition of others. If I breathe, I diminish the stock of oxygen available on the planet. In those far distant ages when Earth shall be as dead as the moon is to-day, my breathing now will have robbed some being then living of the dearest necessity of life.

That the theft is minute, incalculably trifling, is no answer to the moralist, to whom degree is not known; nor to the man of science, who sees the chain of nature miss no link.

If, on the other hand, the store of energy in the universe be indeed constant (whether infinite or no), if personality be indeed delusion, then theft becomes impossible, and to forbid it is absurd. We may argue that even so temporary theft may exist; and that this is so is to my mind no doubt the case. All theft is temporary, since even a millionaire must die; also it is universal, since even a Buddha must breathe.

* The argument that "the animals are our brothers" is merely intended to mislead one who has never been in a Buddhist country. The average Buddhist would, of course, kill his brother for five rupees, or less.

REVIEWS

THE THIRD PRECEPT.

This precept, against adultery, I shall touch but lightly. Not that I consider the subject unpleasant—far from it!—but since the English section of my readers, having unclean minds, will otherwise find a fulcrum therein for their favourite game of slander. Let it suffice if I say that the Buddha—in spite of the ridiculous membrane legend,* one of those foul follies which idiot devotees invent only too freely—was a confirmed and habitual adulterer. It would be easy to argue with Hegel-Huxley that he who thinks of an act commits it (*cf.* Jesus also in this connection, thought he only knows the creative value of desire), and that since A and not-A are mutually limiting, therefore interdependent, therefore identical, therefore identical, he who forbids an act commits it; but I feel that this is no place for metaphysical hair-splitting; let us prove what we have to prove in the plainest way.

I would premise in the first place that to commit adultery in the Divorce Court sense is not here in question.

It assumes too much proprietary right of a man over a woman, that root of all abomination!—the whole machinery of inheritance, property, and all the labyrinth of law.

We may more readily suppose that the Buddha was (apparently at least) condemning incontinence.

We know that Buddha had abandoned his home; true, but Nature has to be reckoned with. Volition is no necessary condition of offence. "I didn't mean to" is a poor excuse for an officer failing to obey an order.

Enough of this—in any case a minor question; since even on the lowest moral grounds—and we, I trust, soar higher!—the error in question may be resolved into a mixture of murder, theft, and intoxication.

(We consider the last under the Fifth Precept.)

THE FOURTH PRECEPT.

Here we come to what in a way is the fundamental joke of these precepts. A command is not a lie, of course; possibly cannot be; yet surely an allegorical order is one in essence, and I have no longer a shadow of a doubt that these so-called "precepts" are a species of savage practical joke.

Apart from this there can hardly be much doubt, when critical exegesis has done its damnedest on the Logia of our Lord, that Buddha did at some time

* Membrum virile illius inmembrana inclusum esse aiunt, ne copulare posset.

commit himself to some statement. "(Something called) Consciousness exists" is, said Huxley, the irreducible minimum of the pseudo-syllogism, false even for an enthymeme, "Cogito, ergo Sum!" This proposition he bolsters up by stating that whoso should pretend to doubt it would thereby but confirm it. Yet might it not be said "(Something called) Consciousness appears to itself to exist," since Consciousness is itself the only witness to that confirmation? Not that even now we can deny some kind of existence to consciousness, but that it should be a more real existence than that of a reflection is doubtful, incredible, even inconceivable. If by consciousness we mean the normal consciousness, it is definitely untrue, since the Dhyanic consciousness includes it and denies it. No doubt "something called" acts as a kind of caveat to the would-be sceptic, though the phrase is bad, implying a "calling." But we can guess what Huxley means.

No doubt Buddha's scepticism does not openly go quite as far as mine—it must be remembered that "scepticism" is merely the indication of a possible attitude, not a belief, as so many good fool-folk think; but Buddha not only denies "Cogito, ergo sum"; but "Cogito, ergo non sum." See *Sabbasava Sutta*, par. 10.

At any rate Sakkyaditthi, the delusion of personality, is in the very forefront of his doctrines; and it is this delusion that is constantly and inevitably affirmed in all normal consciousness. That Dhyanic thought avoids it is doubtful; even so, Buddha is here represented as giving precepts to ordinary people. And if personality be delusion, a lie is involved in the command of one to another. In short, we all lie all the time; we are compelled to it by the nature of things themselves—paradoxical as that seems—and the Buddha knew it!

THE FIFTH PRECEPT.

At last we arrive at the end of our weary journey—surely in this weather we may have a drink! East of Suez,* Trombone-Macaulay (as I may surely say, when Browning writes Banjo-Byron†) tells us, a man may raise a Thirst. No, shrieks the Blessed One, the Perfected One, the Enlightened One, do not drink! It is like the streets of Paris when they were placarded with rival posters:

* "Ship me somewhere East of Suez, where a man may raise a thirst."
R. KIPLING

† "While as for Quilp Hop o' my Thumb there,
Banjo-Byron that twangs the strum-strum there."
BROWNING, *Pachiarotto* (said of A. Austin).

REVIEWS

Ne buvez pas de l'Alcool!
L'Alcool est un poison!

and

Buvez de l'Alcool!
L'Alcool est un aliment!

We know now that alcohol is a food up to a certain amount; the precept, good enough for a rough rule as it stands, will not bear close inspection. What Buddha really commands, with that grim humour of his, is: Avoid Intoxication.

But what is intoxication? unless it be the loss of power to use perfectly a truth-telling set of faculties. If I walk unsteadily it is owing to nervous lies — and so for all the phenomena of drunkenness. But a lie involves the assumption of some true standard, and this can nowhere be found. A doctor would tell you, moreover, that all food intoxicates: all, here as in all the universe, of every subject and in every predicate, is a matter of degree.

Our faculties never tell us true; our eyes say flat when our fingers say round; our tongue sends a set of impressions to our brain which our hearing declares non-existent—and so on.

What is this delusion of personality but a profound and centrally-seated intoxication of the consciousness? I am intoxicated as I address these words; you are drunk—beastly drunk!—as you read them; Buddha was a drunk as a voter at election time when he uttered his besotted command. There, my dear children, is the conclusion to which we are brought if you insist that he was serious!

I answer No! Alone among men then living, the Buddha was sober, and saw Truth. He, who was freed from the coils of the great serpent Theli coiled round the universe, he knew how deep the slaver of that snake had entered into us, infecting us, rotting our very bones with poisonous drunkenness. And so his cutting irony—drink no intoxicating drinks!

When I go to take Pansil,* it is in no spirit of servile morality; it is with keen sorrow gnawing at my heart. These five causes of sorrow are indeed the heads of the serpent of Desire. Four at least of them snap their fangs on me in and by virtue of my very act of receiving the commands, and of promising to obey them; if there is a little difficulty about the fifth, it is an omission easily rectified—and I think we should make a point about that; there is a great virtue in completeness.

* To "Take Pansil" is to vow obedience to these Precepts.

309

THE EQUINOX

Yes! Do not believe that the Buddha was a fool; that he asked men to perform the impossible or the unwise.* Do not believe that the sorrow of existence is so trivial that easy rules easily interpreted (as all Buddhists do interpret the precepts) can avail against them; do not mop up the Ganges with a duster: or stop the revolution of the stars with a lever of lath.

Awake, awake only! let there be ever remembrance that Existence is sorrow, sorrow by the inherent necessity of the way it is made; sorrow not by volition, not by malice, not by carelessness, but by nature, by ineradicable tendency, by the incurable disease of Desire, its Creator, is it so, and the way to destroy it is by the uprooting of Desire; nor is a task so formidable accomplished by any threepenny-bit-in-the-plate-on-Sunday morality, the "deceive others and self-deception will take care of itself" uprightness, but by the severe roads of austere self-mastery, of arduous scientific research, which constitute the Noble Eightfold Path.

O. DHAMMALOYU.

JOHN DEE. By CHARLOTTE FELL SMITH. Constable and Co. 10s. 6d. net.

It is only gracious to admit that this book is as good as could possibly have been produced on the subject—the publishes are cordially invited to quote the last fourteen words, and now I can finish my sentence—by a person totally ignorant of the essence thereof.

Dee was an avowed magician; Miss Smith is an avowed intellectual prig. So she can find nothing better to do than to beg the whole question of the validity of Dee's "actions," and that although she admits that the Book of Enoch is unintelligible to her. Worse, she retails the wretched slanders about me current among those who envied me. I was certainly "wanted" for coining. I happened to have found the trick of making gold at a very early age, but had not the sense to exploit it properly; and when I got any sense I got more sense than to waste time in such follies. The slander that I deluded Dee is as baseless. Again and again I tried to break with him, to show him how utterly unreliable it all was. Only his more than paternal

---

* I do not propose to dilate on the moral truth which Ibsen has so long laboured to make clear: that no hard and fast rule of life can be universally applicable. Also, as in the famous case of the lady who saved (successively) the lives of her husband, her father, and her brother, the precepts clash. To allow to die is to kill —all this is obvious to the most ordinary thinkers. These precepts are of course excellent general guides for the vulgar and ignorant, but you and I, dear reader, are wise and clever, and know better.

310

kindness for me kept me with him. God rest him; I hear he has been reincarnated as W. T. Stead.

For one thing I do most seriously take blame, that my training was too strong for my power to receive spiritual truth. For when the Holy Angels came to instruct me in the great truths, that there is no sin, that the soul passes from house to house, that Jesus was but man, that the Holy Ghost was not a person, I rejected them as false. Ah! have I not paid bitterly for the error? Still, the incarnation was not all loss; not only did I attain the Grade of Major Adept, but left enough secret knowledge (in an available form) to carry me on for a long while. I am getting it back now; with luck I'll be a Magister Templi soon, if I can only get rid of my giant personality. You may say, by the way, that this is hardly a review of a book on my old master, silly old josser! Exactly; I never cared a dump for him. He was just a text for my sermon then; and so he is now.   EDWARD KELLEY.

STRANGE HOUSES OF SLEEP. By ARTHUR EDWARD WAITE. William Rider and Sons, 12s. 6d. net.

I have always held Arthur Edward Waite for a good poet; I am not sure that he is not a great poet; but that he is a great mystic there can be no manner of doubt.

"Strange Houses of Sleep," conceived in the abyss of a noble mind and brought forth in travail of Chaos that hath been stirred by the Breath, is one of the finest records of Mystical Progress that is possible to imagine.

I may be biased in my judgment by this fact, that long ago when first my young heart stirred within me at the sound of the trumpet—perchance of Israfel—and leapt to grasp with profane hands the Holy Grail, it was to Mr. Waite that I wrote for instruction, it was from him that came the first words of help and comfort that I ever had from mortal man. In all these years I have met him but once, and then within a certain veil; yet still I can go to his book as a child to his father, without diffidence or doubt; and indeed he can communicate the Sacrament, the Wafer of his thought, the Wine of his music.

And if in earthly things the instructions of his Master seem contrary to those of mine, at the end it is all one. Shall we cry out if Caesar for his pleasure commandeth his servants to take one the spear and the other the net, and slay each other? Is not service service? Is not obedience a sacrament apart from its accidents?

However this may be, clear enough it is that Mr. Waite has indeed the key to certain Royal Treasuries. Unfortunately, just as to face the title-page he gives us the portrait of a man in a frock-coat, so within the book we have the

Muse in a dress-improver and a Bond Street hat. Never mind; even those who dislike the poetry may love to puzzle out the meaning.

Detailed criticism is here impossible for lack of two illusions, time and space! I will only add that I was profoundly interested in the final book, "The King's Dole." No mystic who is familiar only with Christian symbolism can afford to neglect this Ritual.

Vale, Frater! A. C.

THE CLEANSING OF A CITY. Greening and Co. 1s. net.

"Wherefore I say unto thee, her sins, which are many, are forgiven; for she loved much: but to whom little is forgiven,the same loveth little."

JESUS CHRIST.

"But this German woman, pretending to defend the cause of virtue, and to warn women against the perils of the day, produces a book ('The Diary of a Lost One') which is defilement to touch. ... Before I had skimmed fifty pages I found my brain swimming; I nearly swooned."

REV. R. F. HORTON, D.D.

This book should be printed on vellum and locked up in a fire-proof safe in the British Museum, Great Russell Street W.C.; so that future ecclesiastical historians and ethicists may learn into what a state of mental menorrhagia the adherents of the Christian Church had fallen at the commencement of the twentieth century.

The "cleansing" part of the business seems to consist in pumping filth into everything that is clean. We are not allowed to talk of leg because every leg adjoins a thigh: soon we shall not be able to put a foot into a boot without first looking to see if some nasty mess has not been deposited in it, and why? Because foot adjoins leg! Moreover, foot suggests walking, and walking, like the name of the Rev. Horton, D.D., suggests prostitution—at the thought of this we swoon.

Most of the contributors to this cesspit, like Rev. Horton, have "D.D." after their names. Dr. Bodie has informed us that "M.D." stands for "Merry Devil"; perhaps he can also enlighten us as to the true meaning of these two letters? ANTOINETTE BOUVIGNON.

THE LIFE OF JOHN DEE. Translated from the Latin of DR. THOMAS SMITH by WM. ALEXR. AYTON. The Theosophical Publishing Society. 1s. net.

Wm. Alexr. Ayton's preface to this book deserves a better subject than Dr. Thomas Smith's "Life of John Dee," which is as dreary dull as a life crammed so full of incidents could be made. In fact, if Dr. Smith had collected all Dr. Dee's washing bills and printed them in Hebrew, the result would scarcely have been more oppressive; anyhow it would have been as interesting to read of how many handkerchiefs the famous seer used when he had a cold as to ponder over the platitudes of this rheumy old leech.

Never since reading "Bothwell" and "Who's Who" have we read such ponderous and pedantic pedagogics. The translator in his preface informs us that Moses and Solomon were adepts; verily hast thou spoke, but thou, Wm. Alexr. Ayton, art greater than either, to have survived such a leaden task as this of putting Dr. Smith's bad Latin into good English; at the completion of it you must have felt like Jacob when "he gathered up his feet into the bed, and yielded up the ghost!"

MATTER, SPIRIT, AND THE COSMOS. By H. STANLEY REDGROVE. William Rider and Sons. 2s. 6d.

> Big fleas have little fleas
>   Upon their backs to bite 'em;
> Little fleas have smaller fleas,
>   And so *ad infinitum.*

This book consists of reprinted articles from the *Occult Review*, and some of them are quite entrancing, especially chapter i. "On the Doctrine of the Indestructibility of Matter," and chapters v. and vi. "On the Infinite" and "On the Fourth Dimension."

In the first chapter Mr. Redgrove tries to prove that though matter *cannot* be destroyed, its form can be so utterly changed that it can no longer be treated as such. He illustrates his theory by quoting Sir Oliver Lodge's "knot tied in a bit of string." So long as the knot is, matter is; but when once the knot is untied, though the string remains, the knot vanishes. This, however, is a most fallacious illustration, for, as Gustave le Bon has shown, the destruction of matter implies more than a mere change of "form"; it is an annihilation of gravity itself, and therefore of substance as we understand it. Matter, he shows, goes back unto Equilibrium. But what is Equilibrium? "Nothingness!" this eminent French man of Science declares: "Absolute Nothingness!"

In chapter v. the author points out that as there is an infinite series of infinities, to make Space the "absolute infinite" is the merest of assumptions; he follows up this assertion by declaring that each dimension is bounded by a higher. Thus, the Second Dimension is contained in the Third, and so the Third in the Fourth, *ad infinitum;* each dimension being infinite in itself, and yet contained in a higher, which is again infinite. Thus, we get infinity contained within infinity, just as $\overset{\vee}{\underset{.}{R}}$ is contained in $\overset{\smile}{\underset{.}{R}}$ and $\overset{\smile}{\underset{.}{R}}$ in $\overset{\frown}{\underset{.}{R}}$ and yet $\overset{\frown}{\underset{.}{R}}$ is infinite, and $\overset{\vee}{\underset{.}{R}}$ is infinite and $\overset{\smile}{\underset{.}{R}}$ is infinite, yet there are not three infinites but one infinite, &c. &c.

J. F. C. F.

THE MANIAC. A realistic study of Madness from the Maniac's point of view. Reebman Limited. 5s. net.

Only maniacs are recommended to read this book; its dulness may being them to their senses. For the first chapter is like the second, and the second like the third, and the third like the fourth, which almost proves the Athanasian Creed; for all chapters are but one chapter, which is infinitely dull and dismal. In fact this "realistic study" might well have been translated from Dr. Thomas Smith's "Life of John Dee," and goes a long way to prove Mr. Stanley Redgrove's theory of concentric infinities.

The heroine is a lady journalist, unmarried, and on the wrong side of thirty —there's the whole tragedy in a nutshell. Stimulating work, and thirty years of an unstimulating life. Cut off the first syllable from "unmarried," and this unfortunate lady, in spite of Karezza and the Order of Melchisedec, would never have imagined that she had been seduced by a fiend, or have afflicted us with her dreary ravings.

Therefore we advise—Marry, my good woman, marry, and if nobody will have you, well then, don't be too particular, for anything is better than a second book like this!

BATHSHEBAH TINA.

I found "The Maniac" both entertaining and instructive, a very valuable study of psychology. It is so far as I know the only really illuminating book on madness; and I strongly recommend its perusal to all alienists, psychologists, and members of the grade of Neophyte. It throws an admirable light on the true nature of Obsession and Black Magic.

Two things impressed me in particular. (1) The statement that the arguments held with a patient never reach his consciousness at all, despite his rational answers. This phenomenon is true of my own sane life. I sometimes chat pleasantly to bores for quite a long time without any consciousness that I am doing so. (2) The statement that medical men have no idea of the real contents of a madman's mind. I remember in the County Asylum at Inverness ("Here are the fools, and there are the knaves!" said an inmate, pointing to the city) a man rolling from side to side with an extraordinary regularity and rhythm of swing, emitting a long continuous howl like a wolf. "Last stage of G.P.I." said the doctor; "he feels absolutely nothing." "How interesting!" said I; and thought "How the deuce do you know?" I shall be very glad when it is finally proved and admitted that the consciousness is independent of the senses and the intellect. Hashish phenomena, madness phenomena, magical and mystical phenomena, all prove it; but old Dr. Cundum and young Professor Cuspidor, who can neither of them cure a cold in the head, say it isn't so! The "Imbecile Theologians of the Middle Ages" are matched by the imbecile cacologians of our own. I repeat, a very valuable book; a very valuable book indeed.

FRA: O. M.

SELF SYNTHESIS. A means to Perpetual Life. By CORNWELL ROUND. Simpkin, Marshall and Co. 1s. net.

This is a suggestive little book by a man who revolves a matter in his mind before he writes of it, and whose common sense never quits the hub of his thoughts. Mr. Round never rolls off down a side street, but always keeps to the high road between them all. He does not, so at least we read him, wobble more towards mysticism than towards materialism. He believes that a perfect equilibrium between the Subjective mind—S, and the Objective mind—O, produces the Individual mind, which he symbolises as being neither round nor square, but a simple I or line, connecting the S and O. This I is the self-renewing link between these two, which, when it is truly balanced, renders death the most unnatural, in place of the most natural event, that we may expect once we are born.

METHUSELAH.

THE CASE FOR ALCOHOL. Or the Actions of Alcohol on Body an Soul. By ROBERT PARK, M.D. Rebman Limited. 1s. net.

Dr. Park is an old friend of ours; we enjoyed his masterly translation of Ch: Féré's "The Pathology of Emotions," and his various writings in the days of the old *Free Review* and *University Review*, when J. M. Robertson was worth reading, a review (by the way) which was assassinated by the prurient pot-scourers who would put a pair of "pants" on Phoebus Apollo, and who presumably take their bath in the dark for fear of expiring in a priapic frenzy at the sight of their own nakedness.

Dr. Park in this most admirable little treatise declares that Alcohol is one of "the good creatures of God"; and that Alcohol is a poison is only true relatively.

"It is not true of the stimulant dosage. It is true of it as a narcotic, in narcotic dosage." . . . "So the objection to the use of Alcohol, because in overdosage it is a poison, is not only futile, but stupid."

Further, Dr. Park writes:

"The burden of responsibility must lie upon the person who so misuses his means. Tea, tobacco, coffee, and beef-tea are frequently so misused, but we hear of no socio-political organisations for interfering with the liberty of individuals in regard to the use of these, or trespassing on the rights of traders and purveyors thereof."

"Alcohol," Dr. Park declares, "is a food," and not only a food, but an excellent one at that. Put that in your pipes and smoke it, ye Baptist Bible-bangers—but we forget, you do not smoke, in fact you do nothing which is pleasant; you spend your whole lives in looking for the Devil in the most unlikely places, and declare that the only remedy against his craft and his cunning is total immersion in tonic-water and pine-apple syrup.

F.

AN INTERPRETATION OF GENESIS. By THEODORE POWYS.

This is a most mystical interpretation of the most beautiful of the books of the Old Testament. It consists of a dialogue between the Lawgiver of Israel and Zetetes, who is not exactly the disciple, but rather the Interpreter of the Master's words. Thus it commences:

The Law-giver of Israel:
"In the beginning the Truth created the heaven and the earth."
Zetetes:
"The life that is within and the life that is without, are not these the heaven and the earth that the Truth created?"

Whether the author intends to weave into his interpretation the doctrines of the Qabalah we are not certain, but time after time we came across curious allusions. Thus on p. 3: "Within myself when the truth divided the light from the darkness wisdom arose" . . . "and I knew that every atom of our great Mother giveth light to other atoms . . .". P. 4: "The truth in man is the light of the world. Thus we have known from the beginning, and we shall know it unto the end . . . and the Mother gave unto man her breasts. And man guided by the light within him did eat and was glad." P. 6: "The tree of Life belongeth unto the Father, it groweth in the Mother, but because darkness is still in man he may not eat thereof, but the Truth of the Father that is within man, that Truth may eat and live."

The philosophy of this little book shows that Darkness alone is not evil, and that neither is Light good. Both are beyond: but the mingling twilight begets the illusion of duality, the goodness and wickedness of things external.

It is a little volume which one who reads will grow fond of, and will carry about with him, and open at random in quiet places, in the woods, and under the stars; and it is a little book which one learns to love the more one reads it, for it is inspired by one who at least has crept into the shadow of God's Glory.

J. F. C. F.

REVIEWS

EVOLUTION FROM NEBULA TO MAN. By JOSEPH McCABE. Milner and
Co. 1s.

Mr. McCabe has written another little book on evolution: how many
more of these small, small, small volumes are to appear? The subject seems
a tall order for 128 pages. However, let us be thankful there are not more.

The most interesting fact that we can discover in it, or at least the only
one really original, is, that Erasmus Darwin was born in 1788. This makes
him only thirty years younger than his son Charles; and yet these are the
good people who make such a fuss about Ahaziah being two years older than
his father Jehoram!

THE R. P. A. ANNUAL, 1910. 6d. net.

From the cover of this review we learn that it contains "A striking Poem"
by Eden Phillpotts, whose name evidently tokens his true occupation: it is
called "From the Shades," and might well remain there. Phillpotts informs
us that it was "inspired (!!!) by the spectacle of Paul's statue which now
stands on the triumphal pillar of Marcus Aurelius at Rome." We have read of
many crimes attributed to this unfortunate saint by modern freethinkers, but
none equal to this.

Poor Faustina! We can imagine any self-respecting girl taking to drink
and the street to save herself from such an ethical prig of a husband as the
Phillpottian Marcus. Listen. The Emperor is ousted by the Saint, the
statue of the latter being reared upon the pedestal of the former; this
evidently annoyed the Stoic, for we find his hero worming about in his
shroud—where Paul evidently could not get at him—and saying: "sucks to
you," or to quote:

> " A man named Paul
> Now darkles where aforetimes they set me,
>
> .   .   .   .   .
>
> Keep thou my pillar, Paul; I grudge it not,
> Plebeian-hearted spirit . . ."

just as if Paul could help it!

Outside sudden jars on the ears like "my eyes" and "a euthanasia," and
platitudes like "Now Pontifex is Caesar, but no more is Caesar Pontifex";
and esoteric jabs presumably at poor Faustina, such as: "that biting thing is
only precious in the tart . . ." we find some masterly twaddle, regular
Phillpotts:

> " Two thousand years of fooled humanity,
>   Christ, they have prostituted thee and raped

THE EQUINOX

Thy virgin message till at last it stands
No more than handmaid to their infamy."
(Phillpotts really means harlot, but he is afraid of shocking the inhabitants of
  Torquay.)
       " Some flight of years
       And the inevitable, tireless hand
       Gropes and grips fast, and draws it gently down—

   .   .   .   .   .

       To sublimation. . . ."

What in the name of Narcissus is this all about?

And yet Mr. Ford Madox Hueffer takes for one of his recent texts: "We have not got a great Poet." Well here at least is one, who, if he can do nothing else, can Phillpotts!

THE MARTYRDOM OF FERRER. By JOSEPH MCCABE, R. P. A. 6*d*.

One of the most remarkable points about this interesting brochure is, that no sooner was Señor Ferrer dead than out it came as speedily as if it had been blown from the muzzle of one of his executioner's rifles. It is a true and straightforward account of a man who did not support the blasphemy laws, and who would not have sneaked and shuffled about the Boulter prosecution.

On finishing this book we almost exclaim: "Bravo, Ferrer!" but our enthusiasm was seriously damped when on opening the *Literary Guide,* we read that Miss Sasha Kropotkin has stated in the *The Westminster Gazette* that Señor Ferrer's books on comparative religion "are quite similar in thought and tone to those published in England by the Rationalist Press Association." If so — *Viva Alfonso!*

THE HAND OF GOD. By GRANT ALLEN. 6*d*.

Grant Allan is always exciting, and this posthumous volume of essays quite keeps up his reputation of being the G. A. Henty of Rationalism. We remember reading "The Woman who Did" a dozen and more years ago now, shortly after having closed "A Child of the Age"—both in the delightful Keynote Series. And what a difference! Rosy Howlet, a lazy rosebud, a little sweetheart and nothing else, but Herminia Barton—Lower Tooting with a dash of Clement's Inn. "As beneath so above."

HISTORY OF CHEMISTRY. By SIR EDWARD THORPE, R.P.A. Vol. I. 1*s*.
HISTORY OF ASTRONOMY. By GEORGE FORBES, R.P.A. 1*s*.

Excellent! In every way excellent! After munching through all this heavy pie-crust, we are beginning to feel like little Jack Horner when he pulled out the plum. If only schools would adopt these most interesting little histories, in place of cramming a lot of ridiculous formulae and equations down children's throats, they might become places where time is not altogether wasted.

Twenty years ago I remember learning some two hundred chemical formulæ, the only two which I can remember now being H_2S, because I emptied a bottle into my tutor's desk, and H_2SO_4, because I poured some on his chair to see if it would turn his trousers red, with the result that what lived beneath mine turned very pink shortly after he had discovered who the miscreant was. How I should have learnt to love Chemistry instead of hating it, if I had been taught from Sir Edward Thorpe's little book! There is more elementary education in chapter iv.—The Philosopher's Stone—than ever I learnt in five years with Newth and Thompson; and after all, should not school teach us to love knowledge instead of hating it? should not school teach us the pretty little fables of great men's lives that we can use them in our conversation afterwards, rather than scores of musty dry-as-dust facts, which can only help us to pass dry-as-dust and useless examinations?

Give us more of these, Mr. Watts, dozens more, and we will forgive you "From the Shades." Best wishes to these little volumes, may you sell a million of each, but "in the sunlight," please.   A. QUILLER.

THE SURVIVAL OF MAN. By SIR OLIVER LODGE. Methuen. 7s. 6d. net.

One of the most unfortunate results of the divorce between Science and Religion has been the attempt of each of the partners to set up housekeeping for itself, with the most disastrous results. I shall not run my simile to death, but I shall explain how this train of thought began in my mind.

Sir Oliver's book is mainly a defence of the Society for Psychical Research, and a plea for more scientific investigation of psychic or spiritistic phenomena; and it seems to the reviewer that a scientific society that needs a defence at all, after nearly thirty years' work, has confessed itself to be largely a failure.

Sir Oliver Lodge, and indeed Spiritualism generally, suffer enormously from their lack of knowledge, from their being devoid of theory.

Phenomena! Phenomena! Phenomena! Until the noumenon behind is obscured and disbelieved in and explained away.

This is what makes modern spiritualism so hideous and Qliphothic a thing, and "psychic researchers" such bad mystics.

There is nothing in the book under review that is fresh—nothing that was not known forty years ago—see Emma Hardinge Britten's "Modern American Spiritualism"; nothing that was not commonplace yesterday—see the current issue of *Light*.

The real Occult knowledge of Plato, of Paracelsus, of Boehme, of Levi, was based upon theories whereby all the phenomena of modern psychism had their place, and were awarded their proper value.

The pseudo-occultism and watery mysticism of the modern spiritualistic philosophers—we call them by this noble title by courtesy—is due to their complete lack of knowledge.

What serious student of religion and occultism cares for the vapourings of Ralph Waldo Trine, the philosophising of the Rev. R. J. Campbell, the poetry of Ella Wheeler Wilcox? The prototypes of these people are utterly, or almost utterly, forgotten. One recalls now with how much difficulty the names of the Rev. H. R. Haweis, of A. H. Davis, of Lizzie Doten! For there is no virtue in those who have strayed from the path to linger among the Shells of the Dead and the demons of Matter.

The line of tradition is unbroken, and the way is straight and hard; too hard for "mediums" and New Thoughtists, whose spiritual capital consists of falsehood, and sentimentality, and sham humanitarianism.

Sir Oliver Lodge is always careful and painstaking and entirely honest; he is probably as well fitted to carry on his S.P.R. work as any student in England.

And to those who are unacquainted with the phenomena of spiritualism, "The Survival of Man" is as useful a book as could be read. But to the student of religion its value is *nil*, because the occult knowledge is *nil*.

In fairness it should be added that this review is written from the point of view of a mystic; to spiritualists the book will be welcome as yet another "proof" of "spirit-return," "thought-transference," and so on.

V. B. NEUBURG.

This book is a singularly lucid and complete statement of the work of many noble lives. We believe that the S.P.R. has taken up a most admirable position, and wish greater success to their work in the future. If they would only train themselves instead of exercising patience on fraudulent people, whose exploits no sane person would believe if God Himself came down from heaven to attest them, they might get somewhere.

A. C.

THE KEY TO THE TAROT. By A. E. WAITE. W. Rider and Sons, Limited.

Mr. Waite has written a book on fortune-telling, and we advise servant-girls to keep an eye on their half-crowns. We have little sympathy or pity for the folly of fashionable women; but housemaids need protection—hence their affection for policemen and soldiers—and we fear that Mr. Waite's apologies will not prevent professional cheats from using his instructions for their frauds and levies of blackmail.

REVIEWS

As to Mr. Waite's constant pomposities, he seems to think that the obscurer his style and the vaguer his phrases, the greater initiate he will appear.

Nobody but Mr. Waite knows *all* about the Tarot, it appears; and he won't tell. Reminds one of the story about God and Robert Browning, or of the student who slept, and woke when the professor thundered rhetorically, "And what *is* Electricity?" The youth jumped up and cried (from habit), "I know, sir." "Then tell us." "I *knew*, sir, but I've forgotten." "Just my luck!" complained the professor, "there was only one man in the world who knew — and he has forgotten!"

Why, Mr. Waite, your method is not even original.

When Sir Mahatma Agamya Paramahansa Guru Swamiji (late of H. M. Prisons, thanks to the unselfish efforts of myself and a friend) was asked, "And what of the teaching of Confucius?"—or any one else that the boisterous old boy had never heard of—he would reply contemptuously, "Oh, him? He was my disciple." And seeing the hearer smile would add, "Get out you dog, you a friend of that dirty fellow Crowley. I beat you with my shoe. Go away! Get intellect! Get English!" until an epileptic attack supervened.

Mr. Waite, like Marie Corelli, in this as in so many other respects, brags that he cares nothing for criticism, so he won't mind my making these little remarks, and I may as well go on. He has "betrayed" (to use his own words) the attributions of some of the small cards, and Pamela Coleman Smith has done very beautiful and sympathic designs, though our own austerer taste would have preferred the plain cards with their astrological and other attributions, and occult titles. (These are all published in the book "777," and a pack could be easily constructed by hand. Perhaps we may one day publish one at a shilling a time!) But Mr. Waite has not "betrayed" the true attributions of the Trumps. They are obvious, though, the moment one has the key (see "777"). Still, Pamela Coleman Smith has evidently been hampered; her designs are cramped and forced. I am infinitely sorry for any artist who tries to draw after dipping her hands in the gluey dogma of so insufferable a dolt and prig.

Mr. Waite, I believe, is perfectly competent to produce indefinite quantities of Malted Milk to the satisfaction of all parties; but when it comes to getting the pure milk of the Word, Mr. Waite gets hold of a wooden cow.

And do for God's sake, Arthur, drop your eternal hinting, hinting, hinting, "Oh what an exalted grade I have, if you poor dull uninitiated people would only perceive it!"

Here is your criticism, Arthur, straight from the shoulder.

Any man that knows Truth and conceals it is a traitor to humanity; any man that doesn't know, and tries to conceal his ignorance by pretending to be the guardian of a secret, is a charlatan.

Which is it?

We recommend every one to buy the pack, send Mr. Waite's book to the kitchen so as to warn the maids, throw the Major Arcana out of window, and play bridge with the Minor Arcana, which alone are worth the money asked for the whole caboodle.

The worst of it all is: Mr. Waite really does know a bit in a muddled kind of way; if he would only go out of the swelled-head business he might be some use.

But if you are not going to tell your secrets, it is downright schoolboy brag to strut about proclaiming that you possess them.

Au revoir, Arthur.

ALEISTER CROWLEY.

It is an awkward situation for any initiate to edit knowledge concerning which he is bound to secrecy. This is the fundamental objection to all vows of this kind. The only possible course for an honest man is to preserve absolute silence.

Thus, to my own knowledge Mr. Waite is an initiate (of a low grade) and well aware of the true attribution of the Tarot. Now, what I want to know is this: is Mr. Waite breaking his obligation and proclaiming himself (to quote the words of his own Oath) "a vile and perjured wretch, void of all moral worth, and unfit for the society of all upright and just persons," and liable in addition to "the awful and just penalty of submitting himself voluntarily to a deadly and hostile current of will . . . by which he should fall slain or paralysed as if blasted by the lightning flash"—or, is he selling to the public information which he knows to inexact?

When this dilemma is solved, we shall feel better able to cope with the question of the Art of Pamela Coleman Smith.

II.

THE VISION. By MRS. HAMILTON SYNGE. Elkin Mathews. 1s. 6d. cloth.

It was with no small degree of pleasurable anticipation that we picked up a volume by the distinguished authoress of "A Supreme Moment" and "The Coming of Sonia." The first vision, alas! was an atrocity after Watts, R.A., but we persisted.

Chapter i. is jolly good.

Chapter ii. might have been better with less quotation.

REVIEWS

Chapter iii. is first rate. Mystics can only conquer the Universe when they can prove themselves better than the rest of the world even in worldly things, and that by virtue of their mystic attainment.

We cannot, however, subscribe to her doctrine of the agglutination of the Virttis to the Atman, save only in due order and balance in the case of the adept. Yet we would not deny the possibility of her theory being correct.

In chapter iv. she puts a drop of the Kerosene of Myers into her good wine.

In chapter v. we begin to suspect that the authoress's brain is a mass of ill-digested and imperfectly understood pseudo-science; yet it ends finely—our task is to learn "how to love"—and we refer the reader to Mrs. Synge's other books.

Chapter vi. is more about James. We love our William dearly, but we hate to see dogs trotting about with his burst waistcoat-buttons in their mouths. But the clouds lift. We get Ibsen, and Browning, and Blake; and end on the right note. Oh that Mrs. Synge would come and take up serious occultism seriously; leave vague theorising and loose assertion, and her "larger Whole" for our "narrow Way!"

CHRISTOBEL WHARTON.

THE TRAGIC LIFE-HISTORY OF THE MAN WILLIAM SHAKESPEARE. By FRANK HARRIS. 7s. 6d.

It has always been a source of harmless amusement, in our leisure hours, to watch our learned men grappling with Shakespeare. To study him, the Knower of man's heart, they have withered their own; to interpret the Witness of Life, they have refused to live, and, surrounded by a thousand foolish folios, have sat gloomily in the mouldering colleges of Oxford, or walked the horrid marshes of Cambridge, and produced uncounted pages of most learned drivel.

Frank Harris had another way than that. He took life in both hands and shook it; he made his own study of the heart of man, enlarging, not restricting, his own; and many a night has he lain under the stars on the savannah or the sierra, with Shakespeare for his pillow.

His result is accordingly different. His knowledge of Shakespeare is a living, bleeding, Truth; there is no room in his great heart and brain for the lumber of the pedants.

More, Frank Harris is himself a creative artist, a Freeman of the City of God, and knows that as there is no smoke without fire, so is there no speech without thought.

Whenever a poet writes of something that he does not know, he makes a botch of it; whenever a poet gives detail, and gives it right, he has probably observed it directly. There is nothing in *Hamlet* which need make us think that Shakespeare was ever in Denmark; but from the description in *King Lear* it is likely that he knew Dover.

In the hands of an acute critic this method is perfectly reliable; and Mr. Harris's familiarity with the text, his power of concentration and his sense of proportion, have made it possible for him to see Shakespeare steadily and see him whole.

We are perfectly convinced of the truth of the main theory which Frank Harris presents, the enslaving of his gentle spirit by the bold black-eyed harlot Mary Fitton, and we are even shaken in that other hypothesis which attributes to Shakespeare the vice of Caesar, Goethe, Milton, Michael Angelo, and of so many other good and great men that time and space would fail us to enumerate them.

Yet Mr. Harris only shakes the fabric of proof; he cannot the foundation—instinct.

And it is strange that he, the friend of Oscar Wilde through honour and dishonour, has not perceived the amazing strength of the theory propounded in "The portrait of Mr. W. H." Surely this theory should have been lashed and smashed, had it been possible. For where there is no definite evidence, we must accept the theory which contains least contradiction in itself.

Now, there is nothing monstrous in the supposition that Shakespeare was great enough to understand and feel all the overmastering passions which enrapture and torment, enslave and emancipate mankind; it would have been astonishing had he not done so. Oscar Wilde's theory does not explain Rosalind and Tamora and the dark lady of the Sonnets; but Frank Harris forgets the ambiguous Rosalind and Viola and Imogen, or at least fails to attach to them the immense importance which they are bound to possess for any one who is capable of emotional sympathy with such modern writers as Symonds, Pater, Whitman, FitzGerald, Burton, Wilde, Bloomfield, and a hundred others.

Everything is significant to sympathy, nothing to antipathy; and if sometimes sympathy o'erleaps itself and falls on the other, seeing a camel where there is only a cloud, the error is rarely so great as the opposite. We cannot help thinking that in this one instance Frank Harris has emulated Nelson at Copenhagen.

He will forgive us for dwelling on the one point of disagreement where the points of agreement are so many, where we gladly welcome his book as the sole real light that has ever been shed upon the life and thought of Shakespeare, the light of Frank Harris's soul split up by the prism of his mind

REVIEWS

into wit, style, insight, intelligence, pathos, history, comedy, tragedy, that adorn his book.

As for Staunton, Sidney Lee, Raleigh, Garrett, Bradley, Haliwell-Phillips, Fleay and the rest, their learning is lumber and their theories trash.

A. C.

The *English Review* was enlivened in November by a brilliant article on The Law of Divorce from the fascinating pen of Mr. E. S. P. Haynes.

While sympathising to a large extent with the writer's learned views so lucidly expressed, we are of opinion that there is no middle course between the extreme position of the Catholic Church, that marriage is so holy a bond that nothing can break it, and to accept and even to encourage fornication rather than tamper with it, and the other extreme of allowing a marriage to determine as soon as the parties desire it, proper provision being of course made for the welfare of any offspring.

The problem is really insoluble so long as sexual relations give rise to bitter feeling of any sort. Polygamy is perhaps the most decent and dignified of the systems at present invented.

But the present degrading and stupid farce must be ended.

As things are in these islands to-day, nine-tenths of all divorces, at least in good society, are the result of cheerful agreement between the parties. Adultery on both sides is so common that a genuine grievance is a rare as a truthful witness.

In a case that recently came under my notice, for example, the nominal defendant was really the plaintiff. He had compelled his wife—for sufficient reason—to divorce him by the threat that unless she did so he would break off friendly relations with her. Next came a weary struggle to manufacture evidence, the plaintiff's lawyers keeping up the irritating wail: "Lord—is so strict. *We must have more adultery.*" So the already overworked defendant was kept busy all the summer faking fresh evidence to satisfy the morbid appetite of a Scotch judge, while at the same time he was obliged to hold constant and clandestine intercourse with his own wife, lest she should lose her temper and withdraw proceedings!

This may have been an exceptional case—we hope so. But that any such mockery can take place anyhow and anywhere is a scandal and a reproach to the nation whose laws and customs make it possible.

We hope to hear much more from Mr. Haynes, and that he will throw fearlessly the whole weight of his genius and energy into the cause of radical reform of these monstrous and silly iniquities.

ARIEL.

THE EQUINOX

THE QUEST. No. II. J. M. Watkins. 2s. 6d.

This periodical is the dullest and most sodden slosh possible. No one should fail to buy a copy; a perfect bedside book.

R. N. W.

We beg to apologise for having referred in our last number to G.R.S.Mead, Esquire, B.A., M.R.A.S., as Mr. G.R.S.Mead, B.A. B.A. (Baccalaureus Artium) is indeed the proud distinction awarded to our brightest and best intellects. M.R.A.S. does not mean Mr. Ass; but is a mark of merit so high that dizzy imagination swoons at its contemplation. We grovel.

A. C.

PARACELSUS. Edited by A. E. WAITE. Two vols. Wm. Rider and Son. 25s.

The only edition of the great mediaeval occultist, the discoverer of opium, hydrogen, and zinc. Mr. A. E. Waite in this as in his other translations is altogether admirable, adding a delightful wit to ripe scholarship, and illuminating comment to rational criticism.

A. C.

THE OPEN ROAD (Monthly. C. W. Daniel) is apparently the organ of Mrs. Boole. We leave it at that. A. QUILLER.

THE BLUE BIRD. Translated by ALEXANDER TEXEIRA DE MATTOS. Methuen. 1s. net.

Was it merely an unfortunate accident? As I opened the book my eye fell on these words: "They are my apples and they are not the finest at that! . . . They will all be alike when I am alive." . . . My memory of the play—sole comrade of my wanderings in the Sahara—said no! no! So I turned up the passage, and read—"Toutes seront de même quand je serai vivant."

My memory was right, and Mr. de Mattos had completely failed to grasp the sense of a simple sentence of eight easy words.

I did not continue my inquiry.

A. C.

AN APOLOGY FOR PRINTING HONEST REVIEWS

THE Editor of THE EQUINOX is well aware of the tendency of modern journalism to print only favourable reviews of books, and to praise on the recommendation of the Advertisement Manager rather than that of the Literary Adviser. But he believes that this policy defeats its own end, that praise in THE EQUINOX will really sell copies of the book receiving it, and that appreciation of this fact on the part of publishers will result in the enrichment of his advertising columns.

THE SHADOWY DILL-WATERS

OR

MR. SMUDGE THE MEDIUM

" 'Tis like the howling of Irish wolves agains the moon."
As You Like it.

IN our investigation of the trumpery tin Pantheon of Aunt
Sallies which our country calls 'literary gents," one of the
most striking figures is a certain lame duck that suggests a
mixed ancestry of Bringand manqué and the Ghost in the Bab
Ballads.

Historically, too, the subject has its advantage, for not only
does the work of Weary Willie suggest primal Chaos, but
himself recalls the Flood. He seems to have desired to
emulate Noah, but the modern tendency to specialisation has
led him to confine his attentions to the Insect World, and the
remarkable jumping qualities of some of his specimens have
their correspondence in the metre of those treacly emulsions
which it is our present purpose to study.

Come with me! Behold the scene of action. What? You
can see nothing? Of course not. It's out of focus, and the
limelight is but a farthing dip. Never mind; take the slide,

and hold it to the light! Ah! there's a well—a druid well; a wood—a druid wood; a boat (druid) on a druid sea. Why Druid? Because Willie is not a British workman. The expletive is harmless enough. Look! more wells and woods and boats and apple-blossoms. When in doubt, play apple-blossom. Try and scan it as a dactyl. You can't? He can.

Oh! there are some people in the boat. Druid people. A queen with hair like the casting-net of the stars. What's that? Never mind. There's nothing rude or offensive about the casting-net of the stars? Very good, then; let's get on. What are they doing? Drifting. That's dead sure, any-way. Drifting. Drifting. That's the beautiful Celtic glamour of it. Druidically drifting Druids on a druid sea of apple-blossom in the middle distance. Foreground, a well in a wood. Background, a casting-net of the stars. Dotted about, hounds of various colours, usually red. Let's have another slide. Same thing, with a fairy floating about. Tired? Yes. Well, sit down and talk about it. Tut! Tut! . . .

How on earth does anybody ever deliberately produce this sort of thing? He doesn't. It just happens. All the Gregory Powder in the world won't produce it; it's true Asiatic Cholera, and you can't imitate it. I didn't mean dill-wates; I meant rice-waters.

Now let no one think that we object to an atmo-sphere in Art. Maeterlinck is doubtless just as misty in his symbolism; equally he uses a leitmotiv; equally he relies on mystery to shroud his figures with fascination, terror, or glamour.

But the images are themselves perfectly clear and precise. In the mistiest of all, "Les Aveugles," one can condense the plot into a single phrase of simplest English. On this clean model, Greek in its simplicity, the master has thrown draperies of cleanly woven fabric, delicate and frail as spiders' webs—and as silvery and strong as they.

This is a craftsmanship exquisitely subtle and severe, a style of almost superhuman austerity.

In our shadowy choleraic we have the imitation of this, its reflection in a dull and dirty mind.

Smudge.

When Ruskin reproached Whistler for his ability to distinguish between colours less violent than vermilion and emerald, he was no doubt a Philistine. But how much worse is the Bohemian who thinks—"Since I cannot see anything but muddiness in these silver-grey quarter-tones, I can easily rival Whistler." Forthwith he mixes up all the colours in his box, daubs a canvas with them and——? Certainly he deceives Ruskin, but he deceives nobody else.

Genius, O weary one, is not an infinite capacity for taking pains; but genius has to take pains to express itself, and expression is at least half the battle. You, I think, have neither genius nor application; neither a healthy skin nor the soap-travail which might reveal it. Still, one can never be sure; you might give a trial to the soap.

If we had not a sufficiency of hard work before us in interpreting the masters of old, we might be tempted to waste more time on you; but there is Blake. Blake is more obscure than you are; but we have this guarantee, based on experience, that when we do attain to his meaning, it starts up luminous, Titanic, splendid. With you, we discover only commonplace—the commonplace of a maudlin undertaker replying to the toast of the Ladies at the Annual Dinner of the Antique Order of Arch-Druids.

Blake fashioned his intricate caskets of symbol to conceal pearls; you pile up dead leaves to cover rotten apples.

You are Attis with a barren fig-leaf.

It is true that a sort of dreary music runs monotonously through your verses, only jarred by the occasional discords. It is as if an eternal funeral passed along, and the motor-hearse had something wrong with the ignition—and the exhaust.

It is as if a man were lost upon a lonely marsh in the flat country and constantly slipped and sat down with a splash in a puddle. These be ignoble images, my masters!

The fact is that you are both myopic and tone-deaf. You peer into the darkly splendid world, the abyss of light—for it is light, to the seer—and you see but "unintelligible images, unluminous, formless, and void." Then you return and pose as one who has trodden the eternal snows.

You are like a man who puts a penny into a mutoscope that is out of order; and, rather than admit that he has been swindled, pretends to have enjoyed it. You are like a parvenu with an ill-cooked chop at a swagger restaurant who eats it rather than incur the frown of the waiter.

Better abandon mysticism outright than this. But we suppose it is impossible; you must trim, and compromise, and try to get round the Boyg, O Peer Gynt without his courage and light-heartedness, O onion with many a stinking sheath, and a worm at the heart!

330

THE SHADOWY DILL-WATERS

Yes, if nothing else were wrong with you—and everything else *is* wrong—you would still be damned for your toadying to Mrs. Grundy and the Reverend Robert Rats.

We thought to sum you up on a page, and that page a page of but four corners; on mature consideration we think it could be done in a word, and that word a word of but four letters.

A. QUILLER, JR.

LIBER DCCCCLXIII

A∴ A∴ Publication in Class B.
Issued by Order:

D.D.S. 7° = 4° Præmonstrator
O.S.V. 6° = 5° Imperator
N.S.F. 5° = 6° Cancellarius

LIBER
ΘΕΣΑΥΡΟΥ ᾿ΕΙΔΩΛΩΝ

SVB FIGVRA
DCCCLXIII

צטרת צטרה
Corona, Corolla;
Sic vocatur Malchuth
quando ascendit usque
ad Kether
The Kabbala.

(The Probationer should learn by heat the chapter corresponding to the Zodiacal Sign that was rising at his birth; or, if this be unknown, the chapter "The Twelvefold Unification of God.")

93	108	123	138	153	168	1	16	31	46	61	76	91
107	122	137	152	167	13	15	30	45	60	75	90	92
121	136	151	166	12	14	29	44	59	74	89	104	106
135	150	165	11	26	28	43	58	73	88	103	105	120
149	164	10	25	27	42	57	72	87	102	117	119	134
163	9	24	39	41	56	71	86	101	116	118	133	148
8	23	38	40	55	70	85	100	115	130	132	147	162
22	37	52	54	69	84	99	114	129	131	146	161	7
36	51	53	68	83	98	113	128	143	145	160	6	21
50	65	67	82	97	112	127	142	144	159	52	20	35
64	66	81	96	111	126	141	156	158	4	19	34	49
78	80	95	110	125	140	155	157	3	18	33	48	63
79	94	109	124	139	154	169	2	17	32	47	62	77

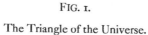

FIG. 1.

The Triangle of the Universe.

Three Veils of the Negative—not yellow; not red; not blue; but therefore symbolised by the "flashing" colours of these three; purple (11); emerald (12) and orange (13). Within their triangle of Yonis is the Lingam touching and filling it. Positive, as they are negative; in the Queen Scale of colour, as they are in the King Scale. Ten are the Emanations of Unity, the parts of that Lingam, in Kether, TARO = 78 = 6 × 13, the Influence of that Unity in the Macrocosm (Hexagram). The centre of the whole figure is Tiphareth, where is a golden Sun of six rays. Note the reflection of the Yonis to the triad about Malkuth. Also note that the triangle of Yonis is hidden, even as their links are secret. From Malkuth depends the Greek Cross of the Zodiac and their Spritual Centre (Fig. 2). For Colour Scales see 777.

A∴A∴
Publication in Class A

A NOTE UPON LIBER DCCCCLXIII

1. Let the student recite this book, particularly the 169 Adorations, unto his Star as it ariseth.

2. Let him seek out diligently in the sky his Star; let him travel thereunto in his Shell; let him adore it unceasingly from its rising even unto its setting by the right adorations, with chants that shall be harmonious therewith.

3. Let him rock himself to and fro in adoration; let him spin around his own axis in adoration; let him leap up and down in adoration.

4. Let him inflame himself in the adoration, speeding from slow to fast, until he can no more.

5. This also shall be sung in open places, as heaths, mountains, woods, and by streams and upon islands.

6. Moreover, ye shall build you fortified places in great cities; caverns and tombs shall be made glad with your praise.

7. Amen.

THE TREASURE-HOUSE OF IMAGES

Here beginneth the Book of
the Meditations on the
Twelvefold Adora-
tion, and the
Unity of
GOD.

𝕿𝖍𝖊 𝕮𝖍𝖆𝖕𝖙𝖊𝖗 𝖐𝖓𝖔𝖜𝖓 𝖆𝖘
𝕿𝖍𝖊 𝕻𝖊𝖗𝖈𝖊𝖕𝖙𝖎𝖔𝖓 𝖔𝖋 𝕲𝖔𝖉
𝖙𝖍𝖆𝖙 𝖎𝖘 𝖗𝖊𝖛𝖊𝖆𝖑𝖊𝖉 𝖚𝖓𝖙𝖔 𝖒𝖆𝖓 𝖋𝖔𝖗 𝖆 𝖘𝖓𝖆𝖗𝖊

♦   ♦   ♦   ♦   ♦   I   ♦   ♦   ♦   ♦   ♦
♦   ♦   ♦   ♦   ♦   adore   ♦   ♦   ♦   ♦   ♦
♦   ♦   ♦   ♦   Thee by the   ♦   ♦   ♦   ♦
♦   ♦   ♦   ♦   Twelvefold Snare   ♦   ♦   ♦   ♦
♦   ♦   ♦   ♦ and by the Unity thereof   ♦   ♦   ♦   ♦

000. In the Beginning there was Naught, and Naught spake unto Naught, saying: Let us beget on the Nakedness of Our Nothingness the Limitless, Eternal, Identical and United: And without will, intention, thought, word, desire, or deed, it was so.

00. Then in the depts of Nothingness hovered the Limitless, as a raven in the night; seeing naught, hearing naught, and understanding naught: neither was it seen, nor heard, nor understood; for as yet Countenance beheld not Countenance.

0. And as the Limitless stretched forth its wings, an unextended unextendable Light became; colourless, formless, conditionless, effluent, naked, and essential, as a crystalline dew of creative effulgence; and fluttering as a dove betwixt Day and Night, it vibrated forth as a lustral Crown of Glory.

1. And out of the blinding whitness of the Crown grew an Eye, like unto an egg of an humming-bird cherished on a platter of burnished silver.

2. Thus I beheld Thee, O my God, the lid of whose Eye is as the Night of Chaos, and the pupil thereof as the marshalled order of the sphere.

3. For, I am but as a blind man, who wandering through the noontide preceiveth not the loveliness of day; and even as he whose eyes are unenlightened beholdeth not the greatness of this world in the depths of a starless night, so am I who am not able to search the unfathomable dephs of Thy Wisdom.

4. For what am I that I durst look upon Thy Countenance, purblind one of small understanding that I am, blindly groping through the night of mine ignirance like unto a little maggot hid in the dark depths of a corrupted corpse?

5. Therefore, O my God, fashion me into a five-pointed star of ruby burning beneath the foundations of Thy Unity, that I may mount the pillar of Thy Glory, and be lost in adoration of the triple Unity of Thy Godhead, I beseech Thee, O Thou who art to me as the Finger of Light thrust through the black clouds of Chaos; I beseech Thee, O my God, hearken Thou unto my cry!

6. Then, O my God, am I not risen as the sun that eateth up ocean as a golden lion that feedeth on a blue-grey wolf? So shall I become one with Thy Beauty, worn upon Thy breast as the Centre of a Sixfold Star of ruby and of sapphire.

7. Yea, O God, gird Thou me upon Thy thigh as a warrior girdeth his sword! Smith my acuteness into the earth, and as a sower casteth his seed into the furrows of the plough, do Thou beget upon me these adorations of Thy Unity, O My Conqueror!

8. And Thou shalt carry me upon Thine hip, O Thou flashing God, as a black mother of the South Country carrying her babe. Whence I shall reach my lips to Thy paps, and sucking out Thy stars, shed them in these adorations upon the Earth.

9. Moreover, O God my God, Thou who hast cloven me with Thine amethystine Phallus, with Thy Phallus adamantine, with Thy Phallus of Gold and Ivory! thus am I cleft in twain as two halves of a child that is split asunder by the sword of the eunuchs, and mine adorations are divided, and one contendeth against his brother. Unite Thou me even as a split tree that closeth itself again upon the axe, that my song of praise unto Thee may be One Song!

10. For I am Thy chosen Virgin, O my God! Exalt thou me unto the throne of the Mother, unto the Garden of Supernal Dew, unto the Unutterable Sea!

Amen,
and Amen of Amen,
and Amen of Amen of Amen
and Amen of Amen of Amen of Amen.

♈ The Chapter known as The Twelvefold Affirmation of God and the Unity thereof

◆ ◆ ◆ ◆ ◆ I ◆ ◆ ◆ ◆ ◆
◆ ◆ ◆ ◆ ◆ adore ◆ ◆ ◆ ◆ ◆
◆ ◆ ◆ ◆ Thee by the ◆ ◆ ◆ ◆
◆ ◆ ◆ ◆ Twelve Affirmations ◆ ◆ ◆ ◆
◆ ◆ ◆ ◆ and by the Unity thereof ◆ ◆ ◆ ◆

1. O Thou snow-clad volcan of scarlet fire, Thou flame-crested pillar of fury! Yea, as I approach Thee, Thou departest from me like unto a wisp of smoke blown forth from the window of my house.

2. O Thou summer-land of eternal joy, Thou rapturous garden of flowers! Yea, as I gather Thee, my harvest is but as a drop of dew shimmering in the golden cup of the crocus.

3. O Thou throbbing music of life and death, Thou rhythmic harmony of the world! Yea, as I listen to the echo of Thy voice, my rapture is but as the whisper of the wings of a buterfly.

4. O Thou burning tempest of blinding sand, Thou whirlwind from the depths of darkness! Yea, as I struggle through Thee, through Thee, my strength is but as a dove's down floating forth on the purple nipples of the storm.

5. O Thou crownèd giant among great giants, Thou crimson-sworded solider of war! Yea, as I battle with Thee, Thou masterest me as a lion that slayeth a babe that is cradled in lilies.

6. O Thou shadowy vista of Darkness, Thou cryptic Book of the fir-clad hills! Yea, as I search the key of Thy house I find my hope but as a rushlight sheltered in the hands of a little child.

7. O Thou great labour of the Firmamanent, Thou tempest-tossed roaring of the Aires! Yea, as I sink in the depths of Thine affliction, mine anguish is but as the smile on the lips of a sleeping bnabe.

8. O Thou depths of the Inconceivable, Thou cryptic, unutterable God! Yea, as I attempt to understand Thee, my wisdom is but as an abacus in the lap of an aged man.

9. O Thou transfigured dream of blinding light, Thou beatitude of wonderment! Yea, as I behold Thee, mine understanding is but as the glimpes of a rainbow through a storm of blinding snow.

10. O Thou steel-girdered mountain of mountains, Tho crested summit of Majesty! Yea, as I climb Thy grandeur, I find I have but surmounted one mote of dust floating in a beam of Thy Glory.

11. O Thou Empress of Light and of Darkness, Thou pourer-forth of the stars of night! Yea, as I gaze upon Thy Countenance, mine eyes are as the eyes of a blind man smitten by a torch of burning fire.

12. O Thou crimson gladness of the midnight, Thou flamingo North of brooding light! Yea, as I rise up before Thee, my joy is but as a raindrop smitten through by an arrow of the Western Sun.

13. O Thou golden Crown of the Universe, Thou diadem of dazzling brightness! Yea, as I burn up before Thee, my

light is but as a falling star seen between the purple fingers
of the Night.

O Glory be unto Thee through all Time
and through all Space : Glory,
and Glory upon Glory,
Everlastingly. Amen,
and Amen, and
Amen.

♉ The Chapter known as The Twelvefold Renunciation of God and the Unity thereof

♦ ♦ ♦ ♦ ♦ I ♦ ♦ ♦ ♦ ♦
♦ ♦ ♦ ♦ ♦ adore ♦ ♦ ♦ ♦ ♦
♦ ♦ ♦ ♦ Thee by the ♦ ♦ ♦ ♦
♦ ♦ ♦ ♦ Twelve Renunciations ♦ ♦ ♦ ♦
♦ ♦ ♦ ♦ and by the Unity thereof ♦ ♦ ♦ ♦

1. O my God, Thou mighty One, Thou Creator of all things, I renounce unto Thee the kisses of my mistress, and the murmur of her mouth, and all the trembling of her firm young breast; so that I may be rolled a flame in Thy fiery embrace, and be consumed in the unutterable joy of Thine everlasting rapture.

2. O my God, Thou mighty One, Thou Creator of all things, I renounce unto Thee the soft-lipp'd joys of life, and the honey-sweets of this world, and all the subtilities of the flesh; so that I may be feasted on the fire of Thy passion, and be consumed in the unutterable joy of Thine everlasting rapture.

3. O my God, Thou mighty One, Thou Creator of all things, I renounce unto Thee the ceaseless booming of the waves, and the fury of the storm, and all the turmoil of the wind-swept waters; so that I may drink of the porphyrine foam of Thy lips, and be consumed in the unutterable joy of Thine everlasting rapture.

4. O my God, Thou mighty One, Thou Creator of all things, I renounce unto Thee the whispers of the desert, and the moan of the simoom, and all the silence of the sea of

dust; so that I may be lost in the atoms of Thy Glory, and be consumed in the unutterable joy of Thine everlasting rapture.

5. O my God, Thou mighty One, Thou Creator of all things, I renounce unto Thee the green fields of the valleys, and the satyr roses of the hills, and the nymph lilies of the meer; so that I may wander through the gardens of Thy Splendour, and be consumed in the unutterable joy of Thine everlasting rapture.

6. O my God, Thou mighty One, Thou Creator of all things, I renounce unto Thee the sorrow of my mother, and the threshold of my home, and all the labour of my father's hands; so that I may be led unto the Mansion of Thy Light, and be consumed in the unutterable joy of Thine everlasting rapture.

7. O my God, Thou mighty One, Thou Creator of all things, I renounce unto Thee the yearning for Paradise, and the dark fear of Hell, and the feast of the corruption of the grave; so that as a child I may be led unto Thy Kingdom, and be consumed in the unutterable joy of Thine everlasting rapture.

8. O my God, Thou mighty One, Thou Creator of all things, I renounce unto Thee the moonlit peaks of the mountains, and the arrow-shapen kiss of the firs, and all the travail of the winds; so that I may be lost on the summit of Thy Glory, and be consumed in the unutterable joy of Thine everlasting rapture.

9. O my God, Thou mighty One, Thou Creator of all things, I renounce unto Thee the goatish ache of the years, and the cryptic books, and all the majesty of their enshrouded words; so that I may be entangled in Thy wordless Wisdom. and be consumed in the unutterable joy of Thine everlasting rapture.

10. O my God, Thou mighty One, Thou Creator of all things, I renounce unto Thee the wine-cups of merriment, and the eyes of the wanton bearers, and all the lure of their soft limbs; so that I may be made drunk on the vine of Thy splendour, and be consumed in the unutterable joy of Thine everlasting rapture.

11. O my God, Thou mighty One, Thou Creator of all things, I renounce unto Thee the hissing of mad waters, and the trumpeting of the thunder, and all Thy tongues of dancing flame; so that I may be swept up in the breath of Thy nostrils, and be consumed in the unutterable joy of Thine everlasting rapture.

12. O my God, Thou mighty One, Thou Creator of all things, I renounce unto Thee the crimson lust of the chase, and the blast of the brazen war-horns, and all the gleaming of the spears; so that like an hart I may be brought to bay in Thine arms, and be consumed in the unutterable joy of Thine everlasting rapture.

13. O my God, Thou mighty One, Thou Creator of all things, I renounce unto Thee all that Self which is myself, that black sun which shineth in Self's day, whose glory blindeth Thy Glory; so that I may become as a rushlight in Thine abode, and be consumed in the unutterable joy of Thine everlasting rapture.

O Glory be unto Thee through all Time
and through all Space : Glory,
and Glory upon Glory,
Everlastingly. Amen,
and Amen, and
Amen.

♊ The Chapter known as The Twelvefold Conjuration of God and the Unity thereof

```
◆   ◆   ◆   ◆   ◆      I      ◆   ◆   ◆   ◆   ◆
◆   ◆   ◆   ◆   ◆    adore    ◆   ◆   ◆   ◆   ◆
◆   ◆   ◆   ◆    Thee by the      ◆   ◆   ◆   ◆
◆   ◆   ◆   ◆  Twelve Conjurations   ◆   ◆   ◆   ◆
◆   ◆   ◆   ◆ and by the Unity thereof ◆   ◆   ◆   ◆
```

1. O Thou Consuming Eye of everlasting light set as a pearl betwixt the lids of Night and Day; I swear to Thee by the formless void of the Abyss, to lap the galaxies of night in darkness, and blow the meteors like bubbles into the frothing jaws of the sun.

2. O Thou ten-footed soldeir of blue ocean, whose castle is built upon the sands of life and death; I swear to Thee by the glittering blades of the waters, to cleave my way within Thine armed hermitage, and brood as an eyeless corpse beneath the coffin-lid of the Mighty Sea.

3. O Thou incandescent Ocean of molten stars, surging above the arch of the Firmament; I swear to Thee by the mane-pennoned lances of light, to stir the lion of Thy darkness from its air, and lash the sorceress of noontide into fury with serpents of fire.

4. O Thou intoxicating Vision of Beauty, fair as ten jewelled virgins dancing about the hermit moon; I swear to Thee by the peridot flagons of spring, to quaff to the dregs Thy Chalice of Glory, and beget a royal race before the Dawn flees from awakening Day.

5. O Thou unalterable measure of all things, in whose lap

lie the destinies of unborn worlds; I swear to Thee by the balance of Light and Darkness, to spread out the blue vault as a looking-glass, and flash forth therefrom the intolerable lustre of Thy Countenance.

6. O Thou who settest forth the limitless expanse, I swear to Thee by the voiceless dust of the dest, to soar above the echoes of shrieking life, and as an eagle to fear for ever upon the silence of the stars.

7. O Thou flame-tipped arrow of devouring fire that quiverest as a tongue in the dark mouth of Night; I swear to Thee by the thurible of Thy Glory, to breathe the incense of mine understanding, and to cast the ashes of my wisdom into the Valley of Thy breast.

8. O Thou ruin of the mountains, glistening as an old white wolf above the fleecy mists of Earth; I swear to Thee by the galaxies of Thy domain, to press Thy lamb's breasts with the teeth of my soul, and drink of the milk and blood of Thy subtlely and innocence.

9. O Thou Eternal river of chaotic law, in whose depths lie locked the secrets of Creation; I swear to Thee by the primal waters of the Deep, to such up the Firmament of Thy Chaos, and as a volcano to belch forth a Cosmos of coruscanting suns.

10. O Thou Dragon-regent of the blue seas of air, as a chain of emeralds round the neck of Space; I swear to Thee by the hexagram of Night and Day, to be unto Thee as the twin fish of Time, which being set apart never divulged the secret of their unity.

11. O Thou flame of the hornèd storm-clouds, that sunderest their desolation, that outroarest the winds; I swear

to Thee by the gleaming sandals of the stars, to climb beyond
the summits of the mountains, and rend Thy robe of purple
thunders with a sword of silvery light.

12. O Thou fat of an hundred fortresses of iron, crimson as
the blades of a million murderous swords; I swear to Thee by
the smoke-wreath of the volcano, to open the secret shrine of
Thy bull's breast, and tear out as an augur the heart of Thine
all-pervading mystery.

13. O Thou silver axle of the Wheel of Being, thurst
through with wings of Time by the still hand of Space; I swear
to Thee by the twelve spokes of Thy Unity, to become unto
Thee as the rim thereof, so that I may clothe me majestically
in the robe that has no seam.

O Glory be unto Thee through all Time
and through all Space : Glory,
and Glory upon Glory,
Everlastingly. Amen,
and Amen, and
Amen.

 **The Chapter known as The Twelvefold Certitude of God and the Unity thereof**

◆　◆　◆　◆　◆　　I　　◆　◆　◆　◆　◆
◆　◆　◆　◆　◆　adore　◆　◆　◆　◆　◆
◆　◆　◆　◆　Thee by the　◆　◆　◆　◆
◆　◆　◆　◆　Twelve Certitudes　◆　◆　◆　◆
◆　◆　◆　◆　and by the Unity thereof　◆　◆　◆　◆

1. O Thou Sovran Warrior of steel-girt volour, whose scimitar is a flame between day and night, whose helm is crested with the wings of the Abyss. I know Thee! O Thou four-eyed guardian of heaven, who kindleth to a flame the hearts of the downcast, and girdeth about with fire the loins of the unarmed.

2. O Thou Sovran Light and fire of loveliness, whose flaming locks stream downwards through the æthyr as knots of lightning deep-rooted. I know Thee! O Thou winnowing flail of brightness, the passionate lash of whose encircling hand scatters mankind before Thy fury as the wind-scud from the stormy breast of Ocean.

3. O Thou Sovran Singer of the revelling winds, whose voice is as a vestal troop of Bacchanals awakened by the piping of a Pan-pipe. I know Thee! O thou dancing flame of frenzied song, whose shouts, like unto golden swords of leaping fire, urge us onwards to the wild slaughter of the Worlds.

4. O Thou Sovran Might of the most ancient forests, whose voice is as the murmur of unappeasable winds caught up in the arms of the swaying branches. I know Thee! O

Thou rumble of conquering drums, who lulleth to a rapture of deep sleep those lovers who burn into each other, flame to fine flame.

5. O Thou Sovran Guide of the star-wheeling circles, the soles of whose feet smite plumes of golden fire from the outermost annihilation of the Abyss. I know Thee! O Thou crimson sword of destruction, who chasest the comets from the dark bed of night, till they speed before Thee as serpent tongues of flame.

6. O Thou Sovran Archer of the darksome regions, who shooteth forth from Thy transcendental crossbow the many-rayed suns into the fields of heaven. I know Thee! O Thou eight-pointed arrow of light, who smiteth the regions of the seven rivers until they laugh like Mænads with snaky thyrsus.

7. O Thou Sovran Paladin of self-vanquished knights, whose path lieth through the trackless forests of time, winding athrough the Byss of unbegotten space. I know Thee! O thou despiser of the mountains, Thou whose course is as that of a lightning-hoofed steed leaping along the green bank of a fair river.

8. O Thou Sovran Surging of wild felicity, whose love is as the overflowing of the seas, and who makest our bodies to laugh with beauty. I know Thee! O Thou outstrider of the sunset, who deckest the snow-capped mountains with red roses, and strewest white violets on the curling waters.

9. O Thou Sovran Diadem of crownèd Wisdom, whose work knowleth the path of the sylphs of the air, and the black burrowings of the gnomes of the earth, I know Thee! O Thou master of the ways of life, in the palm of whose hand all the

arts lie bounden as a smoke-cloud betwixt the lips of the mountain.

10. O Thou Sovran Lord of primæval Baresarkers, who huntest with dawn the dappled deer of twilight, and whose engines of war are blood-crested comets. I know Thee! O Thou flame-crowned Self-luminous One, the lash of whose whip gathered the ancient worlds, and looseth the blood from the virgin clouds of heaven.

11. O Thou Sovran Moonstone of pearly loveliness, from out whose many eyes flash the fire-clouds of life, and whose breath enkindleth the Byss and the Abyss. I know Thee! O Thou fountain-head of fierce æthyr, in the pupil of whose brightness all things lie crouched and wrapped like a babe in the womb of its mother.

12. O Thou Sovran Mother of the breath of being, the milk of whose breasts is as the fountain of love, twin-jets of fire of fire upon the blue bosom of night. I know Thee! O Thou Virgin of the moonlit glades, who fondleth us as a drop of dew in Thy lap, ever watchful over the cradle of our fate.

13. O Thou Sovran All-Beholding eternal Sun, who lappest up the constellations of heaven, as a thirsty thief a jar of ancient wine. I know Thee! O Thou dawn-wing'd courtesan of light, who makest me to reel with one kiss of Thy mouth, as a leaf cast into the flames of a furnace.

O Glory be unto Thee through all Time
and through all Space : Glory,
and Glory upon Glory,
Everlastingly. Amen,
and Amen, and
Amen.

The Chapter known as
The Twelvefold Glorification of God
and the Unity thereof

                I
              adore
          Thee by the
       Twelve Glorifications
    and by the Unity thereof

1. O Glory be to Thee, O God my God; for I behold Thee in the Lion Rampant of the dawn: Thou hast crushed with Thy paw the crouching lioness of Night, so that she may roar forth the Glory of Thy Name.

2. O Glory be to Thee, O God my God; for I behold Thee in the lap of the fertile valleys: Thou hast adorned their strong limbs with a robe of poppied corn, so that they may laugh forth the Glory of Thy Name.

3. O Glory be to Thee, O God my God; for I behold Thee in the gilded rout of dancing-girls: Thou hast garlanded their naked middles with fragrant flowers, so that they may pace forth the Glory of Thy Name.

4. O Glory be to Thee, O God my God; for I behold Thee in the riotous joy of the storm; Thou hast shaken the gold-dust from the tresses of the hills, so that they may chaunt forth the Glory of Thy Name.

5. O Glory be to Thee, O God my God; for I behold Thee in the stars and meteors of Night: Thou hast caprarisoned her grey coursers with moons of pearl, so that they may shake forth the Glory of Thy Name.

6. O Glory be to Thee, O God my God; for I behold Thee

in the precious stones of the black earth: Thou hast lightened her with a myriad eyes of magic, so that she may wink forth the Glory of Thy Name.

7. O Glory be to Thee, O God my God; for I behold Thee in the sparkling dew of the wild glades: Thou hast decked them out as for a great feast of rejoicing, so that they may gleam forth the Glory of Thy Name.

8. O Glory be to Thee, O God my God; for I behold Thee in the stillness of the frozen lakes: Thou hast made their faces more dazzling than a silver mirror, so that they may flash forth the Glory of Thy Name.

9. O Glory be to Thee, O God my God; for I behold Thee in the smoke-veil'd fire of the mountains. Thou hast inflamed them as lions that scent a fallow deer, so that they may rage forth the Glory of Thy Name.

10. O Glory be to Thee, O God my God; for I behold Thee in the contenance of my darling: Thou hast unclothed her of white lilies and crimson roses, so that she may blush forth the Glory of Thy Name.

11. O Glory be to Thee, O God my God; for I behold Thee in the weeping of the flying clouds: Thou hast swelled therewith the blue breasts of the milky rivers so that they may roll forth the Glory of Thy Name.

12. O Glory be to Thee, O God my God; for I behold Thee in the amber combers of the storm: Thou hast laid Thy lash upon the sphinxes of the waters, so that they may boom forth the Glory of Thy Name.

13. O Glory be to Thee, O God my God; for I behold Thee in the lotus-flower within my heart: Thou hast

emblazoned my trumpet with the lion-standard, so that they I
blare forth the Glory of Thy Name.

O Glory be unto Thee through all Time
and through all Space : Glory,
and Glory upon Glory,
Everlastingly. Amen,
and Amen, and
Amen.

 The Chapter known as
The Twelvefold Beseechment of God
and the Unity thereof

◆ ◆ ◆ ◆ ◆ I ◆ ◆ ◆ ◆ ◆
◆ ◆ ◆ ◆ ◆ adore ◆ ◆ ◆ ◆ ◆
◆ ◆ ◆ ◆ Thee by the ◆ ◆ ◆ ◆
◆ ◆ ◆ ◆ Twelve Beesechments ◆ ◆ ◆ ◆
◆ ◆ ◆ ◆ and by the Unity thereof ◆ ◆ ◆ ◆

1. O Thou mighty God, make me as a fair virgin that is clad in the blue-bells of the fragrant hillside; I beseech Thee, O Thou great God! That I may ring out the melody of Thy voice, and be clothed in the pure light of Thy loveliness: O Thou God my God!

2. O Thou Mighty God, make me as a Balance of rubies and jet that is cast in the lap of the Sun; I beseech Thee, O Thou great God! That I may flash forth the wonder of Thy brightness, and melt into the perfect poison of Thy Being: O Thou God, my God!

3. O Thou Mighty God, make me as a brown Scorpion that creepeth on through a vast desert of Silver; I beseech Thee, O Thou great God! That I may lose myself in the span of Thy light, and become one with the glitter of Thy Shadow: O Thou God, my God!

4. O Thou mighty God, make me as a green arrow of Lightning that speedeth through the purple clouds of Night; I beseech Thee, O Thou great God! That I may wake fire from the crown of Thy Wisdom, and flash into the depths on Thine Understanding: O Thou God, my God!

5. O Thou mighty God, make me as a flint-black goat that

pranceth in a shining wilderness of steel; I beseech Thee, O Thou great God! That I may paw one flashing spark from Thy Splendour, and be welded into the Glory of Thy might: O Thou God, My God!

6. O Thou mighty God, make me as the sapphirine waves that cling to the shimmering limbs of the green rocks; I beseech Thee, O Thou great God! That I may chant in foaming music Thy Glory, and roll forth the eternal rapture of Thy Name: O Thou God, my God!

7. O Thou mighty God, make me as a silver fish darting through the vast depths of the dim-peopled waters; I beseech Thee, O Thou great God! That I may swim through the vastness of Thine abyss, and sink beneath the waveless depths of Thy Glory: O Thou God, my God!

8. O Thou mighty God, make me as a white ram that is athirst in a sun-scorched desert of bitterness; I beseech Thee, O Thou great God! That I may seek the deep waters of Thy Wisdom, and plundge into the whiteness of Thine effulgence: O Thou God, my God!

9. O Thou mighty God, make me as a thunder-smitted bull that is drunk upon the vintage of Thy blood; I beseech Thee, O Thou great God! That I may bellow through the universe Thy Power, and trample the nectar-sweet graps of Thine Essence: O Thou God, my God!

10. O Thou mighty God, make me as a black eunuch of song that is twin-voiced, yet dumb in either tongue; I beseech Thee, O Thou great God! That I may hush my melody in Thy Silence, and swell into the sweet ecstasy of Thy Song. O Thou God, my God!

11. O Thou mighty God, make me as an emerald crab that

crawleth over the wet sands of the sea-shore; I beseech Thee, O Thou great God! That I may write Thy name across the shores of Time, and sink amongst the white atoms of Thy Being. O Thou God, my God!

12. O Thou mighty God, make me as a ruby lion that roareth from the summit of a white mountain; I beseech Thee, O Thou great God! That I may echo forth thy lordship through the hills, and dwindle into the nipple of Thy bounty. O Thou God, my God!

13. O Thou mighty God, make me as an all-consuming Sun ablaze in the centre of the Universe; I beseech Thee, O Thou great God! That I may become as a crown upon Thy brow, and flash forth the exceeding fire of Thy Godhead: O Thou God, my God!

O Glory be unto Thee through all Time
and through all Space : Glory,
and Glory upon Glory,
Everlastingly. Amen,
and Amen, and
Amen.

The Chapter known as
The Twelvefold Gratification of God
and the Unity thereof

♦   ♦   ♦   ♦   ♦   I   ♦   ♦   ♦   ♦   ♦
♦   ♦   ♦   ♦   ♦   adore   ♦   ♦   ♦   ♦   ♦
♦   ♦   ♦   ♦   Thee by the   ♦   ♦   ♦   ♦
♦   ♦   ♦   ♦   Twelve Gratifications   ♦   ♦   ♦   ♦
♦   ♦   ♦   ♦   and by the Unity thereof   ♦   ♦   ♦

1. O Thou green-cloaked Mænad in labour, who bearest beneath Thy leaden girdle the vintage of Thy kisses; release me from the darkness of Thy womb, so that I may cast off my infant wrappings and leap forth as an armed warrior in steel.

2. O Thou snake of misty countenance, whose braided hair is like a fleecy dawn of swooning maidens; hunt me as a fierce wild boar through the skies, so that Thy burning spear may gore the blue heavens red with the foaming blood of my frenzy.

3. O Thou cloudy Virgin of the World, whose breasts are as scarlet lilies paling before the sun; dandle me in the cradle of Thine arms, so that the murmur of Thy voice may lull me to a sleep like a pearl lost in the depths of a silent sea!

4. O Thou wine-voiced laughter of fainting gloom, who art as a naked faun crushed to death between millstones of thunder; make me drunk on the rapture of Thy song, so that in the corpse-clutch of my passion I may tear the cloud-robe from off Thy swooning breast.

5. O Thou wanton cup-bearer of madness, whose mouth is as the joy of a thousand thousand masterful kisses; intoxicate me on Thy loveliness, so that the silver of Thy

merriment may revel as a moon-white pearl upon my tongue.

6. O Thou midnight Vision of Whiteness, whose lips are as pouting rosebuds deflowered by the deciduous moon; tend me as a drop of dew in Thy breast, so that the dragon of Thy gluttonous hate may devour me with its mouth of adamant.

7. O Thou effulgence of burning love, who pursueth the dawn as a youth pursueth a rose-lipped maiden; rend me with the fierce kisses of Thy mouth, so that in the battle of our lips I may be drenched by the snow-pure fountains of Thy bliss.

8. O Thou black bull in a field of white girls, whose foaming flanks are as starry night ravished in the fierce arms of noon; shake forth the purple horns of my passion, so that I may dissolve as a crown of fire in the bewilderment of Thine ecstasy.

9. O Thou dread arbiter of all men, the hem of whose broidered skirt crimsoneth the white battlements of Space; bare me the starry nipple of Thy breast, so that the milk of Thy love may nurture me to the lustiness of Thy virginity.

10. O Thou thirsty charioteer of Time, whose cup is the hollow night filled with the foam of the vintage of day; drench me in the shower of Thy passion, so that I may pant in Thine arms as a tongue of lightning on the purple bosom of night.

11. O Thou opalescent Serpent-Queen, whose mouth is as the sunset that is bloody with the slaughter of day; hold me in the crimson flames of Thine arms, so that at Thy kisses I may expire as a bubble in the foam of Thy dazzling lips.

12. O Thou Odalisque of earth's palace, whose garments are scented and passionate as spring flowers in sunlit glades;

roll me in the sweet perfume of Thy hair, so that Thy tresses of gold may anoint me with the honey of a million roses.

13. O Thou manly warrior amongst youths, whose limbs are as swords of fire that are welded in the furnace of war; press Thy cool kisses to my burning lips, so that the folly of our passion may weave us into the Crown of everlasting Light.

O Glory be unto Thee through all Time
and through all Space : Glory,
and Glory upon Glory,
Everlastingly. Amen,
and Amen, and
Amen.

The Chapter known as
The Twelvefold Denial of God
and the Unity thereof

♦ ♦ ♦ ♦ ♦ I ♦ ♦ ♦ ♦ ♦
♦ ♦ ♦ ♦ ♦ adore ♦ ♦ ♦ ♦ ♦
♦ ♦ ♦ ♦ Thee by the ♦ ♦ ♦ ♦
♦ ♦ ♦ ♦ Twelve Denials ♦ ♦ ♦ ♦
♦ ♦ ♦ ♦ and by the Unity thereof ♦ ♦ ♦ ♦

1. O Thou God of the Nothingness of All Things!

Thou who art neither the Formless breath of Chaos; nor the exhaler of the ordered spheres:

O Thou who art not the cloud-cradled star of the morning; nor the sun, drunken upon the midst, who blindeth men!

I deny Thee by the powers of mine understanding;

Guide me in the unity of Thy might, and lead me to the fatherhood of Thine all-pervading Nothingness;

for Thou art all and none of these in the fullness of Thy Not-being.

2. O Thou God of the Nothingness of All Things!

Thou who art neither the vitality of worlds; nor the breath of star-entangled being:

O Thou who art not horsed 'mid the centaur clouds of night; nor the twanging of the shuddering bowstring of noon!

I deny Thee by the powers of mine understanding;

Throne me in the unity of Thy might, and stab me with the javelin of Thine all-pervading Nothingness;

for Thou art all and none of these in the fullness of Thy Not-being.

3.   O Thou God of the Nothingness of All Things!

Thou who art neither the Pan-pie in the forest; nor life's blue sword wrapped in the cloak of death:

O Thou who art not found amongst the echoes of the hills; nor in the whisperings that wake within the valleys!

I deny Thee by the powers of mine understanding;

Crown me in the unity of Thy might, and flash me as a scarlet tongue into Thine all-pervading Nothingness;

for Thou art all and none of these in the fullness of Thy Not-being.

4.   O Thou God of the Nothingness of All Things!

Thou who art neither the Crown of the flaming storm; nor the opalescence of the Abyss:

O Thou who art not a nymph in the foam of the sea; nor a whirling devil in the sand of the desert!

I deny Thee by the powers of mine understanding;

Bear me in the unity of Thy might, and pour me forth from out the cup of Thine all-pervading Nothingness;

for Thou art all and none of these in the fullness of Thy Not-being.

5.   O Thou God of the Nothingness of All Things!

Thou who art neither the formulator of law; nor the Cheat of the maze of illusion:

O Thou who art not the foundation-stone of existence; nor the eagle that broodeth upon the egg of space!

I deny Thee by the powers of mine understanding;

Swathe me in the unity of Thy might, and teach me wisdom from the lips of Thine all-pervading Nothingness;

for Thou art all and none of these in the fullness of Thy Not-being.

6. O Thou God of the Nothingness of All Things!

Thou who art neither the fivefold root of Nature; nor the fire-crested helm of her Master:

O Thou who art not the Emperor of Eternal Time; nor the warrior shout that rocketh the Byss of Space!

I deny Thee by the powers of mine understanding;

Raise me in the unity of Thy might, and suckle me at the swol'n breasts of Thine all-pervading Nothingness;

for Thou art all and none of these in the fullness of Thy Not-being.

7. O Thou God of the Nothingness of All Things!

Thou who art neither the golden bull of the heavens; nor the crimson fountain of the lusts of men:

O Thou who reclinest not upon the Waggon of Night; nor restest Thine hand upon the handle of the Plough!

I deny Thee by the powers of mine understanding;

Urge me in the unity of Thy might, and drench me with the red vintage of Thine all-pervading Nothingness;

for Thou art all and none of these in the fullness of Thy Not-being.

8. O Thou God of the Nothingness of All Things!

Thou who art neither starry eyes of heaven; nor the forehead of the crownèd morning:

O Thou who art not perceived by the powers of the mind; nor grasped by the fingers of Silence of of Speech!

I deny Thee by the powers of mine understanding;

Robe me in the unity of Thy might, and speed me into the blindness of Thine all-pervading Nothingness;

for Thou art all and none of these in the fullness of Thy Not-being.

9. O Thou God of the Nothingness of All Things!

Thou who art neither the forge of eternity; nor the thunder-throated womb of Chaos:

O Thou who art not found in the hissing of the hail-stones; nor in the rioting of the equinoctial storm!

I deny Thee by the powers of mine understanding;

Bring me in the unity of Thy might, and feast me on the honeyed manna of Thine all-pervading Nothingness;

for Thou art all and none of these in the fullness of Thy Not-being.

10. O Thou God of the Nothingness of All Things!

Thou who art neither the traces of the chariot; nor the pole of galloping delusion:

O Thou who art not the pivot of the whole Universe; nor the body of the woman-serpent of the stars!

I deny Thee by the powers of mine understanding;

Lead me in the unity of Thy might, and drawn me unto the threshold of Thine all-pervading Nothingness;

for Thou art all and none of these in the fullness of Thy Not-being.

11. O Thou God of the Nothingness of All Things!

Thou who art neither the moaning of a maiden; nor the electric touch of fire-thrilled youth:

O Thou who art not found in the hardy kisses of love; nor in the tortured spasms of madness and of hate.

I deny Thee by the powers of mine understanding;

Weight me in the unity of Thy might, and roll me in the poisoned rapture of Thine all-pervading Nothingness;

for Thou art all and none of these in the fullness of Thy Not-being.

THE TREASURE-HOUSE OF IMAGES

12. O Thou God of the Nothingness of All Things!

Thou who art neither the primal cause of causes; nor the soul of what is, or was, or will be:

O Thou who art not measured in the motionless balance; nor smitten by the arrow-flights of man!

I deny Thee by the powers of mine understanding;

Shield me in the unity of Thy might, and reckon me aright in the span of Thine all-pervading Nothingness;

for Thou art all and none of these in the fullness of Thy Not-being.

13. O Thou God of the Nothingness of All Things!

Thou who art neither the breathing influx of life; nor the iron ring i' the marriage feast of death:

O Thou who art not shadowèd forth in the songs of war; nor in the tears and lamentaitons of a child!

I deny Thee by the powers of mine understanding;

Sheathe me in the unity of Thy might, and kindle me with the grey flame of Thine all-pervading Nothingness;

for Thou art all and none of these in the fullness of Thy Not-being.

O Glory be unto Thee through all Time
and through all Space : Glory,
and Glory upon Glory,
Everlastingly. Amen,
and Amen, and
Amen.

The Chapter known as The Twelvefold Rejoicing of God and the Unity thereof

```
 ◆   ◆   ◆   ◆   ◆        I        ◆   ◆   ◆   ◆   ◆
 ◆   ◆   ◆   ◆   ◆      adore      ◆   ◆   ◆   ◆   ◆
 ◆   ◆   ◆   ◆    Thee by the     ◆   ◆   ◆   ◆
 ◆   ◆   ◆   ◆   Twelve Rejoicings  ◆   ◆   ◆   ◆
 ◆   ◆   ◆   ◆  and by the Unity thereof ◆   ◆   ◆   ◆
```

1. Ah! but I rejoice in Thee, O Thou my God;
Thou seven-rayed rainbow of perfect loveliness;
Thou light-rolling chariot of sunbeams;
Thou fragrent scent of the passing storm:
Yea, I rejoice in Thee, Thou breath of the slumbering valleys;
O Thou low-murmering ripple of the ripe corn-fields!
I rejoice, yea, I shout with gladness! till. as the mingling blushes of day and night, my song weaveth the joys of life into a gold and purple Crown, for the Glory and Splendour of Thy Name.

2. Ah! but I rejoice in Thee, O Thou my God;
Thou zigzagged effulgence of the burning stars;
Thou wilderment of indigo light;
Thou grey horn of immaculate fire:
Yea, I rejoice in Thee, Thou embattled cloud of flashing flame;
O Thou capricious serpent-head of scarlet hair!
I rejoice, yea, I shout with gladness! till my roaring filleth

the wooded mountains, and like a giant forceth the wind's head through the struggling trees, in the Glory and Splendour of Thy Name.

3. Ah! but I rejoice in Thee, O Thou my God;
Thou silken web of emerald bewitchement;
Thou berylline mist of marshy meers;
Thou flame-spangled fleece of seething gold:
Yea, I rejoice in Thee, Thou pearly dew of the setting moon;
O Thou dark purple storm-cloud of contending kisses!
I rejoice, yea, I shout with gladness! till all my laughter, like enchaunted waters, is blown as an iris-web of bubbles from the lips of the deep, in the Glory and Splendour of Thy Name.

4. Ah! but I rejoice in Thee, O Thou my God;
Thou who broodeston the dark breasts of the deep;
Thou lap of the wave-glittering sea;
Thou bright vesture of the crested floods:
Yea, I rejoice in Thee, Thou native splendour of the Waters;
O Thou fathomless Abyss of surging joy!
I rejoice, yea, I shout with gladness! till the mad swords of my music smite the hills, and rend the amethyst limbs of Night from the white embrace of Day, at the Glory and Splendour of Thy Name.

5. Ah! but I rejoice in Thee, O Thou my God;
Thou cloud-hooded bastion of the stormy skies;
Thou lightning anvil of angel swords;
Thou gloomy forge of the thunderbolt:

Yea, I rejoice in Thee, Thou all-subduing Crown of Splendour;

O Thou hero-souled helm of endless victory!

I rejoice, yea, I shout with gladness! till the mad rivers rush roaring through the woods, and my re-echoing voice danceth like a ram among the hills, for the Glory and Splendour of Thy Name.

6. Ah! but I rejoice in Thee, O Thou my God;

Thou opalescent orb of shattered sunsets;

Thou pearly boss on the shield of light;

Thou tawny priest at the Mass of lust:

Yea, I rejoice in Thee, Thou chalcedony cloudland of light;

O Thou poppy-petal floating upon the snowstorm!

I rejoice, yea, I shout with gladness! till my frenzied words rush through the souls of men, like a blood-red bull through a white herd of terror-stricken kine, at the Glory and Splendour of Thy Name.

7. Ah! but I rejoice in Thee, O Thou my God;

Thou unimperilled flight of joyous laughter;

Thou eunuch glaive-armed before joy's veil;

Thou dreadful insatiable One:

Yea, I rejoice in Thee, Thou lofty gathering-point of Bliss;

O Thou bridal-bed of murmuring rapture!

I rejoice, yea, I shout with gladness! till I tangle the black tresses of the storm, and lash the tempest into a green foam of twining basilisks, in the Glory and Splendour of Thy Name.

8. Ah! but I rejoice in Thee, O Thou my God;
Thou coruscating star-point of Endlessness;
Thou inundating fire of the Void;
Thou moonbeam cup of eternal life:
Yea, I rejoice in Thee, Thou fire-sandalled warrior of
steel;
O Thou bloody dew of the field of slaughter and death!
I rejoice, yea, I shout with gladness! till the music of my
throat smiteth the hills as a crescent moon waketh a nightly
field of sleeping comets, at the Glory and Splendour of Thy
Name.

9. Ah! but I rejoice in Thee, O Thou my God;
Thou jewel-work of snow on the limbs of night;
Thou elaboration of oneness;
Thou shower of universal suns:
Yea, I rejoice in Thee, Thou gorgeous, Thou wildering one;
O Thou great lion roaring over a sea of blood!
I rejoice, yea, I shout with gladness! till the wild thunder
of my praise breaketh down, as a satyr doth a babe, the nine
and ninety gates of Thy Power, in the Glory and Splendour of
Thy Name.

10. Ah! but I rejoice in Thee, O Thou my God;
Thou ambrosia-yielding rose of the World.
Thou vaulted dome of effulgent light;
Thou valley of venemous vipers:
Yea, I rejoice in Thee, Thou dazzling robe of the soft rain-
clouds;
O Thou lion-voiced up-rearing of the goaded storm.
I rejoice, yea, I shout with gladness! till my rapture, like

unto a two-edged sword, traceth a sigil of fire and blasteth the banded sorcerers, in the Glory and Splendour of Thy Name.

11. Ah! but I rejoice in Thee, O Thou my God;
Thou Crown of unutterable loveliness;
Thou feather of hyalescent flame;
Thou all-beholding eye of brightness:
Yea, I rejoice in Thee, Thou resplendent everlasting one:
O Thou vast abysmal ocean of foaming flames!
I rejoice, yea, I shout with gladness! till the stars leap like white courses from the night, and the heavens resound as an army of steel-clad warriors, at the Glory and Splendour of Thy Name.

12. Ah! but I rejoice in Thee, O Thou my God;
Thou star-blaze of undying expectation;
Thou ibis-throated voice of silence;
Thou blinding night of understanding:
Yea, I rejoice in Thee, Thou white finger of Chaotic law;
O Thou creative cockatrice twined amons the waters!
I rejoice, yea, I shout with gladness! till my cries stir the night as the burnished gold of a lance thrust into a poisonous dragon of adamant, for the Glory and Splendour of Thy Name.

13. Ah! but I rejoice in Thee, O Thou my God;
Thou self-luminous refulgent Brilliance;
Thou eye of light that hath no eyelid;
Thou turquoise-studded sceptre of deed:
Yea, I rejoice in Thee, Thou white furnace womb of Energy;

THE TREASURE-HOUSE OF IMAGES

O Thou spark-whirling forge of the substance of the worlds;

I rejoice, yea, I shout with gladness! till I mount as a white beam unto the crown, and as a breath of night melt into the golden lips of Thy dawn, in the Glory and Splendour of Thy Name.

O Glory be unto Thee through all Time
and through all Space : Glory,
and Glory upon Glory,
Everlastingly. Amen,
and Amen, and
Amen.

 The Chapter known as
The Twelvefold Humiliation of God
and the Unity thereof

					I					
♦	♦	♦	♦	♦		♦	♦	♦	♦	♦
♦	♦	♦	♦	♦	adore	♦	♦	♦	♦	♦
♦	♦	♦	♦	Thee by the		♦	♦	♦	♦	♦
♦	♦	♦	♦	Twelve Humiliations		♦	♦	♦	♦	♦
♦	♦	♦	♦	and by the Unity thereof		♦	♦	♦	♦	♦

1. O my God, behold me fully and be merciful unto me, as I humble myself before Thee; for all my searching is as a bat that seeks some hollow of night upon a sun-parched wilderness.

2. O my God, order me justly and be merciful unto me, as I humble myself before Thee; for all my thoughts are as a dust-clad serpent wind at noon that danceth through the ashen grass of law.

3. O my God, conquer me with love and be merciful unto me, as I humble myself before Thee; for all the striving of my spirit is as a child's kiss that struggles through a cloud of tangled hair.

4. O my God, suckle me with truth and be merciful unto me, as I humble myself before Thee; for all my agony of anguish is but as a quail struggling in the jaws of an hungry wolf.

5. O my God, comfort me with ease and be merciful unto me, as I humble myself before Thee; for all the toil of my life is but as a small white mouse swimming through a vast sea of crimson blood.

6. O my God, entreat me gently and be merciful unto me, as I humble myself before Thee; for all my toil is but as a threadless shuttle of steel thrust here and there in the black loom of night.

7. O my God, fondle me with kisses and be merciful unto me, as I humble myself before Thee; for all my desires are as dewdrops that are sucked from silver lilies by the throat of a young god.

8. O my God, exalt me with blood and be merciful unto me, as I humble myself before Thee; for all my courage is but as the fang of a viper that striketh at the rosy heel of dawn.

9. O my God, teach me with patience and be merciful unto me, as I humble myself before Thee; for all my knowledge is but as the refuse of the chaff that is flung to the darkness of the void.

10. O my God, measure me rightly and be merciful unto me, as I humble myself before Thee; for all my praise is but as a single letter of lead lost in the gilded scriptures of the rocks.

11. O my God, fill me with slumber and be merciful unto me, as I humble myself before Thee; for all my wakefulness is but as a cloud at sunset that is like a snake gliding through the dew.

12. O my God, kindle me with joy and be merciful unto me, as I humble myself before Thee; for all the strength of my mind is but as a web of silk that bindeth the milky breasts of the stars.

13. O my God, consume me with fire and be merciful unto me, as I humble myself before Thee; for all mine under-

standing is but as a spider's thread drawn from star to
star of a young galaxy.

> O Glory be unto Thee through all Time
> and through all Space : Glory,
> and Glory upon Glory,
> Everlastingly. Amen,
> and Amen, and
> Amen.

 The Chapter known as
The Twelvefold Lamentation of God
and the Unity thereof

◆ ◆ ◆ ◆ ◆   I   ◆ ◆ ◆ ◆ ◆
◆ ◆ ◆ ◆ ◆   adore   ◆ ◆ ◆ ◆ ◆
◆ ◆ ◆ ◆ Thee by the ◆ ◆ ◆ ◆
◆ ◆ ◆ ◆ Twelve Lamentations ◆ ◆ ◆ ◆
◆ ◆ ◆ ◆ and by the Unity thereof ◆ ◆ ◆ ◆

1. O woe unto me, my God, woe unto me; for all my song is as the dirge of the sea that moans about a corpse, lapping most mournfully against the dead shore in the darkness. Yet in the sob of the wind do I hear Thy name, that quickeneth the cold lips of death to life.

2. O woe unto me, my God, woe unto me; for all my praise is as the song of a bird that is ensnared in the network of the winds, and cast adown the drowning depths of night. Yet in the faltering notes of my music do I mark the melody of universal truth.

3. O woe unto me, my God, woe unto me; for all my works are as a coiled-up sleeper who hath overslept the day, even the dawn that hovereth as a hawk in the void. Yet in the gloom of mine awakening do I see, across the breasts of night, Thy shadowed form.

4. O woe unto me, my God, woe unto me; for all my labours are as weary oxen laggard and sore stricken with the goad, ploughing black furrows across the white fields of light. Yet in the scrawling trail of their slow toil do I descry the golden harvest of Thine effulgence.

5. O woe unto me, my God, woe unto me; for all the hope

of my heart hath been ravished as the body of a virgin that is fallen into the hands of riotous robbers. Yet in the outrage of mine innocnece do I disclose the clear manna of Thy purity.

6. O woe unto me, my God, woe unto me; for all the passion of my love is mazed as the bewildered eyes of a youth, who should wake to find his belovè d fled away. Yet in the crumpled couch of lust do I behold as an imprint the sigil of Thy name.

7. O woe unto me, my God, woe unto me; for all the joy of my days lies dishonoured as the spangle-veil'd Virgin of night torn and trampled by the sun-lashed stallions of Dawn. Yet in the frenzy of their couplings do I tremble forth the pearly dew of ecstatic light.

8. O woe unto me, my God, woe unto me; for all the aspirations of my heart ruin as in time of earthquake the bare hut of an hermit that he hath built for prayer. Yet from the lightning-struck tower of my reason do I enter Thy house that Thou didst build for me.

9. O woe unto me, my God, woe unto me; for all my joy is as a cloud of dust blown athwart a memory of tears, even across the shadowless brow of the desert. Yet as from the breast of a slave-girl do I pluck the fragrant blossom of Thy Crimson Splendour.

10. O woe unto me, my God, woe unto me; for all the feastings of my flesh have sickened to the wormy hunger of the grave, writhing in the spasms of indolent decay. Yet in the maggots of my corruption do I shdow forth sunlit hosts of crownè d eagles.

11. O woe unto me, my God, woe unto me; for all my

craft is as an injured arrow, featherless and twisted, that should be loosed from its bowstring by the hands of an infant. Yet in the wayward struggling of its flight do I grip the unwavering courses of Thy wisdom.

12. O woe unto me, my God, woe unto me; for all my faith is as a filthy puddle in the sinister confines of a forest, splashed by the wanton foot of a young gnome. Yet like a wildfire through the trees at nightfall do I divine the distant glimmer of Thine Eye.

13. O woe unto me, my God, woe unto me; for all my life sinks as the western Sun that struggles in the strangling arms of Night, flecked over with the starry foam of her kisses. Yet in the very midnight of my soul do I hold as a scarab the signet of Thy name.

O Glory be unto Thee through all Time
and through all Space : Glory,
and Glory upon Glory,
Everlastingly. Amen,
and Amen, and
Amen.

The Chapter known as
The Twelvefold Bewilderment of God
and the Unity thereof

♦ ♦ ♦ ♦ ♦ I ♦ ♦ ♦ ♦ ♦
♦ ♦ ♦ ♦ ♦ adore ♦ ♦ ♦ ♦ ♦
♦ ♦ ♦ ♦ Thee by the ♦ ♦ ♦ ♦
♦ ♦ ♦ ♦ Twelve Bewilderments ♦ ♦ ♦ ♦
♦ ♦ ♦ ♦ and by the Unity thereof ♦ ♦ ♦ ♦

1. O what art Thou, O God my God, Thou snow-browed storm that art whirled up in clouds of flame?

O Thou red sword of the thunder!

Thou great blue river of ever-flowing Brightness, over whose breasts creep the star-bannered vessels of night!

O how can I plunge within Thine inscrutable depths, and yet with open eye be lost in the pearly foam of Thine Oblivion.

2. O what art Thou, O God my God, Thou eternal incarnating immortal One?

O Thou welder of life and death!

Thou whose breasts are as the full breasts of a mother, yet in Thy hand Thou carriest the sword of destruction!

O how can I cleave the shield of Thy might as a little wanton child may burst a floating bbble with the breath-feather of a dove.

3. O what art Thou, O God my God, Thou mighty worker laden with the dust of toil?

O Thou little ant of the earth!

Thou great monster who infuriatest the seas, and by their vigour wearest down the strength of the cliffs!

O how can I bind Thee in a spider's web of song, and yet remain one and unconsumèd before the raging of Thy nostrils?

4. O what art Thou, O God my God, Thou forkèd tongue of the purple-throated thunder.

O Thou silver sword of lightning!

Thou who rippest out the fire-bolt from the storm-cloud, as a sorcerer teareth the heart from a black kid!

O how can I posess Thee as the dome of the skies, so that I may fix the keystone of my reason in the arch of Thy forehead?

5. O what art Thou, O God my God, Thou amber-seal'd one whose eyes are set on columns?

O Thou sightless seer of all things!

Thou spearless warrior who urgest on Thy steeds and blindest the outer edge of darkness with Thy Glory!

O how can I grasp the whirling wheels of Thy splendour, and yet be not smitten into death by the hurtling fury of Thy chariot?

6. O what art Thou, O God my God, Thou red fire-fang that gnawest the blue limbs of night?

O Thou devouring breath of flame!

Thou illimitable ocean of frenzied air, in whom all is one, a plume cast into a furnace!

O how can I dare to approach and stand before Thee, for I am but as a withered leaf whirled away by the anger of the storm?

7. O what art Thou, O God my God, Thou almighty worker ungirded of slumber?

O Thou Unicorn of the Stars!

Thou tongue of flame burning above the firmament, as a lily that blossometh in the drear desert!

O how can I pluck Thee from the dark bed of Thy birth, and revel like a wine-drenched faun in the banqueting-house of Thy Seigniory?

8. O what art Thou, O God my God, Thou dazzler of the deep obscurity of the day?

O Thou golden breast of beauty!

Thou shrivelled udder of the storm-blasted mountain, who no longer sucklest the babe-clouds of wind-swept night!

O how can I gaze upon Thy countenance of eld, and yet be not blinding by the black fury of Thy dethronèd Majesty?

9. O what art Thou, O God my God, Thou seraph-venom of witch-vengeance enchaunted?

O Thou coiled wizardry of stars!

Thou one Lord of life triumphant over death, Thou red rose of love nailed to the cross of golden light!

O how can I die in Thee as sea-foam in the clouds, and yet possess Thee as a frail white mist possesses the stripped limbs of the Sun?

10. O what art Thou, O God my God, Thou soft pearl set in a bow of effulgent light?

O Thou drop of shimmering dew!

Thou surging river of bewildering beauty who speedest as a blue arrow of fire beyond, beyond!

O how can I measure the poisons of Thy limbeck, and yet be for ever transmuted in the athanor of Thine understanding?

11. O what art Thou, O God my God, Thou disrober of the darkness of the Abyss?

O Thou veil'd eye of creation!

Thou soundless voice who, for ever misunderstood, rollest on through the dark abysms of infinity!

O how can I learn to sing the music of Thy name, as a quivering silence above the thundering discord of the tempest?

12. O what art Thou, O God my God, Thou teeming desert of the abundance of night?

O Thou river of unquench'd thirst!

Thou tongueless one who lickest up the dust of death and casteth it forth as the rolling ocean of life!

O how can I possess the still depths of Thy darkness, and yet in Thine embrace fall asleep as a child in a bower of lilies?

13. O what art Thou, O God my God, Thou shrouded one veiled in a dazzling effulgence?

O Thou centreless whorl of Time!

Thou illimitable abysm of Righteousness, the lashes of whose eye are as showers of molten suns!

O how can I reflect the light of Thine unity, and melt into Thy Glory as a cloudy chaplet of chalcedony moon

O Glory be unto Thee through all Time
and through all Space : Glory,
and Glory upon Glory,
Everlastingly. Amen,
and Amen, and
Amen.

The Chapter known as
The Twelvefold Unificiation of God
and the Unity thereof

◆ ◆ ◆ ◆ ◆   I   ◆ ◆ ◆ ◆ ◆

◆ ◆ ◆ ◆ ◆   adore   ◆ ◆ ◆ ◆ ◆

◆ ◆ ◆ ◆   Thee by the   ◆ ◆ ◆ ◆

◆ ◆ ◆ ◆ Twelve Unifications ◆ ◆ ◆ ◆

◆ ◆ ◆ ◆ and by the Unity thereof ◆ ◆ ◆ ◆

1. O Thou Unity of all things: as the water that poureth through the fingers of my hand, so art Thou, O God my God. I cannot hold Thee, for Thou art everywhere; lo! though I plunge into the heart of the ocean, there still shall I find Thee, Thou Unity of Unities, Thou Oneness, O Thou perfect Nothingness of bliss!

2. O Thou Unity of all things: as the hot fire that flameth is too subtle to be held, so art Thou, O God my God. I cannot grasp Thee, for Thou art everywhere; lo! though I hurl me down the scarlet throat of a volcano, there still shall I find Thee, Thou Unity of Unities, Thou Oneness, O Thou perfect Nothingness of bliss!

3. O Thou Unity of all things: as the moon that waneth and increaseth in the heavens, so art Thou, O God my God. I cannot stay Thee, for Thou art everywhere; lo! though I devour Thee, as a dragon devoureth a kid, there still shall I find Thee, Thou Unity of Unities, Thou Oneness, O Thou perfect Nothingness of bliss!

4. O Thou Unity of all things: as the dust that danceth over the breast of the desert, so art Thou, O God my God. I cannot seize Thee, for Thou art everywhere; lo! though I lick up with my tongue the bitter salt of the plains, there still

shall I find Thee, Thou Unity of Unities, Thou Oneness, O Thou perfect Nothingness of bliss!

5. O Thou Unity of all things: as the air that bubbleth from the dark depths of the waters, so art Thou, O God my God. I cannot catch Thee, for Thou art everywhere; lo! though I net thee as a goldfish in a kerchief of silk, there still shall I find Thee, Thou Unity of Unities, Thou Oneness, O Thou perfect Nothingness of bliss!

6. O Thou Unity of all things: as the cloud that flitteth across the white horns of the moon, so art Thou, O God my God. I cannot pierce Thee, for Thou art everywhere; lo! though I tangle Thee in a witch-gossamer of starlight, there still shall I find Thee, Thou Unity of Unities, Thou Oneness, O Thou perfect Nothingness of bliss!

7. O Thou Unity of all things: as the star that travelleth along its appointed course, so art Thou, O God my God. I cannot rule Thee, for Thou art everywhere; lo! though I hunt Thee across the blue heavens as a lost comet, there still shall I find Thee, Thou Unity of Unities, Thou Oneness, O Thou perfect Nothingness of bliss!

8. O Thou Unity of all things: as the lightning that lurketh in the heart of the thunder, so art Thou, O God my God. I cannot search Thee, for Thou art everywhere; lo! though I wed the flaming circle to the enshrouded square, there still shall I find Thee, Thou Unity of Unities, Thou Oneness, O Thou perfect Nothingness of bliss!

9. O Thou Unity of all things: as the earth that holdeth all precious jewels in her heart so art Thou, O God my God. I cannot spoil Thee, for Thou art everywhere; lo! though I burrow as a mole in the mountain of Chaos, there still shall I

find Thee, Thou Unity of Unities, Thou Oneness, O Thou perfect Nothingness of bliss!

10. O Thou Unity of all things: as the pole-star that burneth in the centre of the night, so art Thou, O God my God. I cannot hide Thee, for Thou art everywhere; lo! though I turn from Thee at each touch of the lodestone of lust, there still shall I find Thee, Thou Unity of Unities, Thou Oneness, O Thou perfect Nothingness of bliss!

11. O Thou Unity of all things: as the blue smoke that whirleth up from the altar of life, so art Thou, O God my God. I cannot find Thee, for Thou art everywhere; lo! though I inter Thee in the sarcophagi of the damned, there still shall I find Thee, Thou Unity of Unities, Thou Oneness, O Thou perfect Nothingness of bliss!

12. O Thou Unity of all things: as a dark-eyed maiden decked in crimson and precious pearls, so art Thou, O God my God. I cannot rob Thee, for Thou art everywhere; lo! though I strip Thee of Thy gold and scarlet raiment of Self, there still shall I find Thee, Thou Unity of Unities, Thou Oneness, O Thou perfect Nothingness of bliss!

13. O Thou Unity of all things: as the sun that rolleth through the twelve manions of the skies, so art Thou, O God my God. I cannot slay Thee, for Thou art everywhere; lo! though I lick up the Boundless Light, the Boundless, and the Not, there still shall I find Thee, Thou Unity of Unities, Thou Oneness, O Thou perfect Nothingness of bliss!

O Glory be unto Thee through all Time
and through all Space : Glory,
and Glory upon Glory,
Everlastingly. Amen,
and Amen, and
Amen.

The Chapter known as
The Hundred and Sixty-Nine Cries of
Adoration and the Unity thereof

◆ ◆ ◆ ◆ ◆ I ◆ ◆ ◆ ◆ ◆
◆ ◆ ◆ ◆ ◆ adore ◆ ◆ ◆ ◆ ◆
◆ ◆ ◆ ◆ Thee by the ◆ ◆ ◆ ◆
◆ ◆ ◆ ◆ Hundred and Sixty- ◆ ◆ ◆ ◆
◆ ◆ ◆ ◆ Nine Cries of Adoration ◆ ◆ ◆ ◆
◆ ◆ ◆ ◆ and by the Unity thereof ◆ ◆ ◆ ◆

O Thou Dragon-prince of the air, that art drunk on the blood of the sunsets! I adore Thee, Evoe! I adore Thee, IAO!

O Thou Unicorn of the storm, that art crested above the purple air! I adore Thee, Evoe! I adore Thee, IAO!

O Thou burning sword of passion, that art tempered on the anvil of flesh! I adore Thee, Evoe! I adore Thee, IAO!

O Thou slimy lust of the grave, that art tangled in the roots of the Tree! I adore Thee, Evoe! I adore Thee, IAO!

O Thou smoke-shroded sword of flame, that art en-sheathed in the bowels of earth! I adore Thee, Evoe! I adore Thee, IAO!

O Thou scented grove of wild vines, that art trampled by the white feet of love! I adore Thee, Evoe! I adore Thee, IAO!

O Thou golden sheaf of desire, that art bound by a fair wisp of poppies! I adore Thee, Evoe! I adore Thee, IAO!

O Thou molten comet of gold, that art seen through the wizard's glass of Space! I adore Thee, Evoe! I adore Thee, IAO!

O Thou shrill song of the eunuch, that art heard behind the curtain of shame! I adore Thee, Evoe! I adore Thee, IAO!

O Thou bright star of the morning, that art set betwixt the breasts of the night! I adore Thee, Evoe! I adore Thee, IAO!

O Thou lidless eye of the world, that art seen through the sapphire veil of space! I adore Thee, Evoe! I adore Thee, IAO!

O Thou smiling mouth of the dawn, that art freed from the laughter of the night! I adore Thee, Evoe! I adore Thee, IAO!

O Thou dazzling star-point of hope, that burnest over oceans of despair! I adore Thee, Evoe! I adore Thee, IAO!

O Thou naked virgin of love, that art caught in a net of wild roses! I adore Thee, Evoe! I adore Thee, IAO!

O Thou iron turret of death, that art rusted with the bright blood of war! I adore Thee, Evoe! I adore Thee, IAO!

O Thou bubbling wine-cup of joy, that foamest like the cauldron of murder! I adore Thee, Evoe! I adore Thee, IAO!

O Thou icy trail of the moon, that art traced in the veins of the onyx! I adore Thee, Evoe! I adore Thee, IAO!

O Thou frenzied hunter of love, that art slain by the twisted horns of lust! I adore Thee, Evoe! I adore Thee, IAO!

O Thou frozen book of the seas, that art graven by the swords of the sun! I adore Thee, Evoe! I adore Thee, IAO!

THE TREASURE-HOUSE OF IMAGES

O Thou flashing opal of light, that art wrapped in the robes of the rainbows! I adore Thee, Evoe! I adore Thee, IAO!

O Thou purple mist of the hills, that hideth shepherds from the wanton moon! I adore Thee, Evoe! I adore Thee, IAO!

O Thou low moan of fainting maids, that art caught up in the strong sobs of love! I adore Thee, Evoe! I adore Thee, IAO!

O Thou fleeting beam of delight, that lurkest within the spear-thrusts of dawn! I adore Thee, Evoe! I adore Thee, IAO!

O Thou golden wine of the sun, that art poured over the dark breasts of night! I adore Thee, Evoe! I adore Thee, IAO!

O Thou fragrance of sweet flowers, that art wafted over blue fields of air! I adore Thee, Evoe! I adore Thee, IAO!

O Thou mighty bastion of faith, that withstanded all the breachers of doubt! I adore Thee, Evoe! I adore Thee, IAO!

O Thou silver horn of the moon, that gorest the red flank of the morning! I adore Thee, Evoe! I adore Thee, IAO!

O Thou grey glory of twilight, that art the hermaphrodite triumphant! I adore Thee, Evoe! I adore Thee, IAO!

O Thou thirsty mouth of the wind, that art maddened by the foam of the sea! I adore Thee, Evoe! I adore Thee, IAO!

O Thou couch of rose-leaf desires, that art crumpled by the vine and the fir! I adore Thee, Evoe! I adore Thee, IAO!

O Thou bird-sweet river of Love, that warblest through the pebbly gorge of Life! I adore Thee, Evoe! I adore Thee, IAO!

O Thou golden network of stars, that art girt about the cold breasts of Night! I adore Thee, Evoe! I adore Thee, IAO!

O Thou mad whirlwind of laughter, that art meshed in the wild locks of folly! I adore Thee, Evoe! I adore Thee, IAO!

O Thou white hand of Creation, that holdest up the dying head of Death! I adore Thee, Evoe! I adore Thee, IAO!

O Thou purple tongue of Twilight, that dost lap up the lucent milk of Day! I adore Thee, Evoe! I adore Thee, IAO!

O Thou thunderbolt of Science, that flashest from the dark clouds of Magic! I adore Thee, Evoe! I adore Thee, IAO!

O Thou red rose of the Morning, that glowest in the bosom of the Night! I adore Thee, Evoe! I adore Thee, IAO!

O Thou flaming globe of Glory, that art caught up in the arms of the sun! I adore Thee, Evoe! I adore Thee, IAO!

O Thou silver arrow of hope, that art shot from the arc of the rainbow! I adore Thee, Evoe! I adore Thee, IAO!

O Thou starry virgin of Night, that art strained to the arms of the morning! I adore Thee, Evoe! I adore Thee, IAO!

O Thou sworded soldier of life, that art sucked down in the quicksands of death! I adore Thee, Evoe! I adore Thee, IAO!

THE TREASURE-HOUSE OF IMAGES

O Thou brozne blast of the trumpet, that rollest over emerald-tipped spears! I adore Thee, Evoe! I adore Thee, IAO!

O Thou opal mist of the sea, that art sucked up by the beams of the sun! I adore Thee, Evoe! I adore Thee, IAO!

O Thou red worm of formation, that art lifted by the white whorl of love! I adore Thee, Evoe! I adore Thee, IAO!

O Thou mighty anvil of Time, that outshowerest the bright sparks of life! I adore Thee, Evoe! I adore Thee, IAO!

O Thou red cobra of desire, that art unhooded by the hands of girls! I adore Thee, Evoe! I adore Thee, IAO!

O Thou curling billow of joy, whose fingers caress the limbs of the world! I adore Thee, Evoe! I adore Thee, IAO!

O Thou emerald vulture of Truth, that art perched upon the vast tree of life! I adore Thee, Evoe! I adore Thee, IAO!

O Thou lonely eagle of night, that drinkest at the moist lips of the moon! I adore Thee, Evoe! I adore Thee, IAO!

O Thou wild daughter of Chaos, that art ravished by strong son of law! I adore Thee, Evoe! I adore Thee, IAO!

O Thou ghostly night of terror, that art slaughtered in the blood of the dawn! I adore Thee, Evoe! I adore Thee, IAO!

O Thou poppied nectar of sleep, that art curlded in the

still womb of slumber! I adore Thee, Evoe! I adore Thee, IAO!

O Thou burning rapture of girls, that disport in the sunset of passion! I adore Thee, Evoe! I adore Thee, IAO!

O Thou molten ocean of stars, that art a crown for the forehead of day! I adore Thee, Evoe! I adore Thee, IAO!

O Thou little brook in the hills, like an asp betwixt the breasts of a girl! I adore Thee, Evoe! I adore Thee, IAO!

O Thou thou mighty oak of magic, that art rooted in the mountain of life! I adore Thee, Evoe! I adore Thee, IAO!

O Thou sparkling network of pearls, that art woven of the waves by the moon! I adore Thee, Evoe! I adore Thee, IAO!

O Thou wanton sword-blade of life, that art sheathèd by the harlot call'd Death! I adore Thee, Evoe! I adore Thee, IAO!

O Thou mist-clad spirit of spring, that art unrob'd by the hands of the wind! I adore Thee, Evoe! I adore Thee, IAO!

O Thou sweet perfume of desire, that art wafted through the valley of love! I adore Thee, Evoe! I adore Thee, IAO!

O Thou sparkling wine-cup of light, whose foaming is the heart's blood of the stars! I adore Thee, Evoe! I adore Thee, IAO!

O Thou silver sword of madness, that art smitten through the midden of life! I adore Thee, Evoe! I adore Thee, IAO!

THE TREASURE-HOUSE OF IMAGES

O Thou hooded vulture of night, that art gluted on the entrails of day! I adore Thee, Evoe! I adore Thee, IAO!

O Thou pearl-gray arch of the world, whose keystone is the ecstasy of man! I adore Thee, Evoe! I adore Thee, IAO!

O Thou silken web of movement, that art blown through the atoms of matter! I adore Thee, Evoe! I adore Thee, IAO!

O Thou rush-strewn threshold of joy, that art lost in the quicksands of reason! I adore Thee, Evoe! I adore Thee, IAO!

O Thou wild vision of Beauty, but half seen betwixt the cusps of the moon! I adore Thee, Evoe! I adore Thee, IAO!

O Thou pearl cloud of the sunset, that art caught up in a murderer's hand! I adore Thee, Evoe! I adore Thee, IAO!

O Thou rich vintage of slumber, that art crushed from the bud of the poppy! I adore Thee, Evoe! I adore Thee, IAO!

O Thou great boulder of rapture, that leapest adown the mountains of joy! I adore Thee, Evoe! I adore Thee, IAO!

O Thou breather-out of the winds, that art snared in the drag-net of reason! I adore Thee, Evoe! I adore Thee, IAO!

O Thou purple breast of the storm, that art scarred by the teeth of the lightning! I adore Thee, Evoe! I adore Thee, IAO!

O Thou pillar of phosphor foam, that Leviathan spouteth from's nostrils! I adore Thee, Evoe! I adore Thee, IAO!

O Thou song of that harp of life, that chantest forth the perfection of death! I adore Thee, Evoe! I adore Thee, IAO!

O Thou veilèd beam of the stars, that art tangled in the tresses of night! I adore Thee, Evoe! I adore Thee, IAO!

O Thou flashing shield of the sun, as a discus hurled by the hand of Space! I adore Thee, Evoe! I adore Thee, IAO!

O Thou ribald shout of laughter, that echoest among the tombs of death! I adore Thee, Evoe! I adore Thee, IAO!

O Thou unfailing cruse of joy, that art filled with the tears of the fallen! I adore Thee, Evoe! I adore Thee, IAO!

O Thou burning lust of the moon, that art clothed in the mist of the ocean! I adore Thee, Evoe! I adore Thee, IAO!

O Thou one measure of all things, that art Dam of the great order of worlds! I adore Thee, Evoe! I adore Thee, IAO!

O Thou frail virgin of Eden, that art ravished to the abode of Hell! I adore Thee, Evoe! I adore Thee, IAO!

O Thou dark forest of wonder, that art tangled in a gold web of dew! I adore Thee, Evoe! I adore Thee, IAO!

O Thou tortured shriek of the storm, that art whirled up through the leaves of the woods! I adore Thee, Evoe! I adore Thee, IAO!

O Thou dazzling opal of light, that flamest in the crumbling skull of space! I adore Thee, Evoe! I adore Thee, IAO!

O Thou red knife of destruction, that art sheathed in the bowels of order! I adore Thee, Evoe! I adore Thee, IAO!

O Thou storm-drunk breath of the winds, that pant in the bosom of the mountains! I adore Thee, Evoe! I adore Thee, IAO!

O Thou loud bell of rejoicing, that art smitten by the hammer of woe! I adore Thee, Evoe! I adore Thee, IAO!

O Thou red rose of the sunset, that witherest on the altar of night! I adore Thee, Evoe! I adore Thee, IAO!

O Thou bright vision of sunbeams, that burnest in a flagon of topaz! I adore Thee, Evoe! I adore Thee, IAO!

O Thou virgin lily of light, that sproutest between the lips of a corpse! I adore Thee, Evoe! I adore Thee, IAO!

O Thou blue helm of destruction, that art winged with the lightnings of madness! I adore Thee, Evoe! I adore Thee, IAO!

O Thou voice of the heaving seas, that tremblest in the grey of the twilight! I adore Thee, Evoe! I adore Thee, IAO!

O Thou unfolder of heaven, red-winged as an eagle at sunrise! I adore Thee, Evoe! I adore Thee, IAO!

O Thou curling tongue of red flame, athirst on the nipple of my passion! I adore Thee, Evoe! I adore Thee, IAO!

O Thou outrider of the sun, that spurrest the bloody flanks of the wind! I adore Thee, Evoe! I adore Thee, IAO!

O Thou dancer with gilded nails, that unbraidest the star-hair of the night! I adore Thee, Evoe! I adore Thee, IAO!

O Thou moonlit pearl of rapture, clasped fast in the silver hand of the Dawn! I adore Thee, Evoe! I adore Thee, IAO!

O Thou wanton mother of love, that art mistress of the children of men! I adore Thee, Evoe! I adore Thee, IAO!

O Thou crimson fountain of blood, that spoutest from the heart of Creation! I adore Thee, Evoe! I adore Thee, IAO!

O Thou warrior eye of the sun, that shooteth death from the berylline Byss! I adore Thee, Evoe! I adore Thee, IAO!

O Thou Witch's hell-broth of hate, that boilest in the white cauldron of love! I adore Thee, Evoe! I adore Thee, IAO!

O Thou Ribbon of Northern Lights, that bindest the elfin tresses of night! I adore Thee, Evoe! I adore Thee, IAO!

O Thou red sword of the Twilight, that art rusted with the blood of the noon! I adore Thee, Evoe! I adore Thee, IAO!

O Thou sacrificer of Dawn, that wearest the chasuble of sunset! I adore Thee, Evoe! I adore Thee, IAO!

O Thou bloodshot eye of lightning, glowering beneath the eyebrows of thunder! I adore Thee, Evoe! I adore Thee, IAO!

O Thou four-square Crown of Nothing, that circlest the destruction of worlds! I adore Thee, Evoe! I adore Thee, IAO!

O Thou bloodhound whirlwind of lust, that art unleashed by the first kiss of love! I adore Thee, Evoe! I adore Thee, IAO!

O Thou wondrous chalice of light, uplifted by the Mænads of Dawn! I adore Thee, Evoe! I adore Thee, IAO!

O Thou fecund opal of death, that sparklest through a sea of mother-of-pearl! I adore Thee, Evoe! I adore Thee, IAO!

O Thou crimson rose of the Dawn, that art fastened in the dark locks of Night! I adore Thee, Evoe! I adore Thee, IAO!

O Thou pink nipple of Being, thrust deep into the black mouth of Chaos! I adore Thee, Evoe! I adore Thee, IAO!

O Thou vampire Queen of the Flesh, wound as a snake around the throats of men! I adore Thee, Evoe! I adore Thee, IAO!

THE TREASURE-HOUSE OF IMAGES

O Thou tender next of dove's down, built up betwixt the hawk's claws of the Night! I adore Thee, Evoe! I adore Thee, IAO!

O Thou concubine of Matter, anointed with love-nard of Motion! I adore Thee, Evoe! I adore Thee, IAO!

O Thou flame-tipp'd bolt of Morning, that art shot out from the crossbow of Night! I adore Thee, Evoe! I adore Thee, IAO!

O Thou frail blue-bell of Moonlight, that art lost in the gardens of the Stars! I adore Thee, Evoe! I adore Thee, IAO!

O Thou tall mast of wreck'd Chaos, that art crowned by the white lamp of Cosmon! I adore Thee, Evoe! I adore Thee, IAO!

O Thou pearly eyelid of Day, that art closed by the finger of Evening! I adore Thee, Evoe! I adore Thee, IAO!

O Thou wild anarch of the Hills, pale glooming above the mists of the Earth! I adore Thee, Evoe! I adore Thee, IAO!

O Thou moonlit peak of pleasure, that art crowned by the viper tongues of forked flame! I adore Thee, Evoe! I adore Thee, IAO!

O Thou wolfish head of the winds, that frighteth the snow-white lamb of winter! I adore Thee, Evoe! I adore Thee, IAO!

O Thou dew-lit nymph of the Dawn, that swoonest in the satyr arms of the Sun! I adore Thee, Evoe! I adore Thee, IAO!

O Thou mad abode of kisses, that art lit by the fat of murdered fiends! I adore Thee, Evoe! I adore Thee, IAO!

O Thou sleeping lust of the Storm, that art flame-gorg'd as a flint full of fire! I adore Thee, Evoe! I adore Thee, IAO!

O Thou soft dew of the Evening, that art drunk up by the mist of the Night! I adore Thee, Evoe! I adore Thee, IAO!

O Thou wounded son of the West, that gushest out Thy blood on the heavens! I adore Thee, Evoe! I adore Thee, IAO!

O Thou burning tower of fire, that art set up in the midst of the seas! I adore Thee, Evoe! I adore Thee, IAO!

O Thou unvintageable dew, that art moist upon the lips of the Morn! I adore Thee, Evoe! I adore Thee, IAO!

O Thou silver crescent of love, that burnest over the dark helm of War! I adore Thee, Evoe! I adore Thee, IAO!

O Thou snow-white ram of the Dawn, that art slain by the lion of the noon! I adore Thee, Evoe! I adore Thee, IAO!

O Thou crimson spear-point of life, that art thrust through the dark bowels of Time! I adore Thee, Evoe! I adore Thee, IAO!

O Thou black waterspout of Death, that whirlest, whelmest the tall ship of Life! I adore Thee, Evoe! I adore Thee, IAO!

O Thou mighty chain of events, that art strained betwixt Cosmon and Chaos! I adore Thee, Evoe! I adore Thee, IAO!

O Thou towering eagre of lust, that art heaped up by the moon-breasts of youth! I adore Thee, Evoe! I adore Thee, IAO!

THE TREASURE-HOUSE OF IMAGES

O Thou serpent-crown of green light, that art wound round the dark forehead of Death! I adore Thee, Evoe! I adore Thee, IAO!

O Thou crimson vintage of Life, that art poured into the jar of the Grave! I adore Thee, Evoe! I adore Thee, IAO!

O Thou waveless Ocean of Peace, that sleepest beneath the wild heart of man! I adore Thee, Evoe! I adore Thee, IAO!

O Thou whirling skirt of the stars, that art swathed round the limbs of the Æthyr! I adore Thee, Evoe! I adore Thee, IAO!

O Thou snow-white chalice of Love, thou art filled up with the red lusts of Man! I adore Thee, Evoe! I adore Thee, IAO!

O Thou fragrant garden of Joy, firm-set betwixt the breasts of the morning! I adore Thee, Evoe! I adore Thee, IAO!

O Thou pearly fountain of Life, that spoutest up in the black court of Death! I adore Thee, Evoe! I adore Thee, IAO!

O Thou brindle hound of the Night, with thy nose to the sleuth of the Sunset! I adore Thee, Evoe! I adore Thee, IAO!

O Thou leprous claw of the ghoul, that coaxest the babe from its chaste cradle! I adore Thee, Evoe! I adore Thee, IAO!

O Thou assassin word of law, that art written in ruin of earthquakes! I adore Thee, Evoe! I adore Thee, IAO!

O Thou trembling breast of the night, that gleamest with a rosary of moons! I adore Thee, Evoe! I adore Thee, IAO!

O Thou Holy Sphinx of rebirth, that crouchest in the black desert of death! I adore Thee, Evoe! I adore Thee, IAO!

O Thou diadem of the suns, that art the knot of this red web of worlds! I adore Thee, Evoe! I adore Thee, IAO!

O Thou ravished river of law, that outpourest the arcanum of Life! I adore Thee, Evoe! I adore Thee, IAO!

O Thou glimmering tongue of day, that art sucked unto the blue lips of Night! I adore Thee, Evoe! I adore Thee, IAO!

O Thou Queen-Bee of Heaven's hive, that smearest thy thighs with honey of Hell! I adore Thee, Evoe! I adore Thee, IAO!

O Thou scarlet dragon of flame, enmeshed in the web of a spider! I adore Thee, Evoe! I adore Thee, IAO!

O Thou magic symbol of light, that art frozen on the black book of blood! I adore Thee, Evoe! I adore Thee, IAO!

O Thou swathed image of Death, that art hidden in the coffin of joy! I adore Thee, Evoe! I adore Thee, IAO!

O Thou red breast of the sunset, that pantest for the ravishment of Night! I adore Thee, Evoe! I adore Thee, IAO!

O Thou serpent of malachite, that baskest in a desert of turquoise! I adore Thee, Evoe! I adore Thee, IAO!

O Thou fierce whirlpool of passion, that art sucked up by the mouth of the sun! I adore Thee, Evoe! I adore Thee, IAO!

O Thou green cockatrice of Hell, that art coiled around the finger of Fate! I adore Thee, Evoe! I adore Thee, IAO!

O Thou lambet laughter of fire, that art wound round

the heart of the waters! I adore Thee, Evoe! I adore Thee, IAO!

O Thou gorilla blizzard Air, that tearest out Earth's tresses by the roots! I adore Thee, Evoe! I adore Thee, IAO!

O Thou reveller of Spirit, that carousest in the halls of Matter! I adore Thee, Evoe! I adore Thee, IAO!

O Thou red-lipped Vampire of Life, that drainest blood from the black Mount of Death! I adore Thee, Evoe! I adore Thee, IAO!

O Thou little lark of Beyond, that art heard in the dark groves of knowledge! I adore Thee, Evoe! I adore Thee, IAO!

O Thou summer softness of lips, that glow hot with the scarlet of passion! I adore Thee, Evoe! I adore Thee, IAO!

O Thou pearly foam of the grape, that art flecked with the roses of love! I adore Thee, Evoe! I adore Thee, IAO!

O Thou frenzied hand of the seas, that unfurlest the black Banner of Storm! I adore Thee, Evoe! I adore Thee, IAO!

O Thou shrouded book of the dead, that art sealed with the seven souls of man! I adore Thee, Evoe! I adore Thee, IAO!

O Thou writhing frenzy of love, that art knotted like the grid-flames of Hell! I adore Thee, Evoe! I adore Thee, IAO!

O Thou primal birth-ring of thought, that dost encircle the thumb of the soul! I adore Thee, Evoe! I adore Thee, IAO!

THE EQUINOX

O Thou blind flame of Nothingness, as a crown upon my brow! I adore Thee, Evoe! I adore Thee, IAO!

O Glory be unto Thee through all Time
and through all Space : Glory,
and Glory upon Glory,
Everlastingly. Amen,
and Amen, and
Amen.

𝕿𝖍𝖊 𝕮𝖍𝖆𝖕𝖙𝖊𝖗 𝖐𝖓𝖔𝖜𝖓 𝖆𝖘
𝕿𝖍𝖊 𝖀𝖓𝖈𝖔𝖓𝖘𝖈𝖎𝖔𝖚𝖘𝖓𝖊𝖘𝖘 𝖔𝖋 𝕲𝖔𝖉
𝖙𝖍𝖆𝖙 𝖎𝖘 𝖍𝖎𝖉𝖉𝖊𝖓 𝖋𝖗𝖔𝖒 𝖒𝖆𝖓 𝖋𝖔𝖗 𝖆 𝖘𝖎𝖌𝖓.

◆ ◆ ◆ ◆ ◆ I ◆ ◆ ◆ ◆ ◆
◆ ◆ ◆ ◆ ◆ adore ◆ ◆ ◆ ◆ ◆
◆ ◆ ◆ ◆ Thee by the ◆ ◆ ◆ ◆
◆ ◆ ◆ ◆ Twelvefold Sign ◆ ◆ ◆ ◆
◆ ◆ ◆ ◆ and by the Unity thereof ◆ ◆ ◆ ◆

12. The Light of my Life is as the light of two moons, one rising and the other setting, one increasing and the other waning; the one growing fat as the other groweth lean, like a paunchy thief sucking dry a skin of amber wine. Yet though the light of the first devoureth the light of the second, nevertheless the light of the second disgorgeth the light of the first, so that there is neither the desire of light nor the need of light—all being as a woven twilight of day and night, a madness of mingling moons. Yet I behold!

11. Now mine eyes are seven, and are as stars about a star; and the lids of mine eyes are fourteen, two to each eye. Also have I seven arms to do the bidding of the seven eyes; and each arm hath an hand of three fingers, so that I may rule the great ocean and burn it up with the Spirit of Flame, and that I may drown the fire in the Abode of the Waters. Thus I am rendered naked; for neither flame nor water can clothe me; therefore am I as a breath of wind blown over an Earth of Adamant, that knowneth neither sorrow nor rejoicing; then do I abide as a River of Light between the Night of Chaos and the Day of Creation.

10. Two are the moons of my madness, like the horns on

the head of a goat. And between them burneth a pyramid of flame, which consumeth neither but blindeth both, so that the one beholdeth not the other. Notwithstanding, when the one is lost in the water, and the other is burnt up in the flame, they become united in the form of a woman fashioned of Earth and of Air, who without husband is yet mother of many sons.

9. Now the Sons are in truth but one Son; and the one Son but a daughter draped and never naked; for her mother is naked, therefore is she robed. And she is called the Light of my Love, for she in conealed, and cannot be seen, as the Sun burneth over her and drowneth her in fire, whilst below her surgeth the sea, whose waves are as flames of water. When thou hast licked up the oceanthou shalt not see her because of the fire; and when thou hast swallowed the Sun surely shall the waters be driven away from thee, so that though the fire be thine the water hath slipped thee, as a dog its leash. Yet the path is straight.

8. Along it shalt thou journey, and then shalt thou learn that the fear of death is the blood of the world. So the woman dressed herself in the shrouds of the dead, and decked herself with the bones of the fallen; and all feared her, therefore they lived. But she feared life; therefore she wove a dew-moon in her tangled hair as a sign of the fickleness of Death, and wept tears of bitter sorrow that she should live in the blossom of her youth. And her tears crept like scorpions down her cheeks, and sped away in the darkness like serpents; and for each serpent there came an eagle which did carry it away.

7. "Why weep?" said the Balance swinging to the left. "Why laugh?" said the Balance swinging to the right. "Why

not remain still?" answered the Hand that held the Balance. And the Balance replied: "Because on my right laughs Death and on my left weeps a Virgin."

6. Then the Voice of the Hand said to the girl: "Why weep?" And the maid answered: "Because Death maketh jest of my life." Then the Hand stayed the Balance, and at once the girl saw that she as Death, and that Death that had sat opposite her was in truth a motherless babe. So she took the child she had conceived in the arms of fear, and went her way laughing.

5. And the infant grew strong; yet its strength was in its weakness; and though to olook at it from behind was to look upon a man-child, from behind it was a little girl with golden hair. Now, when the child wished to tempt a maid he faced and approached her; and when the child wished to tempt a man she turned her back on him and fled.

4. But one day the child met, at the self-same hour, Love; and the man, seeing a woman, approached her eagerly, and the woman, seeing a man, fled, so that he might capture her. Thus it came about that the child met the child and wondered, not knowing that the child had lost the child. So it was that they walked side by side.

3. Then that part of the child that was man loved and lusted for that part of the child that was woman; and each know not that each was the other, and felt that they were two and yet one, nevertheless one and yet two. And when one said: "Who art thou?" the other answered at the self-same moment: "Who am I?"

2. Soon becoming perplexed if I were Thou, or if Thou were I, it came about that the I mingled with the Thou, and

the Thou with the I, so that six added to ten became sixteen, which is felicity; for it is the interplay of the elements. Four are the elements that make man, and four are the elements that make woman. Thus was the child reborn.

ɪ. But though the man ruleth the woman, and the woman ruleth the man, the Child ruleth both its mother and father, and being five is Emperor over the kingdom of their hearts. To its father it giveth four, and to its mother it giveth four, yet it remaineth five, for it hat of its father an half and of its mother an half; but in itself it is equal to both its father and its mother; for it is father of fathers and mother of mothers.

o. Therefore is it One Whole, and not two halves; and being One is Thirteen, which is called Nothing when it is All-things.

.

Amen
without lie,
and Amen of Amen,
and Amen of Amen of Amen.

FIG. 2.

The Greek Cross of the Zodiac.

♈︎. Emerald on Scarlet.
♉︎. Greenish Blue on Orange-Red.
♊︎. Royal Blue on Orange.
♋︎. Indigo on Amber.
♌︎. Violet on Greenish Yellow.
♍︎. Crimson on Yellow-Green.

♎︎. Scarlet on Emerald.
♏︎. Orange-Red on Greenish Blue.
♐︎. Orange on Royal Blue.
♑︎. Amber on Indigo.
♒︎. Greenish Yellow on Violet.
♓︎. Yellow-Green on Crimson.

Spirit. Black on White.
Serpent. Azure, with Golden Scales.
Border. Gold.

STOP PRESS REVIEWS

NATURE'S HELP TO HAPPINESS. By JOHN WARREN ACHORN, M.D. W. Rider and Sons. 1s. net.

This is the best book ever written on health. Go out and hold naked Nature to your breast; and you will be well.

You sleep in or you sleep out, as luck will have it; sometimes you get food, and sometimes not; it's no odds; you are one with Nature, and find that Nature is one with God.

This is my own practice; every time London can spare me I put on my climbing things and take nothing else but a supply of strong tobacco and a few pounds. Then I think of some place that sounds interesting—Madrid or Fiesole or Timbuktu—and walk there.

When I get back I am strong enough even for book-reviewing.

Go thou and do likewise!

ALEISTER CROWLEY.

MASQUES AND PHASES. By ROBERT ROSS. Arthur L. Humphreys.

A very pleasant collection of witty essays. *O si sic omnes!* Do let us have some more this year.

And thank you so much for the very necessary statements in "There is no decay."

A. C.

AFTER DEATH—WHAT? By CESARE LOMBROSO.

We sent this book to our undertaker for review, but he only wired back "Rot." Why are undertakers always poets?

[The late Cesare Lombroso was a mattoid and degenerate suffering from paranoiac delusions about "criminal types." He would count the hairs in your moustache, and if you had two more on one side than the other, it showed that you would commit forgery. The authorities once sent him a photograph of a murderer, and he proved that not only was he bound to murder somebody, but to do it in just that special way. By an accident, the photograph was that of a blameless grocer, an Arthur Henry Hallam of

THE EQUINOX

grocers.
But he went galumphing on with his monomania, until senile decay
supervened, and he became a spiritualist.
Now he is dead, like Max Nordau.—ED.]

Printed by BALLANTYNE & CO., LIMITED, London

The Equinox by Aleister Crowley -
Hardcover and Paperback

$100 or $250 for 10 volumes!

www.lulu.com/equinox_crowley

Made in the USA
Coppell, TX
12 June 2022

78746247R00233